The **Language** of *Violence*

PETER LANG
New York • Washington, D.C./Baltimore • Bern
Frankfurt am Main • Berlin • Brussels • Vienna • Oxford

Felicity Rash

The Language of Violence

Adolf Hitler's *Mein Kampf*

PETER LANG
New York • Washington, D.C./Baltimore • Bern
Frankfurt am Main • Berlin • Brussels • Vienna • Oxford

Library of Congress Cataloging-in-Publication Data

Rash, Felicity J.,
The language of violence: Adolf Hitler's Mein Kampf / Felicity Rash.
p. cm. — Includes bibliographical references and index.
1. Hitler, Adolf, 1889–1945. Mein Kampf—Criticism, Textual.
2. Hitler, Adolf, 1889–1945—Language. 3. Violence in literature.
4. Nazis—Language. 5. Ideology—Germany—History—20th century.
6. Language and languages—Political aspects—Germany.
7. German language—Rhetoric. I. Title.
DD247.H5A357   943.086092—dc22   2006012702
ISBN 0-8204-8807-0 (hardcover)
ISBN 0-8204-8187-4 (paperback)

Bibliographic information published by **Die Deutsche Bibliothek**.
Die Deutsche Bibliothek lists this publication in the "Deutsche
Nationalbibliografie"; detailed bibliographic data is available
on the Internet at http://dnb.ddb.de/.

Cover design by Sophie Boorsch Appel

The paper in this book meets the guidelines for permanence and durability
of the Committee on Production Guidelines for Book Longevity
of the Council of Library Resources.

© 2006 Peter Lang Publishing, Inc., New York
29 Broadway, New York, NY 10006
www.peterlang.com

All rights reserved.
Reprint or reproduction, even partially, in all forms such as microfilm,
xerography, microfiche, microcard, and offset strictly prohibited.

Printed in the United States of America

Table of Contents

Preface ix

Acknowledgments xi

List of Abbreviations, Punctuation and Typography xiii

Introduction 1

Chapter 1: Historical and Biographical Background 5

1.1	The Wilhelmine and Hapsburg Empires 5
1.2	The Weimar Republic 6
1.3	Adolf Hitler: His Life until 1933 9
1.4	*Mein Kampf* 19
1.5	Hitler's *Weltanschauung* 21

Chapter 2: Hitler's Language 29

2.1	The Language of National Socialism 29
2.2	Possible Influences on Hitler's Language 31
2.3	The Language of *Mein Kampf* 41
2.3.1	Hitler's Rhetoric 42
2.3.2	Hitler's Views on Propaganda and the Spoken Word 44
2.3.3	Hitler's Construction of a *"Feindbild"* 47
2.3.4	Hitler's Glorification of the German *Volk* 55
2.3.5	Hitler's Belief in a Racial Hierarchy 58
2.3.6	The Nature of Hitler's *Kampf* 63
2.3.7	What the Language of *Mein Kampf* Tells us about Hitler . . . 66
2.3.8	How Conventional was the Language of *Mein Kampf*? 71

Chapter 3:	Metaphor in *Mein Kampf*	75
3.1	What is Metaphor?	75
3.2	Other Types of Metaphorical Representation	78
3.2.1	Metonymy	78
3.2.2	Personification	80
3.2.2.1	Personification of Human Experiences in *MK*	81
3.2.2.2	Personification of Non-human Entities in *MK*	82
3.2.3	Idioms	82
3.2.4	Sayings and Proverbs	84
3.2.5	Myth, Legend and Fiction	85
3.2.6	Historical and Biblical Events	88
3.3	Source Domains for Metaphors and Other Figures of Thought	90
3.4	Source Domains for Hitler's Metaphors	91
3.4.1	Container Metaphors	92
3.4.2	Metaphors of Location and Movement	102
3.4.2.1	Location	102
3.4.2.2	Movement	104
3.4.2.3	Lack of Movement	114
3.4.3	THE GREAT CHAIN OF BEING	115
3.4.3.1	Supernatural Beings, Nature and Fate	117
3.4.3.2	Human Beings	120
3.4.3.2.1	Human Hierarchies	120
3.4.3.2.2	Personification	123
3.4.3.2.3	The Human Anatomy	125
3.4.3.2.4	Human Attributes and Capacities	132
3.4.3.2.5	Human Society and Culture	134
3.4.3.2.6	Artifacts and Technologies	143
3.4.3.3	Zoological Metaphors	150
3.4.3.4	Botanical Metaphors	156
3.4.3.5	Non-living Entities	157
3.4.4	Natural Elements, Forces and Processes	161
3.4.4.1	Meteorological Metaphors, Fire, Light and Colours	161
3.4.4.2	Growth and the Processes of Decay	166
3.4.4.3	Other Natural Forces	169
3.5	How Conventional were Hitler's Metaphors?	169

Conclusion		175
Appendix I: Sample Texts		183
Appendix II: Rhetorical Devices		191
1	Superlatives	191
1.1	Grammatical Superlatives	191
1.2	Superlative Meanings	192
1.3	Grammatical Superlatives with Words of Superlative Meaning	193
1.4	Superlatives of Size and Amount	193
1.5	Numerical Superlatives	194
1.6	Time Superlatives	194
2	Repetition	195
2.1	Phonetic Repetition	195
2.2	Morphological Repetition	195
2.3	Grammatical Repetition	196
2.4	Lexical Repetition	198
2.5	Semantic Repetition	199
3	Accumulation *(Häufung)*	200
3.1	Idiomatic Pairs *(Zwillingsformeln)*	200
3.2	Figures of Three *(Dreierfiguren)*	201
3.3	Figures of Four	201
3.4	Figures of Five	202
3.5	Enumeration	202
4	Aggressive and Apocalyptic Vocabulary	203
5	Epithets and Evaluations	205
5.1	Neutral Epithets	205
5.2	Positive Epithets and Evaluations	205
5.3	Pejorative Epithets and Evaluations	211
6	Antithesis	232
7	Irony	233
7.1	Ironic Quotation Marks	233
7.2	Irony Without Inverted Commas	234
7.3	Sarcasm	235
7.4	Ironic Epithets	235

8	Euphemisms	236
9	Involving the Reader	237
9.1	Questions	237
9.2	Addressing the Reader	239
9.3	Appellatives	241
9.4	Imperatives	241
9.5	Exclamations	242
10	Features of Colloquial Language	242
10.1	Clichés	242
10.2	Modal Particles	243
10.3	Pauses	244
11	Narrative Structure	245
12	Archaisms	246
13	Foreign Words	246

Glossary 249

Bibliography 251

Index of Metaphors 257

General Index 259

Preface

I am neither Jewish nor a German; I was not alive during the Second World War and I have never been the victim of severe discrimination or cruelty. I have no special qualification for writing about anti-Semitic discourse, though I believe that if I were Jewish or German, or if I had ever suffered as a result of war or discrimination, I would not have been able to write this book. My initial intention was to be objective in my discussion of *Mein Kampf*, to remain detached from the horror of its content; but while it may have been possible for me to keep subjectivity out of my writing, I have been shocked by the hatred which is evident on nearly every page. Having read the research of Schmitz-Berning, Grieswelle, Sternberger and others, I knew from the outset that Hitler's bible of anti-Semitism was suffused with hatred for the Jews, but not to what extent. Almost every group of people or institution that Hitler despised had, as he saw it, a Jewish connection: Marxism, the press, the arts, Freemasons, Russians; he also expressed disdain for the German bourgeoisie, the proletariat, parliamentarians and democrats.

My earliest experience of the language of *Mein Kampf* was after I was asked to teach a course on German political discourse. I started by reading the chapters which dealt with the language of propaganda and the importance of the spoken word (Book 1, Chapter 6 and Book 2, Chapter 6). I observed many similarities with the political discourse of the nineteenth and early twentieth centuries, such as that of Eugen Thüring (see Cobet, 1973), Friedrich Ludwig Jahn (1810) and Houston Stewart Chamberlain (1899, 1905 and 1925^2). I read much on the language of National Socialism, but few authors dealt in great depth with *Mein Kampf*. I felt there was a significant lacuna in research into the language of National Socialism and that of totalitarianism more generally, and I decided to read *Mein Kampf* in its entirety. I managed to remain relatively dispassionate, concentrating particularly on Hitler's use of metaphor, until I reached page 772. Here I encountered Hitler's statement that 12,000 –15,000 Jews ('diese hebräischen Volksverderber') should have been gassed at the beginning of the Great War, thus sparing the lives of one million worthy Germans ('wertvolle Deutschen', translated by Mh. as 'real Germans').

I began to doubt if *MK* were worthy of any scholarly attention. Yet I still believed that its language should be subjected to thorough scrutiny—not because this was the book which had led the German nation astray, as it was probably less influential than Hitler's later speeches, but because its language must tell us something about the mind of a man who intended to, and eventually did, take a nation to war, and who was ultimately responsible for the death of millions of innocent people, Jews and non-Jews.

Hitler brought little novelty to the rhetoric of hatred, apart from the number and density of the linguistic devices that he used. He commandeered a style and tone already in use in nationalistic discourse and intensified it for his own purposes. The sheer concentration and violence of Hitler's language in *Mein Kampf*, the long-winded repetitive ranting, the sheer length of the book, probably find no parallels in any political work before or since. Hitler's language in *Mein Kampf*, in my opinion, sheds light on the mental processes of an obsessive, arrogant, self-appointed totalitarian leader in the making, and this is sufficient reason for analysing it, particularly for the benefit of the English-speaking scholarly community. Wolfgang Benz's judgement that anti-Semitism is a social paradigm for the formation of prejudices and the construction of *"Feindbilder"* ('images of the enemy') clarifies the need to investigate all of its manifestations to their deepest foundations (cf. Benz and Königseder 2002: 15). The present-day political climate of increased radical right-wing political activity and holocaust denial in various parts of Europe makes this undertaking all the more desirable.

Acknowledgments

I would like express my sincere gratitude to the following people for their practical help and advice: Professor Bill Jones, Professor Andreas Musolff and Professor Katie Wales, all of whom gave their encouragement and expert guidance throughout the project. I would also like to thank my colleagues in the School of Modern Languages at Queen Mary, University of London for their support over the several years that it has taken me to write this book, in particular Professor Leonard Olschner, Dr. Patricia Howe, Dr. Robert Gillet, Dr. Astrid Köhler, Dr. Falco Pfalzgraf, Mr Derek Daniels, Mr Brian Place and Professor Elza Adamowicz. Special thanks are due to Professor Wolfgang Mieder and Professor Rüdiger Görner for their encouragement and suggestions. Dr. Geraldine Horan and Dr. Rebecca Townsend, both of the Department of German, University College London have provided valuable bibliographical references. I am also grateful to Phyllis Korper, Gabriel Miller, Sophie Appel and Brittany Schwartz of Peter Lang, New York, for their help with the production of this volume, and to the Research Committee of the School of Modern Languages for assistance with production costs. Finally, Dr. Peter Orton, my partner, has lived with this book for the last eight years and I thank him most sincerely for his support and patience, and for his indefatigability as a proof-reader and sounding board.

List of Abbreviations

<	derived from	n.	neuter
App.	Appendix	NS	National Socialist
c.	century	NSDAP	*Nationalsozialistische Deutsche Arbeiterpartei*
DAP	*Deutsche Arbeiterpartei*		
DNVP	*Deutschnationale Volkspartei*	OHG	Old High German
		pl.	plural
ENHG	Early New High German	SA	*Sturmabteilung*
f.	feminine	sb.	somebody
KPD	*Kommunistische Partei Deutschlands*	sth.	something
		SPD	*Sozialdemokratische Partei Deutschlands*
m.	masculine		
Mh.	Manheim	SS	*Schutzstaffel*
MHG	Middle High German	VB	*Völkischer Beobachter*
MK	*Mein Kampf*		

Punctuation and Typography

Within the main body of the text, double and single quotation marks are used in accordance with the European system;
Square parentheses surround Manheim's translations into English;
Rounded parentheses surround my translations into English;
Square parentheses plus the 'is equal to' symbol surround additional or contextual information provided within quotations thus [=];
Bold-face is used in quotations from *MK* represents Hitler's *Sperrdruck* (spaced characters);
Italics are used in quotations from *MK* to represent Hitler's Roman type (used for foreign words);
Italics are used in quotations from Mh. as in the original translation;
The "SMALL CAPITALS" system of notation is used to refer to metaphorical mappings.

Introduction

It is widely assumed that a great deal has been written on the language of the Third Reich and on Hitler's language in particular. There is, however, no recent detailed study of the rhetoric of *MK* in English, and this volume, written from the point of view of a linguistician, should go some way towards filling this gap. It is hoped that the provision of quotations from the German original, along with English translations taken from Ralph Manheim's widely available version, will make the book useful to scholars whether or not they know German. It is intended to be of value to linguists, historians and political scientists in both the English-speaking and German-speaking worlds. It is hoped that the research presented here will support future study in the field of critical discourse analysis and add to our understanding of the nature of totalitarian discourse and its persuasive power.

Many of the oldest descriptions of NS language are still considered to be among the best. Victor Klemperer's *LTI* is a case in point. This Jewish philologist characterized the language of National Socialism as a 'Sprachkrankheit' ('a linguistic disease') and 'als Prahlen und Lüge erkannte Propaganda' ('a propaganda recognized as bragging and lies', Klemperer 1996 (1946): 237). *Mein Kampf (MK)* is an early example of such language, and it is the purpose of this book to investigate its language, in particular its use of rhetorical figures, with the aim of shedding some light on Hitler's intentions in writing it and his political stance as a whole.

In 1941, Kenneth Burke marked the publication of the first unexpurgated translation into English of *MK* with an essay on Hitler's propagandist intentions and some of the rhetorical devices he used to achieve them. This essay is perhaps the most enlightening account of *MK* in English to date (cf. Josef Schmidt's warm praise of it in 2004). Burke makes a number of useful generalisations about the content and language of *MK* which show it to have a plain but terrifying message reinforced chiefly by constant repetition of simple concepts. Burke presents Hitler's political aim as a unification of disparate and directionless political factions in a depressed post-First World War Germany. According to Burke, Hitler understood that a single "common enemy" has the power to unite people: 'Men who can unite on nothing else can unite on the basis of a foe shared by all' (Burke 1973: 193). It was for this reason that Hitler constructed his *"Feindbild"* ('image of the enemy'), making the Jews responsible for all Germany's current ills. He allocated a "devil-function" to the Jews, based on his belief in the "curative" effect of being able to hand one's ills to a scapegoat: this he called 'purification by dissociation' (Burke: 202). Burke's central line of argument is that Hitler's "unification device" made corrupt use of religious patterns; that it "bastardized" religious patterns of thought. Much of *MK* could, indeed, be considered blasphemous in its usurping of religious language and images. In this connection, Burke accuses Hitler of 'emotional trickeries' that shifted criticism away from the true locus of Germany's troubles (Burke: 219). Burke further adds to our understanding of *MK* by contextualizing Hitler's persecution mania (as he diagnoses it) with a declaration that this was not genuine but constructed from public materials that he adapted for his own purposes (Burke: 213).

In the present volume, Chapter 1 provides a sketch of the historical period leading up to the Weimar Republic, of the time of the Republic itself, and of Hitler's life before he came to power. The first part of the chapter is intended as a contextual aid for linguists. This chapter also examines Hitler's *Weltanschauung* and how this is realized in *MK*. It is recognized that Hitler's ideology, particularly his anti-Semitism, was not unique, and that his propaganda and its language should be studied against the background of earlier and coexistent right-wing discourse. Chapter 2 concentrates on the language of National Socialism and Hitler's own language. A number of possible and probable influences on Hitler's ideas and language are postulated, exemplified by seven of the texts in Appendix I. This chapter also demonstrates how the author attempted to convince his audience or, if some of his readers were already converts to his ideas, to reinforce their loyalty and reassure them of his trustworthiness and sincerity (we can only guess at the truth behind his image of himself as sincere). In *MK*, Hitler used a variety of stylistic and rhetorical devices to enhance his message of hatred for those people whom he judged to be Germany's enemies. Hyperbolic and aggressive vocabulary, powerful and emphatic style and a very full inventory of metaphors were used to rouse the German people to fight these enemies. Hitler made it clear that only wholehearted, unwavering support for his cause would be enough to achieve success. Chapter 2 also examines Hitler's use of rhetorical devices for specific ideological purposes: for his construction of a *Feindbild*, for his glorification of the German *Volk*, to elucidate his belief in a racial hierarchy, and to define the nature of his *Kampf* and that of National Socialism. These four sections illustrate the prominence of anti-Semitism in Hitler's doctrine and his polarization of relevant human characteristics into Good (i.e. Aryan) and Evil (i.e. Jewish).

Chapter 3 explains the notion of conceptual metaphor and then demonstrates Hitler's use of a wide variety of metaphorical expressions. Most of these he will have encountered in political literature and speeches before he started work on *MK*. He deployed chiefly conventional and well-worn metaphors, although the variety and density of these make *MK* a model of totalitarian discourse. Hitler was especially skilled at creating novel blends of metaphors, extended metaphors and allegorical scenes to illustrate his views. As in Chapter 2, Chapter 3 exposes his *Weltanschauung* as one that only tolerated extremes, for example with unpleasant, dangerous and generally low-level metaphorical source domains representing Jews and other of Germany's "enemies", and pleasant, harmless and higher-level domains representing all that Hitler considered good.

The two analytical chapters of this volume (Chapters 2 and 3) are followed by two appendices in this volume. A third appendix, containing an extensive database of metaphors attested in *MK*, may be accessed on the web site www.qmul.ac.uk/~mlw032. Appendix I documents samples of nationalistic discourse from the nineteenth and twentieth centuries to illustrate how Hitler's *MK* fitted in to a continuum of similar political writing. Appendix II complements Chapter 2 by providing additional textual examples and their English translations.

CHAPTER 1

Historical and Biographical Background

1.1 The Wilhelmine and Hapsburg Empires

Prior to 1871, Prussia, under Hohenzollern kings, and Austria, under Hapsburg emperors, dominated the German-speaking area. Both had been part of the Holy Roman Empire, which by the mid-nineteenth century had completely disintegrated, and their relationship had been unstable since the French Revolution, culminating in the dispute over the rule of Schleswig-Holstein and the subsequent defeat of Austria at the Battle of Königgrätz (1866). Despite moves to develop democratic systems after the French Revolution, both the Hohenzollerns and the Hapsburgs were keen to preserve royal authority. Simultaneously, a progressive and nationalist debate had continued and political parties emerged on both the left and right wings of the political spectrum. In 1848, Karl Marx and Friedrich Engels had produced the Communist Manifesto, which was to inspire the international socialist and communist movements. While absolute rule had continued in Prussia and Austria, the smaller German states had refused to consider power-sharing. A small number of liberals had, however, begun to explore the concept of a single German democratic State (Allinson 2002: 15). Nationalist feelings had grown from the early nineteenth century onwards, particularly among members of the German *Burschenschaften* (student societies), who celebrated German national identity and called for liberal reforms. High food prices and shortages had caused a revolution in 1848, but this had been promptly quashed by the ruling elite. Against this background, the new *Deutsches Reich,* or *"Kaiserreich"*, was formed in 1871. This "Second Empire" was formed as a parliamentary democracy by the Prussian Prime Minister Otto von Bismarck, with Wilhelm I as Emperor until 1888 and Wilhelm II until 1918 (Bismarck remained Chancellor until 1890). The formation of a single state followed Prussia's victory over Napoleon III's French forces in 1870. The Hapsburg Austro-Hungarian Empire was now completely excluded from German affairs. The King of Prussia held the title of *Deutscher Kaiser* in perpetuity, and the *Reichskanzler* (imperial chancellor, i.e. Bismarck) and his ministers were accountable to him. The Kaiser could appoint and dismiss governments and thus the Empire bore the outward trappings of a democracy without being truly democratic at heart.

The Second Empire expired at the end of the First World War, when Wilhelm II abdicated on 9 November 1918, two days before the armistice was signed with the victorious powers. The Treaty of Versailles was signed on 28 June 1919. It contained a "war guilt clause" which led to the imposition of its terms on Germany without negotiation (Allinson: 62). Hitler later harnessed German anger over these terms by topicalizing the treaty in his speeches and writings. Germany lost all of her colonies, and some of the territory on her borders was assigned to France, Poland, Denmark and Belgium. Danzig became a "free city" and a corridor of land, the "Danzig corridor", gave Poland access to the Baltic sea. Most importantly, Germany lost control of the Saarland, upon which she depended for vital coal supplies, to the League of Nations. Union with Austria was proscribed and punitive reparations payments left the German people living in harsh economic circumstances.

1.2 The Weimar Republic

At the end of the First World War, Woodrow Wilson was only prepared to consider peace with a democratic state. Constitutional change was thus forced upon a largely unwilling Germany. A *Nationalversammlung* (National Assembly) was elected in January 1919 with the Social Democrat Friedrich Ebert as its president, replacing the Kaiser as Head of State. The first meeting of the Assembly took place in Weimar, though the capital of Germany remained in Berlin. The new republic was formed from a coalition of moderate parties; the *Sozialdemokratische Partei Deutschlands* (SPD) was the largest party but had no overall majority. The Weimar Republic was unstable from the start, as the new system of proportional representation made it possible for small extremist parties to be elected to the *Reichstag*. Parliamentary democracy was further weakened by the *Reichstag*'s acceptance of the Treaty of Versailles, which angered the right-wing parties and caused widespread resentment within the population. The new republic started to be made a scapegoat for all the ills that befell Germany. In 1921 the allies presented their bill for reparations—132 billion marks. The government resigned and was replaced by a more centrist group under the leadership of the *Zentrum* politician, Joseph Wirth. The new government agreed to pay the reparations bill and Germany's economic situation continued to deteriorate. Inflation increased as large quantities of paper money were printed (the reparations had been calculated on the old gold mark). Political unrest simmered, but attempts to bring down the Weimar government, such as the Kapp putsch of 1920, failed.

Sebastian Haffner highlights 1923 as a year of extraordinary events, and a point at which 'Germans had a spiritual organ removed' (Haffner 2003: 44). Two events stand out: the French occupation of the Ruhr and Hitler's *"Bierkeller"* putsch (further described in Section 1.3 below). The Ruhr occupation unleashed a short burst of patriotic fervour, with crowds chanting the words of the Rütli oath from Schiller's *Wilhelm Tell*: 'Wir wollen sein ein einzig Volk von Brüdern'. During 1923, the value of the mark fell dramatically, with an exchange rate of 20,000 marks to the dollar rising through tens of thousands to hundreds of thousands within months of the Ruhr crisis. By September, a million marks had no practical value. Those who were brave enough dealt in shares, some becoming rich quickly, others losing fortunes just as suddenly. Poverty was the more normal outcome, yet, according to Haffner, an air of light-headedness and licentiousness prevailed. There was talk of revolution, of the dissolution of the republic, a return of the Kaiser. Various right-wing and left-wing political leagues became active once more, people disappeared and "saviours" appeared. Hitler was one possible saviour, giving anti-Semitic speeches. Then, in November of that year, Hitler's failed *Bierkeller* putsch filled the headlines and for a few days people thought that the long-expected revolution had come. No revolution occurred, however; Hitler was arrested and the *Rentenmark* was introduced. The exchange rate against the dollar stabilized, and business and foreign trade started to improve.

Between 1924 and 1929 the German economy recovered and, due to Germany's apparent willingness to pay reparations, diplomatic relations with the western allies and with Russia improved. According to the Dawes Plan of 1924, German reparation payments were linked with the ability to pay. In 1925, the foreign minister, Gustav Stresemann, signed the Locarno Treaty with the western powers, acknowledging the post-1918 frontiers in western Europe, and the Berlin Treaty with the Soviet Union. Following Friedrich Ebert's death in 1925, Field Marshal Paul von Hindenburg was elected president and in 1926 Germany joined the League of Nations, assuring Germany's return to the world stage. But the Weimar Republic had structural problems and Hindenburg, a hero of the First World War and an imperialist, disliked democratic rule. He defended parliamentary rule during the 1920s but did nothing to save the government from collapse in 1930. During the late 1920s unemployment rose. The SPD was weakened and more people voted for the *Kommunistische Partei Deutschlands* (KPD), the Roman Catholic *Zentrum*, and more radical parties. In 1929 Germany was required to settle her financial obligations to the allies according to the terms of the Young Plan. Alfred Hugenberg's *Deutschnationale Volkspartei* (German National People's Party = DNVP), aided by Hitler's *Nationalsozialistische Deutsche Arbeiterpartei* (National Socialist German Workers' Party = NSDAP), led a campaign against the Young Plan. The campaign failed, but Hitler's popularity was strengthened. In October 1929 the Wall Street Crash caused foreign investors to withdraw their funds and Germany's underlying economic weakness became apparent. The coalition government, led by the SPD under Hermann Müller, collapsed in March 1930 and Hindenburg appointed the *Zentrum* politician, Heinrich von Brüning, to the post of *Reichskanzler*. Brüning introduced spending cuts, lower wages and higher taxation as a means of raising funds to honour the Young Plan. Unemployment rose once more: both the working class and the middle class were affected. Brüning became increasingly unpopular, and in the 1930 elections the KPD and the NSDAP, both firmly opposed to the Weimar Republic, were successful. While rejecting the Republic, the NSDAP were unable to provide a viable alternative, but their opposition to the Versailles Treaty made them popular with nationalists.

During the early 1930s, politics were polarized between the KPD and NSDAP, and the centrist parties were weakened. The communist paramilitarist *Roter Frontkämpferbund* and the NSDAP *Sturmabteilung* (SA) and *Schutzstaffel* (SS) fought battles in the streets. As political violence grew, economic decline increased. When Brüning decided to ban the SA and SS, Hindenburg replaced him with Franz von Papen. Support for the NSDAP increased as it seemed to represent the whole of Germany. People wanted a radical break from democracy, which they saw as responsible for hyperinflation, unemployment and the humiliation represented by Germany's acceptance of the Versailles Treaty. On 30 January 1933 Hindenburg appointed Hitler *Reichskanzler* at the head of an authoritarian and nationalist NSDAP-DNVP coalition. The feeling in Germany became more optimistic. Idealists and racists celebrated as fascist Germany was born; the western European powers and many Germans would later regret their continuing belief that Hitler was harmless.

Haffner characterizes the period between the end of the First World War and 1924 as a time when the majority of the younger generation had no direction; when they did find a direction, they became either Nazis or anti-Nazis (Haffner: 58). Prior to 1924 they had depended on political tensions, the practical hardships caused by hyperinflation and the excitement of share-dealing to fill their lives, for they 'had never learned to live from within themselves' (Haffner: 57). With the advent of relative economic and political peace after 1924, they became bored and longed for salvation from what they experienced as a *'horror vacui'*. Older people were uncertain about their ideals, the youth of the bourgeois class were bored, and the masses were disillusioned with Marxism. While peace reigned on the surface, 'under the surface, all was ready for a vast catastrophe' (Haffner: 59). Germany was ready for Hitler.

1.3   Adolf Hitler: His Life until 1933

Adolf Hitler was born in 1889 in Braunau am Inn, on the Austrian side of the German-Austrian border. In 1892 his father Alois Hitler, a customs official, was appointed to the Austrian Customs House in Passau, on the German side of the river Inn. Later, in *Mein Kampf (MK)*, Hitler stated that his early childhood near the border with Germany was providential ('glückliche Bestimmung', *MK*: 1), and that at this early time Fate had decided that he would have a hand in reuniting Austria and Germany (**'Gleiches Blut gehört**

in ein gemeinsames Reich', *MK*: 1). When Hitler was six his father retired, and two years later the family moved to Leonding near Linz in Austria. The young Adolf was educated at the elementary school in Leonding and then at the *Realschule* in Linz. A year later he was moved to the *Realschule* at Steyr near Linz, which he left after one year at the age of fifteen. This was the end of Hitler's formal schooling. He had not been a model schoolboy. He was lazy, opinionated and rebellious, and addicted to the adventure stories of Karl May. He enjoyed playing 'Cowboys and Indians' and war games, taking his encouragement from a book about the Franco-Prussian war of 1870/71. In *MK*, Hitler claimed that his favourite subject at school was history and his favourite teacher Prof. Leopold Pötsch:

> Noch heute erinnere ich mich mit leiser Rührung an den grauen Mann, der uns im Feuer seiner Darstellung manchmal die Gegenwart vergessen ließ, uns zurückzauberte in vergangene Zeiten und aus dem Nebelschleier der Jahrtausende die trockene geschichtliche Erinnerung zur lebendigen Wirklichkeit formte. Wie saßen da, oft zu heller Glut begeistert, mitunter sogar zu Tränen gerührt. (*MK*: 12) [Even today I think back with gentle emotion on this grey-haired man who, by the fire of his narratives, sometimes made us forget the present; who, as if by enchantment, carried us into past times and, out of the millennial veils of mist, moulded dry historical memories into living reality. On such occasions we sat there, often aflame with enthusiasm, and sometimes even moved to tears. (Mh.: 13)]

According to Hitler, this teacher appealed to his pupils' budding sense of national honour and encouraged fanatical (German) nationalism in them (*MK*: 13). This was perhaps the beginning of Hitler's obsession with history and politics, and of his hatred of the Hapsburg monarchy and all non-German residents in the multinational Austro-Hungarian Empire. Linz itself was certainly a firmly German nationalist town and its 60,000 citizens almost homogeneously German (Kershaw: 18). Hitler therefore had little or no contact with Jews before he first visited Vienna in 1906.

Hitler's father died when he was thirteen and his indulgent mother did not force him to stay on at school or to choose a profession. Alois Hitler had wanted his son to follow him into the civil service. While his father was still alive this had caused friction, but with his father dead, Hitler could claim to be an artist and a writer. In 1906, at the age of seventeen, Hitler visited Vienna. One year later, after inheriting his share of his father's estate, Hitler moved to Vienna where he hoped to follow a career as an artist, but he failed the entrance examination to the Academy of Art and was advised to study architecture. Unfortunately he had not taken the necessary school-leaving examinations and subsequently did nothing to remedy this deficiency. Hitler did not tell his mother of his failure, perhaps because of her terminal illness with breast cancer. Klara Hitler died in December 1907 and her son returned to Vienna in February 1908. He had persuaded his friend, August "Gustl" Kubizek, to join him in Vienna. Kubizek was a musician and the two friends visited the opera several evenings a week. It was during this time that Hitler's fanatical love of Wagner developed.

Still pretending to be an art student, Hitler reapplied to the Academy, again unsuccessfully. Hitler left Gustl behind in the rented room that they shared and "dropped out". From this time on he eked out an existence selling drawings of Vienna landmarks. For much of his remaining time in Vienna he lived at a men's hostel at Meldemannstrasse 27, where he was able to rent a cubicle to sleep in and spend his days in the canteen or the smoking-room. In *MK* Hitler remembered this time as one of hunger, hardship and misery ('Elend und Jammer', *MK*: 20), with *Frau Sorge* (Lady Care) taking the place of his loving, complaisant mother. These hard times, he claimed, prepared him for a later life of conflict and endurance:

> (...) und was damals als Härte des Schicksals erschien, preise ich heute als Weisheit der Vorsehung. Indem mich die Göttin der Not in ihre Arme nahm und mich oft zu zerbrechen drohte, wuchs der Wille zum Widerstand, und endlich blieb der Wille Sieger. (*MK*: 20) [(...) and what then seemed to be the harshness of Fate, I praise today as wisdom and Providence. While the Goddess of Suffering took me in her arms, often threatening to crush me, my will to resistance grew, and in the end this will was victorious. (Mh.: 19)]

During Hitler's time as a "down-and-out" in Vienna he was able to read widely on political issues and also to listen to debates in parliament, and according to his account in *MK* it was then that his political beliefs started to form. In fact he claims in *MK* that his eyes were opened to the menace of Jewry and Marxism, and that his beliefs acquired a granite foundation for him to build on for the future ('ein Weltbild und eine *Weltanschauung*, die zum granitenen Fundament meines derzeitigen Handelns wurden', *MK*: 20f., Mh.: 20f.). Hitler's later speeches and writings bear testimony to the fact that his *Weltanschauung* was indeed well-formed before he wrote *MK* and largely unchanged afterwards. Ian Kershaw has suggested that the story of his political "conversion" in Vienna was necessary for the image he constructed for himself in the early 1920s. If he were to portray himself as a "messiah", destined to free Austria and Germany from the evils of "Jewish" Marxism, it was essential that he had started out as a Nobody, that he had studied diligently despite his struggle for survival, and, as a result of such harsh experience, had gained unique insights into the social and political problems of the age. Only thus could he claim the right to leadership (Kershaw: 65). During his time in Vienna, Hitler was influenced in his political development by a number of individuals, such as Jörg Lanz von Liebenfels, who published the racist periodical *Ostara* and later claimed to remember having met Hitler in 1909 (Kershaw: 51). Lanz von Liebenfels was himself inspired by the ideas of Guido von List, whose doctrine included notions of an racially superior Aryan ruling class. It was von List who popularized the swastika, the Hindu sign of the sun, as a symbol of the "Germanic Hero" (Kershaw: 50). Von Liebenfels's followers were enthused by ideas of racial purity and *Ostara* abounded in illustrations of blond women being seduced by ape-like creatures. They advocated racial struggle which would take the form of racial selection and the eradication of socialism, democracy and feminism.

Between February 1908 and May 1913 Hitler was also exposed to the propaganda of political figures such as Karl Lueger, the mayor of Vienna and leader of the *Christlich-Soziale Partei* (Christian Social Party), and Georg Ritter von Schönerer, leader of the anti-Hapsburg, anti-Catholic, anti-socialist, anti-Semitic *Alldeutsche Bewegung* (German National Party). The 'Heil' greeting and the title of 'Führer' derive from Schönerer while Lueger influenced Hitler's own methods of propaganda. In particular Lueger understood the masses, to whom Hitler was later to address his own propaganda. The "masses" comprised the lower middle classes and artisans. To these people the Christian Social Party emphasized its social character. It did not oppose the Church in any way, thus obtaining its support. It had mastered the art of propaganda and had great influence over the masses:

> Sie erkannte den Wert einer großzügigen Propaganda und war Virtuosin im Einwirken auf die seelischen Instinkte der breiten Masse ihrer Anhänger. (*MK*: 130) [It recognised the value of large-scale propaganda and was a virtuoso in influencing the psychological instincts of the broad masses of its adherents. (Mh.: 109)]

The Christian Socialists thus gained a loyal and self-sacrificing following ('eine ebenso treue wie opferwillige Gefolgschaft'). Schönerer advised healthy and moral living if the German people were one day to be strong. He advocated a meat-free diet, abstinence from alcohol, and warned against consorting with prostitutes, from whom men might catch diseases that had originated with clients of an "inferior" race (Kershaw: 44).

Another early influence upon Hitler was the Austrian *Sozial-Demokratische Partei* (Social Democratic Party). He detested their ideology, but admired their propaganda methods, their marches, slogans, songs and salutes, and their whole-heartedness in everything they did: 'Die Psyche der breiten Masse ist nicht empfänglich für alles Halbe und Schwache' [The psyche of the great masses is not receptive to anything that is half-hearted and weak (*MK*: 44; Mh.: 39). Kershaw suggests that Hitler's hatred of the Social Democrats stems from his own status-consciousness (Kershaw: 59). In *MK* he writes of the social barrier between himself, coming as he did from a bourgeois background, and the lower classes. These he speaks of in derogatory terms:

> Dazu kommt noch bei vielen die widerliche Erinnerung an das kulturelle Elend dieser unteren Klasse, die häufige Roheit des Umgangs untereinander, wobei die eigene, auch noch so geringe Stellung im gesellschaftlichen Leben jede Berührung mit dieser überwundenen Kultur- und Lebensstufe zu einer unerträglichen Belastung werden läßt. (*MK*: 22) [To this, in many cases, we must add the repugnant memory of the cultural poverty of this lower class, the frequent vulgarity of its social intercourse; the petty bourgeois' own position in society, however insignificant it may be, makes any contact with this outgrown stage of life and culture intolerable. (Mh.: 21)]

Perhaps the most significant aspect of Hitler's views on socialism was his coupling of Judaism and Marxism, 'die jüdische Lehre des Marxismus' [the Jewish doctrine of Marxism] (*MK*: 69). He believed that the Marxist leadership and press was dominated by Jews.

In 1913 Hitler left Vienna for Munich, possibly to escape military service in Austria, although he claimed that he was fleeing from the 'Völkergemisch von Tschechen, Polen, Ungarn, Ruthenen, Serben und Kroaten usw.' [mixture of Czechs, Poles, Hungarians, Ruthenians, Serbs, and Croats] and, worse still, the 'ewiger Spaltpilz der Menschheit—Juden und wieder Juden' [the eternal mushroom of humanity—Jews and more Jews (the usual translation for *Spaltpilz* is 'bacterium')] (*MK*: 135; Mh.: 113). His dislike of the Hapsburg

Empire is well documented. Like the pan-Germans, he could see no future for German-Austrians in this multiethnic and multilingual empire. While he enjoyed visiting the imperial parliament during his time in Vienna, he was exposed to the spectacle of the delegates from different nations arguing with one another. Hitler agreed with the pan-Germans that the language of parliament should be German, for delegates were allowed to speak in their own languages with no interpreters provided (Hamann 1999: 118). The majority in parliament was, however, non-German, and the situation could not be changed.

Once in Munich, Hitler registered as an artist and was able to exist on his share of his father's inheritance, which had come to him on his twenty-fourth birthday. Hitler joined the German army at the outbreak of the First World War, being caught up, like tens of thousands of German men, in a frantic war euphoria. He joined the 16th Bavarian Infantry Regiment as a corporal and *Meldegänger* (dispatch runner), and was awarded the Iron Cross (Second Class) in December 1914 and the Iron Cross (First Class) in August 1918. At the end of the war Hitler was temporarily blinded by mustard gas. While he was in hospital in Pasewalk (near Stettin in Pomerania) the war ended, and revolution broke out on land and mutiny at sea. These events had a traumatic effect upon Hitler, who claimed in *MK* that he had decided to enter politics at this time.

In 1919, Hitler, now in the 2nd Bavarian Infantry Regiment, became involved in a propaganda offensive against communism, organized by Captain Karl Mayr to counter the propaganda of the Communists and Independent Socialists. Hitler became an Army Education Officer *(Bildungsoffizier)* and now had the opportunity to speak out about the Jews, possibly for the first time in public:

> (...) und was ich früher immer, ohne es zu wissen, aus dem reinen Gefühl heraus einfach angenommen hatte, traf nun ein: ich konnte „reden".' (*MK*: 235) [(...) and the thing that I had always presumed from pure feeling without knowing it was corroborated: I could 'speak'. (Mh.: 196)]

Hitler joined the *Deutsche Arbeiterpartei* [German Workers' Party = DAP], initially as an army observer, and wooed audiences in Munich beerhalls, appealing, as Kershaw puts it, to the 'gutter instincts of his listeners'

(Kershaw: 128). Hitler took over the propaganda of the DAP in early 1920 and he had his first large success at a meeting at the Festsaal of the Hofbräuhaus, which seated 2,000 people. On April 1, 1920, the name of the DAP was changed to the *Nationalsozialistische Deutsche Arbeiterpartei* [NSDAP]. A "leadership cult" started to grow up around Hitler and just three years after he joined the DAP he was known as the "German Mussolini" (Kershaw: 132)

According to Ian Kershaw, the First World War 'made Hitler possible' (Kershaw: 73). After the war, Germany was ready for a demagogue to help it endure the aftermath of military defeat and give it hope for a future as a world power. Germany was accustomed to authoritarianism and militarism. The Second Reich, although nominally a parliamentary democracy, had left Germans expecting to be led by a powerful and strongly militaristic elite. Imperial Germany had fervently desired national unity and post-war Germans were susceptible to an ideology of anti-pluralism and exclusivism. Germany was thus ready for a leader like Hitler and he found a number of powerful backers, such as Helene Bechstein, Elsa Bruckman, and Ernst Hanfstängel. In April 1920 Hitler left the army to devote himself entirely to the party. Later that year he organized a band of rough young men, dressed in brown uniforms and later named the *Sturmabteilung* (Storm Section or Brownshirts = SA), to keep order at party meetings. He also designed the party banner with a black swastika, already the symbol of the *Deutschvölkischer Schutz- und Trutzbund* (German Nationalist Protection and Defiance Federation), on a white circle against a red background. Hitler impressed his audiences with the strength of his conviction and the power of his prejudices. He appealed to the anger, fear and frustration already felt by many Germans and fed their loathing for those "responsible" for the post-war misery with the force of his own hatred. Hitler offered a simple solution to Germany's problems and won thousands of devotees (Kershaw: 123). The figure of the Jew dominated his tirades against Germany's "enemies", his language becoming increasingly genocidal and saturated with metaphors of vermin *(Ungeziefer)*, reptiles, parasites and pathological organisms (Kershaw: 151).

In July 1921 Hitler was elected president of the NSDAP. The basic ideology of the party was the love of all things German, fear of Marxism and hatred of the Jews. The *SA* was transformed into a paramilitary organization by Ernst Röhm, who had access to leading parliamentarians and a supply of weapons. On 14–15 October 1922 Hitler spoke at the *Deutscher Tag* (German Day) in Coburg, on the Thuringian border with north Bavaria. Until this point his sphere of influence had been well within the Bavarian border. A few days later the entire membership of the Franconian *Deutsche Werkgemeinschaft*, headed by Julius Streicher, joined the NSDAP, bringing with them their organ, the *Deutscher Volkswille*. Franconia became a Nazi stronghold. Hitler was seen increasingly as a heroic leader while he grew impatient for action, particularly in spring 1923 after the French occupation of the Ruhr.

On 1–2 September 1923, Hitler spoke at the *Deutscher Tag* in Nuremberg to an audience of 100,000. The NSDAP now merged with the *Reichsflagge* organisation, the *Bund Oberland* and the *Deutscher Kampfbund*. Although Hitler had been responsible for this propaganda coup, it was Erich von Ludendorff who was generally envisaged as the future dictator of Germany (Kershaw: 200). The *Völkischer Beobachter (VB)*, formerly the *Münchener Beobachter*, became a daily newspaper and the party organ in 1923. It was accompanied by Julius Streicher's weekly newspaper, *Der Stürmer*, with its macabre stories of Jewish sexual crimes and ritual murder (Shirer 1959: 50).

When the German economy collapsed later in 1923, Hitler recommended the dissolution of the Weimar Republic and the annulment of the Treaty of Versailles. Against a background of hyperinflation, strikes, unemployment and hatred of foreigners, Hitler came under pressure to act. He planned a putsch for 8 November to take over police stations and town halls and hijack a public meeting at the *Bürgerbräukeller* in Munich. The three political leaders of Bavaria, the Minister President Gustav von Kahr, the Police Chief Hans von Seißer and the Commander of the *Reichswehr* Otto von Lossow, had organized the meeting on the fifth anniversary of the November Revolution with the intention of denouncing Marxism. The SA was sent in at 8.30 p.m., while Kahr was speaking. Hitler stood on a chair, fired his gun and announced that the national revolution had begun. At gunpoint he took the "triumvirate of vons" into a side room. Promising them positions in the new government, he extracted promises that they would support his revolution. This they did and they were allowed to leave the meeting. Later the three "vons" broadcast on radio that they had only promised Hitler support at gunpoint and that they were opposed to the putsch. Hitler and Ludendorff marched through the streets of Munich at the head of 3,000 SA troops but were met in the Residenzstraße by state police. A bloody battle ensued and fourteen putschists and four policemen lost their lives. Hitler was spirited away and taken to the residence of Ernst Hanfstängel. It was here that he was arrested on 11 November.

While Hitler was imprisoned in the Landsberg, Alfred Rosenberg took charge of the now banned Nazi party. Hitler had time to read (Nietzsche, Treitschke, Houston Stewart Chamberlain) and to ponder and refine his *Weltanschauung*. By the time he started to write the first volume of *MK*, the final element had been added to his world-view, namely that Germany needed more lebensraum, and that this should be gained at the expense of Russia (Kershaw: 241). At this time Hitler's supporters began to form a "*Führer* cult" around him and he started to see himself as a predestined leader. By the time that he left the Landsberg he had a fully-fledged vision of how he would rebuild the Nazi movement and save Germany. He saw himself as indispensable and the party came to see him as the one and only *Führer*. In February 1925, the ban on the NSDAP and the *VB* was lifted and Hitler could make plans for the future. He intended to nationalize the "masses" through propaganda and mobilize them for an eventual takeover of the state and for external conquest. Hitler's first major speech after his release from prison took place at the *Bürgerbräukeller* on 27 February 1925. The NSDAP was now officially relaunched, but a subsequent ban on public speaking prevented Hitler from addressing other than private, closed meetings until March 1927. He continued working behind the scenes, protected by the SS.

The NSDAP grew in size between 1924 and 1929, and had 100,000 members by October 1928. Its sphere of influence spread from Bavaria into the rest of Germany and it was in a strong position to exploit the economic crisis in 1929. By this time it had few right-wing rivals and had been restructured into a well-organized movement. Goebbels was *Gauleiter* of Berlin and Gregor Strasser, organizer of National Socialism in North Germany, was Leader of Party Propaganda until late 1927, when Hitler took over from him. Joseph Goebbels started to publish a weekly (soon to be twice weekly) newspaper, *Der Angriff*, and was shortly after made Chief of Propaganda. Baldur von Schirach was appointed leader of the Nazi Students' Federation. Later he was to head the *Hitlerjugend* (Hitler Youth).

The NSDAP was disappointed by the results of the *Reichstag* election of May 1928, in which there were unexpected gains by the SPD and KPD. Only

12 Nazis, including Gregor Strasser, Wilhelm Frick, Gottfried Feder, Joseph Goebbels, General Ritter von Epp and Hermann Göring gained seats (Kershaw: 303). Results in the cities had been devastating, but in the rural areas there seemed to be more hope for the future and Hitler started to woo voters in the country areas. In January 1929 the *Landvolk* was founded by a group of radical peasants. This was a protest group with violent leanings and closely allied with the NSDAP. By this time Hitler was speaking at meetings all over Germany, with reparation payments as a major theme. According to the terms of the Young Plan, payments to the World War I allies were greatly reduced, but the issue was still capable of inflaming Germans, especially as Hitler stressed that they had been sold out by Jews and Communists at the Treaty of Versailles.

On 1–4 August 1929, Hitler spoke at a rally in Nuremberg to an audience of over 30,000. By the time of the Wall Street stock-market crash on 24 October his mastery of the Nazi movement was complete. The crash was greatly to the advantage of the NSDAP, as countless small German loans were underwritten by American banks and the German population was severely affected. During 1930, Germany's economic crisis deepened. Hitler offered hope to a public driven by hatred of a government which had failed them and of the Jews who they believed were forcing them out of their businesses and jobs. The NSDAP began to win an increased percentage of the votes in state and city elections (in Baden, Lübeck, Berlin and Thuringia). It was now a dynamic national party holding some hundred meetings a day. At the University of Jena a chair was endowed for *Rassenfragen* (Racial Questions) and *Rassenkunde* (Racial Knowledge).

Goebbels organized the campaign for the *Reichstag* elections of 14 October 1930. 34,000 meetings were planned for the final four weeks of the campaign. Hitler gave twenty speeches in the last six weeks, with his main theme the collapse of the German economy under democratic rule and the lack of unity among the German people. He presented a utopian picture of a united, classless Germany. The youth of the nation, who had never experienced prosperity, were particularly impressed with Hitler's message. They looked forward to a homogenous, racially pure national community *(Volksgemeinschaft)* with an authoritarian leader to look up to. The Nazis did well at the 1930 elections, gaining six million votes (107 seats). NSDAP membership grew accordingly. By now the foreign press had begun to notice Hitler and he became an international figure. The party continued its policy of agitation and organized 70,000 meetings for the ensuing period.

The Weimar State finally disintegrated in 1932. Hindenburg dissolved the *Reichstag* and set elections for 31 July. The NSDAP received 37·4% of the vote and won 230 seats in the *Reichstag*, and Hitler could have taken a role in Hindenburg's cabinet, but he was prepared to occupy no office other than the Chancellorship. He tried to negotiate with Hindenburg, who refused to allow the "Bohemian corporal" to take over as Chancellor from Franz von Papen. Hitler continued in his "all-or-nothing" strategy while Germany's economic depression deepened. Von Papen acted as an intermediary between Hindenburg and Hitler and eventually Hindenburg appointed Hitler Chancellor. On 30 January 1933 Hitler was sworn in as Chancellor of Germany. That evening a torchlight procession of SA and SS men through the centre of Berlin, watched from a window by Hindenburg and Hitler, heralded the new era of German Nazism.

1.4 *Mein Kampf*

Hitler wrote the first volume of *MK* in 1924 while he was imprisoned in the old fortress at Landsberg am Lech, and it was published in July 1925. During his early incarceration he would dictate each chapter to his chauffeur, Emil Maurice, then type Maurice's transcript in his cell. Later, after his arrival at the Landsberg, Rudolf Heß helped Hitler to formulate his ideas, and also took dictation and relieved him of some of the typing. The second volume of *MK* was written after Hitler's release from prison in July 1924 and it was published in December 1926. He had wanted to call his book *Viereinhalb Jahre gegen Lügen, Dummheit und Feigheit (Four and a Half Years of Struggle against Lies, Stupidity and Cowardice)*, but his publisher, Max Amann, found the title cumbersome and shortened it to *Mein Kampf* (usually translated into English as *My Struggle*). Amann had hoped for an exciting account of Hitler's rise from a casual worker in Vienna to an internationally renowned political figure. When the book appeared it contained some autobiography but was largely a political treatise in which Hitler aired his views on the Jews, on Marxism and parliamentarianism, and on such diverse topics as syphilis and prostitution, both of which he claimed to have been caused by the Jews. During the years following its publication, *MK* sold in modest numbers of some thousands of copies per annum. Hitler was at least able to live on the royalties; indeed, this was the first time that he had received a regular income. In the year following his appointment as Reich Chancellor in 1933, *MK* sold over one million copies; only the Bible was more popular. Most households had at least one copy of *MK* and it became customary to present a copy to newly-wed couples, although many more people owned a copy of the book than actually read it.

Hitler saw his book as a work of propaganda. He set out his aspirations as a propagandist in Chapter 6 of Book I of *MK*. His main aim was to convey the basic elements of his *Weltanschauung* to ordinary people, to the *"breite Masse"* ('the broad masses'), not necessarily as a direct result of their reading *MK*, but via the intermediary propagandists who would read and interpret his message and then deliver it according to his instructions on language use as documented in the work. Hitler recommended that a very simple message be used to woo the "common man", whom he believed to have a limited intellect:

> Die Aufnahmefähigkeit der großen Masse ist nur sehr beschränkt, das Verständnis klein, dafür die Vergeßlichkeit groß. Aus diesen Tatsachen heraus hat sich jede wirkungsvolle Propaganda auf nur sehr wenige Punkte zu beschränken und diese schlagwortartig so lange zu verwerten, bis auch bestimmt der Letzte unter einem solchen Worte das Gewollte sich vorzustellen vermag. (*MK*: 198) [The receptivity of the great masses is very limited, their intelligence is small, but their power of forgetting is enormous. In consequence of these facts, all effective propaganda must be limited to a very few points and must harp on these in slogans until the last member of the public understands what you want him to understand by your slogan. (Mh.: 165)]

Hitler saw subjectivity as vital to the psychology of propaganda: he intended to use one-sided arguments to appeal to the irrational nature of the masses, whom he saw as having no capacity for differentiation. He aimed his propaganda at people's emotions rather than at their minds:

> Das Volk ist in seiner überwiegenden Mehrheit so feminin veranlagt und eingestellt, daß weniger nüchterne Überlegung, vielmehr gefühlsmäßige Empfindung sein Denken und Handeln bestimmt. (*MK*: 201) [The people in their overwhelming majority are so feminine by nature and attitude that sober reasoning determines their thoughts and actions far less than emotion and feeling. (Mh.: 167)]

Hitler's message was one of hatred. He criticized the German propaganda of the First World War, the failure of which he considered as having resulted from its tendency to ridicule the enemy rather than portray it as a truly awful menace. The American and British propaganda of the time had succeeded in properly preparing their armies for the horrors of war by portraying the Germans as Huns and barbarians (*MK*: 199). The Germans, on the other hand, had been left at the end of the war with the feeling of having been misinformed and swindled. What had been lacking in the German propaganda had been an understanding of the psychology of the masses. In future they would have to feel rage and hatred *(Wut und Haß)* if their courage were not to flag (*MK*: 199; Mh.: 165). Germany's propaganda during the First World War had worked like a 'geradezu umgekehrt arbeitende Aufklärung' [an unparalleled example of an 'enlightenment' service working in reverse] (MK: 199; Mh.: 166). Hitler condemned it as ambiguous and ineffectual, 'fades Pazifistenspülwasser' [insipid pacifist bilge] (*MK*: 202, Mh.: 168), the product of weak thinkers. He believed that only simple and persistent emotive rhetoric would 'fire men's spirits till they were willing to die' (Mh.: 168). Hitler's later speeches, so similar in style and content to *MK*, were to unite audiences in an incomparable euphoria and spirit of joint purpose. Hitler's propaganda remained one of his most powerful weapons throughout the 1920s and 1930s and until the Second World War was nearly at its end.

1.5 Hitler's *Weltanschauung*

Michael Burleigh writes of the Third Reich as an era in which 'ordinary people chose to abdicate their individual faculties in favour of a politics based on faith, hope, hatred and sentimental collective self-regard for their own race and nation' (Burleigh 2001: 1). The faith of these people was put in Adolf Hitler and in the politics of violence and hatred that he promoted in his speeches and writings. Burleigh explains that the masses of ordinary German people were encouraged by self-interested sections of an elite class to pay heed to a ridiculous figure and his flawed, fanatical world-view. Many contemporary critics likened Nazism to a pseudo-religion under a sectarian-style leader, and Hitler's rhetoric encouraged this view. The First World War and its aftermath led to the revival of a pseudo-religious style of politics which helped console survivors but also gave the Far Right a new lease of life (Burleigh: 8). Hitler subscribed to this type of politics, as he recognized that a religion can touch emotions beyond the reach of political discourse. The NS philosophy of Hitler and his kind looked back to Germanic myths as reflecting a world where 'heroic doom was regarded positively, and where the stakes were all or nothing' (Burleigh: 12). According to Burleigh, Hitler's National Socialism merged the pseudo-science of eugenics and a 'bastardised Christianity', this being one of its few creative features. To Hitler, Nazism was the expression of God's scientific laws; it was a sacred science with Hitler as chief scientist on a mission to rid Germany of pathogens, i.e. human beings whom he considered inferior, according to God's will. Ian Kershaw summarizes Hitler's ideology as a belief that three values determined a people's fate: 'blood-' or 'race-values', the 'value of personality', and *Kampfsinn* ('sense of struggle') or *Selbsterhaltungstrieb* ('self-preservation drive'). These values were embodied in the Aryan race and were opposed by three Jewish vices: democracy, pacifism and internationalism (Kershaw 1998: 289). This typically *"völkisch"* world-view, consisting of extreme nationalism, anti-Semitism and pan-Germanism, was not new to the Germany of the 1920s and certainly not unique to Hitler.

During Hitler's early life the Austro-Hungarian Empire was home to a multinational community of Hungarians, Serbs, Croats and Slovaks. It was this medley of inhabitants as well as the large Jewish population that Hitler took against when living in Vienna (1908–1913). His home town of Linz was largely populated with German-speakers, but less than half of the population of Vienna had been born there and it was home to over 175,000 Jews (8·6% of the population): 'Mir erschien die Riesenstadt als die Verkörperung der Blutschande' [To me the giant city seemed the embodiment of racial desecration] (*MK*: 135; Mh.: 113). To Hitler the only solution was the reincorporation of Austria into the German Reich and the recognition of the "Jewish problem" as a matter of race rather than of religion (*MK*: 131). The superiority of the Aryan race was incontrovertible to Hitler: all the triumphs of art, science and technology were to be attributed to Aryans, who were the prototypes *(Urtyp)* of all higher humanity. To Hitler, the Aryan was the Prometheus of mankind 'aus dessen lichter Stirn der göttliche Funke des

Genies zu allen Zeiten hervorsprang' [from whose bright forehead the divine spark of genius has sprung at all times] (*MK*: 317; Mh.: 263).

In *MK*, Hitler states that his *Weltanschauung* was complete by the time he left Vienna for Munich in 1913 (*MK*: 21). While in Vienna he had taken great interest in newspapers such as the *Neue Freie Presse*, the *Wiener Tageblatt* and the overtly anti-Semitic *Deutsches Volksblatt*. It is also likely that he was familiar with anti-Jewish views before 1908, during his time in Linz, where he would have known the anti-Semitic *Linzer Fliegende Blätter* (Maser 1970: 60). Vienna was one of the most fanatically anti-Semitic cities in Europe at this time. Extremists demanded that sexual liaisons between Jews and Christians be punished as sodomy and Jews watched over at Easter time to prevent ritual child-murder (Kershaw: 65). This cannot have failed to have affected Hitler and he claims in *MK* that his anti-Semitism was fully fledged by the time he left the Austrian capital; he pins his enlightenment down to a specific episode, which he claims sparked his interest in anti-Semitic literature:

> Als ich einmal so durch die innere Stadt strich, stieß ich plötzlich auf eine Erscheinung in langem Kaftan mit schwarzen Locken.
> Is dies ein Jude? war mein erster Gedanke.
> So sahen sie freilich in Linz nicht aus. Ich beobachtete den Mann verstohlen und vorsichtig, allein je länger ich in dieses fremde Gesicht starrte und forschend Zug um Zug prüfte, um so mehr wandelte sich in meinem Gehirn die erste Frage zu einer anderen Frage:
> Ist dies auch ein Deutscher? (*MK*: 59)
> [Once, as I was strolling through the Inner City, I suddenly encountered an apparition in a black caftan and black hair locks. Is this a Jew? was my first thought.
> For, to be sure, they had not looked like that in Linz. I observed the man furtively and cautiously, but the longer I stared at this foreign face, scrutinising feature for feature, the more my first question assumed a new form:
> Is this a German? (Mh.: 52)]

Ian Kershaw believes it unlikely that this episode actually took place and suggests that Hitler's hatred of the Jews finally crystallized after the loss of the First World War and the 1918 Revolution in Germany (Kershaw: 69).

When Hitler joined the mobilized German troops in 1914 he was in the company of ordinary soldiers who had rushed to defend their homeland in a flurry of patriotic fervour. Much of their inspiration derived from the mythologization of the German nation and the anti-French rhetoric of the nineteenth century (Gregor 2005: 25). Starting with Fichte's *Reden an die deutsche Nation* in 1807, a tradition of national education *(Nationalerziehung)* developed according to which young Germans should learn to be proud of their specifically Germanic natures. During the early nineteenth century, authors such as Kleist, Iffland, Rückert and Kotzebue expressed anti-Napoleonic feelings and stressed the importance of blood-ties and of the individual as a 'Glied in einer Kette' ('link in a chain', Johnston 1990: 58f.). Other noteworthy patriots included Freiherr vom Stein, Ernst Moritz Arndt and Friedrich Schleiermacher, who became involved in paramilitary activities and secret societies, such as the *Lesende und schießende Gesellschaft* (Reading and Shooting Association) and the *Tugendbund* (League of Virtue), whose major stated aim was the improvement of individual moral conduct. Such societies aimed to involve themselves with matters of State, most notably the Prussian State, in order to influence policies vis-à-vis Napoleonic France. An extreme case of anti-French patriotism was encountered in the ideas of Friedrich Ludwig Jahn, which were directed at the youth of the lower middle class whom he hoped would save Germany from her foreign enemies, and build and defend a new nation (Johnston: 167). Many of Jahn's ideas seem to have been gleaned from contemporary popular philosophers, such as Thomas Abbt, Joseph von Sonnenfels and K.G. Kapf: Johnston describes Jahn's *Deutsches Volkstum* (1810) as containing references to a potpourri of literary sources but as agreeing broadly with similar nineteenth-century patriotic authors, especially in its aim to prepare young Germans for military action (Johnston: 176). Nineteenth-century secret societies, such as the *Tugendbund*, and authors such as Jahn continued to set the tone for German nationalism throughout the First World War and through the 1920s.

In 1912 the *Verband gegen Überhebung des Judentums* (League against Jewish Arrogance) was formed, publishing a periodical, *Auf Vorposten*, between 1912 and 1924. Hitler may well have read this periodical, and he certainly read and believed in the authenticity of the *Protokolle der Weisen von Zion* (first published in German in 1920), an anti-Semitic work propagating the myth of a Jewish conspiracy to control the entire world (*MK*: 337). Heinrich Claß, chairman of the *Alldeutscher Verband* (Pan-German League) from 1918, advocated that his members should support the idea of a dictatorship for Germany, and his deputy, Konstantin Freiherr von Gebsattel, urged members to use Jews as lightning conductors ('Blitzableiter für alles

Unrecht', Pfahl-Traughber 2003: 202). The *Deutschvölkischer Schutz- und Trutzbund* (German Nationalist Protection and Defiance Federation) was founded in 1919 under the aegis of the *Alldeutscher Verband* and became a gathering point for anti-Semitic and folkish groups. It published brochures and leaflets with explicit titles, for example: *Der Jude im Weltkrieg*, *Die Verjudung des Bank- und Börsenwesens* and *Ganz Israel bürgt füreinander* (Pfahl-Traughber: 203). It is inconceivable that Hitler would not have read this sort of literature. He must also have been familiar with the sentiments expressed through the statutes of the *Alldeutscher Verband*, the last two clauses of which recommended the planned racial improvement of the German *Volk* ('planmäßige rassische Höherentwicklung des deutschen Volkes') and the fight ('Bekämpfung') against Jewish hegemony ('Vorherrschaft', *Alldeutsche Blätter* 1919: 310). The *Reichshammerbund*, founded in 1912 by Theodor Fritsch and others, was already spreading the myth of a Jewish world conspiracy, and during the post-war period its periodical, *Der Hammer. Blätter für deutschen Sinn*, published anti-Semitic articles such as 'Freimaurerei während des Weltkriegs' (1918) and 'Geheime Gesellschaften im Dienste Judas' (1924). The Hammer-Verlag (Hammer publishing house) produced books and brochures such as *Der jüdische Plan* (1920) and *Die Geldherrschaft und das Haus Rothschild* (1921) as well as a German translation of Henry Ford's *The International Jew* in 1920 (Pfahl-Traughber: 204). Thus Germany was well supplied with anti-Semitic literature at the time when Hitler was at his most receptive to the views of other people.

Hitler records in *MK* that he had been able to observe anti-German Jewish behaviour for himself. In 1916, for example, while on leave in Munich, he noticed (or so he claims in *MK*) that a very large percentage of clerical jobs were held by Jews who, he thought, should have been at the front. Whilst in hospital at Pasewalk in November 1918, Hitler heard of the communist German Revolution and blamed Jewish *'Drahtzieher'* ('wire-pullers', *MK*: 585): 'ein paar Judenjungen waren die „Führer" in diesem Kampfe um die „Freiheit, Schönheit und Würde" unseres Volksdaseins' [a few Jewish youths were the 'leaders' in this struggle for the 'freedom, beauty, and dignity' of our national existence] (*MK*: 21; Mh.: 184). According to his account of the revolution in *MK*, Hitler decided to enter politics at precisely this time (*MK*: 225; Mh.: 187). Ian Kershaw, however, maintains that Hitler's entry into politics was not an act of personal determination; he was "discovered" by Karl Mayr in Munich after the end of the war, and it is possible that Mayr ordered him to attend his first meeting of the *Deutsche Arbeiterpartei* (German Workers' Party, Kershaw: 126). Kershaw further claims that Hitler did not make a firm connection between Bolshevism and Judaism until 1919, a year after his time at Pasewalk, where he did no more than rationalize his existing prejudices (Kershaw: 104). It was also in 1919 that Hitler became close to the anti-Semitic journalist and writer, Dietrich Eckart (1868–1923), to whom he expresses his gratitude in the final lines of *MK*.

Later, while incarcerated in the Landsberg, Hitler came to see himself as a heroic leader with a mission to save his nation. He looked up to Martin Luther, Frederick the Great and Wagner as his role-models. He is believed to have read Nietzsche, although there is no way of knowing precisely which texts. It is possible that he derived from Nietzsche his own belief in the existence of a naturally superior type of human being and the coming of a master race with one superior leader. If he read *Zur Genealogie der Moral, Erste Abhandlung* (Nietzsche 1956: 771–798) his own polarized view of the world would have been reinforced. It is possible that he read such texts on a very superficial level, simplifying their ideas in order to underpin his own nascent philosophy. Thus he might have concluded that Aryans were good and Jews were evil, the latter capable only of negative feelings such as hatred. He would also have become acquainted with Nietzsche's views on the disorientation *(Orientierungslosigkeit)*, decay *(Verfall)* and eventual downfall *(Untergang)* of mankind (von Polenz 1999: 552). It should be remembered, however, that Nietzsche's philosophy had been filtered through the editorial transformations of his racist sister, Elisabeth, before Hitler would have read the works that might have influenced him, such as *Der Wille zur Macht (The Will to Power)*. Hitler and his followers came to revere Nietzsche as an anti-Semite and proto-Nazi. He was, in fact, neither, and it was for this reason that he fell out with Richard Wagner (Kaufmann 1974: 45). After his release from prison Hitler visited the Nietzsche archive seven times and formed a friendship with Elisabeth Förster-Nietzsche; she, in turn, admired both Hitler and Nazism. The so-called "Nietzsche legend" (Kaufmann: 1) was, indeed, no more than a myth created by Elisabeth Förster-Nietzsche's over-enthusiastic editorship.

According to Kershaw, Hitler's lebensraum ideology started to take shape in 1922 alongside his anti-Semitism (Kershaw: 241). His ideas on lebensraum are clearly expressed in *MK*, where he stresses the importance of regaining territories lost to Germany after the First World War and adding to these land gained at Russia's expense. Basing his argument on Hitler's *Second Book*, Neil Gregor explains Hitler's world-view vis-à-vis lebensraum and the human struggle for survival as belonging to a 'vulgarized form of Darwinian thinking' (Gregor: 40). For Hitler, human history had been dominated by the struggles for survival of individuals and nations. He believed that nations and races exist in a perpetual struggle for self-preservation and self-perpetuation, and they are thus in competition with one another for living-space, food and, ultimately life itself. Hitler believed that it was the duty of each individual to subordinate his needs to the greater needs of his race or nation, and that war was the natural expression of the eternal competition for space. Ultimately it would be the physically stronger and mentally and spiritually superior people who would survive.

By the time *MK* was published, Hitler believed that he had 'found the key to the ills of the world in a doctrine of anti-Semitism' (Kershaw: 52) and that he was the man to cure those ills. In the second volume of *MK* he had written of *Führerfähigkeit* ('ability as a leader'), *Führergenialität* ('genius of a leader') and *Führerschwung* ('energy of a leader') as the characteristics of a leader who would be psychologist, demagogue, organizer and agitator all at the same time: **Denn Führen heißt: Massen bewegen können** *[For leading means: being able to move masses]* (*MK*: 650f.; Mh.: 528). Doubtless Hitler was thinking of himself here. He believed that he had an individual fight ahead of him for which he would be able to rally his fellow Germans. The uncompromising message of *MK* was one of total hatred for the enemies of Germany. Hitler believed that Germany would either become a world power or would cease to exist altogether: **'Deutschland wird entweder Weltmacht oder überhaupt nicht sein'** (*MK*: 742; Mh.: 597); half-measures *(Halbheiten)* were anathema to Hitler and not an option for his German followers. His descriptions of Jews echo the common stereotypes that have existed for centuries: that they are unwashed, ugly, dishonest and arrogant in their claims to be the "chosen people". Hitler saw his task as a holy mission: **'Indem ich mich des Juden erwehre, kämpfe ich für das Werk des Herrn'** [by defending myself against the Jew, I am fighting for the work of the Lord] (*MK*: 70; Mh.: 60). His mission consisted of constructing a terrifying image of the Jews as the deadly enemies of the German *Volk* (see Chapter 2, Section 2.3.3 on the construction of a *Feindbild*). Hitler did not consider the Jews to be Germany's only enemy, but they were certainly the worst. His aim was to unify all Aryans behind him in a battle to free Germany from its enemies and secure for it a glorious future. His ideology was totalitarian in that he disregarded individual freedom and loathed liberal democracy. He would lead Germany and Germans would obey him. There would be no place for discussion or individual choice, and the individual would overcome self-interest to the point where he would sacrifice his own life, if necessary, for the good of the German *Volk* as a whole.

Neil Gregor has examined the question of whether Hitler explicitly advocated the mass murder of his enemies in *MK*. Gregor believes that Hitler's medical imagery provides the key to recognizing the 'implicitly genocidal message' in Hitler's writings in that he used the language of hygiene to portray Germany as a sick body needing to be cured and cleansed. The cure would involve the eradication of the dirt- and disease-bringing pathogens, namely the Jews and the Marxists they controlled (Gregor: 56). A more explicit message of planned genocide is to be found in Book II, Chapter 13 of *MK*, where Hitler writes that it is not enough to fight for a *Weltanschauung* with verbal means. He scoffs at 'tapfere Herren Wortprotestler' [brave lip-service protesters] and states that a physical encounter must be planned: 'Wehe, wenn auch unsere Bewegung, statt das Fechten vorzubereiten, sich in Protesten üben würde!' (*MK*: 712; Mh.: 574). Only a sharp sword ('ein geschliffenes Schwert') and a bloody fight ('blutige(n) Kampf') would win back the territories lost after the Great War (*MK*: 710; Mh.: 574).

CHAPTER 2

Hitler's Language

2.1 The Language of National Socialism

The language of the National Socialists has long been a fertile field of academic study, the first major milestone being Manfred Pechau's doctoral dissertation of 1935. A self-proclaimed National Socialist, Pechau used *MK* as one of his major primary sources. Like Hitler, he characterized propaganda as *Kampf*, seeing NS language as a 'Sprache der Kampfformen' ('language of violence') and its style as a 'Gewaltstil' ('style of violence', Pechau 1935: 95f.). Such language reflects the purpose of the 'revolutionäre Kampfbewegung' ('revolutionary fighting movement') which was National Socialism (Pechau: 10). According to Pechau, NS language had already been dubbed the 'Stil des 20. Jahrhunderts' by the 1930s. He claimed, however, that it would not become a self-contained *(abgeschlossen)* style of the twentieth century until National Socialism had led the entire German *Volk* to the ideal of a national will and of socialist justice ('zum Ideal des nationalen Wollens und der sozialistischen Gerechtigkeit', Pechau: 96). Pechau warned against a dilution of the language through over-repetition of terms such as *Gleichschaltung*, and pleaded for a strong, powerful means of hammering in basic truths *(Grundwahrheiten)*:

> Diese Anwendung von Gewaltformen entspricht ganz dem Wesen des Kampfes der Bewegung und dem stürmischen Wollen seiner jungen Förderer. (The use of violent language entirely matches the war-like character of the movement and the stormy desires of its young supporters.) (Pechau: 96).

Heinz Paechter published the first comprehensive study in English of NS language in 1944: *Nazi-Deutsch, A Glossary of Contemporary German Usage*. This is a revised and enlarged edition of the *Dictionary of Nazi Terms* compiled for the Office of European Research. Its sources were German newspapers and magazines, German military dictionaries, the *Brockhaus*, and a list of germanizations of foreign technical terms issued by the Reich Patent Office. Unfortunately Paechter's glossary is held by very few European libraries. More readily available is Victor Klemperer's *LTI. Notizbuch eines Philologen*[1] (1996, first published in 1947), an indispensable aid to the study of NS language. It is a contemporary record not only of the linguistic features of NS language, but also of the social position of Jews during the NS era. According to Klemperer, the *LTI* was 'arm und eintönig' ('poor' (or, possibly, 'meagre') and 'monotonous'), 'bettelarm' ('as poor as a beggar'), and its basic features were laid down with the publication of *MK*: 'es war immer, gedruckt und gesprochen, bei Gebildeten und Ungebildeten, dasselbe Klischee und dieselbe Tonart' (Klemperer: 25f.). Very few words were coined during the time of National Socialism, *coventrieren* ('to raze to the ground' (like the city of Coventry)) being one of the few that one can be sure about. Kenneth Burke's 1941 essay in English on the rhetoric of *MK* is more narrowly focused and concentrates chiefly on Hitler's propagandist methods, his 'acts and attitudes of persuasion' (Schmidt 2004, second footnote).

The major landmarks in more recent study of NS language include Cornelia Schmitz-Berning's series of articles published in *Zeitschrift für deutsche Wortforschung* (Berning 1960–63) and her dictionary: *Vokabular des Nationalsozialismus* (Schmitz-Berning 1998). Her alphabetical word lists have been central to many valuable studies of NS language since the 1960s, as has her taxonomy of the style and metaphors used by the National Socialists. Schmitz-Berning concludes that, except for necessary neologisms to designate new political and military organisations, the language of the National Socialists underwent only minor developments after 1933 (Berning 1963: 92f.). She places the language of 1930s German fascism within a long tradition of anti-Semitic discourse and acknowledges a number of earlier influences upon Adolf Hitler's world-view and language. Other valuable contributions in the second half of the twentieth century include those of Eugen Seidel and Ingeborg Seidel-Slotty (1960), Sigrid Frind (1966), Siegfried Bork (1970), Detlef Grieswelle (1972), Utz Maas (1984 and 1991), Wolfgang

---

[1] *LTI* stands for *Lingua Tertii Imperii*: the Language of the Third Reich.

Mieder (1983, 1994 and 1997), Dolf Sternberger, Gerhard Storz and Wilhelm E. Süskind (1985), and Gerhard Bauer (1988).

Konrad Ehlich stands out as an author and editor of recent work on language under fascism. He explains the title of his book, *Sprache im Faschismus* (1989), as referring to the wide-ranging linguistic results of fascist discourse: "language *in* fascism" includes the language of those who suffered under the fascist regime and those who were coerced into using fascist language (Ehlich 1989: 31). Ehlich's 1989 collection of essays includes valuable contributions by Claus Ahlzweig, Gerd Simon, Jan Wirrer, Wolfgang Werner Sauer, Otto Ludwig, Johannes Volmert, Utz Maas, Willi Minnerup, Christoph Sauer and Siegfried Jäger (who demonstrates the place of the Neo-Nazi language of the 1980s in fascist propaganda). In his 1990 analysis of Hitler's speeches between 1920 and 1933, Ulrich Ulonska sheds light on some vital aspects of his early rhetoric. Ulonska concludes that Hitler relied on a balance of *ethos* and *pathos* in his presentation of himself as a trustworthy protector of the German people. While the publication since 1990 of works about NS language has not stagnated, few, apart from Schmitz-Berning, have dealt at all with Hitler's political discourse before 1933.

As Peter von Polenz points out (1972: 165), work on the language of National Socialism tends to focus mostly on vocabulary (cf. Schmitz-Berning 1998). Von Polenz recommends that political vocabulary should be studied in context, perhaps with the aid of "readers" containing entire texts. Geraldine Horan has ventured beyond the lexis in her study of the discourse of NS women. This fascinating contribution to the linguistic study of political discourse promises to guide the way for a new type of research into the language of National Socialism (Horan 2003). It is also the intention of the present volume to examine rhetorical features of the lexicon and beyond.

2.2 Possible Influences on Hitler's Language

It cannot be disputed that Hitler read avidly—while staying in the men's hostel in Vienna, for example, and later, while imprisoned in the Landsberg fortress, which he called his 'university at the expense of the state' (Kershaw 1998: 240). He claims in *MK* to have read authors such as Nietzsche and

Treitschke, and remembers having been influenced by anti-Semitic pamphlets while in Vienna (*MK*: 60). He quotes from classical authors, such as Goethe and Schiller, in *MK*, although he may not have read the entire texts himself; as Brigitte Hamann points out, he would have encountered quotations from great German men of letters in German-national newspapers from his time in Vienna onwards (Hamann 1999: 74). Hitler would also have read entire novels serialized in newspapers, and it is possible that he saw *Faust II* at the Vienna Burgtheater in 1908 (Hamann: 75). Thus there were many literary influences, both direct and indirect, on his vocabulary, style and choice of images. In *MK*, Hitler writes that to read is to do more than absorb information: reading should be instrumental in the formation of one's world-view. For him, reading was 'nicht Selbstzweck, sondern Mittel zu einem solchen' [no end in itself, but a means to an end] (*MK*: 36; Mh.: 33). He claims to understand the 'Kunst des Lesens' ('art of reading') better than did 'der große Durchschnitt unserer sogenannten „Intelligenz"' [the average member of our so-called 'intelligentsia'], who could not differentiate between valuable and useless information (*MK*: 36; Mh.: 33). Scepticism is, however, frequently expressed regarding Hitler's reading skills. An extreme view, held by Neil Gregor, is that his writing contains echoes of semi-assimilated political, philosophical and scientific writings of the nineteenth and early twentieth centuries, and that his writings are 'examples of the vulgarization of key elements' of these texts. Many of Hitler's ideas were, according to Gregor, acquired 'second-hand' from 'second-rate' literature (Gregor 2005: 39).

It was while he was living in Vienna that the young Hitler was first introduced to politics and its discourse. He read political pamphlets and listened to speeches in parliament, and he would also have read the anti-Semitic *Deutsches Volksblatt*. Hitler was further influenced by his fellow countryman, Guido von List, whose followers formed a Guido-von-List-Bund that was closely connected to the *Thule-Gesellschaft*. The Thule, which had grown out of the older *Germanenorden*, was a right-wing *völkisch* society, one of whose central tenets was the purity of its members' blood: it blamed all illnesses and social evils on racial mixture. Later, after arriving in Munich, Hitler joined the "philosopher of the NSDAP", Dietrich Eckart, as a guest at meetings of the *Thule-Gesellschaft*. According to Berning, Guido von List was the originator of the following expressions: *Volkskörper*, *Mischehe* (referring to the marriage of Aryans with Jews), *Rassenchaos* ('racial chaos') and *Dünger des Blutes* ('fertilizer of the blood', Berning 1963: 96). Von List referred to pure Germans as *Edelrassige* ('of noble race') and *Herrenmenschen* ('master people') and all non-Aryans as 'minderrassige Herdenmenschen' ('herd-living people of a lesser race', Berning, 1963: 97), and he recommended strict marriage laws to prevent "mixed" liaisons. Hitler also knew Jörg Lanz von Liebenfels, who in turn had known Guido von List. Von Liebenfels belonged to the List-society and von List was a member of von Liebenfels's Orden des Neuen Tempels, a society which only admitted blond, blue-eyed men; both von List and von Liebenfels frequently quoted one another in their writings. The symbol of von Liebenfels's Order was the swastika and its organ, *Ostara*, regularly included articles by List-society members. Berning quotes some of the typical vocabulary of *Ostara*, which Hitler is known to have read: *Erbsünde* (in its meaning of 'mixed marriage'), *Rassenchaos*, *Völkerbrei* and *Volksgenosse*; blond people were named *"Asinge"* ('heavenly ones') and people from non-Germanic races *"Äfflinge"* ('apelings') (Berning 1963: 101).

While still in Vienna, Hitler visited the opera as frequently as he could, often as many as three times weekly. His favourite composer was Richard Wagner (1813–1883), a fanatical anti-Semite who also despised the bourgeoisie and disapproved of parliaments and democracies. Wagner's operas embodied the spirit and much of the substance of Germanic myth and he classed the operas of the *Ring* cycle as characteristically Aryan (Lincoln 1999: 61). Hitler was inspired by Wagner's operas. He had seen his first opera, *Lohengrin*, in Linz with his friend Gustl, and it remained his favourite throughout his life. He loved the stories of ancient Germanic heroes fighting pagan gods, demons and dragons; he, and later the Nazi party, adopted their sense of destiny, of virtuous lives and noble deaths.

An investigation into the possible influence upon Hitler of Wagner's *libretti* is beyond the scope of the present study, but future research may reveal valuable insights. A brief examination of one work, *Lohengrin*, will serve here as a case study. The action of *Lohengrin* takes place in Antwerp in the early tenth century. Germany is under threat of a Hungarian invasion. King Heinrich reminds his followers of how often Germany has been under threat from the East ('Soll ich euch erst der Drangsal Kunde sagen, die deutsches Land so oft aus Osten traf', Act 1: 217). Heinrich's purpose is to protect Germany's honour in a battle against the Hungarians and to supervise the trial of Elsa of Brabant, who has been accused of killing her brother, Gottfried. Justice will be achieved by means of a dual between Friedrich von Telramund, Elsa's accuser, and Elsa's champion, Lohengrin, who appears upon a barge drawn by a swan. Lohengrin promises to marry Elsa if he wins, on condition that she does not ask him who he is or where he is from. After Lohengrin's victory over Friedrich, Ortrud, Friedrich's wife, suggests a means of revenge, namely that she should persuade Elsa to ask Lohengrin about his identity. Ortrud claims that he was assisted in his brave deed by magical power and seeds of doubt are sown in Elsa's mind. Believing she has seen the swan coming to fetch Lohengrin and fearful that he will leave without her, Elsa asks his name. He reveals himself to be Parsifal's son and a knight of the Grail. Lohengrin explains that he was sent to save a maiden in distress, but now that she has broken the protective spell that surrounds him by causing him to name himself he must return alone to Montsalvat, the castle of the Grail. Before he leaves, however, Lohengrin is able to prophesy that King Heinrich will be victorious over the invaders from the East: Dir Reinem ist ein großer Sieg verlieh'n!' ('To you, pure being, a great victory has been given', Act 3, Scene 2: 260). The swan arrives and Lohengrin gives Elsa his horn, his ring and his sword to pass on to her brother. As Lohengrin walks towards the river bank, the swan turns into Gottfried, whom Lohengrin proclaims as the future leader of Brabant: 'Zum Führer sei er euch genannt!' ('Let him be proclaimed your leader', Act 3, Scene 2: 262). Hitler would surely have loved the rousing speeches and emotive vocabulary with which *Lohengrin* abounds; the martial theme; the horns blowing the 'Kampfruf' ('call to arms', 228); the calls of 'Sieg!' and 'Heil!' when Lohengrin is victorious. Violent and apocalyptic vocabulary, similar to that which Hitler used in *MK* (see App. II, Section 4), is present in each Act: *Schmerz und Klagen* ('pain and lament', Act 1: 218), *Bang' und Grau'n* ('fear and horror', Act 1: 225); *zertrümmern, zerbrechen, verfluchen* ('to shatter', 'to smash', 'to curse', Act 2: 230); *grimmig (...) gedroht* ('fiercely (...) threatened', Act 2: 232); *schauerlich und klagend* ('horrifying and plaintive', Act 2: 234); *zerreißen, verdammen, Jammer, Unglück* ('to tear', 'to damn', 'wailing', 'sorrow', Act 2: 235); *erschlagen, klagen* ('to strike dead', 'to lament', Act 3: 256). Lohengrin is more than once praised in terms that Hitler might have chosen for himself; Elsa hails him 'Mein Held, mein Retter!' ('My hero, my saviour', 225), 'Mein Schirm! Mein Engel! Mein Erlöser!' ('My protector! My angel! My saviour!', 226), 'hehrer, wonnevoller Mann' ('glorious, delightful man', 226); she calls him 'mein teurer Held' ('my dear hero', 242), 'der hehre Mann' ('noble man', 242); and she speaks of his 'Sendung' ('Mission').

Perhaps the major folkish author to have influenced Hitler was Wagner's son-in-law, Houston Stewart Chamberlain (1855–1927), the son of an English admiral and the nephew of Field Marshal Sir Neville Chamberlain. He was a friend of Artur, Comte de Gobineau, author of *Essai sur l'inégalité des races humaines* (1853), and influenced by his theory that the white race was the 'only one that had the will and power to build up a cultural life' (Cassirer 1946: 226). Gobineau praised the Aryan Brahmans for having established a caste system and believed that men attain glory as a result of their racial instincts and origins (Cassirer: 229–238). Chamberlain's major work, *Grundlagen des neunzehnten Jahrhunderts (Foundations of the Nineteenth Century*, 1899), entered many editions and had sold more than a quarter of a million copies by the outbreak of the Second World War. It introduced a firm anti-Semitic bias to Gobineau's "race worship" and became a 'foundational text for the development of Nazi ideology' (Lincoln 1999: 61). Kaiser Wilhelm II was one of its first and most avid readers, and it was popular with the German upper classes as it seemed to confirm what they wanted to believe: that the Germans were the master race and that Jesus was not a Jew but an Aryan. Chamberlain thought that Hitler had been sent by God to lead the German people out of the wilderness and foresaw the coming of the Third Reich (Shirer: 103). Hitler saw Chamberlain as an unrecognized prophet, mentioning what he saw as his under-appreciated contribution to NS ideology in *MK* (296; see also the description of a passage from Chamberlain's *Arische Weltanschauung* below). Chamberlain's biography of Wagner was one of the books mentioned in Ernst Hanfstaengel's memoirs as having adorned Hitler's book-shelves before 1923. Others included Treitschke's *Deutsche Geschichte*, Clausewitz's *Vom Kriege*, histories of the First World War by Stegemann and Ludendorff, Kugler's history of Frederick the Great and Gustav Schwab's *Schönste Sagen des klassischen Altertums* (Zentner 2004: 15).

In his description of German political vocabulary between the French Revolution and the Weimar Republic, Peter von Polenz places NS language in its historical context (von Polenz 1999: 539–547). Whereas expressions such as *Vernunft* ('reason') and *Humanität/Menschheit* ('humanity') had been key concepts of the late eighteenth century, words such as *Nation*, *Volkstum* ('national character'), *Volksgeist* ('national spirit') and *Deutschheit* ('Germanness') came to the fore in the early nineteenth century. At the beginning of the Second Reich the notion of the *Reichsfeind* ('enemy of the Reich') was propagated to refer to the French, Prussian Poles and Danes, Catholics, Jews and Liberals, all of whom were designated *vaterlandsfeindlich* ('enemies of the fatherland'). Prussian nationalist-chauvinistic associations railed against the eastern Slavic population using words such as: *Polyp* ('polyp'), *Bazillen* ('bacilli'), *Parasiten* ('parasites'), *Polenkrebs* ('Polish cancer'), *vernichten* ('to destroy'), *ausrotten* ('to eradicate'), *ausmerzen* ('to eradicate'), *Lebensraum* and *Germanisierung des Bodens* ('germanization of the land', von Polenz: 539). Von Polenz also presents evidence from school essays written during the months after the outbreak of the First World War. He explains that many teachers must have been members of nationalist associations and would therefore have influenced their pupils. Von Polenz lists vocabulary from a number of fields: conservative-bourgeois moralistic vocabulary: *anständig* ('decent, respectable'), *gerecht* ('just'), *heilig* ('holy'), *Hingabe* ('devotion'), *Schuldigkeit* ('sense of duty'), *treu* ('loyal'); martial and acquiescent vocabulary: *brav* ('honest, brave'), *dienen* ('to serve'), *ehrenvoll* ('honourable'), *eisern* ('iron'), *entschlossen* ('decisive'), *gewaltig* ('huge, powerful'), *glorreich* ('glorious'), *Größe* ('greatness'), *hassen* ('to hate'), *Helden* ('heroes'), *kolossal* ('colossal'), *Macht* ('power'), *opferwillig* ('willing to sacrifice oneself'), *Pflicht* ('duty'), *ruhmreich* ('glorious, celebrated'), *sieg-reich* ('victorious'), *stolz* ('proud'), *tapfer* ('brave'), *zornig* ('angry'); nationalistic-ideological vocabulary: *Aar* ('eagle'), *Gaue* ('district'), *germanisch* ('Germanic'), *hehr* ('glorious, noble'), *Nibelungentreue* ('the loyalty of the Nibelungs (unquestioning loyalty, loyalty unto death)'), *Schild* ('shield'), *Scholle* ('the sod'), *Schwert* ('sword'), *Volk der Dichter und Denker* ('nation of poets and thinkers'), *deutsches Wesen* ('German character'); vocabulary from the Kaiser's speeches: *Volkskrieg* ('people's war'), *heiliger Krieg* ('holy war'), *Kreuzzug* ('crusade'), *Gut und Blut einsetzen* ('to risk everything'), *bis zum letzten Mann* ('up until the last man'); and terms describing the attributes and behaviour of Germany's "enemies": *böse* ('evil'), *feige* ('cowardly'), *frech* ('impudent'), *frivol* ('frivolous'), *hinterlistig* ('deceitful, treacherous'), *gewissenlos* ('unscrupulous'), *Habgier* ('greed'), *Hass* ('hate'), *Machwerk* ('shoddy effort'), *Neider* ('envious people'), *Niedrigkeit* ('lowness'), *räuberisch* ('predatory'), *ruchlos* ('heinous'), *schändlich* ('disgraceful'), *schnöde* ('despicable'), *Tücke* ('guile'), *verblendet* ('blinded'), *verhetzt* ('inflamed'), *Verleumder* ('slanderer'), *Verräter* ('traitor') (von Polenz: 541). Using Cobet (1973) as his source, von Polenz also describes the anti-Semitic discourse of the nineteenth century, listing nature metaphors such as *Abschaum* ('scum'), *entartet* ('degenerate'), *Krebs* ('cancer'), *Parasit* ('parasite'), *Schädling* ('pest'), *Schlange* ('snake'), *schleichen* ('to creep, sneak'), *Ungeziefer* ('vermin'), *Versumpfung* ('becoming swampy, going to the dogs'), *Volksbrei* ('porridge of nations') and *Zersetzung* ('decay'), all of which are found in *MK* (von Polenz: 534). He reminds us that much of the anti-Semitic language current in nineteenth-century Germany originated in the Middle Ages, some of it attested in the writings of Martin Luther (on Luther's anti-Semitism see Robert Michael and Karin Doerr 2002).

In order to illustrate the similarities in political discourse throughout the period from 1848 to 1943, Peter von Polenz provides seven short texts (von Polenz 1972: 165–167). I have followed his example in App. I in order to show the place of Hitler's language within a tradition of distinctive, largely nationalistic German rhetoric. Texts 1 and 2 are from Friedrich Ludwig Jahn's *Von deutschem Volkstum* (1810), Text 3 from Houston Stewart Chamberlain's *Arische Weltanschauung* (1905), Text 4 from Kaiser Wilhelm II's speech to the German people at the beginning of the First World War, and Text 5 is a piece of anti-British propaganda taken from a popular periodical of the sort that Hitler may have read, the *Bibliothek der Unterhaltung und des Wissens* (1919).

Text 1 is a passage glorifying the German *Volk* and explaining the notion of *Volkstum*. The *Volk* is hyperbolized as the 'höchste und größeste und umfassendste Menschengesellschaft' ('highest and greatest and most all-embracing human society', line 4). The *Einigungskraft* ('unifying power') of the *Volkstum* is stressed and supported with the verb *verknüpft* ('tied') and the adjectives *umfassend* ('inclusive, extensive') and *schönverbunden* ('beautifully united'); the inclusive nature of the *Volk* is further stressed by the repetition of *All*, *binden* and *verbinden* in lines 2 and 3 and the creation of *Allverbindung* in line 11. The metaphor of the individual parts of the *Volk* rising up and uniting to form *Sonnenreichen und Welten* ('sun-realms and worlds') is an example of the hyperbole commonly used in totalitarian literature. Human capacities are listed in pairs (lines 8–10) and stressed as being *volkstümlich*. The accumulation of faculties in this list reminds one of Hitler's style in *MK* (cf. App. II, Section 3). A vitally important human faculty, repeatedly mentioned as a virtue by Hitler, is given weight in the tautologous *Wiedererzeugungskraft* and *Fortpflanzungsfähigkeit*' ('ability to reproduce', lines 6f.).

Text 2 similarly stresses the unity of the *Volk*. It is likened to a high-growing tree with strong roots to support it ('einem festgewurzelten, hochstämmigen Baume vergleichbar'). This is a splendid tree with many branches, twigs and leaves (*vielastig, vielzweigig, vielblättrig*), like a body with many limbs *(vielgliedriger Leib)* which cannot be torn asunder. This body will need space to grow or it will be crippled *(verkrüppeln)*. If it is limited to existence in a small space it will waste away *(verkümmern und verbauern)*. Such apocalyptic images are also common in *MK*. Anaphora is a type of repetition often used for hyperbolic purposes and favoured by Hitler (see App. II, Section 2); it is found in Text 2, lines 10f.:

> Es [das Volk] darf nicht auf einer einzigen Scholle kleben, an *einem* Strome entlang ufern, in einem einzigen Gau hocken, in einem einzigen Tale hausen. (It may not stick to one single sod, settle on the bank of *one* river, inhabit one region, live in one valley.)

Text 3, with its pseudo-anthropological content, is uncannily reminiscent of *MK*, and it is known that Hitler read and admired Chamberlain's work. Non-German peoples are repeatedly dehumanized as *Elemente*, a noun which is often qualified as *fremd* ('foreign') and in one instance as 'fremde, ethnisch stark vermischte und geistig minderwertige Elemente' (line 19). The dangers of mixing German with non-German (not necessarily Jewish) blood are stressed with vocabulary that Hitler later adopted, such as *verderben* ('to spoil', line 16), *vergiften* ('to poison', line 16) and 'den Segen zum Fluch kehrend' (lines 16f.), and an apocalyptic vision of the results of tolerance is presented: 'wir steuern auf das Chaos zu' (lines 39f.). The non-German is presented as the enemy who will cause this chaos. The purity of German "(breeding)-stock" is stressed as paramount (line 25), as it was later by Hitler in *MK*. The notion of a German 'Kampf um das eigene Dasein' ('fight for existence'), a justified and holy battle ('durchaus berechtigter, ja heiliger Kampf'), is found in lines 32f. Rhetorical questions ask what the German *Volk*, included in the questions as *wir*, should do to protect itself. The answer is that it must wake up (*erwachen*, line 40) and become 'Herren im eigenen Hause' ('masters of their own house', lines 41f.). Also, and most significantly, Germans must understand that it will be necessary to fight their enemies ('die Notwendigkeit des Kampfes', line 34). Text 3 is a mere extract from one book written by Chamberlain, and it is conceivable that Hitler read all or at least most of them. As all of the features just described are present in *MK*, I believe it is safe to assume that Chamberlain's discourse had a significant influence on that of *MK* and Hitler's speeches. It is also likely that Chamberlain read Nietzsche, and that Hitler derived some of his Nietzschean ideas indirectly from Chamberlain. Furthermore, in his 1917 essay, *Deutsche Weltanschauung*, Chamberlain quoted from Schiller, Goethe and Clausewitz, and praised Wagner, Kant, Treitschke, Bismarck and Luther as founders of the German *Weltanschauung* (Chamberlain 1925): Hitler refers to all of these in *MK*.

Hitler would certainly have heard or read Text 4, the Kaiser's speech of 6 August 1914. The phrase *Sein oder Nichtsein* ('to be or not to be') occurs twice—at the beginning of consecutive sentences. The first occurrence is linked with 'unseres Reiches' and 'unsere Väter' (lines 10f.), the second with 'deutscher Macht und deutschen Wesens' (lines 11f.). In propagandist texts the audience is constantly reminded of the need to fight for their existence on earth (cf. reference to *Dasein und Wesen*, Text 2, line 13). Hitler believed that with his help Germany would either *be* or *not be*, and the sentiment expressed by this Shakespearean phrase echoes throughout *MK*; indeed it is the heart of Hitler's message. In Text 4, *entschlossener Treue* ('decisive loyalty'), *Verantwortung* ('responsibility') and *Kraft* ('strength') are contrasted with *Schwanken* ('wavering') and *Zögern* ('hesitation'); just as in *MK*. The enemy is described as *tückisch* ('deceitful') and accused of attacking Germany. Like Chamberlain, the Kaiser includes his audience in a *wir*-form. The fight is portrayed as holy ('Vorwärts mit Gott'; 'forwards with God') and the entire world is seen as the enemy (line 9). Hyperbole intensifies the image of Germany's future battle 'zum letzten Hauch von Mann und Roß' ('unto the last breath of man and horse', lines 12f.). The sword *(Schwert)*, a metonymy for fighting popular with Hitler, must decide the outcome. Germans are called to arms in forthright language 'Darum auf! zu den Waffen!'; a call which Hitler himself followed. Kaiser Wilhelm's text reminds the German people that they are surrounded by dangerous enemies, just as *MK* would do later, and, like *MK*, it shows the German *Volk* as being more entitled to freedom than other peoples.

Text 5 is similar to *MK* in the way it constructs a *Feindbild* of the English during the First World War. It ironizes England's supposed picture of itself as a humanitarian nation: '(das) stets von Humanität übertriefende England' ('England, which is always dripping wet with humanity', lines 3f.), and employs pairs of evaluative adjectives and nouns to demonize the deeds of its people: *widerwärtiger Grausamkeit* ('disgusting cruelty', line 4) and *völkerrechtswidrige Greueltat* ('atrocity which is against international law', line 9) The weapons used by the English are *berüchtigt* ('disreputable', line 5), *grauenhaft tückisch* ('horribly deceitful', line 12), *erstickend* ('suffocating', line 3) and *betäubend* ('anaesthetic', line 3). A terrifying picture of the English enemy is thus created in just a few lines.

In Text 6, taken from Hitler's New Year's address of 1943, we see that he continues the theme from *MK* of Germans fighting for their existence, *Sein oder Nichtsein* (line 5). He includes his audience in the *wir* of *unser Volk* (line 9) and paints an apocalyptic picture of the *Verfall* ('decline', line 9), *Zersplitterung* ('fragmentation', line 10) and *Ohnmacht* ('impotence', line 10) of the first German *Reich*. His portrayal of Germany's plight is supported by hyperbole: Germany has suffered from centuries of decline (*Verfall*, line 9) and 'ungezählte Millionen Deutscher' ('countless millions of Germans') have been forced to leave their homes in search of their "daily bread" (*das tägliche Brot*, line 13). The American President Wilson is dubbed *verlogen* ('mendacious') and *heuchlerisch* ('hypocritical'), adjectives which later became firmly embedded in Hitler's repertoire. A metaphor of downward movement *(heruntergesunken)* describes Germany's position in the world as only worthy to supply *Kulturdünger* ('cultural fertilizers') for other nations (cf. *MK*: 735).

If one compares Text 7, apparently written by a housewife and mother of four, with Text 1, the similarities are not obvious. If, however, one considers all eight texts as points along a continuum of discourse styles, similarities span them all. Text 7 shares many features with the previous six: exclamations, rhetorical questions, hyperbole ('aller Menschen auf der ganzen Welt' and the title of the text) and repetition (e.g. of *Neubeginn*). *Wir*-forms are also present, as are warnings and accumulations of apocalyptic vocabulary: 'Denken Sie an die Not, das Elend, den Hunger, die Tragödien, das Blutvergießen!' ('Think about the poverty, the misery, the hunger, the tragedies, the loss of blood!', lines 10f.) and 'retten Sie Deutschland vor den vernichtenden Folgen weiteren Schweigens' ('save Germany from the shattering consequences of further silence', lines 12f.). The narrator's allegiance to *Volk* and *Reich* is clearly expressed, along with reference to being German and to an enemy who threatens weaker sections of society.

2.3 The Language of *Mein Kampf*

Hitler was a self-proclaimed master of the "art" of propaganda *(Herr dieser Kunst)* (*MK*: 522), acknowledging no influence from those rhetoricians from whom he must have learnt his art. His language was aggressive and oppositional, the rhetoric of a fanatical demagogue. Hitler overwhelmed his audience with stark black-and-white classifications and emphatic claims. He admired the methods of agitation developed in Leninist Russia and apodictic declarations that invited no argument (*MK*: 532). Hitler's forceful statements about people and situations were intended to work like the strokes of a hammer on people's emotions: 'die Worte, die Hammerschlägen ähnlich die Tore zum Herzen eines Volkes zu öffnen vermögen' [words which like hammer blows can open the gates to the heart of a people] (*MK*: 116; Mannheim: 98). To Hitler, objectivity was a type of weakness, and not what his audiences expected or wanted: 'Die Psyche der breiten Masse ist nicht empfänglich für alles Halbe und Schwache' [The psyche of the great masses is not receptive to anything that is half-hearted or weak] (*MK*: 44; Mh.: 39). He coined the term *"Objektivitätsfimmel"* ('mania for objectivity'), for what he claimed to be a particularly German trait. Fascism was 'eine Lehre, die keine andere neben sich duldet' [a doctrine, tolerating no other beside itself] (*MK*: 44; Mh.: 39f.); the masses favoured uncompromising partisanship from their leaders and expected to be commanded and not entreated: 'die Masse [liebt] mehr den Herrscher als den Bittenden ('the masses love a ruler more than a supplicant', *MK*: 44). Thus, when Hitler claimed that propaganda involves 'Belehrung und Aufklärung' ('instruction and enlightenment', *MK*: 535) he was not thinking of enabling his audience to form their own views on the basis of clear and accurate information, but only of the propagation of his own opinions.

Hitler made it clear throughout *MK* that his message was for 'die breite Masse' ('the broad masses'), but he wrote about the masses rather than for them. In his introduction to Mannheim's translation, D. Cameron Watt claims that *MK* was a reference work of Nazi ideology for use by National Socialist propagandists who would spread his doctrine to the "common man":

> It need not be read; or comprehended; in fact it is better that it should not be too easily comprehensible in its entirety. Its message must, of course, be capable of reduction to simplicity; that is the task of the movement's propagandists and educators. But its own complexity and obscurity are an advantage, since they demonstrate the profundity of the leader's vision and understanding, his ability to grapple with the problems which his followers have admitted their inability to handle. (...) It was enough for them that it existed, a guarantee of their leader's intellectual genius and respectability (...). (Hitler 1992: xiv)

One might therefore assume that ordinary people did not have to read *MK*. They absorbed its ideology through the intermediacy of Hitler's minions: these would read and digest the message and reproduce it according to Hitler's advice on the language of propaganda in Book 1, Chapter 6 and Book 2, Chapter 6.

2.3.1 Hitler's Rhetoric

Hitler's early political speeches have been analyzed in some detail by Ulrich Ulonska (1990). Apart from their organization, which Ulonska demonstrates to be a firm tripartite structure, the speeches are very similar to *MK* in language and content. Ulonska shows how Hitler's speeches emphasized certain human values, the most important of which were bravery, justice, diligence and patriotism, and linked these with the emotions of his audience. In the first section of his speeches he would explain in a rational tone how these very German values were in danger from outside influences, in the second section he would launch into an emotional defamation of the "enemies" that were threatening German values, and in the third section he would present himself as a trustworthy saviour *(Erlösergestalt)* of the people, telling his audience how much he had already achieved and promising them a brighter future (Ulonska: 286). According to Ulonska, Hitler did not woo people with his charisma, as is often assumed, but with the passion of his outpourings of hatred: he shouted 'Haßappell an Haßappell" ('one outburst of hatred after the other'), presenting himself as the super-ego of the assembled masses (Ulonska: 274). He combined two rhetorical styles: *pathos* and *ethos*, with *pathos* reaching the greater extreme of intensity. Ulonska quotes from Ueding's *Einführung in die Rhetorik* (1976) in order to illustrate the two styles:

> Mit *pathos (movere)* bezeichnet man die wilden, mitreißenden, erschütternden und entsetzenden Gefühlsregungen wie Leidenschaft, Zorn, >>Schauder und Jammer<<. (...) Das *ethos (delectare)* benennt man die sanften, anmutenden, gelassenen und unterhaltenden Gemütsbewegungen, die gleichmäßiger und dauerhafter als die heftigen Emotionen sind. (Ulonska: 222) (The term *pathos (movere)* refers to wild, fervent, shocking and horrifying emotions such as passion, anger, "trembling and wailing". (...) *Ethos (delectare)* refers to gentle, pleasant, calm and amusing emotions, which are steadier and longer-lasting than violent emotions.)

The pathos of *MK* is supported by hyperbole: superlative forms and meanings, excessive repetition, accumulation *(Häufung)* of words and phrases, aggressive and apocalyptic vocabulary, and exaggerated evaluative descriptions of people and institutions that he despised (see App. II, Sections 4 and 5). Hitler's hyperbolic language served a number of purposes in *MK*, all of which were closely linked and interdependent: derogation of his enemies, glorification of the German *Volk*, exposition of his belief in a racial hierarchy, and the nature of his *Kampf* and that of the NS movement. In *MK*, Hitler also assailed his audience with appeals, questions (many of which he answered himself), imperatives, and exclamations (see App. II, Sections 9 and 10). They are joined by descriptions, explanations, examples, comparisons, recapitulations and summaries to form the basis of his propaganda. These are all features of argumentational discourse. Perelman and Olbrechts-Tyteca describe the goal of argumentation as being 'to create or increase the adherence of minds to the theses presented for their assent' (Perelman and Olbrechts-Tyteca 1969: 45). Hitler desired to create assent where necessary and increase it in those who already adhered to his views. He presented justifications and what he considered to be logical arguments in order to persuade his audience to share his views and prepare to act on them. Argumentation tends to look towards the future and present an optimistic view of the results of future action (Perelman and Olbrechts-Tyteca 1969: 47). Hitler's argumentation looked backwards more than it did forwards in order to illustrate mistakes made in the past, but his vision of Germany's future under a strong leadership was optimistic and confident. Much of what he wrote had an epidictic quality in that he appealed to universal truths, God and Nature. He presented certain values as unquestionable and aimed to strengthen existing values as well as instilling new ones in those of his audience still to be persuaded.

According to Clemens Ottmer, argumentation is most commonly employed where the content of a text is controversial (Ottmer 1996: 73): the rhetorician has to deal with disagreements and answer questions both before and after they are posed; he has to prove his point with adequate ratiocination and, possibly, with recourse to "authorities". This Hitler did on occasion, quoting, for example, from Clausewitz on the subject of war in Book 2, Chapter 15. He further supported his argument with what was perhaps his most pervasive rhetorical figure, antithesis, as the idea of opposition lay at the core of his entire *Weltanschauung*. Each of the following sections will illustrate how Hitler emphasized the stark contrast he saw between the Aryan *Volk* and Jews, the aggression of many of his antithetical images reflecting his personal hatred for half-measures: if Aryans had been created in God's image, then Jews had not, indeed they were incarnations of the devil (see, for example, *MK*: 340; Mh.: 282).

2.3.2 Hitler's Views on Propaganda and the Spoken Word

In the sixth chapters of both Books 1 and 2 of *MK*, Hitler aired his own views on the successful composition and dissemination of political rhetoric. A message had to be straightforward and uncompromising, *einheitlich*, if it were to work on the emotions of the masses:

> Es gibt hierbei nicht viel Differenzierungen, sondern ein Positiv oder ein Negativ, Liebe oder Haß, Recht oder Unrecht, Wahrheit oder Lüge, niemals aber halb so und halb so oder teilweise usw. (*MK*: 201) [It does not have multiple shadings; it has a positive and a negative; love or hate; right or wrong; truth or lie, never half this way and half that way, never partially, or that kind of thing. (Mh.: 167)]

Effective agitatory discourse should involve the repetition of a few basic ideas. It should be bold, powerful and authoritarian, and the rhetorician should exercise perseverance and patience:

> (...) Konzentration auf wenige Punkte, immerwährende Wiederholung derselben, selbstsichere und selbstbewußte Fassung des Textes in den Formen einer apodiktischen Behauptung, größte Beharrlichkeit in der Verbreitung und Geduld im Erwarten der Wirkung. (*MK*: 401f.) [(...) concentration on a few points, constant repetition of the same, self-assured and self-reliant framing of the text in the forms of an apodictic statement, greatest perseverence in distribution and patience in awaiting the effect. (Mh.: 332)]

For Hitler, practical propaganda was a *"Werbetätigkeit"* ('advertising campaign'). Where possible the message would be delivered orally, and if written texts were needed, posters and pamphlets were the ideal vehicles, as in advertising, because of their brevity and compact nature. Both advertising and propaganda are most successful if they give a simple, uniform message ('gleichmäßige Einheitlichkeit' [continuity and sustained uniformity], *MK*: 203; Mh.: 169). As in advertising, the propaganda campaign must be 'genial und psychologisch richtig' ('brilliant and psychologically sound') (*MK*: 510; Mh.: 416, where *genial* is translated as 'with (...) wisdom'). Like advertising, propaganda has to promise the impossible. According to Hitler, Germany had been incapable of doing this during the First World War, unlike her enemies, who had known how to represent hell as heaven and the most wretched life as a paradise ('einem Volke (kann) selbst der Himmel als Hölle vorgemacht werden und umgekehrt das elendste Leben als Paradies', *MK*: 302).

Hitler admired the subjectivity of advertising: an objective comparison of different goods is unlikely to result in increased sales of one over the other:

> Was würde man zum Beispiel über ein Plakat sagen, das eine neue Seife anpreisen soll, dabei jedoch auch andere Seifen als „gut" bezeichnet? (*MK*: 200) [What, for example, would we say about a poster that was supposed to advertise a new soap and that described other soaps as 'good'? (Mh.: 166)]

Hitler's own message is one of pure subjectivity—it is an undisguised rant against the Jews, the Marxists, the German press and all other "enemies" of the German people. Hitler ignores his own recommendations on brevity, however, and gets totally carried away by the flood of his own ideas.

The importance of the spoken word for political discourse forms a significant part of the message of *MK*. Hitler was doubtless thinking of himself when he described the powers of the 'überragende Redekunst einer beherrschenden Apostelnatur' [the superior oratorical art of a dominant preacher (*MK*: 532; Mh.: 432). As a politican, he saw himself as Germany's saviour; as a propagandist, he saw himself as a rhetorician rather than a writer. In his preface, Hitler is almost apologetic about the need to publish his doctrine in written form, as the 'foundation stones' *(Bausteine)* for the NS movement and as a reference work for his followers:

> Ich weiß, daß man Menschen weniger durch das geschriebene Wort als vielmehr durch das gesprochene zu gewinnen vermag, daß jede große Bewegung auf dieser Erde ihr Wachsen den großen Rednern und nicht den großen Schreibern verdankt (*MK*, *Vorwort*) [I know that men are won over less by the written than by the spoken word, that every great movement on this earth owes its growth to great orators and not to great writers. (Mh., Preface)]

Hitler's own style in *MK* is frequently colloquial, using modal particles and clichés, exclamations and questions to appeal to his audience (for examples see App. II, Sections 9 and 10). At the time of writing *MK*, he looked back upon his childhood as the time when his talent for speaking developed, for he remembered himself as a ring-leader among the local youth in Linz (*MK*: 3). It was, however, in 1919, when he was appointed to the post of *Bildungsoffizier*, that Hitler discovered his gift for speaking in public: 'ich konnte „reden"'(*MK*: 235). During the early years of the Nazi party he developed as a 'Massenversammlungs redner' [speaker for mass meetings] (*MK*: 524; Mh.: 426); he became practised in the pathos that speaking to a large audience requires:

> daß mir das Pathos geläufig wurde und die Geste, die der große, tausend Menschen fassende Raum erfordert' [that I became practised in the pathos and the gestures which the great hall, with its thousands of people, demands (*MK*: 524; Mh.: 426).

In Book 2, Chapter 6 Hitler talks in general terms about how to replace the audience's emotions and prejudices with one's own (*MK*: 530). To him, the spoken word has magical powers *(Zauberkraft, MK*: 116); only spoken rhetoric is capable of bringing about 'gewaltige, weltumwälzend Ereignisse' [great, world-shaking events] (*MK*: 525; Mh.: 426). The violence of which the spoken word is capable should not be underestimated: it can shatter, blow by blow, the foundations of the audience's existing *Weltanschauung* ('Schlag um Schlag das Fundament ihrer bisherigen Einsichten (...) zertrümmern', *MK*: 522) in order to make way for a new ideology. The art of the rhetorician lies, in Hitler's view, in domination of the audience, 'Beeinträchtigung der Willensfreiheit des Menschen' [encroachment upon man's freedom of will] (*MK*: 531; Mh.: 431) and a 'Schwächung ihrer Widerstandskraft in natürlichster Weise' [a weakening of their force of resistance in the most natural way] (*MK.*: 532; Mh.: 432). Hitler likens his methods to those of the Catholic Church, where a mysterious twilight reigns, and burning incense relaxes people and dulls their wills ('ihrer geistigen und willensmäßigen Spannkraft', *MK*: 532). Even the timing of speeches is important—people are more passive and receptive to propaganda in the evenings (*MK*: 530–532). A political meeting is like a wrestling match: in the evening it is easier for the fighter with the stronger will to break the resistance of his opponent (*MK*: 532). Hitler refers back to the French Revolution as a time when demagogues whipped up *(aufpeitschten)* the passions of a tormented people, not with theories and written texts but with words. He also remembers the Bolshevist Revolution, which succeeded not because of Lenin's writing but because of 'die haßaufwühlende rednerische Betätigung zahlloser größter und kleinster Hetzapostel' [the hate-fomenting oratorial activity of countless of the greatest and the smallest apostles of agitation] (*MK*: 532; Mh.: 432).

2.3.3 Hitler's Construction of a *"Feindbild"*

Bernhard Pörksen defines a *"Feindbild"* as a negative image constructed by political or ideological groups of their opponents which serves to stabilize their own group. Such images are disseminated to the public at large as well as to their own sympathizers, in the latter case helping to deepen the notional divide between the "in-group" and the "out-group" or "Other" (Pörksen 2000: 34–38). The gulf between the in-group and the Other is deepened by the construction by the former of a "reality" in which it presents itself as superior to the out-group. This *"Imagepflege"* is intended to attract new followers whilst at the same time discrediting the enemy Other:

> Zwischen der eigenen und der als feindselig wahrgenommenen Gruppe gibt es keine Verständigung mehr, sondern nur noch Kampf, keine Kompromisse, sondern nur noch Sieg oder Niederlage; Andersdenkende und -lebende werden nicht mehr als Konfliktpartner gesehen, mit denen Verständigung prinzipiell möglich sein muß. (Pörksen 2000: 38) (Agreement between the in-group and its perceived enemy is no longer possible, only conflict remains; no compromises are possible, there can only be victory or defeat; groups which think and live differently are no longer seen as opponents with whom agreement must, in principle, be possible.)

This was exactly Hitler's philosophy. The reader of *MK* quickly becomes aware of Hitler's sense of personal persecution: he felt under threat and believed that the entire German nation was at the mercy of enemies that included Jews, Marxists, Social Democrats, Freemasons, the press, Slavs, the British (whom he on one occasion accused of being *'britisch-jüdisch'*, MK: 724), the French and the Russians. Almost anybody who was not a nationalistically inclined and pure-blooded German was demonized as the Other. In order to convince his audience that they were in danger, Hitler created images of this Other as a dangerous enemy (cf. Kenneth Burke's 1941 account of the Jewish scapegoat's "devil function"). Hitler's skill in instilling fear into the German people, and his concentrated exaggeration of the Other as a force of evil (which only he knew how to control), was a major factor in his eventual political success.

Hitler's *MK* could be taken as a prototype for the expression of prejudices and the demonization of enemies with the intention of infecting a wider audience. His main targets were Jews: any other enemy was seen as being under Jewish influence. In my preface, I mentioned that anti-Semitism may be taken as a paradigm for the construction of more widespread *Feindbilder* (Benz and Königseder 2002: 15). *MK* can be studied as such a paradigm, as one of its major purposes, perhaps *the* major purpose, was to present a picture of the German *Volk* as the victim of a Jewish conspiracy to dominate the world. Hitler described Germany's leaders in the field of foreign affairs as being 'im Dienste des jüdischen Welteroberungsgedankens und -kampfes' [in the service of the Jewish idea and struggle for world conquest] (*MK*: 761; Mh.: 611). The notion that Jews want nothing less than to be rulers of the world is still widespread in anti-Semitic discourse. Hitler presented the supposed Jewish desire to expand their race, especially through the "judaisation" of other races, as dangerous and aggressive (*MK*: 349; Mh.: 288). Jewish expansion by intermarriage is referred to in *MK* as 'jüdische Bastardierung' [Jewish bastardisation] (*MK*: 629; Mh.: 512) and 'Blutschande' [racial desecration] (*MK*: 135; Mh.: 113). An increased population would compel the Jewish people to seek new lebensraum: 'Sein Sich-Weiterverbreiten aber ist eine typische Erscheinung für alle Parasiten; er sucht immer neuen Boden für seine Rasse' [His spreading is a typical phenomenon for all parasites; he always seeks a new feeding ground for his race] (*MK*: 334; Mh.: 276). Hitler wanted such land for an expanded German *Volk*. Jews were a threat not only to German living-space, but also to Aryan breeding-stock: 'das ahnungslose Mädchen, das er mit seinem Blute schändet und damit seinem, des Mädchens Volke raubt' [the unsuspecting girl whom he defiles with his blood, thus stealing her from her people] (*MK*: 357; Mh.: 295). Hitler reinforced these terrifying images by referring to the myth that Jews drank the blood of Christian children in ceremonies of ritual slaughter, implying that this practice would continue: 'der Jude fräße tatsächlich die Völker der Erde' [the Jew would really devour the peoples of the earth] (*MK*: 504; Mh.: 411). In *MK*, we read of the Jews' flayed victims ('abgehäutete Opfer', *MK*: 343; Mh.: 284), and of their lust for blood and money: 'dieser blut- und geldgierigen jüdischen Völkertyrannen' [these blood-thirsty and avaricious Jewish tyrants of nations] (*MK*: 703; Mh.: 568). Hitler taught that it was the Jews' intention to let folkish Germans bleed to death in a religious war: he expressly stresses the German *'verbluten lassen'* ('Und ich betone das Wort verbluten lassen' (*MK*: 632; Mh.: 513f.). Such a battery of violent and terrifying images must have struck fear into the hearts of susceptible readers. Present-day racist discourse in many European nations makes use of similar notions, especially that of foreigners stealing living accommodation, jobs, and social services from the native residents of a country (cf. Kässner 2004, Zschaler 2004). Even in its most extreme form, however, it does not incline towards accusations that outsiders are ready to eat native populations; merely that they are prepared to take food from the mouths of "our" children and that (where black male people are concerned) they wish to appropriate "our" women (cf. App. I, Text 7).

The anti-Semitic message of *MK* is supported by a generally aggressive language which suffuses any part of the text where enemies are denigrated. In the section entitled 'Der Werdegang des Judentums' (Book 1, Chapter 11: 338–347), the following verbs of violence are attested: *ausplündern* ('to plunder'), *zugrunde richten* ('to destroy'), *aussaugen* ('to suck (blood)'), *abzapfen* ('to tap off (blood)'), *auspressen* and *herauspressen* ('to squeeze'), *herausschinden* ('to grind'), *quälen* ('to torment'), *rauben* ('to rob'), *umklammern* ('to ensnare'), *umgarnen* ('to grip, ensnare'), *vergiften* ('to poison'). Adjectives and nouns include *blutsaugerisch* ('blood-sucking'), *Tyrannei* ('tyranny'), *Erpressung* ('blackmail'), *Einschläferung* ('putting to sleep'), *Ausplünderung* ('plundering'), *Auspressung* ('squeezing out'), *Umgarnung* ('ensnarement'), *Verfechtung* ('fighting') and *Volksvergifter* ('poisoner of the people'). (For a fuller list of aggressive vocabulary see App. II, Section 4).

Just as odious as the vocabulary of violence in *MK* is its suffusion with pejorative epithets for every group of people that Hitler despised and feared. He judged everybody and everything and appears to have revelled in finding varied ways to revile his enemies and the weaker members of his own *Volk*. App. II, Section 5.3.1.2 categorizes the negative epithets applied to Jews and Hitler's other enemies, most of whom he saw as having a Jewish connection. Jews are categorized as outsiders, liars and cheats, bandits, tyrants, seducers, mimics, physically degenerate and dirty; they are likened to a variety of animals, especially to vermin and blood-sucking creatures; and they are portrayed as monstrosities *(Mißgeburten)*. They are also deindividualized as **der** Jude, **der** internationale Jude, along the lines of scientific abstraction (see von Polenz 1972: 169). Hitler further mocks the Jews by means of ironic epithets: '„Wohltäter" der Menschheit' ['benefactor' of mankind] (*MK*: 343; Mh.: 284), '„Freund der Menschen" ['friend of mankind'] (*MK*: 343; Mh.: 284), 'diese Zierden des menschlichen Geschlechtes' [these ornaments of the human race] (*MK*: 341; Mh.: 282). Marxists and the press are derided in similar terms as bringers of disease and as the diseases themselves, as murderers, traitors, plunderers, rapists, scoundrels and cowards.

App. II, Section 5.3.2.2 records a selection of references to the general attributes and behaviour of Jews. These include the desire to expand their race; the desire for world domination; dishonesty, deception and hypocrisy; lack of conscience; seduction, exploitation and secrecy; imitation of other races; subversion and agitation; selfishness, cowardice and greed; brutality; impertinence, flattery and slyness; and an adverse influence on parliament and on Germany's cultural life. Hitler also mentions some common, stereotypically Jewish attributes, considered positive in other races, in order to challenge them, for example:

> Es ist also grundfalsch aus der Tatsache des Zusammenstehens der Juden im Kampfe, richtiger ausgedrückt in der Ausplünderung ihrer Mitmenschen, bei ihnen auf einen gewissen idealen Aufopferungssinn schließen zu wollen. (*MK*: 331) [So it is absolutely wrong to infer any ideal sense of sacrifice in the Jews from the fact that they stand together in struggle, or, better expressed, in plundering of their fellow men. (Mh.: 274)]

Hyperbole aggravates Hitler's images of Germany's supposed enemies. The adjective *ewig* has a particularly sinister effect when used with anti-Semitic epithets, for example: 'gegen den ewigen Blutegel' [against the eternal bloodsucker] (*MK*: 339; Mh.: 281) and 'ewiger Spaltpilz der Menschheit' [the eternal mushroom of humanity] (*MK*: 135; Mh.: 113—*Spaltpilz* would normally be translated as 'bacterium'). Klemperer documents the noun *Welt* as having intrinsic superlative connotations: in *MK*, Hitler favours the word in compound epithets for his Jewish enemy: 'vom Gift des internationalen Weltjuden' [the poison of the international world Jew] (*MK*: 629; Mh.: 512); **'das Gezische der jüdischen Welthydra'** *[the hissing of the Jewish world hydra]* (*MK*: 721; Mh.: 581; see also App. II, Section 1; *Weltpest* [world plague] could also refer to Social Democrats (*MK*: 46), another of Hitler's targets). A further type of hyperbole is the accumulation or listing of words describing enemies, as in the figure of five referring to the Jews as 'Repräsentanten der Lüge, des Betrugs, des Diebstahls, der Plünderung, des Raubes' [champions of deceit, lies, theft, plunder, and rapine] (*MK*: 750; Mh.: 604; see App. II, Section 3).

During his time as a propagandist Hitler used a number of common metaphors to demonize Jews (see Chapter 3 and App. III). Many of his favoured metaphors are also commonly employed in modern right-wing discourse to discredit both Jews and foreigners. Bernhard Pörksen documents eight common source domains used in the construction of *Feindbilder*: the body, disease, the animal kingdom (usually lower-order animals), natural catastrophes, houses and their upkeep (for example decorating and cleaning), the theatre, religion and the military sphere (Pörksen 2000: 179). Hitler used metaphorical expressions from all of these domains (most notably *Volkskörper* ('body of the people'), *-organismus* ('organism of the people'); *Pest* ('plague'), *Krebs* ('cancer'), *Geschwür* ('ulcer'), *Bazillus* ('bacillus'); *Flut* ('flood'), *Strom* ('stream, river'), *Welle* ('wave'); *satanisch* ('satanic'), *teuflisch* ('devilish'); *Front* ('front'), *Waffe* ('weapon'), *Truppen* ('troops'). In *MK*, Jews are accused, metaphorically, of strangling, consuming, corroding, dissolving, ensnaring, enslaving, attacking, robbing and sucking the blood of their German victims, and of undermining, ruining and contaminating German institutions and culture (see App. II, Section 4 and App. III, A.2.10). Jews are dehumanized as animals, as parts of a machine ('jüdische Welteroberungsmaschine', *MK*: 528) and as instruments ('dieses Instrument einer maßlosen Erpressung und schmachvollsten Erniedrigung', *MK*: 714; Mh.: 577); they are metaphorized as the causers of diseases and as the diseases themselves *(Seuche, Pest, Pestilenz)*; they are ironized as apostles ('Weltversöhnungsapostel', *MK*: 248); and they are described as devils, vampires and poisoners *(Volksvergifter)*. A group of metaphors relating light and darkness to good and evil, or to truth and lies, shows Jews as haters of daylight *(das Tagelicht scheuend)* and lovers of the dark (e.g. as moths). The following particularly repulsive image shows the effect of light upon those who are not used to it:

> Sowie man nur vorsichtig in eine solche Geschwulst hineinschnitt, fand man, wie die Made im faulenden Leibe, oft ganz geblendet vom plötzlichem Lichte, ein Jüdlein. (*MK*: 61) [If you cut even cautiously into such an abscess, you found, like a maggot in a rotting body, often dazzled with sudden light—a kike! (Mh.: 53)]

Similarly, Jews are depicted as black, although obviously not literally black-skinned, and Aryans are portrayed as white: thus, for example, the former are portrayed as black parasites of the nation ('diese schwarzen Völkerparasiten') who defile inexperienced young blonde girls ('unsere unerfahrenen, jungen, blonden Mädchen', *MK*: 630; Mh.: 512).

Jews are particularly commonly metaphorized as herd animals and lower-level animals (rats, snakes, insects, blood-sucking creatures, maggots, etc.), just as they are portrayed as occupying a lower level than Germans in the human hierarchy (cf. App. II, Section 5.3.1.2). They are shown as corrupters and bringers of harm: 'Er wird dadurch „zum Ferment der Dekomposition" von Völkern und Rassen und im weiteren Sinne zum Auflöser der menschlichen Kultur' [He becomes 'a ferment of decomposition' among peoples and races, and in the broader sense a dissolver of human culture] (*MK*: 498; Mh.: 406). Hitler's most disgusting metaphors are reserved for the Jews, the following quotation being one of his more imaginative:

> Wo immer man so einen Apostel angriff, umschloß die Hand qualligen Schleim; das quoll einem geteilt durch die Finger, um sich im nächsten Moment schon wieder zusammenzuschließen. (*MK*: 67) [Whenever you tried to attack one of these apostles, your hand closed on a jelly-like slime which divided up and poured through your fingers, but in the next moment collected again. (Mh.: 58)]

Whether one takes the medical rendering of the word *Schleim* (mucus) or imagines any type of slimy substance, the image is equally repulsive. A further sinister image is that of the possible "switching off" (Mh. has 'exclude') of the light-bringing Aryan by the hand of his enemy: 'Man schalte ihn aus—und tiefe Dunkelheit wird vielleicht schon nach wenigen Jahrtausenden sich abermals auf die Erde senken' [Exclude him—and perhaps after a few thousand years darkness will again descend on the earth] (*MK*: 317f.; Mh.: 263; Schmitz-Berning records the use of *Ausschaltung* only with reference to the 'Ausschaltung der Juden aus dem Wirtschaftsleben', 1998: 82). Jews are accused of using other human beings as inanimate tools, the 'willenlose Werkzeuge in seiner Faust' [will-less tools in his fist] (*MK*: 723; Mh.: 583), and as instruments with which to attain their goals:

> (...) und hat in der ihm vollständig verfallenen Freimaurerei ein vorzügliches Instrument zur Verfechtung wie aber auch zur Durchschiebung seiner Ziele. (*MK*: 345) [(...) and in Freemasonry, which has succumbed to him completely, he has an excellent instrument with which to fight for his aims and put them across. (Mh.: 285)]

The Jews are also portrayed in *MK* as the enslavers of the German people, and their methods of making money are shown as particularly harmful to the nation, which was in danger of succumbing to 'das Sklavenjoch des internationalen Kapitals und seiner Herren, der Juden' [the slave's yoke of international capital and its masters, the Jews] (*MK*: 265; Mh.: 221). Such a message was especially potent at a time when so many Germans were experiencing financial hardship. Hitler reminds his readers that slavery is the very worst of all fates ('Das Unschönste, was es im menschlichen Leben geben kann', *MK*: 195; Mh.: 163). Equally menacing to the Christian reader, however, was the notion that the mixture of Aryan with Jewish blood was akin to the fall from paradise *(Sündenfall)* and into hell (*MK*: 320 and 233). Hitler liked to portray himself as the one leader who could save Germany from eternal damnation at the hands of such absolute enemies.

In *MK*, Jews are contrasted with the Aryan *Volk* with stark linguistic antitheses, such as 'das eine ergibt dann eben arische Arbeits- und Kulturstaaten, das andere jüdische Schmarotzerkolonien' [the one results in Aryan states based on work and culture, the other in Jewish colonies of parasites]. They are the epitome of what Hitler calls *Unnatur*, the opposite of all that is natural (*MK*: 65; Mh.: 56), indeed they are the antithesis of all that is pure and good; they are pitiless *(unbarmherzig)* (*MK*: 343; not translated by Mh.), shameless *(unverschämt)* (*MK*: 354; Mh. 292), and the embodiment of intolerance *(Unduldsamkeit)* (*MK*: 506; MK: 336). Hitler portrayed the Jews, indeed all of his enemies, as unable to compromise and negotiate, thus justifying his own totalitarian stance: 'Mit dem Juden gibt es kein Paktieren, sondern nur das harte Entweder-Oder' [There is no making pacts with Jews; there can only be the hard: either-or] (*MK*: 225; Mh.: 187). Such stark alternatives instilled fear into the hearts of his followers, thus ensuring that their hatred for these major enemies would be increased.

The message of *MK* is that the ultimate goal of Germany's chief enemy, the Jew, was world conquest, both in the economic sphere ('wirtschaftliche Eroberung') and the realm of politics ('politische Unterjochung') (*MK*: 352; Mh.: 291). A supposed Jewish plan to subjugate Germans not by means of honest work, but by feeding parasitically on German cultural, economic and technical achievements, was fundamental to Hitler's *Feindbild*. While Marxists, Socialists, the press and any other group associated with Jews were portrayed as enemies, it is the Jews whom Hitler demonized beyond the understanding of most reasonable readers. Fear, however, can overpower reason, when it is expressed in such extreme terms as in the following image of Judaism: 'dann wird seine Krone der Totentanz der Menschheit sein' [his crown will be the funeral wreath of humanity] (*MK*: 69f.; Mh.: 60). Jews, according to Hitler, were at the root of all evil, so that:

> (...) niemand zu wundern braucht, wenn in unserem Volke die Personifikation des Teufels als Sinnbild alles Bösen die leibhaftige Gestalt des Juden annimmt. (*MK*: 355) [(...) no one need be surprised if among our people the personification of the devil as the symbol of all evil assumes the living shape of the Jew. (Manheim: 294)]

2.3.4 Hitler's Glorification of the German *Volk*

Hitler saw his task and that of National Socialism as a holy mission *(heilige Mission, heilige Aufgabe)* to protect and improve the lot of the German *Volk* through the creation of a Germanic state populated by pure-blooded Aryans. He saw his role, and that of National Socialism, as *heilig* (holy) and *weihevoll* (sacred) (see especially *MK*: 626; Mh.: 509). Hitler felt able to prophesy a glorious and eternally secure future for a *Volk* of German citizens as long as they supported him (*MK*: 475); love and pride would be their binding elements:

> **Dann wird dereinst ein Volk von Staatsbürgern erstehen, miteinander verbunden und zusammengeschmiedet durch eine gemeinsame Liebe und einen gemeinsamen Stolz, unerschütterlich und unbesiegbar für immer.** (*MK*: 475) [*Then a people of citizens will some day arise, bound to one another and forged together by a common love and a common pride, unshakable and invincible forever.* (Mh.: 388)]

The notion that the German Reich was the natural home of all racial Germans was fundamental to Hitler's *Weltanschauung*: **'Gleiches Blut gehört in ein gemeinsames Reich'** *[One blood demands one Reich]* (*MK*: 1; Mh.: 1). Hitler declared his aim of protecting the *Volkskörper* (body of the people) from its enemies, seeing the Jews in particular as conspiring to poison folkish blood through intermarriage, which he termed *Rassenschande* [defilement of the race] (*MK*: 444; Mh.: 366). In *MK*, Hitler describes the *Volk* as a body with superlatives such as 'im Kerne urgesund' [at the core (...) robust and healthy] (*MK*: 9; Mh.: 10). They always willingly give their 'teuerstes Blut' [most precious blood] (*MK*: 219; Mh.: 182) for the good of their race, a blood which is constantly under threat of Jewish attack: 'Er vergiftet das Blut der anderen, wahrt aber sein eigenes' [He poisons the blood of others, but preserves his own] (*MK*: 346; Mh.: 286).

Hitler saw the preservation and expansion of the Aryan racial "stock" as a fundamental virtue, often using compounds formed with *-erhaltung* ('preservation') as their second element *(Selbsterhaltung, Erhaltungswille, Selbsterhaltungswille, Forterhaltung, Forterhaltungswille, Arterhaltung)*, sometimes qualified by the adjective *völkisch*, as in 'der völkische Selbsterhaltungstrieb bei Niederkämpfung eine solchen Macht' [the national instinct of preservation, in overthrowing such a power] (*MK*: 104; Mh.: 88). App. II, Section 5.2.2 records a sample of the good qualities and behaviour which Hitler attributes to the German *Volk*, or which he believes they are capable of displaying. These include their desire for racial unity ('starker Rasseinstinkt', *MK*: 443); self-sacrifice and loyalty ('Aufopferungsfähigkeit und Aufopferungswille', *MK*: 167); courage and heroism ('strahlendes Heldentum', *MK*: 169); selflessness and honesty ('Uneigennützigkeit und Redlichkeit', *MK*: 309); mental agility ('geistige Elastizität und schöpferische Fähigkeit', *MK*: 443); health, strength and will ('Wille und Kraft', *MK*: 371); ruthlessness and brutality ('rücksichtslose Brutalität', *MK*: 229); fanaticism and hysteria (**'fanatische, ja hysterische Leidenschaften'**, *MK*: 475); nationalist sentiments ('nationale Willenskraft', *MK*: 457); and physical superiority ('stählerne Geschmeidigkeit', *MK*: 453). In App. II, Section 5.2.2, I have documented over 100 positive German qualities identified by Hitler. This is in stark contrast to Ulrich Ulonska's findings in relation to his speeches, i.e. that he favoured certain qualities over others. Ulonska concentrates his analysis on four "dominant" and five "secondary" values (dominant: *Tapferkeit* (bravery), *Gerechtigkeit* (justice), *Patriotismus*, *Fleiß* (diligence); secondary: *Gleichheit* (equality), *Aufrichtigkeit* (honesty, sincerity), *Zuverlässigkeit* (reliability), *Frömmigkeit* (piety), *Zuversicht* (confidence) (Ulonska 1990: 130–214).

To Hitler, the German *Volk* was everything that its enemies were not. The glory of the good German is further highlighted by its contrast with the characteristics of unworthy Germans. As can readily be seen from App. II, Section 5, Hitler was generally quicker to criticize than he was to praise. Pejorative epithets are recorded in App. II, Section 5.3 and describe the following types of people: the incapable, stupid and ignorant ('Nichtskönner und Nichtstuer', *MK*: 399); the lazy, weak and generally degenerate ('den Wankelmütigwerdenden und den Schwachen', *MK*: 781); cowards and pacifists (**'tränenreiche pazifistische Klageweiber'**, *MK*: 438); crawlers and climbers ('Kriecher und Schliefer', *MK*: 259); monarchists and hangers-on at Court ('Hofgaul', *MK*: 57); liars and cheats ('verlogene, heimtückische Duckmäuser', *MK*: 400); traitors and thieves ('ein schuftiger Waffenverräter', *MK*: 610); and general rabble and scoundrels ('Gelichter', *MK*: 219 and 'Kanaillen', *MK*: 610; see also Section 5.3.1.1). It was even possible to be too "folkish". Hitler criticized what he considered to be old-fashioned and excessively overt folkish behaviour, including the use of archaic vocabulary ('altgermanische Ausdrücke') [old Germanic expressions] (*MK*: 395; Mh.: 326); he used very little archaic language himself, apart from the *ward*-form for the third person singular preterite of *werden*, see App. II, Section 12.

Hitler's recommendation for the members of his new folkish movement was that they should be healthy and physically resilient: 'Flink wie Windhunde, zäh wie Leder und hart wie Kruppstahl' [swift as greyhounds, tough as leather, and hard as Krupp steel] (*MK*: 392) (Mh.: 324). A healthy body is a prerequisite for a healthy mind. The following passage links national pride with the feeling of belonging to a healthy folkish body:

> **Erst wenn ein Volkstum in allen seinen Gliedern, an Leib und Seele gesund ist, kann sich die Freude, ihm anzugehören, bei allen mit Recht zu jenem hohen Gefühl steigern, das wir mit Nationalstolz bezeichnen. Diesen höchsten Stolz aber wird auch nur der empfinden, der eben die Größe seines Volkstums kennt.**
> **Die innige Vermählung von Nationalismus und sozialem Gerechtigkeitssinn ist schon in das junge Herz hineinzupflanzen. Dann wird dereinst ein Volk von Staatsbürgern erstehen, miteinander verbunden und zusammengeschmiedet durch eine gemeinsame Liebe und einen gemeinsamen Stolz, unerschütterlich und unbesiegbar für immer.** (*MK*: 474f.) [*Only when a nation is healthy in all its members, in body and soul, can every man's joy in belonging to it rightfully be magnified to that high sentiment which we designate as national pride. And this highest pride will only be felt by a man who knows the greatness of his nation.*
> *An intimate coupling of nationalism and a sense of social justice must be implanted in the young heart. Then a people of citizens will some day arise, bound to one another and forged together by a common love and a common pride, unshakable and invincible forever.* (Mh.: 388)]

In Chapter 3, I describe the conceptual metaphor A STATE IS A BODY. Hitler saw the German *Volk* as one living organism (*MK*: 362; Mh.: 299) which had to be kept healthy. In the above quotation, Hitler stresses the necessity of a body being healthy in all of its limbs (Mh.'s translation is 'members') if it is to be able to feel pride. He writes of a marriage (*Vermählung*, Mh. has 'coupling') of nationalism and social justice, a joining of the two forces which were at the heart of Hitler's vision for Germany's future. The passage gives an image of a united *Volk* coming out of a period of decline in words frequently associated with Christ's resurrection (see also App. III, A.1.3.2). The optimistic tone of the final sentence, the reference to love, pride and sharing, and the promise of permanence, is an example of the type of rhetoric in *MK* which may have blinded budding National Socialists to the true message of the book.

2.3.5 Hitler's Belief in a Racial Hierarchy

The writings of Friedrich Nietzsche were a major influence upon Hitler while the latter was developing his racial doctrine. Nietzsche's notion that some humans were naturally of a higher order than others may well have come to Hitler through the Nietzsche *"Nachlaß"*, edited and corrupted by Elisabeth Förster-Nietzsche. To Hitler, of course, the superior human beings belonged to the so-called "Aryan" race, against which he contrasted non-Aryans, particularly the Jews. He saw Aryans as innately superior, a state ordained by God and Nature together. He metaphorized the Jews as a black race and the Aryans as white (e.g. *MK*: 705, Mh.: 569), while not forgetting to mention other races that he considered less worthy than his own:

> (...) daß es eine Versündigung am Willen des ewigen Schöpfers ist, wenn man Hunderttausende und Hunderttausende seiner begabtesten Wesen im heutigen proletarischen Sumpf verkommen läßt, während man Hottentotten und Zulukaffern zu geistigen Berufen hinaufdressiert. (*MK*: 479) [(...) that it is a sin against the will of the Eternal Creator if His most gifted beings by the hundreds and hundreds of thousands are allowed to degenerate in the present proletarian morass, while Hottentots and Zulu Kaffirs are trained for intellectual professions. (Mh.: 391)]

Hitler's text portrays African races as no better, even in the sight of God, than well-trained animals. In his translation of *hinaufdressieren* as 'to train' Manheim disregards the notion of upward movement in *hinauf* as well as the fact that the verb *dressieren* usually refers to the training of animals.

In *Zur Genealogie der Moral* Nietzsche makes a link, based on the etymology of the words *arya* and *bonum*, between the Aryan, as the noble 'Eroberer- und Herren-Rasse' ('conquering- and master-race'), and the German words *gut*, *göttlich* and *Goten* ('good, godly and Goths', Nietzsche 1956: 776f.). The Jews are portrayed as the race who altered worldly values so that only those who are poor, wretched and powerless are deemed to be good ('die Elenden sind allein die Guten, die Armen, Ohnmächtigen, Niedrigen sind allein die Guten', 779). Nietzsche claims that priests are the greatest haters *(Hasser)* in the world and the most evil of enemies because they are powerless; he goes on to describe the Jews as a priest-like people ('priester-liches Volk'), introducing words like '(das) Giftigste' ('most poisonous thing') and 'Rache' ('revenge') into his discussion. Later in the same text he uses the term *Blutvergiftung* ('blood-poisoning') to describe racial mixture. Such a text must have been exactly what Hitler was looking for to reaffirm his own convictions. If he was as uneducated as Victor Klemperer believed, he may not have perfectly understood Nietzsche's writings (Klemperer 1996: 25f.). He may, however, gladly have accepted a simplified interpretation as a pillar to support his own opinions, and he possibly found the writings of Houston Stewart Chamberlain more accessible than those of Nietzsche. In Chamberlain's essay of 1900, 'Die Rassenfrage', for example, he would have seen his own ideas on race echoed, particularly in the following words, quoted from the Jewish-British politician Benjamin Disraeli:

> Rasse ist alles; es gibt keine andere Wahrheit. Und jede Rasse muß zugrunde gehen, die ihr Blut sorglos Vermischungen hingibt' (Race is everything; there is no other truth. And every race that carelessly allows its blood to be mixed will perish) (Chamberlain, 1925: 80).

In Chapter 2.3.5, I demonstrate how Hitler used well-worn metaphors to present images of the Aryan race as higher in the racial hierarchy than other races. He makes use of the deeply grounded conceptual metaphor of THE

GREAT CHAIN OF BEING. Jews in particular are portrayed as lower-level beings: insects, parasites, vermin and bacteria. Within the conceptual metaphors SUPERIORITY IS UP and PROGRESS IS MOVEMENT UPWARDS, the Aryan is judged to be the founder of all higher humanity (*MK*: 317; Mh.: 263) and the NS movement to have the highest obligation ('eine höchste Verpflichtung') to protect the Aryan race (*MK*: 32; Mh.: 590). App. III, B.2.1.3.1.9 records verbs (*fallen, (nieder)senken, (unter)sinken, stürzen and hintunterziehen*) and nouns (*Abgrund, Niedergang* and *Sündenfall*) which refer to the "lowering" (i.e. devaluation) of racial characteristics and cultural gifts as a result of contamination largely by the Jews. According to Hitler, the Aryan was the highest of all human races and the 'Begründer höheren Menschentums überhaupt' [the founder of all higher humanity] (*MK*: 317; Mh.: 263). Metaphors of light and darkness similarly denote superiority and inferiority. Light metaphors show the Aryan as the racial founder of the German *Volk*, as a bringer of light ('Lichtbringer', *MK*: 320; Mh.: 265) and the Prometheus of mankind (*MK*: 317; Mh.: 263). Jews are contrasted with Aryans as bringers of darkness and haters of daylight ('das Tagelicht scheuender Schliefer') (*MK*: 99; Mh.: 83).

Book 1, Chapter 11 of *MK*, entitled 'Volk und Rasse', presents Hitler's Darwinian-style racial theories as 'Wahrheiten' (truths) and 'Binsenweisheiten' (truisms) (*MK*: 311; for an excellent summary of Hitler's racial philosophy as expressed in Chapter 11 see Zehnpfennig 2002). He believed that every race and species in Nature was sharply differentiated and that the races existed in perpetual strife, the stronger always living at the expense of the weaker. Lack of differentiation within species and races was a form of *"Halbheit"* (half-heartedness) that did not conform to Hitler's uncompromising view of race. He referred to the mixing of races as *Blutvergiftung* and *Erbsünde* (see App. III, A.1.1 and A.2.9). One of the Hitler's most distinctive types of metaphor involves foodstuffs which are concocted from a mixture of ingredients: *Völkerbrei* [medley of nations], *Einheitsbrei* [unified mash] and *Rassenbrei* [general racial porridge] (*MK*: 23, 444 and 439; Mh.: 22, 365 and 361). Manheim's translation of *Brei* as 'medley' supports the image of a porridge blended from several ingredients. For Hitler, racial mixture was as unappetizing as these "porridges" sound. Chapter 11 also stresses the Christian message that man should be willing to subordinate his own ego to the good of the community. Hitler depicted Aryans as having an inborn predisposition to selflessness:

> Der Selbsterhaltungtrieb hat bei ihm die edelste Form erreicht, indem er das eigene Ich dem Leben der Gesamtheit willig unterordnet und (...) auch zum Opfer bringt. (*MK*: 326) [In him the instinct of self-preservation has reached the noblest form, since he willingly subordinates his own ego to the life of the community and (...) even sacrifices it. (Mh.: 270)]

The Jews, on the other hand, are portrayed in *MK* as egoists, who put their individual aims above the general good (*MK*: 168; Mh.: 140).

Hitler portrayed biological selection as an *Existenzkampf*, a *Lebenskampf*, or a *Kampf ums Dasein* (fight for survival) (see App. III, A.2.7). This was a battle in which the Aryan would (in Hitler's view rightfully) prevail. He saw the State as a weapon in Germany's 'großen ewigen Lebenskampfes um das Dasein' [great, eternal life struggle for existence] (*MK*: 440; Mh.: 362). According to Hitler, Nature had already selected the Aryan as the 'Urtyp' [prototype] which encapsulated everything 'was wir unter dem Worte „Menschen" verstehen' [that we understand by the word 'man'] (*MK*: 317; Mh.: 263). It was now the task of pure-blooded Aryans to recognize that some races are more valuable than others ('daß Volk nicht gleich Volk ist') and select only their own kind as mates:

> (...) der Versuch, die innerhalb der Volksgemeinschaft als rassisch besonders wertvoll erkannten Elemente maßgeblichst zu fördern und für ihre besondere Vermehrung Sorge zu tragen. (*MK*: 492f.) [(...) an attempt to promote in the most exemplary way those elements within the national community that have been recognised as especially valuable from the racial viewpoint and to provide for their special increase. (Mh.: 402)].

Hitler eschewed the Marxist view that all men are equal and called for a recognition of the aristocratic principle of human categorization. He invoked Darwinian theories to support his claim that in the battle between Jews and Aryans the latter would be the natural victor. Even intermarriage would not be able to raise Jews or any other "lower" race to the level of Aryans:

> Jede Kreuzung zweier nicht ganz gleich hoher Wesen gibt als Produkt ein Mittelding zwischen der Höhe der beiden Eltern. Das heißt also: das Junge wird wohl höher stehen

als die rassisch niedrigere Hälfte des Elternpaares, allein nicht so hoch wie die höhere. Folglich wird es im Kampf gegen diese höhere später unterliegen. (*MK*: 312) [Any crossing of two beings not at exactly the same level produces a medium between the level of the two parents. This means: the offspring will probably stand higher than the racially lower parent, but not as high as the higher one. Consequently, it will later succumb in the struggle against the higher level. (Mh.: 258ff.)]

Hitler took the notion of racial hierarchy a step further when writing of the ranking of individuals within races. By analogy with the principle that 'Volk (ist) nicht gleich Volk' [peoples are not equal] (*MK*: 492; Mh.: 402), people are similarly not equal within the broad category of their race. Hitler's idea of giving the world to the "best" people (**'dem besten Volk, also den höchsten Menschen'**) followed an aristocratic principle of only conferring leadership to the people with the best minds:

(...) **innerhalb dieses Volkes wieder dem gleichen aristokratischen Prinzip gehorchen und den besten Köpfen die Führung und den höchsten Einfluß im betreffenden Volke sichern.** (*MK*: 493) [*(...) obey the same aristocratic principle within this people and make sure that the leadership and the highest influence in this people fall to the best minds.* (Mh.: 403)]

We may assume that he considered himself to belong to the category of people with the best minds.

One of Hitler's most vital tasks, as he saw it, was to preach that Aryan blood should be protected from contamination (*MK*: 444; Mh.: 365). In this he may have been following Houston Stewart Chamberlain, who wrote that racial purity was the holiest of all religious laws: 'die Reinheit der Rasse als das heiligste aller religiösen Gesetze' (Chamberlain 1925: 80). It appeared imperative to Hitler that the folkish State be composed only of those human beings whom he judged to be closer to God's image than all others, i.e. Aryans. The purpose of marriage in a folkish State should be the creation of: **'Ebenbilder des Herrn (...) und nicht Mißgeburten zwischen Mensch und Affe'** [*images of the Lord and not monstrosities halfway between man and ape*] (*MK*: 445; Mh.: 366). According to Hitler, the Aryans alone had a God-given mission on earth: '**(der) auch ihm vom Schöpfer des Universums zugewiesenen Mission'** [*the mission allotted it by the creator of the universe*] (*MK*: 234; Mh.: 195). Hitler not only portrayed Aryans as special in God's eyes and close to His image; he also maintained that the Aryans had built paradise for themselves ('im Paradiese, das er sich selbst geschaffen hatte', *MK*: 324; Mh.: 268).

2.3.6 The Nature of Hitler's *Kampf*

It is apparent from the text of *MK* that at the time of writing Hitler saw his own life and his political efforts in terms of conflict—not yet a physical fight perhaps, but a violent battle of words and ideas. *Mein Kampf* was a major weapon in Hitler's fight, one of its aims being to enlist followers to support his cause. On the first page of *MK* he acknowledged the necessity of wars for human progress 'aus den Tränen des Krieges erwächst für die Nachwelt das tägliche Brot' [and from the tears of war the daily bread of future generations will grow]. However the word *Krieg* seldom refers to future combat in *MK*, whereas the term *Kampf* occurs on nearly every page and denotes Hitler's present and future fights. The fight would be for Germany and all German people (in which category he included "Aryan" Austrians) and against an assortment of enemies, of which he portrayed the Jews as the most evil.

In *MK*, references to war using the word *Kampf* are open to various interpretations. Some are clearly metaphorical, others are likely to be meant literally; few are as direct as the following reference to a counterattack against the Jews: 'Kein Volk entfernt diese Faust anders von seiner Gurgel als durch das Schwert' [No nation can remove this hand from its throat except by the sword] (*MK*: 738; Mh.: 595). The careful reader will, however, be in no doubt that Hitler's plans for a folkish state would involve a fierce battle rather than a gentle argument:

> Wenn man also versuchen will, das ideale Bild eines völkischen Staates in die reale Wirklichkeit zu überführen, dann muß man (...) nach einer neuen Kraft suchen, die gewillt und fähig ist, den Kampf für ein solches Ideal aufzunehmen. Denn um ein Kampf handelt es sich hierbei, insofern die erste Aufgabe nicht heißt: Schaffung einer völkischen Staatsauffassung, sondern vor allem: Beseitigung der vorhandenen jüdischen. (*MK*: 504f.) [And so, if we wish to transform the ideal image of a folkish state into practical reality, we must (...) seek a new force that is willing and able to take up the struggle for such an idea. For it will take a struggle, in view of the fact that the first task is not creation of a folkish state conception, but above all elimination of the existing Jewish one. (Mh.: 411)]

Within the conceptual metaphor POLITICS IS WAR, further discussed in Chapter 3, the noun *Kampf* and its verb *kämpfen*, as well as the synonyms *fechten* and *ringen*, could mean anything from a political argument to full-blown physical combat (as undertaken by Hitler's *"Ordnertruppe"*). POLITICS IS WAR had a tradition in political rhetoric before *MK*, but nowhere before or since have the term *Kampf* and its synonyms been used with such force and frequency. Hitler certainly used the term to refer to non-physical political arguments, possibly in order to give his book an aggressive tone and thus make his message appear more urgent. Yet he saw his personal fight and that of National Socialism as active and forceful. It is not certain, however, to what degree he was already thinking of war. The following quotation certainly refers to physical combat:

> **(...) daß man verlorene Gebiete nicht durch die Zungenfertigkeit geschliffener parlamentarischer Mäuler zurückgewinnt, sondern durch ein geschliffenes Schwert zu erobern hat, also durch einen blutigen Kampf.** (*MK*: 710) [(...) *that lost territories are not won back by sharp parliamentary big-mouths and their glibness of tongue, but by a sharp sword; in other words, by a bloody fight.* (Mh.: 574)]

But can we be certain that Hitler intended the 'bloody fight' to be interpreted literally, or was he using the expression metaphorically and hyperbolically? Von Polenz reminds us of the euphemistic usage of the term *Kampf* for *Krieg* in NS discourse (von Polenz 1972: 170), but to what extent is this true of *MK*?

Whether Hitler thought of his fight and that of his followers as physical or verbal, or both, *MK* is saturated with expressions of hatred and of the need for combat. The terms *Kampf* or *kämpfen* are found on almost every page, often more than once. For Hitler, life was a battle, a notion which he often qualified with the adjective *ewig*:

> Vor Gott, insofern wir auf diese Welt gesetzt sind mit der Bestimmung des ewigen Kampfes um das tägliche Brot (...) (*MK*: 739) [(...) before God, since we have been put down on this earth with the mission of eternal struggle for our daily bread (...) (Mh.: 596)]

Hitler saw himself as leading a fight for existence *(Existenzkampf/Lebenskampf /Kampf ums Dasein)* on behalf of the Aryan race, a fight which involved biological selection—those of the German masses who did not understand Darwinian theory would be moved by the simpler message that they must fight for their daily bread). In App. III, A.2.7 (www.qmul.ac.uk/~mlw032), I have attempted to categorize Hitler's usage of the word *Kampf* as follows: the fight for the Aryan race; the fight against Jews, Marxists and Social Democrats; the fight for a *Weltanschauung*; the National Socialist struggle; the fight for Germany as a nation; the fight to keep German culture alive; the fight for freedom, human rights and progress; the fight against parliamentary democracy; the fight against centralisation; the fight for economic independence; and the moral fight against syphilis. A fight solely with intellectual and spiritual weapons *(geistige Waffen)* was considered inadequate, and Hitler warned strongly of the consequences of not fighting:

> Wird dieser Kampf aber aus Bequemlichkeit oder auch Feigheit nicht ausgefochten, dann möge man sich in 500 Jahren die Völker ansehen. (*MK*: 280) [But if out of smugness, or even cowardice, this battle is not fought to its end, then take a look at the peoples five hundred years from now. (Mh.: 233)]

Those who are willing to fight are contrasted unfavourably with cowards, such as those who in 1918 quickly exchanged the halberd *(Hellebarde)* for the walking-stick *(Spazierstock)* (*MK*: 261; Mh.: 217f.).

Hitler's martial vocabulary in *MK* includes those expressions used metaphorically to stress the intensity of his political views and to give the entire work an aggressive tone. The following is a list of terms which refer variously to the martial acts of Germans and of their enemies (cf. App. III, A.2.7 for a fuller documentation): *Angriff* (attack), *angreifen* (to attack), *Ausplünderung* (pillaging), *Beutezug* (campaign of pillage), *erobern* (to conquer), *Eroberung* (conquest), *Fehde ansagen* (to declare a seige), *zu Feld ziehen* (to assail), *aus dem Feld schlagen* (to drive from the field), *Feldzug* (campaign), *Front machen* (to oppose, resist), *Gegenwehr* (counterattack) (*MK*: 629; Mh.: 511); *geißeln* (to flay), *Geißelhiebe* (scourge), *Krieg* (war), *Lager* (camp), *Leichenfeld* (battle-field covered with dead bodies), *Ramme* (battering-ram), *Ritter* (knight), e.g. 'der Ritter mit dem „geistigen" Schwert' [knights of the spiritual sword] (MK: 399; Mh.: 329), *rüsten* (to arm, prepare), *Schlacht* (battle), *Schlachtfeld* (battlefield), *Schwert* (sword), *Sieg* (victory), *siegen* (to conquer), *Speer* (speer), *Sturm* (storm, assault), *Sturm laufen, stürmen* (to storm, assault), *Waffe* (weapon), *entwaffnen* (to disarm).

Hitler summarizes the nature of his own fight and that of his fellow Aryans as the fulfilment of a holy mission. The gullible and the doubters among his readers may have been swayed by the following words:

> **Für was wir zu kämpfen haben, ist die Sicherung des Bestehens und der Vermehrung unserer Rasse und unseres Volkes, die Ernährung seiner Kinder und Reinhaltung des Blutes, die Freiheit und Unabhängigkeit des Vaterlandes, auf daß unser Volk zur Erfüllung der auch ihm vom Schöpfer des Universums zugewiesenen Mission heranzureifen.** (*MK*: 234) [*What we must fight for is to safeguard the existence and reproduction of our race and our people, the sustenance of our children and the purity of our blood, the freedom and independence of the fatherland, so that our people may mature for the fulfilment of the mission allotted it by the creator of the universe.* (Mh.: 195)]

What fight is more urgent than one to feed one's children? And who is better justified in attacking his enemies than a person who is following God's command.

2.3.7 What the Language of *Mein Kampf* Tells us about Hitler

In his 1933 monograph in Hitler's honour, Hans Wendt praised *MK* as the 'Zeugnis einer nach Totalität und neuen schöpferischen Wegen suchenden Persönlichkeit' (testimony to a personality who seeks totality and new creative roads) (Wendt 1933: 19). Hitler would have found such a tribute fitting: it is clear to any reader of *MK* that this was what he thought of himself. First conceived as an autobiography, Hitler's *MK* is a first-person narrative: everything in it is seen from Hitler's personal and very radical point of view, even when he is not giving autobiographical information and appears to retreat into the background. He does attempt, however, to engage his readership with a generally colloquial style and occasional inclusion of the audience in his deliberations (see App. II, Section 9). His extensive use of questions appears on the surface to be part of an attempt to involve his readers, but most of his open questions contain their answer within them or form part of question and answer sequences (see App. II, Section 9.1). Hitler used the first person plural more sparingly than some totalitarian politicians, and his voice is more aloof than one of solidarity. He does make it clear, however, that he assumes a basic common cause with his audience: '**Wir, als Arier (...)**, *MK*: 434; Mh.: 358). He may also adopt a stance of collaboration 'ich wende mich an die (...) [I address myself to those] (*MK*: 136; Mh.: 114), and he asks people to recall shared knowledge 'so bitte ich nicht zu vergessen, daß (...)' [I beg you not to forget that (...)] (*MK*: 502; Mh.: 410). Hitler's own involvement with his text is signalled by exclamations such as: 'Fürchterlich, fürchterlich!' [Terrible, terrible!] (*MK*: 241; Mh.: 201); 'Pfui Teufel und wieder Pfui Teufel!' [Phooey, I say, and again phooey!] (*MK*: 540) (Mh.: 439; see App. II, Section 9.5). He also uses spaced letters *(Sperrdruck)* to highlight what he considers to be especially important passages. Occasionally these passages cover several pages, for example pages 474–476, where a passage entitled 'Weckung des Nationalstolzes' reaches poetic, almost spiritual heights.

The reader of *MK* will soon notice Hitler's unwavering belief that he was right, especially in his frequent use of the modal particles *ja* and *doch*, often together, with *ja* appearing as many as three times in one sentence (see App. II, Section 10.2). One also notices his affirmation of his own superior knowledge: 'Ich betone es und bin fest davon überzeugt, daß (...)' [I emphasize the fact, and I am firmly convinced of it (...)] (*MK*: 765; Mh.: 615); and, with added arrogance, 'Man darf folgenden Satz als ewig gültige Wahrheit aufstellen: (...)' [The following theorem may be established as an eternally valid truth: (...)] (*MK*: 168; (Mh.: 140). When Hitler proclaims that the NS movement will not admit weaklings or the hesitant to its ranks he closes his statement with a biblical: 'Und das war gut so' [And this was good] (*MK*: 658; Mh.: 533).

Along with his belief that he was always right, Hitler assumed that most other people were stupid. He saw the masses in particular as unable to understand even the most basic of ideas unless these were constantly restated:

> Diese [die Masse] aber braucht in ihrer Schwerfälligkeit immer eine bestimmte Zeit, ehe sie auch nur von einer Sache Kenntnis zu nehmen bereit ist, und nur einer tausendfachen Wiederholung einfachster Begriffe wird sie endlich ihr Gedächtnis schenken. (*MK*: 203) [But the masses are slow-moving, and they always require a certain time before they are ready even to notice a thing, and only after the simplest ideas are repeated thousands of times will the masses finally remember them. (Mh.: 169)]

Each chapter of *MK* hammers its message home by the repetition of these simplest ideas, and some less simple ones. Hitler often signals that he is about to recapitulate a group of ideas, as in: 'Man kann also zuzammenfassend folgendes festhalten: (...)' [Thus, in summing up, we can establish the following (...)] (*MK*: 189; Mh.: 158); and he also promises to return to a particular vital point later: 'wie ich später nachweisen will' [as I shall later demonstrate] (*MK*: 569; Mh: 463). He deliberately and frequently recapitulates and paraphrases, perhaps in case an unintelligent reader should not have understood him: 'Das heißt mit anderen Worten folgendes: (...)' [This, in other words, means the following: (...)] (*MK*: 654; Mh.: 531).

Hitler's excessive use of tautology also falls into the category of repetition and must have been part of his strategy for hammering his message home (see App. II, Section 2). Why else would he have used such pointless combinations as 'die heutige Gegenwart' [the present time] (*MK*: 292; Mh.: 242) or 'alle acht Tage, also wöchentlich einmal' [every seven days; in other words, once a week] (*MK*: 518; Mh.: 421)? Did he think his audience so stupid that they had to be given two or three alternative lexemes for each concept, as in 'dem Ausgange zuwälzte, zuschob und zudrängte' [to move, shove and press towards the exit] (*MK*: 406; Mh.: 336)? Or was he simply showing off, demonstrating the wide range of vocabulary at his disposal? On one occasion he even thought it necessary to point out that he was speaking metaphorically: 'Das heißt freilich, nur bildlich gesprochen „gegen sich selbst"' ['Against himself' is only figuratively speaking] (*MK*: 349; Mh.: 289). One can also deduce from Hitler's writing that he was obsessed with precision and perfection: perhaps this explains some of his tautologous lists, as in: **'vier Millionen emsig arbeitenden, fleißigen, schaffenden Menschen'** *[four million hard-working, producing people]* (*MK*: 628; Mh.: 510)

Hitler was inordinately forthright throughout *MK*. Von Polenz writes (1972: 170) that totalitarian language makes widespread use of euphemisms as a form of gentle seduction towards conformity and self-affirmation ('sanfte Verführung zur Anpassung und Selbstbestätigung'), but Hitler uses relatively few in *MK* (see App. II, Section 8). The verb *beseitigen* (to eliminate) and its noun *Beseitigung* (elimination), and the deverbal adjective *korrigierend* (corrective) refer to what one assumes are drastic measures to dispose of unwanted people, such as the Jews:

> Zwölftausend Schurken zur rechten Zeit beseitigt, hätte vielleicht einer Million ordentlicher, für die Zukunft wertvoller Deutschen das Leben gerettet. (*MK*: 772) [(...) twelve thousand scoundrels eliminated in time might have saved the lives of a million real Germans, valuable for the future. (Mh.: 620)].

This sentence follows the most disturbing sentence in the entire work, namely that in which Hitler openly asserts that if twelve to fifteen thousand Jews had been gassed at the beginning of the First World War, a million German lives would have been saved.

Von Polenz writes about the tendency of totalitarian language to simplify complicated situations by means of aggressive polarization, particularly that of Jewish/Aryan or non-Aryan/Aryan (169). Antithesis was one of Hitler's favourite linguistic tools in enforcing the sharp polarity at the base of his *Weltanschauung*. In *MK* he constantly created clear binary divisions between good and bad, right and wrong, truth and lies, strength and weakness, body and mind, energy and apathy, bravery and cowardice, health and sickness, love and hate, and, most importantly, Aryan and Jew, whereby he refers to Jews as *"international"* and Germans as *"national"* (see App. II, Section 6). Hitler juxtaposed opposite views not in order to weigh them against one another, but to emphasize that only one of them was correct. One of his favoured ways of presenting his views as facts was with *nicht ... sondern ..., kein ... sondern, nie/niemals ... sondern* or *niemals ... immer* constructions. Hitler's use of antithesis illustrates one of the most basic and obvious traits of his character: he hated indecision and compromise, which he referred to as *Halbheit*:

> Die Nationalisierung der breiten Masse kann niemals erfolgen durch Halbheiten, durch schwaches Betonen eines Objektivitätsstandpunktes, sondern durch rücksichtslose und fanatisch einseitige Einstellung auf das nun einmal zu erstrebende Ziel. (*MK*: 370) [The nationalisation of the broad masses can never be achieved by half-measures, by weakly emphasising a so-called objective standpoint, but only by a ruthless and fanatically one-sided orientation towards the goal to be achieved. (Mh.: 306)].

Hitler believed in the dynamic power of subjectivity and that mankind's emotional side is of more use to him than the ability to reason, as reasoning gives rise to uncertainty, compromise and weakness: 'In politischen Angelegenheiten entscheidet nicht selten das Gefühl richtiger als der Verstand' [In political matters feeling often decides more correctly than reason] (*MK*: 190; Mh.: 159).

Hitler further employed antithesis to assert his view of justice and human rights. Pure-blooded Aryans enjoyed human rights, and, as a consequence of their omission from his reasoning, non-Aryans did not. Thus we can deduce that, in Hitler's view, non-Aryans were not human beings, or, at best, that they were beings with fewer rights than Aryans:

> **Nein, es gibt nur ein heiligstes Menschenrecht, und dieses Recht ist zugleich die heiligste Verpflichtung, nämlich: dafür zu sorgen, daß das Blut rein erhalten bleibt (...)**. (*MK*: 444) *[No, there is only one holiest human right, and this right is at the same time the holiest obligation, to wit: to see to it that the blood is preserved pure (...).* (Mh.: 365f.)]

Antithesis is also apparent in Hitler's descriptions of his friends and enemies. He shows sympathy for the former and callousness with regard to the feelings of the latter—indeed, when one examines his rich inventory of pejorative epithets, one may imagine that he thought of his enemies as having no feelings at all. This hostility is in stark contrast to his feelings of self-pity and self-admiration.

Hitler presented himself almost exclusively in a positive light, often with antithetical statements, such as 'Für mich war es dann keine vorübergehende Spielerei, sondern blutiger Ernst' [For me it was no passing game, but grim earnest] (*MK*: 242) (Mh.: 202). Hitler here contrasts his own attitudes with those of individuals who do not take things seriously. He sings his own praises and extols the qualities of a hypothetical *Führer* with characteristic hyperbole: (e.g. 'stürmische Begeisterung' [stormy enthusiasm] (*MK*: 177; Mh.: 148) and 'Feuereifer' [ardent zeal] (*MK*: 57; Mh.: 49).

Hitler portrayed himself as a fighter and a hero (see especially *MK*: 379; Mh.: 313). He was stubborn and obsessively determined to get his message across. His desire to communicate was perfectly sincere, as was his belief that his message was valuable, even vital. Furthermore, he was absolutely confident that his message would be understood. Hitler's generally emphatic style and aggressive vocabulary in *MK* were never replaced by a softer pleading or reasoning. He showed no doubt that he was to be *Führer* of the German *Volk*, and, perhaps most disturbingly, saw his task on earth as ordained by God. When he spoke of an apparently hypothetical leader as a 'dafür begnadeter Mann' ('man with a divine gift', Mh. has 'endowed') he meant himself: he believed he was the saviour who would bring 'lang ersehnte Erfüllung' to Germany (*MK*: 570; Mh.: 464; Mh.'s 'long yearned-for fulfilment' lacks the overtly Biblical tone of Hitler's words). Hitler believed that he had unlimited, God-given authority over his followers ('höchste unumschränkte Autorität'), balanced by an equally unlimited responsibility toward God and mankind ('die letzte und schwerste Verantwortung', *MK*: 379; Mh.: 313). Such a sense of duty would have been to his credit if he had been willing to serve all mankind, not just the German *Volk*.

2.3.8 How Conventional was the Language of *Mein Kampf*?

In Chapter 3.5, I claim that Hitler used chiefly conventional and well-worn metaphors; that it is chiefly their number and density within the text that is unusual. Above (2.1) I have quoted Klemperer's view that the language of the Third Reich was 'bettelarm' ('as poor as a beggar'; he includes *MK* among his examples of *LTI*). Hitler's book contains vivid and varied language, however, even though much of it was "begged" from other sources. He made the excessive repetition of his ideas more interesting by the use of synonyms, such *Heilung*, *Gesundung* and *Genesung* for healing, and *Fäulnis*, *Verfall*, *Verwesung*, *Zerfall*, *Zersetzung* and *Dekomposition* for decay. And while his ideas and many linguistic features were borrowed from other writers with similar views, Hitler put these together in a unique patchwork, tailored to his own needs.

In October 2004, I had a conversation with Swiss friend who had recently read a newspaper article about Hitler. My friend informed me that as I was writing a book about Hitler I should read this article, for it contained some useful facts: for example, that Hitler hated foreign words and that he had invented thousands of new words. These are fairly widespread myths. If Hitler had invented thousands of new words, *MK* would be more interesting than it actually is. In my opinion, one of the few unique features of *MK* is the outrageous exaggeration on every page—it is like other nationalist and totalitarian language, but more so. In App. I, I have reproduced texts which are similar in tone and language, but I have selected passages with a particularly high frequency of features; few entire texts are as intense as *MK*.

While contradicting my friend's "facts", however, I realized that two notable features of *MK* are, in fact, Hitler's predilection for foreign words, a selection which are found in App, 1, Section 13, and some unusual instances of word-formation.

As far as foreign words are concerned, some Nazis liked them, some did not. Hitler was not a linguistic purist and he probably used foreign words to impress and befuddle his audience: 'Das Fremdwort imponiert, es imponiert um so mehr, je weniger es verstanden wird' (Foreign words impress, and they impress all the more when they are less well understood, Klemperer: 268). According to Klemperer, the largely self-educated Hitler was 'nicht etwa halb-, sondern allerhöchstens zehntelgebildet' (not even half-educated, but at the most one-tenth educated). Klemperer feels that Hitler was self-conscious about his lack of formal education and tried to make up for this with a skilful use of vocabulary.

As far as Hitler's creative use of vocabulary is concerned, he used a wide selection of unusual compounds, some of which he may have encountered elsewhere, others perhaps his own creations, such as the following pejorative epithets: *schafsgeduldig* [patient lamblike] (*MK*: 685; Mh.: 555); „*verantwortlichseinsollend*" [should be responsible] (*MK*: 685; Mh.: 555); *weniggeistig* [unintellectual] (*MK*: 509; Mh.: 415); *hochnäsig-arrogant* [supercilious, arrogant] (*MK*: 727; Mh.: 587); *kindlich-blödsinnig* [absurd childish] (*MK*: 505; Mh.: 412); *kleinherzig-partikularistisch* [small-hearted, particularistic] (*MK*: 644; Mh.: 523); *sadistisch-pervers* [perverted sadistic] (*MK*: 704; Mh.: 569); „*weltbürgerlich*", *pazifistisch-ideologisch* ['cosmopolitan', pacifistic-ideological] (*MK*: 703; Mh.: 569); *witzig-ulkig* [cute and kittenish] (*MK*: 489; Mh.: 400; this is one of Mh.'s less felicitous translations). Hitler also varied his vocabulary considerably: one only has to glance at the selection of negative qualities listed in App. I, Section 5.3.2.1 and the epithets in Section 5.3.1 to see that he was not satisfied with mere tens of ways to insult people. He used pejorative vocabulary with such bravado and apparent delight that one wonders if he did not think he was amusing his audience. His message was, however, far from amusing, and it is to be regretted that it was not taken seriously enough in the period running up to the Second World War.

As a written work of propaganda, *MK* is remarkable for its excessive length. In his autobiographical novel, *Was soll aus dem Jungen bloß werden?*,

Heinrich Böll remembers that as a schoolboy he was given pages of *MK* to summarize: four pages would ideally be reduced one and a half without any significant loss of content (Böll 1983: 57). Thus the book could have given its message in 300 pages or less. But to Hitler, if a job was worth doing, it was worth doing well. He followed his own recommendations for political speeches, namely that a message must be hammered home by means of the constant repetition of mainly simple ideas, and it took him 781 pages to do so. Only truly dedicated followers could have been impressed by this. To a reader who does not appreciate Hitler's views, the journey from beginning to end feels like wading through a bog. Hitler aimed to give an impression of ideological consistency and firmness, and of his own dedication to his cause, and he succeeded, but one does not need to read all 781 pages to be convinced of this.

CHAPTER 3

Metaphor in *Mein Kampf*

3.1 What is Metaphor?

In terms of the classical rhetorical tradition, a metaphor is a "figure of speech", the main purpose of which is to embellish innovative or sophisticated texts, such as poetry and political discourse. Within traditional metaphor theory, the linguistic sign that represents the literal meaning of an object, concept or experience is replaced by a figurative sign: thus *arrival* "stands for" *birth* (BIRTH IS ARRIVAL) and *departure* "stands for" *death* (DEATH IS DEPARTURE)[1] (Nash 1989: 121). This theory does not, however, account for all of the possibilities of metaphoricity within the more recently conceived conceptual model, as described in Lakoff and Turner's seminal work: here we read that metaphors operate within the conceptual "schemas" that organize human knowledge (for example, the conceptual metaphor LIFE IS A JOURNEY includes DEATH IS THE END OF A JOURNEY, DEATH IS REST and DEATH IS DEPARTURE, Kövecses 2002: 44). According to this model, metaphor is a cognitive process by means of which we understand one conceptual domain (the "target domain") in terms of another (the "source domain") (Lakoff and Turner 1989: 112). Metaphor is therefore a "process of thought" and is at the base of all types of language, both everyday and unconventional. The individual domains which are substituted one for the other are referred to as "conceptual" metaphors (for example GOOD IS UP), and the individual linguistic expressions based on these conceptual mappings are called "metaphorical expressions". Later research by Lakoff and Johnson suggests that metaphorical structure underlies every mode of human thought; that the

---

[1] Throughout this chapter I will use the "SMALL CAPITALS" system of notation when referring to types of metaphorical mapping.

unconscious mind uses metaphor to 'define our unconscious metaphysics' (Lakoff and Johnson 1999: 12). They believe that it is the sensorimotor system which enables human beings to conceptualize and reason, and that it is unconscious metaphorical thought processes that make this possible. Their view that there is no such thing as disembodied truth or reason runs counter to the well-established tenet of Western philosophy that the world has a rational structure, independent of human beings, the categories of which are 'characterized by a *transcendent* or *universal* reason' (Lakoff and Johnson 1999: 21).

Within the "experientialist" framework of metaphorical theory described by cognitive linguists such as Lakoff, Turner and Johnson, the kind of link between conceptual domains exemplified by LIFE IS A JOURNEY is understood as being closely related to the conceptual categories by means of which human beings make sense of the world around them. Our basic bodily experience provides a natural link between conceptual categories and many of the metaphors that we use (Lakoff 1987: 272f.). For example, we experience our bodies as containers into which food is ingested and air breathed. This physical experience enables us to construct metaphorical links with other objects that have an exterior and an interior, such as houses and rooms, and also with abstract concepts, such as wakefulness and life. We also conceive of our minds as containers, where we 'chew over' and 'digest' ideas, indeed it would be difficult for us to picture the mind as an entity if we did not have access to such metaphors. In this last example the following mappings of source domain on to target domain are possible:

cooking	→	thinking
chewing	→	considering
swallowing	→	accepting
digesting	→	understanding
nourishment	→	mental well-being

(adapted from Kövecses 2002: 73)

We all have a subliminal understanding of common source and target domains and use these automatically and effortlessly. The German expression 'er kochte vor Zorn', for example, paralleled in the English 'he boiled with rage', in which 'boiling' is the source and 'anger' the target, is used so instinctively that many people do not realize they are using a metaphor. Such instinctively understood phrases are often referred to as "dead metaphors" because the (understood) relationship between source and target has been lost over time. However, as Raymond Gibbs explains, many, if not most, dead metaphors have 'vitally alive metaphorical roots' and are based on the common cognitive experience of the human race (Gibbs 1994: 277). The metaphor 'er kochte vor Zorn', for instance, is easily decoded because we can feel heat and internal pressure when we get angry; our scientific knowledge also tells us that feelings of anger are embodied via our automatic nervous system, causing our pulse rate and skin temperature to rise (Lakoff 1987: 407).

Most people employ familiar and well-used "conventionalized" metaphors. Kövecses writes of a "scale of conventionality" (Kövecses 2002: 31), with common, everyday metaphors at one extreme and novel, "unconventionalized" metaphors at the other. Understanding a conventional metaphor depends on conventional knowledge: 'In order to understand a target domain in terms of a source domain, one must have appropriate knowledge of the source domain' (Lakoff and Turner 1989: 69). In the case of basic image schemas, the resemblance of source and target domain is clear, and we are able to understand the links unconsciously and automatically. Thus, darkness, night and cold may be linked with the physical discomfort and fear that they cause, while light, day and warmth may by similarly linked with physical well-being and optimism. When basic metaphors are extended, social and cultural experience often plays a part. Darkness, for example, which is analogous with fear and inability to see, may be extended to represent ignorance and irrationality; light and the ability to see may signify knowledge and rationality.

While the present chapter accepts and develops the recent view of metaphor as omnipresent and embodied, forming part of everyday, largely unconscious human thought processes, it will also examine the exploitation of traditionally conceived decorative metaphors in public discourse as used by politicians such as Adolf Hitler. Hitler used the stock of conceptual metaphors employed, often unconsciously, by all human beings and exploited ornamental "figures of speech" which would have required more effort to decode on the part of his audience. Most of his metaphors were conventional and well worn in the field of political discourse, but, as will be demonstrated in the final section of this chapter, a modest quantity were, if not entirely fresh, used creatively.

3.2 Other Types of Metaphorical Representation

This section will describe a number of linguistic figures and non-linguistic devices considered by Raymond Gibbs (1994) and Zoltán Kövecses (2002) to belong to the basic realizations of metaphoricity. Other realizations include similes, metonymies, personification, proverbs, sayings and idioms, and myths and legends; these all play a role in our cognitive activities and involve some type of substitution—a source entity provides mental access to a target entity (Kövecses: 143). Traditional linguistic and literary scholarship does not tend to think of these devices as metaphors *per se*, but it is clear that, from the point of view of cognitive linguistics, they function as "figures of thought", and help us understand one conceptual domain by analogy with another in the same way as do metaphors. As Hitler used metaphors and similes for the same purpose and based them on the same range of source domains, I will use the term "metaphor" to refer to similes as well unless otherwise indicated.

3.2.1 Metonymy

Metonymy may involve either the evocation of a whole conceptual entity by mentioning part of that entity, e.g. a 'lane' evoking an entire 'journey', or, alternatively, one element of a conceptual entity may stand for another element of the same entity, as in a poem by Yeats in which a rocking cradle stands for the baby which is lying in it, which in turn represents Christ (Lakoff and Turner: 100f.). Examples of a source entity representing a target entity, as illustrated by Kövecses (144), are: THE PRODUCER/INSTRUMENT FOR THE PRODUCT ('She loves Picasso'); THE PLACE FOR THE EVENT ('America doesn't want another Pearl Harbour'); THE PLACE FOR THE INSTITUTION ('Washington is negotiating with Moscow'); THE CONTROLLER FOR THE CONTROLLED ('Ozawa (the conductor) gave a terrible concert last night'); AN OBJECT USED FOR THE USER ('The sax had flu today'), THE CONTAINER FOR THE CONTAINED ('The kettle's boiling'), EFFECT FOR CAUSE ('It's a slow road'), WHOLE FOR PART ('America for United States'), and PART FOR WHOLE ('All hands on deck!').

Metonymy differs from metaphor in that the source and target domains of metaphors are conceptually distant from one another, as with IDEAS ARE FOOD; whereas the vehicle and target entities of metonymies belong to the same domain, as with PART FOR WHOLE or THE PRODUCER FOR THE PRODUCT (see Radden and Kövecses 1999: 19 on the notion of 'contiguity'). Metaphor and metonymy can interact in such cases as 'to shoot one's mouth off' (related to German *losschießen*). In the English example, the mouth stands for the faculty of speech, i.e. it is a metonymy, and the foolish use of a firearm is a metaphor for foolish talk. Metonymic relationships may underlie conceptual metaphors, for example the conceptual metaphor ANGER IS HEAT has a metonymy EFFECT FOR CAUSE (BODY HEAT FOR ANGER) at its base: the metonymic vehicle becomes the source of the metaphor by means of the generalization BODY HEAT BECOMES HEAT (Kövecses: 156f.).

The following examples from *MK* represent well-known metonymic categories:

THE PART FOR THE WHOLE

Mouths *(Mäuler)* for people:
(...) **die Zungenfertigkeit geschliffener parlamentarischer Mäuler** (...) (*MK*: 710) [*(...) sharp parliamentary big-mouths and their glibness of tongue (...)* (Mh.: 574)]

Blood *(Blut)* for a person's life:
Teuerstes Blut gab sich da freudig hin im Glauben, dem Vaterlande so seine Unabhängigkeit und Freiheit zu bewahren. (*MK*: 219) [The most precious blood there sacrificed itself joyfully, in the faith that it was preserving the independence and freedom of the fatherland. (Mh.: 182)]

The head *(Kopf)* for an intelligent person:
Leider handelt es sich hier aber zumeist überhaupt um keine „Köpfe" (...) [= in parliament] (*MK*: 97) [Unfortunately we are here confronted, for the most part, not with 'thinkers' (...) (Mh.: 81)]

The sod or soil *(Scholle)* for the farm or the farming profession:
(...) der sich auch weiter redlich auf der bäuerlichen Scholle ernährende. (*MK*: 25) [(...) the brother who continues to make an honest living from the peasant sod. (Mh.: 24)]

THE INSTRUMENT FOR THE PRODUCT

A feather *(Feder)* or a quill *(Keil)* for writing:
> (...) die größten Umwälzungen auf dieser Welt sind nie durch einen Gänsekiel geleitet worden! Nein, der Feder blieb es immer nur vorbehalten, sie theoretisch zu begründen. (*MK*: 116) [(...) the greatest revolutions in this world have never been directed by a goose-quill! No, to the pen it has always been reserved to provide their theoretical foundations. (Mh.: 98)]

The fist *(Faust)* for violence and the mind *(Geist)* for conciliation:
> (...) in Zeiten, in denen nicht der Geist, sondern die Faust entscheidet (...) (*MK*: 277) [In times when not the mind but the fist decides (...) (Mh.: 230)]

AN OBJECT USED FOR THE USER (THE CLOTHING FOR THE WEARER)

The crown *(Krone)* for a monarchy:
> (...) die Krone (...) rief sie einen Geist wach, den sie selber zunächst freilich nicht für möglich gehalten hatte. (*MK*: 102) [(...) the crown aroused a spirit which at the outset it had not considered possible. (Mh.: 85)]

3.2.2   Personification

Kövecses explains personification as a form of ontological metaphor where abstract experiences are interpreted in terms of physical entities. He observes that 'personification makes use of the best source domains we have—ourselves' (Kövecses 2002: 35). Thus non-human objects, such as life, cancer, or computers are given human characteristics, such as cheating, eating and dying. Hitler made extensive use of personifications in *MK*. These are listed in Sections A.2.3.1 and B.2.1.2 of App. III. He also "depersonified" certain categories of human being, in particular Jews and Marxists, but also larger groups, such as the "masses" of ordinary German citizens. The groups of whom Hitler disapproved were either "dehumanized" (represented as non-human living entities, such as animals, reptiles or bacteria) or "de-animated" (represented as non-living entities, such as metals and rocks). Depersonification will be dealt with alongside personifications in Section 3.4.3 below as belonging to THE GREAT CHAIN OF BEING.

3.2.2.1 *Personification of Human Experiences in MK*

In *MK*, Hitler relied on two categories in particular, that of professions (App. III, A.2.3.1), and emotions and capacities (App. III, B.2.1.2) to dynamize the portrayal of his political beliefs. In general he used respected and useful professions, occupations and roles to metaphorize what he regarded as beneficial and neutral entities such as historical education *(stiller Mahner, MK*: 11; Mh.: 13), reason *(Führerin, MK*: 753; Mh.: 606), the Christian Social Party *(Virtuosin, MK*: 130; Mh.: 109), the NSDAP *(Siegerin, Vorkämpfer, Repräsentantin, MK*: 575 and 514; Mh.: 467 and 419), and his own will to resist 'und endlich blieb der Wille Sieger' [and in the end this will was victorious] *(MK*: 20; Mh.: 19). Certain roles are metaphorized for ironic effect, such as the *Menschheitsfreundin* ('friend of humanity') that was Social Democracy *(MK*: 53; Mh.: 46), or they are used in a negative sense, for example civilization as the enemy *(Feindin)* of a high standard of thinking and living *(MK*: 282; Mh.: 234). Hunger is ambiguously portrayed as the faithful bodyguard *(getreuer Wächter)* who accompanied Hitler during much of his time in Vienna—the pangs of hunger were unpleasant, but the insight into human hardship that he gained assisted the development of his political philosophy. Human emotions and capacities are not personified as having a particular occupation or role but are portrayed as agencies acting as if they were a person: reason, physical strength, care and hardship, hunger, madness, willpower, and ideas are used in this way. Lady Care *(Frau Sorge)*, for example, became Hitler's new mother when Time (also personified) pulled him out of the comfort, portrayed as a feather bed, which he had hitherto enjoyed *(MK*: 20; Mh.: 20). This occurred during Hitler's time in Vienna, when his emotions and his reason were frequently at war with one another:

> (...) erst nach monatelangem Ringen zwischen Verstand und Gefühl begann der Sieg sich auf die Seite des Verstandes zu schlagen. Zwei Jahre später war das Gefühl dem Verstande gefolgt, um von nun an dessen treuester Wächter und Warner zu sein. *(MK*: 59) [(...) only after months of battle between my reason and my sentiments did my reason begin to emerge victorious. Two years later, my sentiment had followed my reason, and from then on became its most loyal guardian and sentinel. (Mh.: 51)]

The will is shown in *MK* to be one of the least dispensable of human capacities. Hitler relied upon it in himself and hoped for its presence in his followers: it would cause men and women alike to feel such hatred and shame at the current situation in Germany that it would grow as hard as steel and rise up with the cry: '**Wir wollen wieder Waffen!** *[Give us arms again!]* (*MK*: 715; Mh.: 577). Similarly, a young victorious idea (**'eine junge sieghafte Idee'**) would refuse to wear fetters that could prevent it from pushing itself forward (*Vorwärtstreiben*, *MK*: 648; Mh.: 605).

3.2.2.2 *Personification of Non-human Entities in MK*

Hitler personifies a variety of non-human entities in *MK*, such as music and architecture, both of which he termed 'die Königin der Künste' [the queen of arts] (*MK*: 35; Mh.: 32), the economy ('bestimmende Herrin des Staates' [the dominant mistress of the state], *MK*: 255f.; Mh.: 213), and the German Reich as 'Herrin des Erdballs' [mistress of the globe] (*MK*: 437f.; Mh.: 360). History is personified as the 'Göttin einer höheren Wahrheit und eines besseren Rechtes' [the goddess of a higher truth] (*MK*: 780; Mh.: 626), and as an avenger ('Rächende Geschichte!', *MK*: 637; Mh.: 518; App. III, A.2.5). Nature and Fate are forces especially suitable for personification and Hitler often personifies both in *MK*.

3.2.3   Idioms

An idiom is a multi-word, formulaic expression with a meaning of its own that is not apparent from the meanings of its individual words. According to Kövecses, idioms are like metaphors in that they are 'products of our conceptual system and not simply a matter of language (i.e. a matter of the lexicon)' (Kövecses 2002: 201). This is true for many, if not most, idioms. They are understood not merely in relation to the meanings of their constituent parts but in relation to our 'more general knowledge of the world embodied in our conceptual systems' (201).

There are a number of different types of idiom, of which the most important for this study are metaphors ('to see red'/*bei etwas rot sehen*); similes ('to fight like cats and dogs'/*wie Hund und Katze sein*); metonymies ('it has already passed through many pairs of hands'/*es ist bereits durch viele Hände gegangen*); pairs of words ('through thick and thin'/*auf Biegen und Brechen*); and grammatical idioms ('let alone'/*geschweige denn*). Metaphorical and metonymic idioms are particularly numerous; the motivation for an idiom may, indeed, be both metaphorical and metonymic, as with 'to gain the upper hand'/*die Oberhand haben*, which is probably motivated by the metonymy THE HAND STANDS FOR CONTROL and the conceptual metaphor CONTROL IS UP. Similarly, the idiom 'to get one's hands dirty'/*sich die Hände schmutzig machen*, meaning 'to act unethically', is based on the metonymy THE HAND STANDS FOR THE ACTIVITY and the conceptual metaphor ETHICAL IS CLEAN (Kövecses: 210). On the other hand, an idiom may simply be motivated by conventional knowledge, as in 'to have one's hands full'/*die Hände voll haben*, where it is commonly understood that if one is holding something in one's hands one cannot use them for another activity, i.e. if we are busy with things already in hand, we cannot engage in another activity (Kövecses: 207f.).

Political rhetoric, in particular Hitler's propaganda, makes frequent use of idioms of all types. Such fixed strings of words are quickly understood because their associations already exist in peoples' minds. They have persuasive power over us because we do not have to think deeply about them and because we share them with the rest of our language community. Hitler was fond of idioms which involve parts of the body: *an der Nase führen* (*MK*: 132)/'to lead by the nose'; *an den Ohren haben* (*MK*: 132)/'to have by the ears'; *auf die leichte Schulter nehmen* (*MK*: 272)/'not to take seriously' (literally 'to take it on one's light shoulder'); *mit Füßen treten* (*MK*: 771)/'to trample on somebody'; *den Kopf zerbrechen* (*MK*: 445)/'to rack one's brains'; *zu Leibe gehen* (*MK*: 278)/'to tackle something, to set about something'; *vom Halse schaffen* (*MK*: 186: 237)/'to rid from' (literally 'to get it off one's neck'); *mit offenen Augen* (*MK*: 200)/'with open eyes'; *in die Arme treiben* (*MK*: 283)/'to drive into somebody's arms'; *jmdm. auf die Finger sehen* (*MK*: 264)/'to keep a sharp eye on somebody'; *die Zügel in die Hand geben* (*MK*: 657)/'to hand over the reins, to give control'; *an die Gurgel springen* (*MK*: 623)/'to go for somebody's throat'; *Stoß ins Herz* (*MK*: 266)/'thrust to the heart'; *das Rückgrat brechen* (*MK*: 265)/'to break somebody's backbone, to break somebody's resistance'.

3.2.4 Sayings and Proverbs

Proverbs are particular types of idiom as described in Section 3.2.3 above. They are short, pithy sayings used to express social norms and moral concerns (Gibbs 1994: 98). As with idioms, they have a message which is understood independently of the meanings of their individual lexical components. Like metaphors, proverbs which are less familiar may take longer to decode than others: they may need to be analyzed at the literal level before their figurative sense can be recognized. The generic-level metaphor GENERIC IS SPECIFIC helps us understand proverbs such as 'The early bird catches the worm' (Kövecses 2002: 39): the early bird stands for anyone who achieves or obtains something before others do, catching is obtaining something, and the worm is whatever is achieved or caught. This generic structure can be applied to a wide range of situations, such as being first in a queue at the summer sales. The German equivalent to this proverb, *Morgenstunde hat Gold im Munde*, can be applied to similar situations. Proverbs communicate their message concisely and quickly and are easily memorized; they are thus useful aids to teaching and to the rhetoric of persuasion. As Wolfgang Mieder reminds us: "A proverb is worth a thousand words" (Mieder 1993: x). Many English proverbs have exact or close equivalents in German, e.g. 'a bird in the hand is worth two in the bush'/*ein Spatz in der Hand ist besser als eine Taube auf dem Dach*, and they may stem from a time when these related languages were less differentiated than they are now.

Wolfgang Mieder has counted over 500 proverbs and proverbial expressions in *MK*, i.e one proverbial utterance for every page and a half (Mieder, 1995). Many of these 500 fall into the category of idiom as I have defined it in Section 3.2.3 above. The closely related category that I see as the "full" proverb, comprising a complete sentence, often in two parts which may have end-rhymes, is much less common in *MK* than in Hitler's later speeches and Nazi rhetoric after 1933, and there is no clear evidence that he made direct use of collections of anti-Semitic proverbs such as that of Sally Simon Tilles (*Jude im Citat und im Sprichwort*, 1892), although he may have been influenced by the characterizations of Jews that they contained.

Apart from the biblical proverbs described in Section 3.2.6 below, two traditional German examples have been identified. The first, 'Mit dem Hute in der Hand kommt man durch das ganze Land' [with hat in hand, he travels all about the land] (*MK*: 258; Mh.: 216), teaches that he who is polite to all will be welcome everywhere. Here Hitler is referring to the reputation of Germans as compliant people who put themselves in the service of other nationalities, particularly when it comes to sharing their knowledge. The second example, 'Was der Bauer nicht kennt, das frißt er nicht' [What the peasant doesn't know, he won't eat] (*MK*: 184; Mh.: 154), may be better translated as 'You can't change the habits of a lifetime'. One of Hitler's favourites, 'Gemeinnutz geht vor Eigennutz' ('the common good should be put before self-interest'), which he had used in speeches as early as 1920 (Mieder 1993: 236), does not feature in *MK*, although its sentiment is expressed, as in the following quotation: 'im Jagen nach dem eigenen Glück stürzen die Menschen aus dem Himmel erst recht in die Hölle' [in the chase after their own happiness men fall from heaven into a real hell] (*MK*: 328; Mh.: 272).

3.2.5 Myth, Legend and Fiction

The Greek word *mythos* means 'story'. Myths are traditional stories originating in pre-literate times about supernatural beings, heroes or ancestors. They are true stories in the sense that they 'reflect the power of metaphor to breathe life into the essential human story, the story of the relationship between the known and the unknown (...), the story of the search for identity in the context of the inward struggle between order and chaos' (Gibbs 1994: 187). In other words they have, over the centuries, helped human beings to categorize the world they live in and make sense of their own existence. Other fictional or legendary stories may be viewed as having a similar function.

Kövecses explains the riddle in the Oedipus myth in terms of metaphor. Oedipus is given a riddle by the Sphinx: 'Which animal has four feet in the morning, two at midday, and three in the evening?' Oedipus correctly gives the answer as Man: Man crawls when he is a baby, walks upright when he is mature, and supports himself with a stick in old age. Oedipus is able to solve the riddle due to his knowledge of the conceptual metaphor THE LIFE OF HUMAN BEINGS IS A DAY: morning corresponds to infancy, midday to adulthood, and evening to old age (Kövecses: 9). In this case a conceptual metaphor functions as a key element in a myth and the myth is in itself a metaphor (in that myths help human beings make sense of the world).[2] Individual mythological figures may also function as metaphors; for example the Greek god of the sea can represent uncontrollable external events according to the general metaphor UNCONTROLLABLE EXTERNAL EVENTS ARE LARGE, MOVING OBJECTS (Kövecses: 60). In *MK*, Hitler used the part-historical, part-legendary figure of the Germanic hero Siegfried three times as a metaphor for the German *Volk* struggling against seemingly irrepressible external forces:

> Ein Feuer war entzündet, aus dessen Glut dereinst das Schwert kommen muß, das dem germanischen Siegfried die Freiheit, der deutschen Nation das Leben wiedergewinnen soll. (*MK*: 406; cf. also p. 163 and p. 336) [A fire was kindled from whose flame one day the sword must come which would regain freedom for the Germanic Siegfried and life for the German nation. (Mh.: 336)].

Hitler's references to mythological and literary figures and events would have appealed to the better-educated members of his readership. Writing about the right-wing political propaganda of the late twentieth century, Siegfried Jäger suggests that most middle-class Germans have been brought up with strong traditional values, which would involve them having read or been read folk-tales and stories from classical mythology as children (Jäger 1989: 303–305). As with Hitler's audiences, they may not remember enough of these stories to know if political propagandists are using the names of folk and mythological figures correctly, but they will recognize those names and be reassured that the writer has experienced the same upbringing as themselves.

Stories of heroes and their journeys are popular in many cultures, not least that of the German-speaking world (Gibbs 1994: 188). Mythological or legendary heroes undertake long and dangerous journeys, often into a supernatural world, ostensibly in search of knowledge and new powers, but ultimately in search of self-knowledge. Hitler's own story must have been seen by some of his followers as the journey of a hero; a journey of self-sacrifice, of 'Jammer und Elend' [hardship and misery] (*MK*: 20; Mh.: 20), with freedom for the German people as his destination. Hitler himself saw his journey through life as a journey towards self-knowledge and towards the

---

[2] Hitler refers to the German army as a terrifying sphinx (*MK*, p. 590; Mh., p. 480). Siegfried was a common metaphor for the German army (Berger 2004: 120).

wider knowledge which would qualify him to act as Germany's saviour. Hitler certainly knew whom he judged to be heroes. The journey of the National Socialist (NS) party, his own creation, is shown as the journey of uncompromising heroes:

> **Große, wahrhaft weltumwältzende Revolutionen geistiger Art sind überhaupt nur denkbar und zu verwirklichen als Titanenkämpfe von Einzelgebilden, niemals aber als Unternehmen von Koalitionen.** (*MK*: 578) [*Great, truly world-shaking revolutions of a spiritual nature are not even conceivable and realisable except as the titanic struggles of individual formations, never as enterprises of coalitions.* (Mh.: 470)].

German heroes are similarly portrayed as climbing the steps to Valhalla, the pagan Scandinavian hall of immortality, after their death in the First World War, outnumbered by cowards who had remained at home (*MK*: 583; Mh.: 474).

Hitler also quotes from medieval and more modern literature in *MK*, assuming his audience's familiarity with the *Nibelungenlied*, the Pied Piper of Hameln, and the works of Goethe, Schiller and Kleist (see App. III, A.2.13.1). He refers to democracy as a Gessler's hat (*MK*: 640; Mh.: 520f.) and the Jews as hiding behind a 'Tarnkappe der Lüge' [tarn-cap of lies] (*MK*: 185; Mh.: 154f.; for further explanation see App. III, A.1.6). Hitler's reference to the *Nibelungenbündnis* ('Nibelungen alliance') is not a direct reference to literature, but is a term coined after the First World War, based on the medieval *Nibelungenlied* and alluding to the supposedly treacherous part played by socialists and revolutionaries in persuading Germany to agree to the Treaty of Versailles (Berger: 120). The gulf between Aryan and Jew is expressed by reference to Jews as vampires (*MK*: 358; Mh.: 296), or to the 'jüdische Welthydra' (*MK*: 721; Mh.: 581), alluding to the many-headed hydra slain by Hercules, and to the Aryan as the light-bringing 'Prometheus der Menschheit' [Prometheus of mankind] (*MK*: 317; Mh.: 263), referring to the Titan Prometheus who stole fire from heaven for the benefit of mankind. The press is portrayed as Aphrodite, the Greek goddess of love and vanity, arising from the waves (*MK*: 94; Mh.: 79); some priests are deemed to be Ephialteses, the personification of betrayal (*MK*: 126; Mh.: 106); and the so-called "November parties" are described as intellectual Cyclopses (*MK*: 705; Mh.: 570).

Overall, mythological and literary references fail to lend an erudite tone to the text of *MK*, as they are mostly well known and are relatively few in number. Viewed alongside Hitler's historical and biblical references they do, however, show that he was as well read and educated as his readers might have expected a political leader to be.

3.2.6 Historical and Biblical Events

Historical and biblical events may function as non-linguistic metaphors for more recent events and even provide models for the makers of history. Key events in the Bible, for example, commonly act as metaphors for more recent events; when the Mormons migrated west to Salt Lake City, for example, they saw their journey in terms of the Jews' flight from Egypt to Israel (Kövecses 2002: 61). Hitler frequently likened the plight of the Aryan race, whose physical existence and genetic purity he considered threatened by other races, to the expulsion of Adam and Eve from paradise:

> Der Arier gab die Reinheit seines Blutes auf und verlor dafür den Aufenthalt im Paradiese, das er sich selbst geschaffen hatte. (*MK*: 324) [The Aryan gave up the purity of his blood and, therefore, lost his sojourn in the paradise which he had made for himself. (Mh.: 268)]

Hitler commonly referred to the return to world power of the German State[3] and a return to good fortune of the German people as resurrection (*Auferstehung*, *MK*: 248, or *Wiederauferstehung*, *MK*: 403; see App. III, A.1.3.2).

In *MK*, Hitler was able to demonstrate his acquaintance with biblical proverbs and other passages that would have been readily recognizable to most of his readers: the daily bread which he portrays as something mankind had to fight for (*MK*: 739; Mh.: 596), the lost sheep (*MK*: 128; Mh.: 107), the golden calf (*MK*: 140; Mh.: 117) and the camel passing through the eye of a needle (*MK*: 96; Mh.: 81). He issued warnings based on passages from the Bible, such as: 'Die heutige Gegenwart erntet nur, was die letzte

---

[3] In this chapter I will refer to political States with an upper-case initial character and a state, i.e. set of circumstances or a condition, with a lower-case initial *s*.

Vergangenheit gesät hat' [The present time is only harvesting what the past has sown] (*MK*: 292; Mh.: 242; *Matthew* 25, 24–26; *Proverbs* 22, 8; *Hosea* 87, 7). With Ulonska (1990: 271), I believe that one of Hitler's main aims was to make himself appear trustworthy to his audience: he could have found no better means of achieving this than to demonstrate his knowledge of the Bible.

Well-known biblical locations occasionally feature, such as Sodom and Gomorrha to represent a place of sin (*MK*: 271; Mh.: 226), and Babylon to represent the members of different language groups living in the Hapsburg Empire (*MK*: 79 and 138; Mh.: 67 and 116). The biblical figures which appear in *MK* include Ahasver, the wandering Jew (*MK*: 397; Mh.: 328), Methuselah, personifying old, worn-out ideas (*MK*: 396; Mh.: 327), and Mammon, the personification of worldly greed and avarice (*MK*: 255f. and 272; Mh.: 213 and 226). A number of biblical episodes appear in *MK* which refer to Jewish "misdeeds", such as the killing of Abel by his brother Cain (*MK*: 583; Mh.: 474) and the betrayal of Jesus by Judas for a reward of thirty pieces of silver or *Judaslohn* (*MK*: 368, 608 and 719; Mh.: 304, 494 and 580).

In *MK*, Hitler shows a familiarity with well-known historical, or partly legendary and partly historical figures, artifacts and events. He saw the Germanic race as following in the footsteps of great heroes, such as Alexander the Great (*MK*: 743; Mh.: 598f.), and as being the only people with the right to climb the steps of the 'Pantheon of history' (*MK*: 100; Mh.: 84). He refers back to historical figures of ancient Greece, such as Pericles, whom he claims small-minded German parliamentarians do not attempt to emulate (*MK*: 88; Mh.: 75), and Demosthenes, a great orator, who represents any speaker whose voice is drowned out by his audience (*MK*: 399; Mh.: 330). The name of the alchemist Theophrastus Paracelsus is used ironically to refer to the "magic trick" *(Zauberstück)* of bestowing citizenship upon foreigners (*MK*: 489; Mh.: 400). There is also reference to the 'mummy of the state' *(staatliche Mumie)*, i.e. Austria (*MK*: 155; Mh.: 130), and the eggs of Columbus *(die Eier des Kolumbus)*, which represent easy solutions and also the notion that it takes a great person to lead those who are less capable (as Columbus discovered America for those who would follow him, *MK*: 311; Mh.: 258; see App. III, A. 2 5).

3.3 Source Domains for Metaphors and Other Figures of Thought

In metaphor generally, only certain aspects of the source domain are "utilized" to highlight particular aspects of the target domain (Kövecses 2002: 84–90). While metaphorical mapping involves only some aspects of both target and source, other aspects of both types of domain remain hidden or "unutilized". The metaphor ARGUMENT IS A BUILDING, for example, utilizes the construction process and strength of a building, but not usually its structural components such as roofs, windows and doors. Thus one can "build" a strong argument, but it would be highly unconventional to talk of the "roof" of an argument.

Typically, more than one source domain is needed for the full understanding of a target. Kövecses illustrates how a number of metaphors jointly characterize happiness: BEING HAPPY IS BEING UP, as in 'She was on cloud nine/in heaven'; HAPPINESS IS LIGHT, 'When she heard the news, she lit up'; HAPPINESS IS VITALITY, 'He was alive with joy'; HAPPINESS IS FLUID IN A CONTAINER, 'She brimmed over with joy when she saw him', HAPPINESS IS A PLEASURABLE PHYSICAL SENSATION, 'He was wallowing in a sea of happiness'; HAPPINESS IS INSANITY, 'They were crazy with happiness'; HAPPINESS IS A NATURAL FORCE, 'He was swept off his feet' (Kövecses: 85–89). The fact that so many source domains are needed to represent the concept of happiness fully illustrates the richness and complexity of this human emotion.

According to Lakoff and Turner (1989: 63), when a group of people share knowledge of a conventional metaphorical schema, such as LIFE IS A JOURNEY, which has amongst its components TRAVELLER, PATH, DESTINATION, IMPEDIMENTS, ARRIVAL, the metaphors have power over them: because they are shared with other people their persuasive force is more readily accepted. Hitler understood this fact and relied on it for his production of propaganda: he saw himself as an expert in the psychology of wooing the masses with simple and direct language, and he used a wide range of mostly conventional metaphors to do this.

Zoltán Kövecses lists thirteen major source domains: The Human Body, Health and Illness, Animals, Plants, Buildings and Construction, Machines and Tools, Games and Sport, Money and Economic Transactions, Cooking and Food, Heat and Cold, Light and Darkness, Forces (such as gravitational, magnetic, electrical and mechanical), and Movement and Direction (Kövecses 2002: 16–20). This list of source domains, predominantly based on the *Cobuild Metaphor Dictionary*, parallels my own categorization of source domains for Hitler's most commonly used metaphors in *MK*, a categorization which emerged naturally from my empirical study of the work. It is not at all remarkable, of course, that English and German should share their basic stock of source domains if one assumes that many conceptual metaphors originated in times when the common ancestors of present-day speakers of English and German belonged to the same group of Germanic tribes sharing the same basic bodily and mental experiences. Many such metaphors are, indeed, found throughout Europe, having been disseminated via literature, such as the Bible.

3.4 Source Domains for Hitler's Metaphors

In *MK*, Hitler makes use in his metaphorical expressions of each of the thirteen source domains listed by Kövecses, and many more that commonly appear in political discourse, such as War, Growth and Location. The few parts of *MK* that are not overtly political, notably the section giving an account of his childhood, are also rich in metaphors and similes. Most of the categories of image used by Hitler in *MK* can be allocated to one of three major categories of image schema, as described in detail by Lakoff and Turner (1989) and Lakoff and Johnson (1999):

1. CONTAINER metaphors, including metaphors of MOVEMENT and LOCATION;
2. THE GREAT CHAIN OF BEING;
3. Natural elements, forces and processes used as metaphors.

This method of categorization accords with the notion of metaphor as grounded in human bodily experience and is favoured by many critical linguists (e.g. Andreas Musolff and Christina Schäffner) as particularly well suited to the analysis of political discourse. The first two schemata contain all of the categories presented by Jonathan Charteris-Black as being central to the language of party political manifestos, namely conflict metaphors, building metaphors, journey metaphors, plant metaphors and religious metaphors (Charteris-Black 2004: 69–79). Further support for this choice of domains is found in Andreas Musolff's *Metaphor and Political Discourse* (2004a), in which he elucidates the mapping of the human body on to sociopolitical institutions, as with A STATE IS A BODY, which may be strong and healthy or weak and sick (Chapter 5), and the use of JOURNEY metaphors in political discourse (Chapter 3). The choice of THE GREAT CHAIN OF BEING is my own and derives from my reading of *MK* as a political tract greatly concerned with Hitler's particular views on racial hierarchy. To Hitler, the higher-level human beings belonged to the so-called "Aryan" race, against which he contrasted lower-level non-Aryans, most particularly Jews. He saw Aryans as innately superior, a state ordained by God and Nature together. Hitler saw biological selection as an *Existenzkampf*, a *Lebenskampf*, or a *Kampf ums Dasein* ('fight for survival', *MK*: 195, 440, 496,; Mh.: 163, 362, 405) in which the superior, stronger race would conquer the inferior, weaker races.

3.4.1 Container Metaphors

At the beginning of this chapter it was pointed out that, according to the experientialist philosophical framework, all basic metaphors are embodied (Lakoff and Johnson, 1999: 231) and that one of the most fundamental of our bodily experiences is that of the body as a container. Contained by our bodies, our stomachs are containers for food, our hearts are seen as containers for a variety of emotions, our brains containers for knowledge and ideas, and so on. By analogy, States, buildings, ships, rooms and many other items associated with human society are conceptualized as containers and used as sources for metaphors. True containers, such as bottles and cooking pots, are also useful sources of metaphors. Containers may be opened or kept closed, they may leak or, as a result of heat or pressure building up inside, they may burst or explode. Our experience tells us that these phenomena are possible, and, unconsciously, our bodily experience of emotions is mapped on to images of these phenomena. For example, a State experiencing political difficulties can be seen as sick like a human body; it can explode into violence like an angry person; people may wish to escape it; and they may or may not be contained by the State's borders if they wish to escape.

A STATE IS A CONTAINER

The metaphor A STATE IS A CONTAINER was fundamental to Hitler's political vision. He explicitly conceptualized Germany as a container, filled with desirable and undesirable citizens. In particular he saw Jews as threatening the purity of the contents of the container-State, as pouring into *(sich ergießen)* its 'Wirtschaftsbetriebe und Verwaltungsapparate' [economic concerns and administrative apparatuses] (*MK*: 644; Mh.: 524). The following quotation clarifies Hitler's understanding that the vessel of the State must protect its contents or be doomed:

> Wir haben schärfstens zu unterscheiden zwischen dem Staat als einem Gefäß und der Rasse als dem Inhalt. Dieses Gefäß hat nur dann einen Sinn, wenn es den Inhalt zu erhalten und zu schützen vermag; im anderen Falle ist es wertlos. (*MK*: 434) [We must distinguish in the sharpest way between the state as a vessel and the race as its content. This vessel has meaning only if it can preserve and protect the content: otherwise it is useless. (Mh.: 358)]

A STATE IS A BODY/THE *VOLK* IS A BODY

Closely related to this container metaphor is A STATE IS A BODY. In political discourse, States are commonly referred to as living organisms, and for Hitler the future German State was to be a *folkish* organism:

> (...) ein Staat (...), der nicht einen volksfremden Mechanismus wirtschaftlicher Belange und Interessen, sondern einen völkischen Organismus darstellt: *Einen germanischen Staat deutscher Nation.* (*MK*: 362) [(...) a state (...) which represents, not an alien mechanism of economic concerns and interests, but a national organism: **A Germanic State of the German Nation.** (Mh.: 299)]

Similarly, the German *Volk* was metaphorized in *MK* as one single body, a *Volkskörper*. This image may derive from Friedrich Ludwig Jahn, who, for example, depicted the German *Volk* as a 'vielgliedriger Leib' ('many-limbed body') (see App. I, Text 2, lines 3f.), In *MK*, Hitler represented the State and its *Volk* as a body kept alive by a healthy blood circulation *(Blutlauf)*. He saw the "hereditary" territories of the German Reich as its heart, pumping fresh blood into the circulation of political and cultural life, and Vienna as its brain and will (*MK*: 74 and 109; Mh.: 63 and 92, see App. III, B.1.2.1.3). This metaphor simultaneously belongs to the conceptual metaphor HAVING CONTROL IS BEING AT THE CENTRE, as the heart is at the centre of the body and controls the blood circulation without which life is impossible (on heart-based metaphors in EU debates see Musolff 2004b: 61–70). States possess nerve centres *(Nervenzentren, MK*, 654) which are occupied by the ruling political party (see App. III, B.1.2.1.4). Policies can also be portrayed as bodies, kept upright by a strong *Rückgrat* ('backbone'). For Hitler, propaganda, indispensable for the dissemination of ideology, had to have a 'firm backbone' (*MK*: 655, Mh.: 531). The National Socialists would break both the backbones and necks of opposing political movements: 'Man besaß ja nun (...) eine Gebrauchsanweisung, die der bisherigen Gewaltpolitik ein für allemal das Genick brechen sollte' [we possessed a recipe which was expected to break the neck of the former policy of violence] (*MK*: 157; Mh.: 131)]

As a living organism, a State can remain healthy or fall ill, live or die (Musolff 2003: 329). According to Hitler, the enemies of the German *Volk* were intent on bleeding Germany dry *(ausbluten, MK*: 749), translated by Mh. as 'bled white' (603). Hitler saw the events leading up to the First World War as the symptoms of an illness that had to reach a point of crisis before it could be cured. His melodramatic portrayal of acute disease as preferable to chronic illness reflects his personal dislike of all that is half-hearted or moderate *(Halbheit)*; *Rücksichtslosigkeit* ('ruthlessness'), the opposite of *Halbheit*, was required if a cure were to be effected. Hitler claimed (*MK*: 253f.) that the catastrophe of the war cut short Germany's drawn-out political problems. Just as mankind had mastered the plague more easily than tuberculosis, the diseased *Volkskörper* was made aware of its problems more rapidly and effectively by an acute problem (*MK*: 253; Mh.: 211f.; see App. III, B.2.1.1.1 for full quotation). The message of *MK* is, however, that the *Volkskörper* was not yet cured. Before the First World War the *Volkskörper* was being eaten at by 'giftige Geschwüre' [poisonous abscesses], poisoned by an 'immerwährender Giftstrom bis in die äußersten Blutgefäße dieses einstigen Heldenleibes' [a continuous stream of poison (...) being driven into the outermost blood-vessels of this once heroic body], and suffering from 'Lähmungen der gesunden Vernunft, des einfachen Selbsterhaltungstriebes' [progressively greater paralysis of sound reason and the simple instinct of self-preservation] (*MK*: 169; Mh.: 141; App. III, B.2.1.1.1). After the war, according to Hitler, Germany was still suffering from an 'Erkrankung der sittlichen, sozialen und rassischen Instinkte' [sickening of the moral, social, and racial instincts].

Hitler believed that it was possible to heal the German nation of its political sickness if the right person were to identify the causes of the disease:

> So wie man zur Heilung einer Krankheit nur zur kommen vermag, wenn der Erreger derselben bekannt ist, so gilt das gleiche auch vom Heilen politischer Schäden. (*MK*: 246) [The cure of a sickness can only be achieved if its cause is known, and the same is true of curing political evils. (Mh.: 206)]

One of the obvious reasons for Hitler writing *MK* was to expose the causes of Germany's weakness. He saw himself as the one man who could recognize and explain the causes of the problem, and one may assume that he saw himself as the only man with enough courage to expose and then cure Germany's ills: **'Wer diese Zeit, die innerlich krank und faul ist, heilen will, muß zunächst den Mut aufbringen, die Ursache dieses Leides klarzulegen'** *[anyone who wants to cure this era, which is inwardly sick and rotten, must first of all summon up all the courage to make clear the causes of this disease]* (*MK*: 485; Mh.: 396; see also *Genesung* and *Gesundung*, App. III, B.2.1.1.10).

Hitler's use of bodily images goes beyond a mere explanation of a past historical situation. After the end of the First World War, the *Volkskörper* was in peril. He saw this danger in terms of infectious disease, and in *MK*, the terms *Pest* ('plague') and *Seuche* ('epidemic, scourge') are most commonly used to refer to Jews, Marxists, the press, cowardice, and a lack of *Tatentschlossenheit* ('readiness to act', *MK*: 169; Mh.: 141) among the rulers of Germany and the population in general. Jews were considered the chief infecting agents; cowardice was a moral flaw which the Germans had to shun if they were to save themselves. Hitler considered Marxists to be under Jewish control and labelled them a *"Weltpest"* [world plague] (*MK*: 85; Mh.: 72). Through *MK*, Hitler tried to convince the German people that the Jews aimed to cause the nation to bleed to death *(verbluten)* (*MK*: 632; Mh.: 513f.; see also App. III, B.1.3.11 for blood-sucking creatures).

A sickly State may appear dead only to rise again. This was Hitler's hope for Austria as expressed in the following quotation:

> Es ist dann oft so, als befinde sich in einem solchen Körper keinerlei Leben mehr, als wäre er tot und abgestorben, bis plötzlich der Totgewähnte sich wieder erhebt (...) (*MK*: 78) [At such times it often seems as though there were no more life in such a body, as though it were dead and done for, but one fine day the supposed corpse suddenly rises (...) (Mh.: 67)] (See App. III, A.1.3.2 for references to resurrection.)

A small number of vivid images of birth and death also accompany descriptions of the former Reich and present day Germany in *MK*: Hitler likens the foundation of the former to an 'einzige Geburt und feurige Taufe' [unique birth and baptism of fire] (*MK*: 246; Mh.: 205) and the state of the latter to a drowning man catching at straws ('dem Ertrinkenden, der nach jedem Strohhalm greift', *MK*: 746; Mh.: 600). Germany's allies during the First World War are described as **'faulige staatliche Leichname'** *[putrid state corpses]* (*MK*: 756; Mh.: 608).

A NATION/STATE IS A BUILDING

The representation of States and nations as buildings is common in political discourse and *MK* contains a wide variety of metaphors taken from the fields of architecture and building (App. III, A.2.18), and also demolition (App. III, A.2.10.3). Hitler writes of the edifice of State *(Staatsgebäude*, *MK*: 580; Mh.: 472; *Staatsbau* (*MK*: 52; Mh.: 45) and of the dangers to which it is exposed, described with verbs such as *untergraben* and *unterhöhlen* ('to undermine'), *zertrümmern* ('to shatter'), *anfressen* ('to corrode'), *einreißen* ('to tear down') and *zum Einsturz bringen* ('to cause to collapse'). Hitler describes Germany at the end of the First World War as 'das zertrümmerte Reich' [the shattered Reich] at the mercy of Bolshevism (*MK*: 624; Mh.: 507)].

As with buildings, States can be seen as vessels containing people of different types, some welcome and some not. They may be well built and safe, or in a state of disrepair or collapse; they may need renovation or even demolition in preparation for rebuilding. Revolutions, according to Hitler, do not require total demolition of the State; only the rotten parts of the building need to be torn down and rebuilt:

> Der Sinn und Zweck von Revolutionen ist dann nicht der, das ganze Gebäude einzureißen, sondern schlecht Gefügtes oder Unpassendes zu entfernen und an der dann wieder freigelegten gesunden Stelle weiter- und anzubauen. (*MK*: 286) [Thus the meaning and purpose of revolutions is not to tear down the whole building, but to remove what is bad or unsuitable and to continue building on the sound spot that has been laid bare. (Mh.: 237)]

In *MK*, Hitler portrays a future German Reich as a 'Vaterhaus' [father's house], a safe place with its doors open to the right type of person (*MK*: 136; Mh.: 114). At the turn of the twentieth century, Houston Stewart Chamberlain had already written of Germany as 'allein auf Erden der Hort wahrer Freiheit' (the only place on earth which is a refuge of true freedom) (Chamberlain 1905: 16), and, as it is known that Hitler was influenced by Chamberlain, it reasonable to assume that this influence is manifest in Hitler's portrayal of the German Empire as 'ein mächtiger Hort des Friedens' [a mighty haven of peace] (*MK*: 178; Mh.: 149).

A building has foundations *(Fundamente)*, which must be deep and fully supportive, and walls *(Mauern)* which must keep in the right human elements and keep out those which are undesirable. Hitler portrays the future NS State as one which will be protected by a patriotic people:

> (...) nicht Festungswälle werden ihn beschirmen, sondern die lebendige Mauer von Männern und Frauen, erfüllt von höchster Vaterlandsliebe und fanatischer Nationalbegeisterung. (*MK*: 473) [(...) no fortress walls will protect it, but a living wall of men and women filled with supreme love of their fatherland and fanatical national enthusiasm. (Mh.: 387)]

It is each young person's duty to build up his or her nation, to be a builder *(Bauherr)* of the future (*MK*: 450; Mh.: 369); the genius of youth must provide the building plans and materials ('Baustoffe und Zukunftspläne') for a new Germany (*MK*: 21; Mh.: 21).

Nests, too, are a type of building, and provide a romantic and cosy image to represent "home", both in the narrower sense of one's personal dwelling and in the broader sense of *Heimat*:

> Dieser Kampf gegen die eigene Art, das eigene Nest, die eigene Heimat war ebenso sinnlos wie unbegreiflich. Das war unnatürlich. (*MK*: 65) [This struggle against their own species, their own clan, their own homeland, was as senseless as it was incompre-

hensible. It was unnatural. (Mh.: 56)]. Cf. the *Lieblingsnest* of the Jew (*MK*: 269; Mh.: 224). Notably, Manheim does not retain the image of a nest in his translation.

Related to A NATION IS A BUILDING are some less common building metaphors:

MANKIND IS A BUILDING

Eine wirklich segensvolle Erneuerung der Menschheit wird immer und ewig dort weiter zu bauen haben, wo das letzte gute Fundament aufhört. (*MK*: 286) [A really beneficial renascence of humanity will always have to continue building where the last good foundation stops. (Mh.: 237)]

THE *VOLK* IS A BUILDING

(...) die erste allen sichtbare katastrophale Folge einer sittlichen und moralischen Vergiftung (...), die schon seit vielen Jahren die Fundamente des Volkes und Reiches zu unterhöhlen begonnen hatte. [= military collapse] (*MK*: 252) [(...) this was the first consequence, catastrophic and visible to all, of an ethical and moral poisoning (...) which for many years had begun to undermine the foundations of the people and the Reich. (Mh.: 210)]

AN ERA IS A BUILDING

(...) jenen allgemeinen Stil (...), der dann einst die neue Zeit als eine wirklich innerlich festfundierte erscheinen läßt (...) (*MK*: 674) [(...) that universal style which will some day make the new era seem really solidly founded (...) (Mh.: 547)]

IDEAS ARE BUILDINGS/KNOWLEDGE IS A BUILDING

The most vital component of every edifice, whether it be made of bricks or political ideas, is its foundations. According to Hitler, the NS movement was in need of **'ein neues, weltanschaulich gefestigtes, einheitliches Fundament als Ziel politischen Handelns im Innern'** [*a new philosophically established, uniform foundation as the aim of political activity at home*] (*MK*: 735f.; Mh.: 593). Pillars are needed to support a philosophical edifice: in the case of National Socialism it was race and personality which were to act as the 'Grundpfeiler ihres ganzen Gebäudes' [pillars of its entire edifice] (*MK*: 499f.; Mh.: 408). The popularity of the early Weimar Republic, in contrast, had only a tottering pillar ('schwankende Säule') to support it (*MK*: 584; Mh.: 475). The NS movement would construct steps to lead the *Volk* back up to their former 'Tempel der Freiheit' [temple of freedom] (*MK*: 415; Mh.: 343) and Hitler would provide the building blocks *(Bausteine)* for NS doctrine (*MK*, Preface). Similarly, knowledge may be metaphorized as a building, and reading provides people with the knowledge, the tools and the building materials with which to construct it ('Werkzeug und Baustoffe (...) die der einzelne zu seinem Lebensberufe nötig hat', *MK*: 36; Mh.: 33).

Related to the concept of knowledge as a building is that of HUMAN PROGRESS IS A BUILDING. The following quotation describes Aryans as the superior race who have laid the foundations of human creativity and provided the materials to advance humankind:

> Von ihm stammen die Fundamente und Mauern aller menschlichen Schöpfungen, und nur die äußere Form und Farbe sind bedingt durch die jeweiligen Charakterzüge der einzelnen Völker. Er liefert die gewaltigen Bausteine und Pläne zu allem menschlichen Fortschritt (...) (*MK*: 318) [From him [= the Aryan] originate the foundations and walls of all human creation, and only the outward form and colour are determined by the changing traits of character of the various peoples. He provides the mightiest building stones and plans for all human progress (...) (Mh.: 263)]

The negative counterpart of building and progress is demolition and regression. Ideas can be demolished, and Hitler saw democracy as a system which would lead to the 'Demolierung des Führergedankens überhaupt' [demolition of any idea of leadership] (*MK*: 87; Mh.: 74). Even the strongest opinion can be conquered, as was public opinion at the end of the First World War, due, according to Hitler, to the influence of Marxist propaganda:

> (...) und so eine fabelhafte Kenntnis dieses Menschenmaterials zu gewinnen wußten, was sie erst recht in die Lage versetzte, die richtigen Angriffswaffen auf die Burg der öffentlichen Meinung zu wählen. (*MK*: 529) [(...) and thus were able to acquire a marvellous knowledge of this human material which really put them in a position to choose the best weapons for attacking the fortress of public opinion. (Mh.: 430)]

Other Building Metaphors

In *MK*, the economy is a building with 'wirtschaftlichen Grundmauern' [economic foundations] (*MK*: 51f.; Mh.: 45); education is a building, in need of strong foundations '**als Fundament einer Erziehungsmöglichkeit des einzelnen**' *[as a foundation for the possibility of educating the individual]* (*MK*: 34; Mh.: 31); the Catholic Church is a 'Lehrgebäude' [doctrinal edifice] (*MK*: 512; Mh.: 417); and the monarchy is a building (*MK*: 261; Mh.: 218). Specific types of building offer sanctuary, such as the temple (*MK*: 415; Mh.: 343).

Dams are a type of edifice which can keep out malign influences. One page with the heading 'Sterilisation Unheilbarer', Hitler calls for decisive action in erecting a dam against sexually transmitted diseases (*MK*: 280; Mh.: 232; App. III, A.2.18.4). In a similar vein, useful new members for the NS movement are seen as contained in reservoirs: 'Das Reservoir (...) wird also in erster Linie die Masse unserer Arbeitnehmer sein' [Thus, the reservoir (...) will primarily be the masses of our workers] (*MK*: 374; Mh.: 309).

A STATE IS A SHIP

In general terms, the State, political movements, and even life, may be portrayed as ships on a journey within the LIFE IS A JOURNEY metaphor. Furthermore, following in the pattern of A STATE IS A CONTAINER, ships, as containers, may metaphorize states in political discourse. Hitler wrote in *MK* of the *Reichsschiff* [Reich ship] (*MK*: 765; Mh.: 615) which could be turned around and steered to ram the enemy, and of the Jews, who made their "State" sail under the flag of a "religion" (*MK*: 165; Mh.: 138; cf. *Parteischiff*, *MK*: 113; Mh.: 95). He also wrote of the possibility of a nation running aground (*zugrunde gehen*, *MK*: 253), which Mh. translates as 'going to the dogs' (Mh.: 211) (see App. III, A.2.6). The NS movement is also portrayed as a ship in *MK*, one which must not be allowed to "swim with the stream" (translated by Mh. as 'drifting with the current') or be driven by it (*MK*: 520; Mh.: 423). Capitulation is also described in terms of "trimming one's sails to the wind" (*die Segel nach dem Wind stellen*), i.e. following public opinion (*MK*: 521; Mh.: 423).

THE MIND IS A CONTAINER

The head contains the brain in which reside our intelligence and our minds. Information may be conceptualized as being poured into our brains: Hitler used the verbs *gießen* ('to pour'), *einflößen* ('to cause to flow in'), *einpumpen* ('to pump in'), *eintrichtern* ('to funnel in'), *eindrillen* ('to drill in') and *einpauken* ('to drum in') (see App. III, A.2.17.2). In *MK*, the press is frequently accused of leading people astray by pouring the wrong information into them; schools are criticized for drumming in knowledge but not the ability to analyze it, and for neglecting the training of the body in favour of 'das ausschließliche Einpumpen sogenannter Weisheit' [just the pumping in of so-called wisdom] (*MK*: 278; Mh.: 231). Jews and Marxists are denounced for funnelling *(eintrichtern)* nonsense and madness ('Unsinn und Irrwahn') into the masses (*MK*: 185; Mh.: 154). We also encounter the *Volk* as a container into which ideas can be poured ((wie) das Gift kübelweise in das Volk hineingeschüttet wird [the poison poured into the people by bucketfuls], *MK*: 34; Mh.: 31). Here the *Volk* is seen as a unified whole with one mind.

THE MIND IS A SHIP/MOVING VESSEL

In keeping with the metaphor THE MIND IS A CONTAINER, we encounter in *MK* the notion of the mind as a ship or other type of moving vessel overloaded with useless information *(Ballast)* which weighs it down. Only knowledge which can be retained and used should be passed on to young people in school or to members of political movements who throw their principles overboard when it is expedient for political reasons. The following example may refer to a hot-air balloon: 'wobei Einstellungen und Grundsätze je nach Zweckmäßigkeit wie Sandballast über Bord geworfen werden' [in which convictions and principles are thrown overboard like sand ballast whenever it seems expedient] (*MK:* 414; Mh.: 343; App. III, A.2.6).

THE HEART IS A CONTAINER/ROOM

The heart has long been seen as the seat of the emotions (Spalding 1952 –2000: 1310f.). Within the context of cognitive metaphor theory it is seen as a container which might become too full and overflow, or which might be sealed and will therefore burst if the emotions grow too large or strong to be held in. Hitler writes in *MK* of his heart overflowing *(überquellen)* with pride and joy when he joined the Bavarian Regiment, and bursting *(zerspringen)* with joy when he saw the hall full of people at the beginning of his first mass meeting in 1920 (*MK*: 178f. and 405; Mh.: 149 and 335; cf. 'mir wollte die Brust zu enge werden' [I felt as though my heart would burst] (*MK*: 180; Mh.: 151).

The heart may be portrayed as a room which can be locked and opened with a key; the key is a metaphor for security and power (Spalding: 2147). If, for example, one wishes to convince the masses of the people of the rightness of a certain idea, one must be able to open their hearts with the right words and with one's own fanaticism: 'Wer die breite Masse gewinnen will, muß den

Schlüssel kennen, der das Tor zu ihrem Herzen öffnet' [Anyone who wants to win the broad masses must know the key that opens the door to their heart] (*MK*: 371; Mh.: 306f.). The wrong words may be portrayed as poison, for example that which Hitler accuses the press of pouring into the hearts of its readers (*MK*: 268; Mh.: 223).

Emotions may be portrayed as bursting or overflowing from other types of container, such as the 'Vulkanausbrüche menschlicher Leidenschaften und seelischer Empfindungen' [volcanic eruptions of human passions and emotional sentiments] which metaphorize great political movements (*MK*: 116; Mh.: 98).

3.4.2 Metaphors of Location and Movement

Lakoff and Johnson's definition of LOCATION EVENT-STRUCTURE METAPHORS serves as a framework for the type of metaphors presented in this section. The concepts of cause and event arise from human biology (Lakoff and Johnson 1999: 171), and causation is seen as involving the application of force (most commonly volitional human force) to an object, resulting in motion or other (usually physical) change (177). A movement or other type of change is an event. A change of place or state is conceptualized as a movement from one location to another (183). A location is a bounded region in space with an interior, an exterior and a boundary or edge: it is thus a type of container. A state, such as depression or happiness, can be conceptualized as a location. One can remain *in* a state of depression and one can *come out* of it. Within it, a state can have a vertical dimension, as in *the depths of depression* or *over the moon*. There can be a long distance to travel to escape from the deepest of depressions or to come down from the heights of happiness.

3.4.2.1 *Location*

IMPORTANCE IS BEING AT THE CENTRE

The farthest inner space from the boundary is at the centre of the space (Lakoff and Johnson 1999: 180). In *MK*, the metaphorical expressions *Kern* ('kernel, core, nucleus') and *Herz* ('heart') most commonly exemplify the metaphor IMPORTANCE IS BEING AT THE CENTRE. The core of the National Socialist movement is portrayed as fresh and healthy ('frisch und gesund') (*MK*: 657; Mh.: 532). The racial core of the State, namely the Aryan race, is seen as the 'rassisch wertvollster Kern des Volkes' [the racially most valuable nucleus of the people] (*MK*: 448; Mh.: 368). It is, according to Hitler, the originally creative racial nucleus, the 'ursprünglich schöpferischer Rassekern' (*MK*: 319), which will keep the NS State intact and pure. Hitler saw *MK* as his opportunity to organize and present the central philosophy *(Kernideen)* of National Socialism (*MK*: 423f.; Mh.: 350); a central place with the significance of Mecca or Rome was to become the focal point, the 'zentraler Mittelpunkt', of the new NS State if it were to have the strength to consolidate under one unifying force at its summit *(Spitze)* (*MK*: 381; Mh.: 315). The heart *(Herz)* and nerve centres *(Nervenzentren)*, also seen as having a central position in human and animal bodies, are discussed under THE GREAT CHAIN OF BEING below. A hollow centre is generally portrayed in *MK* in a negative light, such as that of the contemporary State ('innere Hohlheit dieses Staates' [inner hollowness of the state], *MK*: 135; Mh.: 113).

MEDIOCRITY IS BEING IN THE MIDDLE

According to *MK*, location in the middle, between two extremes is a negative trait as exemplified by the mediocre 'Masse der Mitte' ('masses in the middle') that Hitler so despised. For him, racial mixture between higher-level and lower-level human beings would result in a lowering of the quality of mankind in general and of the Aryan race in particular:

> Jede Kreuzung zweier nicht ganz gleich hoher Wesen gibt als Produkt ein Mittelding zwischen der Höhe der beiden Eltern. Das heißt also: das Junge wird wohl höher stehen als die rassisch niedrigere Hälfte des Elternpaares, allein nicht so hoch wie die höhere. Folglich wird es im Kampf gegen diese höhere später unterliegen. (*MK*: 312) [Any crossing of two beings not at exactly the same level produces a medium between the level of the two parents. This means: the offspring will probably stand higher than the racially lower parent, but not as high as the higher one. Consequently, it will later succumb in the struggle against the higher level. (Mh.: 258ff.)]

SUPERIORITY/IMPORTANCE/GOOD IS ABOVE

The notion of hierarchy is presented fully in Section 3.4.3 as the basis of THE GREAT CHAIN OF BEING. The Christian God and other gods may be taken as occupying the highest position (see App. III, A.1.1). Human beings are higher in the hierarchy of nature than animals, and within the category of "animal" and "human" there are secondary hierarchies. Human beings have higher-order abilities and sensitivities than animals, and within human societies status varies according to wealth, birth, and a variety of achievements. In *MK*, the nouns *Höhe* ('height') and *hoch* ('high') indicate higher levels of humanity in accordance with Hitler's *Weltanschauung* of the superiority of the Aryan race, which he considers to be 'der Begründer höheren Menschentums überhaupt' [the founder of all higher humanity] (*MK*: 317; Mh.: 263). These words also describe "higher" human capacities and virtues, such as 'höhere Begeisterung' [higher enthusiasm] (*MK*: 33; Mh.: 31) and 'Geistes- und Lebenshöhe' [high standard of thinking and living] (*MK*: 282; Mh.: 234). Hitler saw his own role as party leader as one of superiority and responsibility toward those over whom he had authority: **'Autorität jedes Führers nach unten und Verantwortlichkeit nach oben'** [*authority of every leader downward and responsibility upward*] (*MK*: 501; Mh.: 409).

Geographical heights and depths, most notably *Gipfel* ('summit') and *Sumpf* ('swamp'), are also used in *MK* to metaphorize the good and the bad, as, for example, in the following description of the Christian Social Party: 'Sie war damals gerade am Gipfel ihres Ruhmes angelangt' [At that time it had just reached the apogee of its glory] (*MK*: 107; Mh.: 90). The mentality of the masses is seen as a low-lying swamp 'Sumpf(e) einer niedrigen Gesinnung' [swamp of a base mentality] from which the press could lead it if it wished (*MK*: 355; Mh.: 293).

3.4.2.2   Movement

Within the framework for metaphor which is based on human bodily experience, a location is a container and change is MOVEMENT FROM ONE CONTAINER TO ANOTHER. Movement is our most basic bodily experience. We are constantly in motion, even if our movement merely involves the unconscious acts of inhaling and exhaling. Perhaps the most basic of the movements of which we are aware is our progress towards physical goals: from babyhood onwards we experience the desire to reach certain objects; initially our "journey" towards the object involves crawling, later we learn to walk and possibly to drive a vehicle; we may encounter obstacles along the way, and we experience a sense of achievement when the object has been attained. Thus our experience of the metaphor LIFE IS A JOURNEY is embodied. Within this metaphor, progress and success are seen as motion forwards, regression and failure are seen as movement backwards. Various aspects of our individual and social lives are seen as journeys, for example education, politics and social movement. In general, upwards movement is seen as positive, downward movement as negative.

LIFE IS A JOURNEY

Life, like time, can only move forwards. Our forward movement is, however, only seen as progress within a set of conventions defined by the society we live in. As with a journey, our goal is usually in front of us, but we may be forced back over old ground if unfavourable circumstances intervene. On rare occasions, on the other hand, a return to previous circumstances may be beneficial. Hitler saw his own life in terms of a journey: 'meine (...) zu spät angetretene irdische Wanderschaft' [my earthly pilgrimage, which (...) had begun too late] (*MK*: 173; Mh.: 145). This quotation suggests that he regarded his role on earth as akin to a divine journey in the service of God and, like Jesus, sacrificing himself for the good of his fellow beings. Within the conceptual metaphor POLITICS IS A JOURNEY, a political strategy can be seen as having a starting point, a progression and a goal. Hitler saw the NS movement as having a point of origin *(Ausgangspunkt)* and a goal *(Endziel)* for its journey forwards (*MK*: 381 and 347; Mh.: 315 and 287; App. III, A.2.15.1). His ambition for the NS movement was for it to lead the German people to a new life of freedom and prosperity which would, in part, be achieved through the acquisition of new lebensraum. The German *Volk* would engage all of its courage and strength to advance ('zum Vormarsch') along the route which would lead it to new pastures (*MK*: 732; Mh.: 590).

In *MK*, political parties are depicted as vehicles for conveying the population along a route leading in either the right or the wrong direction. The right direction, i.e. progress, is metaphorized as movement forwards and/or upwards; the wrong direction is metaphorized as movement backwards and/or downwards. As far as Hitler was concerned, the 'alter Parteiwagen' [old party cart] (*MK*: 410; Mh.: 339) had to be halted and the new movement given 'freie Bahn' [a free path] (*MK*: 551; Mh.: 447). The new movement would stop the 'Wagen des Verhängnisses' [chariot of doom] (*MK*: 409; Mh.: 339) which was drawn by the traditional bourgeois parties. It would guide the nation out of the wilderness of illusion and back to a reality which would ultimately lead to political stability ('aus der Traumwelt wieder in die Wirklichkeit zurückzubringen', *MK*: 753; Mh.: 606).

Political opponents could also take different routes in order to reach the same goal, namely power. According to Hitler each traveller should watch out for competitors whose aim it was to arrive first. Once groups were aware of one another, the successful party could reassess its route, shorten it if possible and expend the necessary extra energy to reach the journey's end first. Thus a political journey is portrayed as a race:

> Marschieren also verschiedene Gruppen auf getrennten Wegen dem gleichen Ziele zu, so werden sie, soweit sie von dem Vorhandensein ähnlicher Bestrebungen Kenntnis genommen haben, die Art ihres Weges gründlicher überprüfen, denselben womöglich abkürzen und unter Anspannung ihrer äußersten Energie versuchen, das Ziel schneller zu erreichen. (*MK*: 571f.) [And so, if different groups march towards the same goal on separate paths, once they have become aware of the existence of similar efforts, they will more thoroughly examine the nature of their own way; where possible they will shorten it, and by stretching their energy to the utmost will strive to reach the goal more quickly. (Mh.: 465)]

In the early days of National Socialism the German people had an arduous journey ahead of them which they would only be able to complete by setting themselves a sequence of smaller goals *(Teilstrecken)*, the ultimate destination being too far away for them to see at the outset:

> (...) ähnlich dem Wanderer, der ebenfalls wohl das Ende seiner Reise weiß und kennt, der aber die endlose Straße besser überwindet, wenn er sich dieselbe in Abschnitte zerlegt und auf jeden einzelnen losmarschiert, als ob er schon das ersehnte Ziel selber wäre. (*MK*: 273f.) [(...) like the wanderer, who likewise knows and recognises the end of his journey, but is better able to conquer the endless highway if he divides it into sections and boldly attacks each one as though it represented the desired goal itself. (Mh.: 228)]

Aryans would have a particularly strenuous journey, which would necessarily involve combat, but it would lead to a more worthwhile final destination than that reached by pacifists. It would be the 'Weg der Wirklichkeit' [road of reality], much harder to follow than the road of the dreamer 'wo der andere die Menschheit gerne hinträumen möchte, von wo er sie aber leider in Wahrheit eher noch entfernt, als daß er sie näherbringt' [where our friend would like to bring humanity by dreaming, but unfortunately removes more than bringing it closer] (*MK*: 323; Mh.: 268).

Writing of the failure of the *Alldeutsche Bewegung*, Hitler uses the image of a mountaineer who, keeping his eye on his goal, and with great determination, sets out for the summit. He should, however, have paid more attention to his route, for he fails to reach his destination:

> (...) den Blick auf das Ziel gerichtet, die Beschaffenheit des Aufstiegs weder sieht noch prüft und daran endlich scheitert. (*MK*: 130) [(...) his eyes are always on his goal, so that he neither sees nor feels out the character of the ascent and thus comes to grief at the end. (Mh.: 109)]

In order to help his own political party to success, Hitler employed an "*Ordnertruppe*" to create 'a free path for the holy mission of our movement' (Mh.: 447) ('der heiligen Mission unserer Bewegung freie Bahn zu schaffen' (*MK*: 551). He promised to guide his followers along the right path and help them avoid obstacles; the aim of his propaganda was to destroy people's existing beliefs and lead them across *(hinüberleiten)* to the place where the NS *Weltanschauung* dwelled (*MK*: 522; Mh.: 424).

PROGRESS IS MOVEMENT FORWARDS / REGRESSION IS MOVEMENT BACKWARDS

As a politician who saw the future of the nation as in his care, Hitler was aware of time as a force which moves relentlessly forwards: 'Der Zeiger der Weltuhr ist seitdem weiter vorgerückt' [The hand of the world clock has moved on since then] (*MK*: 753; Mh.: 606). He saw himself as the heroic leader (*Führer*, *MK*: 379; Mh.: 313) and the NS movement as a pioneer (*Vorkämpferin*) (*MK*: 514; Mh.: 419) whose duty it was to lead Germany forward. The movement was guided by reason *(Vernunft)*, which was in turn personified as a leader *(Führerin)*. He considered the strength of National Socialism as a pushing forwards or to the front a momentous *Weltanschauung (voranstellen)* (*MK*: 409; Mh.: 339; App. III, B.2.1.3.1.2). For Hitler, the spoken word was the medium with sufficient power to start *(ins Rollen bringen)* great political and religious movements (*MK*: 116; Mh.: 98; App. III, B.2.1.3.1.1).

Hitler had little admiration for people who pushed themselves forwards at the expense of others. Those people who struggle for prominence, whether social or political, are portrayed as animals pushing their way to the front of the herd at a feeding-trough:

> (...) dann ist ihr Sinnen und Trachten nur darauf eingestellt, sich, sei es durch Gewalt oder List, in dem Rudel der Auch-Hungrigen wieder nach vorne zu bringen (...) (*MK*: 507f.) [(...) their thoughts and actions are directed solely, whether by force or trickery, towards pushing their way back to the front of the hungry herd (...) (Mh.: 413f.)]

Images of backward movement symbolizing regression are much less common in *MK* than those signifying forward movement. One image of backward movement is, however, aligned with images of racial sinking *(Niedersenkung)* and progressive sickness in Hitler's argument that racial mixture results in regression and hinders the improvement of more valuable races:

> Das Ergebnis jeder Rassenkreuzung ist also, ganz kurz gesagt, immer folgendes:
> a) Niedersenkung des Niveaus der höheren Rasse,
> b) körperlicher und geistiger Rückgang und damit der Beginn eines, wenn auch langsam, so doch sicher fortschreitenden Siechtums. (*MK*: 314)
> [In short, the results of any mixture of races is therefore always the following:
> a) Lowering of the level of the higher race
> b) physical and intellectual regression and hence the beginning of a slowly but surely progressing sickness. (Mh: 260)]

Racial mixture thus ruins the work of higher breeding that has, according to Hitler, taken place over thousands of years in accordance with the will of Nature ('ihre (...) jahrhunderttausendelange Arbeit der Höherzüchtung' [her whole work of higher breeding, over perhaps hundreds of thousands of years] (*MK*: 313; Mh.: 260). In Hitler's view, Jews could not improve their stock by mixing with Aryans, but Aryans may improve their own race.

PROGRESS IS MOVEMENT UPWARDS / REGRESSION/DISASTER IS MOVEMENT DOWNWARDS

Upward movement is a common means of metaphorizing progress in political and other discourses, possibly more common than forward movement. In *MK*, Hitler is concerned with social and political progress and, above all, racial progress. He sees himself as the instigator and leader of the upward movement of Germany under National Socialism. He refers to the leadership of political groupings as a summit with a united following 'eine diese Einheit repräsentierenden Spitze' (*MK*: 381; Mh.: 315). Verbs such as *aufsteigen, emporführen, emporsteigen, sich emporheben, emporreißen, erheben, sich erheben, erklimmen, herausheben, herausführen* (the final two words including the sense of 'outwards') all convey the notion of upward movement and may be applied to circumstances, ideas and emotions, as in the 'Emporsteigen der neuen Idee' [the rising new idea] (*MK*: 392; Mh.: 323f.). Using words such as *Auferstehung* and *Wiederauferstehung* (both meaning 'resurrection'), Hitler portrays Germany as a once great nation striving to rise again after the disaster of the First World War using religious imagery (see App. III, A.1.3.2). Similarly, the NS movement will help the German *Volk* climb up to a 'Tempel der Freiheit' [temple of freedom] (*MK*: 415; Mh.: 343) by erecting and defending the steps of a new *Weltanschauung* (App. III, B.2.1.3.1.4). One of Hitler's burning concerns in *MK* is to convince his audience of the superiority of the Aryan race. He saw the elevation of the Aryan race as possible in his age only as a result of selective breeding, the exclusion of "lower" races from the "pure" Aryan blood stock. He likened the breeding of human beings to the breeding of domestic animals, **'der Höherzüchtung von Hunden, Pferden und Katzen'** [*breeding dogs, horses, and cats*] (*MK*: 449; Mh.: 368f.; cf. *hinaufdressieren, MK*: 497; Mh.: 391).

While racial superiority was desirable and, indeed, natural for Aryans, Hitler did not find praise for the social climber, the *Emporkömmling*, depicting him as less socially adaptable than a member of the upper classes (*MK*: 22; Mh.: 21). It may be that he considered that social and racial hierarchies were given by God and irrefutable, or, more likely, that nobody should rise in society without a struggle. In *MK*, all human progress is portrayed as an arduous uphill struggle, like 'dem Aufstiege auf einer endlosen Leiter' [climbing an endless ladder] (*MK*: 323; Mh.: 268); this was, indeed, how Hitler saw his own life.

In *MK*, the counterpart of upward movement, namely movement downwards, is used as a metaphor for disaster, as with *in den Abgrund reißen/zerren* ('to drag into the abyss') (*MK*: 141, 211 and 212) and *zugrunde gehen* ('to be destroyed') (*MK*: 253), translated by Mh. as 'to go to the dogs' [(Mh.: 211)]. Political decline is also metaphorized as downward movement, as a *Sturz* ('fall'), a *Niederlage* ('defeat', literally 'laying down'), and an *Untergang* ('destruction', literally 'movement downwards'). Chapter 10 of Book 1 deals with the causes of Germany's decline after the First World War, blaming the half-heartedness *(Halbheit)* and uncertainty *(Unsicherheit)* of the German population in all things, both before and during the war, and, of course, of the deeds of the Jews. Germany's fate is portrayed as comprising only one of two extreme possibilities: a future or ruin, 'Zukunft oder Untergang' (*MK*: 274; Mh.: 228).

The sinking of the collective attributes of race ('allgemeine Senkung des Rassenniveaus') will, according to Hitler, have as its consequence a 'Minderung der geistigen Elastizität und schöpferischen Fähigkeit' [diminution of spiritual elasticity and creative ability] (*MK*: 443; Mh.: 364). Such a fate is inevitable if a race does not guard its purity. The terms *Niedergang* ('fall, decline'), *(herab)sinken* ('to sink (down)'), *senken/Senkung* ('to lower/lowering') and *Niedersenkung* ('lowering') are most notably used to refer to the contamination of German blood as a result of intermarriage (App. III, B.2.1.3.1.9). The decline of Aryan blood is mirrored by a rise in the cultural level of the races from which they select their sexual partners:

> **Indem wir uns immer wieder mit anderen Rassen paaren, erheben wir wohl diese aus ihrem bisherigen Kulturniveau auf eine höhere Stufe, sinken aber von unserer eigenen Höhe für ewig herab.**(*MK*: 476) [*By mating again and again with other races, we may raise these races from their previous cultural level to a higher stage, but we will descend forever from our high level.* (Mh.: 389, cf. also pp. 432 and 443)]

The mixing of Aryans with other races, most notably the Jews, is portrayed as a fall from paradise *(Sündenfall)* (*MK*: 320; Mh.: 265, App. III, A.1.3.1). Hitler suggests that the Aryan created paradise for himself (*MK*: 324; Mh.: 268); mankind as a whole will fall from paradise if people put their own wellbeing before that of others: 'im Jagen nach dem eigenen Glück stürzen die Menschen aus dem Himmel erst recht in die Hölle' [in the chase after their own happiness men fall from heaven into a real hell] (*MK*: 328; Mh.: 272).

Hitler also conceived negative forces preventing upward movement as weights which drag the purer races downwards *(hinunterziehen)* and cause a diminution of their endowments. Lack of character, for example, can be like a lead weight *(Bleigewicht)* dragging a nation down until it exists only as a slave race *(Sklavenrasse)* (*MK*: 761; Mh.: 612). The young Hitler was himself dragged down by material hardship, 'niedergedrückt von der Schwere des eigenen Loses' [oppressed by the hardship of my own lot] (*MK*: 55; Mh.: 48). The following quotation, combining an image of inward movement with one of downward movement, is a terrifying image of the type used by Hitler to depict Germany's enemies (cf. Chapter 2.3.3):

> Das deutsche Volk war noch nicht reif, um in den bolschewistischen Blutsumpf hineingezerrt werden zu können, wie dies in Rußland gelang. (*MK*: 585f.) [The German people was not yet ripe for being forced into the bloody Bolshevistic morass, as had happened in Russia. (Mh.: 476)]

Failures can be seen in terms of failure to reach a summit (see above). A forced downward movement *(Niederlage*, literally 'laying down') can, however, be seen in an optimistic light if it motivates increased power in the future:

> (...) dann wird die militärische Niederlage eher zum Antrieb eines kommenden größeren Aufstieges als zum Leichenstein eines Völkerdaseins. (*MK*: 250) [(...) the military defeat will rather be the inspiration of a great future resurrection than the tombstone of a national existence. (Mh.: 209)]

Here Manheim's translation adds a religious dimension not present in the original text.

Other Types of Movement
Movement to Surround/Force Into
The actions of surrounding and restraint are represented in *MK* by verbs such as *umgarnen* ('to ensnare'), *umklammern* ('to grip'), *umspinnen* ('to weave a web around') and *ketten* ('to chain'), and nouns such as *Umstrickung*

('ensnarement'), *Fesseln* ('shackles') and *Garn* ('thread'). Webs are woven, chains and shackles attached, usually by Jews in order to restrict the movement, i.e. the cultural progress, of Aryans. A bond can, however, be a good thing where it unites people in a beneficial way. Education, for example, can unite people by putting them on an equal level:

> (...) um so durch gleiches Wissen und gleiche Begeisterung auch ein gleichmäßig verbindendes Band um die ganze Nation zu schlingen. (*MK*: 471) [(...) thus through like knowledge and like enthusiasm tying a uniform, uniting bond around the entire nation. (Mh.: 386)]

App. III, A.2.8 records images of incarceration, where bonds, fetters, nets, ropes and chains help to contain prisoners. Most commonly it is Jews who are portrayed as robbing the Aryans of their freedom. Verbs such as *umarmen* ('to embrace') have two metaphorical interpretations, one relating to security and love and the other to control and imprisonment. Hitler uses the less common, negative sense. This is illustrated in *MK* with reference to Bolshevism: 'Wie will man unser eigenes Volk aus den Fesseln dieser giftigen Umarmung erlösen, wenn man sich selbst in sie begibt? [How can we expect to free our own people from the fetters of this poisonous embrace if we walk right into it?] (*MK*: 752; Mh.: 605).

Movement Inwards and Movement Outwards
Containers can be entered or left, not by force, as with imprisonment or expulsion, but voluntarily. Places which can be entered and exited include a nation, a building, a party, an organisation, a good place or a place of danger. Hitler writes of his decision that the German parliament should be attacked from outside (*MK*: 112), describing first the question that the NS movement asked itself:

> Sollte man, um das Parlament zu vernichten, in das Parlament gehen, um dasselbe, wie man sich auszudrücken pflegte, „von innen heraus auszuhöhlen", oder sollte man diesen Kampf von außen angriffsweise gegen diese Einrichtung an und für sich führen? (*MK*: 111) [Should its members, to destroy parliament, go into parliament, in order, as people used to say, 'to bore from within', or should they carry on the struggle from outside by an attack on the institution as such. (Mh.: 94)]

Terms such as *angreifen* ('to attack'), *Angriff* ('attack'), *Griff (in)* (*MK*: 767, translated by Mh. as 'blow at'), *Ausplünderung* ('pillaging'), *Beutezug* ('campaign of pillage'), *erobern*, *Eroberung* ('conquest'), *Fehde ansagen* ('to declare seige') describe attempts to force entry into and possibly take items out of a variety of places (see App. III, A.2.7) such as the minds of the masses, an area which, according to Hitler, was regularly attacked by brilliant Marxist orators:

> (...) diese Volksredner auf die Massen einhämmerten und so eine fabelhafte Kenntnis dieses Menschenmaterials zu gewinnen wußten, was sie erst recht in die Lage versetzte, die richtigen Angriffswaffen auf die Burg der öffentlichen Meinung zu wählen. (*MK*: 529) [(...) these people's orators hammered at the masses and thus were able to acquire a marvellous knowledge of this human material which really put them in a position to choose the best weapons for attacking the fortress of public opinion. (Mh.: 429f.)]

Putting Aside/Away
Containers, which may be of a variety of shapes, have a central area, usually seen as more valuable, and outer areas, which, in political discourse, often represent a less favourable environment, In App. III, B.2.1.3.1.12 two such metaphors are recorded: *in die Ecke stellen* ('to put into the corner') and *drängen* ('to force away'), the latter being applied to the House of Hapsburg being forced to the outermost edge of the Empire ('die äußerste Kante des Reiches') (*MK*: 79; Mh.: 67, translated as 'corner').

Change of Direction/State
Within the experientialist framework of metaphor, a change of direction or state is seen as a movement from one container to another. In political discourse a change of direction is a common metaphorization for the change from a positive to a negative state of affairs, or vice versa. I have only found one example in *MK*, namely of the latter (see App. III, B.2.1.3.1.13). The verb *herumreißen* applied to the NS movement has much more metaphoric impact that Mh.'s 'to shake', which does not include the sense of a *change* of direction: 'Da war es notwendig, mit eiserner Faust die Bewegung herumzureißen' [it was necessary to shake the movement with an iron fist] (*MK*: 521; Mh.: 423).

A change of state, conceptualized as the movement from one state to another, frequently metaphorizes a change for the better in *MK*. Three terms recorded in App. III, A.2.11.10 describe arousal from a sleeping state (*erwecken, wach rufen* and *Wiederaufrüttelung*), the latter referring to propaganda as a weapon for shaking awake the nation's spirit: 'die größte Propagandawaffe zur Wiederaufrüttelung der eingeschlafenen Lebensgeister einer Nation' (*MK*: 715; Mh.: 577).

Unbounded Movement
Due to the fact that containers have boundaries that may be crossed, whilst other areas have no perceivable boundaries, we have access to a number of metaphors which help us understand feelings and situations, such as the extremes of emotion metaphorized by boundlessness, as with 'grenzenloser Haß' [boundless hatred] (*MK*: 65; Mh.: 56). The lack of a boundary to restrict movement can be viewed in different ways. It can be seen as a type of freedom to think and feel as one wishes, or it can be seen as a lack of control and discipline. Both may be relished or feared. The adjectives *uferlos* ('boundless' or 'infinite'), *grenzenlos* ('boundless'), *bodenlos* ('bottomless') and *unumschränkt* ('unlimited') generally refer to negative emotions or lack of virtues in *MK* (see App. III, B.2.1.4), with boundlessness appearing particularly dangerous:

> Wer hier die Schranken einreißt, gibt eine Bahn frei, deren Anfang man kennt, deren Ende jedoch sich im Uferlosen verliert. (*MK*: 513; cf. 655) [Once you tear down barriers in this connection, you open a road, the beginning of which is known, but whose end is lost in the infinite. (Mh.: 418)]

If an area has no boundaries or clear network of roads to guide one, the possibility of getting lost is ever-present. In Hitler's mind, control of the masses and lack of individual freedom was vital for the success of his ideas and the NS movement. Furthermore, the individual was expected to sacrifice his own freedom for the greater good.

3.4.2.3   Lack of Movement

While movement upwards/forwards and downwards/backwards are most commonly regarded as metaphors for progress and regression respectively, lack of movement necessarily stands for lack of progress, and impediments to motion stand for difficulties encountered before a particular aim can be achieved. In *MK,* Hitler emphasizes the necessity for the leaders of his movement to be the type of people who will resist stagnation:

> **Die Organisation erfaßt in ihrem Rahmen nur diejenigen, die nicht aus psychologischen Gründen zum Hemmschuh für eine weitere Verbreitung der Idee zu werden drohen.** (*MK*: 652f.) [*(...) the organisation embraces within its scope only those who do not threaten on psychological grounds to become a brake on the further dissemination of the idea.* (Mh.: 529)]

Captivity and illness or paralysis may metaphorize the prevention of progress, as in the following quotation (cf. Sections A.2.8 and B.2.1.1.2):

> **Im übrigen wird eine junge sieghafte Idee jede Fessel ablehnen müssen, die ihre Aktivität im Vorwärtstreiben ihrer Gedanken lähmen könnte.** (*MK*: 648) [*Moreover, a young victorious idea will have to reject any fetter which might paralyse its activity in pushing forward its conceptions.* (Mh.: 526)]

Here the 'idea', namely National Socialism, will keep Germany moving forwards if it repels Marxism and the pacifism that Hitler associated with it ('(der) fortschreitenden pazifistisch-marxistischen Lähmung unseres Volkskörpers'; *MK*: 361; Mh.: 298).

3.4.3 THE GREAT CHAIN OF BEING

Arthur Lovejoy's 1936 book on the GREAT CHAIN OF BEING traces the history of the GREAT CHAIN (also called the "Scale of Being") back to Neo-Platonism and shows how it helped to shape Western philosophy (Lovejoy 1966). Undoubtedly the notion of a hierarchy of earthly things is much older. Within the CHAIN, beings or entities are located on a vertical scale with "higher" beings and properties above "lower" ones. This is called the "gradation principle". Within this hierarchical scale, divine beings are at the top, followed by human beings; humans are followed by animals in appropriate order (for example horses are higher than rats, which, in their turn, are higher than reptiles); these are followed by lesser living forms (for example insects followed by bacteria). Plants are still lower in the hierarchy, having their own higher and lower levels (trees, for example, are higher than algae). Non-living objects follow (stones, metals and so on), with physical properties or size determining their place in the hierarchy. Where human beings are concerned we talk of our "higher faculties" in relation to our moral sense and rationality. Humans also tend to be ranked according to social, financial or cultural criteria, and according to the power that those in a higher position may exert on those lower down the hierarchy.

Hitler's political discourse, as exemplified by *MK*, made full and varied use of metaphors from the GREAT CHAIN, although it is unlikely that this was his conscious intention. In my analysis of Hitler's metaphors I have included the products of human creativity and social formations within the GREAT CHAIN, as I take these to be evidence of the supposed mental and physical superiority of human beings over other animals. In *MK*, Hitler personified many non-living entities, bringing machines and other artifacts into the sphere of THE GREAT CHAIN OF BEING. I have also included metaphors associated with the way in which human beings interact within and between the societies that they organize for themselves, such as POLITICS IS WAR, which is especially pertinent to Hitler's message in *MK*.

Hitler believed that Nature controlled the world and had set in place an "aristocratic principle"; he personified her as wanting higher life forms to be stronger than weaker ones and to survive them. His message in *MK* was that Aryans were high order beings and Jews low. According to Hitler, the inferiority of the Jews was part of Nature's design, and it was inevitable that these "lower" beings would try to poison the higher Aryans or to develop a parasitic dependency upon them. They therefore had to be destroyed. Men before Hitler had expressed similar views, but part of the explicit force of Hitler's message was his own: that of the Jews belonging to a race rather than a religion. The original GREAT CHAIN was characterized by the "principle of continuity" and this was a principle not recognized by Hitler. According to the continuity principle each level in the CHAIN is seamlessly connected with the next level; thus all beings are connected with one another. Hitler, on the other hand, proclaimed a *discontinuity* between Aryan and Jew: there was an gulf between the two, one race being good and the other evil. The gulf could not be bridged with any intermediate being because this would have involved the mixing of German and Jewish blood, something which Hitler considered a sin, indeed an *Erbsünde*. The only possibility for Hitler was a battle to the death between the two opposing forces (cf. *The war of the races* below).

3.4.3.1 Supernatural Beings, Nature and Fate

Arguably at the top of the GREAT CHAIN, above human beings, are the Christian God, and other gods and goddesses. Divine beings were certainly at the top of Hitler's hierarchy, and he made extensive use of religious metaphors in *MK*, with his own political aims and the tenets of National Socialism frequently seen in terms of "holy" work, as a "mission". Heaven is portrayed as the supreme location, while hell is to be avoided, as with the locational conceptual metaphors IMPORTANCE/GOOD IS UP and WORTHLESSNESS/BAD IS DOWN. I have found only one example of a metaphor for the Christian God in *MK*, where He is mentioned as the Highest of the High *(der Allerhöchster)*, translated by Mh. as 'the Almighty'; Hitler's other gods represent forces, both good and evil, such as peace, truth, war, money and suffering. People may worship false gods, such as the 'Götze Mammon' [idol Mammon] (*MK*: 255f.; Mh.: 213), or they may follow a more virtuous path, even at times of war, war making peace possible because 'die milde Göttin des Friedens nur an der Seite des Kriegsgottes wandeln kann' [the gentle Goddess of Peace can walk only by the side of the God of War] (*MK*: 550; Mh.: 447). The negative counterpart to holy figures is the devil, and Hitler metaphorizes groups of people that he despises, most commonly the Jews, as devils *(Teufel)* and Lucifer, also using adjectives such as *teuflisch* ('diabolic'), *satanisch* ('satanic') and *infernalisch* ('infernal') (see App. III, A.1.4).

Heaven and hell represent two extremes of location, one high and divine, the other low and disagreeable (see Sections A.1.2 and A.1.4). The reward for taking the right road in life is a place in heaven, while the wrong road will lead downwards into purgatory or hell: 'im Jagen nach dem eigenen Glück stürzen die Menschen aus dem Himmel erst recht in die Hölle' [in the chase after their own happiness men fall from heaven into a real hell] (*MK*: 328; Mh.: 272). Hitler more than once warns Aryans that they will be responsible for their own fall from paradise if they marry Jews (see App. III, A.1.3.1), paradise having been, to Hitler's mind, created by and for Aryans (*MK*: 324; Mh.: 268).

Hitler saw his life and the political ambitions of his NS movement as a holy mission *(heilige Mission)*, thus putting himself on the highest rung of the human hierarchy, closely followed by those who shared his views (*MK*: 551 and 688; Mh.: 447 and 557). This mission was primarily concerned with the creation of a Germanic State populated by pure-blooded Aryans: 'Ihre Mission liegt (...) in der Schaffung eines germanischen Staates' (*MK*: 380; Mh.: 314). The adjective *heilig* ('holy') is more broadly used in *MK*, but nevertheless most commonly describes the "hallowed" mission of Hitler and his National Socialists, namely the protection of Germany against internal and external enemies, those who fight with real weapons and those who fight with what Hitler believed to be corrupt practices and impure blood:

> **Nein, es gibt nur ein heiligstes Menschenrecht, und dieses Recht ist zugleich die heiligste Verpflichtung, nämlich: dafür zu sorgen, daß das Blut rein erhalten bleibt (...)** (*MK*: 444) [*No, there is only one holiest human right, and this right is at the same time the holiest obligation, to wit: to see to it that the blood is preserved pure (...)* (Mh.: 365)]

Hitler's portrayal of his life as a Christ-like journey ('irdische Wanderschaft' (*MK*: 173), translated as the less provocative 'pilgrimage' by Mh.: 145) verges on blasphemy, while he only uses the words *auserwählt* and *auserkoren* (both meaning 'chosen') ironically, referring to democratically elected politicians. The notion of resurrection and rebirth, on the other hand, frequently appear in *MK* with referrence to Germany's future (see App. III, A.1.3.2). The terms *Auferstehung, Wiederauferstehung, Wiedererstehung, Wiedererhebung* and *Wiedergeburt* are all used to refer to the hoped-for freedom of the *Vaterland* and the strengthening of the Germans' instinct of self-preservation *(Selbsterhaltungstrieb)* (*MK*: 714; Mh.: 576).

Hitler has praise for virtuous human beings who are willing to sacrifice themselves for the common good: they are celebrated in religious terms as 'aufopferungsbereite Helden' [heroes prepared to make sacrifices] (*MK*: 114; Mh.: 96) with *Aufopferungsfähigkeit* and *Aufopferungswille* [the ability and will of the individual to sacrifice himself] (*MK*: 167; Mh.: 140). The ultimate sacrifice is the gift of one's life: **'das heiligste Opfer (ist) das Blut, das man**

für diese Erde vergießt! *[and the most sacred sacrifice the blood that a man sheds for this earth]* (*MK*: 755; Mh.: 607). Similarly, *Weihe* ('consecration') and *Entweihung* ('desecration') represent desired or unwanted political or social outcomes. Hitler further writes in *MK* of political revelations *(Offenbarungen)* (*MK*: 72; Mh.: 61), the *Feuertaufe* ('baptism of fire', *MK*: 219; Mh.: 182) at the beginning of the First World War; and he refers to the audiences of his political meetings as *andächtig* ('pious') (*MK*: 518; Mh.: 421). The thoughts and deeds of heroes are described as *unsterblich* ('immortal') (*MK*: 205; Mh.: 170). The verb *anbeten* ('to worship'), on the other hand, is used with negative connotations to refer to those who read the "Jewish" democratic press (*MK*: 191; Mh.: 159).

Nature and Fate
Nature and Fate are frequently personified in *MK*. A selection of examples is listed at the beginning of App. III, B. In particular, Nature is claimed by Hitler to hold a view close to one of his own, namely that she has little love for the products of racial mixture: 'Sie liebt die Bastarde nur wenig' (*MK*: 441f.; Mh.: 363). Nature is portrayed as favouring the more "highly" bred, stronger living beings which are the product of a strict delimitation of races and species. Hitler writes that it is the way of Nature to endorse the superiority of some animals over others. She watches benignly as the species fight among themselves, because it is a fight for survival:

> Daher entsteht auch hier der Kampf untereinander weniger infolge innerer Abneigung etwa als vielmehr aus Hunger und Liebe. In beiden Fällen sieht die Natur ruhig, ja befriedigt zu. (*MK*: 312f.) [Therefore, here too, the struggle among themselves arises less from inner aversion than from hunger and love. In both cases, Nature looks on calmly, with satisfaction, in fact. (Mh.: 259)]

Fate, in *MK*, is most notably personified as Hitler's mentor, sending him to live in Vienna shortly before the death of his mother (*MK*: 18; Mh.: 18), directing him to the harsh school of the Vienna streets (*MK*: 29; Mh.: 27), and opening his eyes to the evils of Social Democracy, also while he was a young man in Vienna:

Es bedurfte auch hier erst der Faust des Schicksals, um mir das Auge über diesen unerhörtesten Völkerbetrug zu öffnen. (*MK*: 40) [Here again it required the fist of Fate to open my eyes to this unprecedented betrayal of the peoples. (Mh.: 36)]

3.4.3.2 Human Beings

3.4.3.2.1 Human Hierarchies

According to the GREAT CHAIN, human beings are at the top of the hierarchy of mortal living beings. The position of mankind above animals is portrayed as a life in the service of higher ideals:

> Man darf also wohl feststellen, daß nicht nur der Mensch lebt, um höheren Idealen zu dienen, sondern daß diese höheren Ideale umgekehrt auch die Voraussetzung zu seinem Dasein als Mensch geben. So schließt sich der Kreis. (*MK*: 417) [We may therefore state that not only does man live in order to serve higher ideals, but that, conversely, these higher ideals also provide the premise for his existence. Thus the circle closes. (Mh.: 345)]

Within this category of "human being" there is a secondary ordering according to social, financial or cultural criteria, and according to the power that those in a higher position may exert on those lower down the hierarchy. Hitler believed that there were human beings who were naturally of a higher order or lower order. For Hitler the distinction between naturally preeminent and inferior human beings was bound to race, with the so-called "Aryan" race being superior to all others (for a discussion of racial hierarchy see Chapter 2.3.5). He believed that Nature (personified in the following quotation) had honoured such superior beings with this position:

> Der Stärkste an Mut und Fleiß erhält dann als ihr liebstes Kind das Herrenrecht des Daseins zugesprochen. (*MK*: 147) [She [Nature] then confers the master's rights on her favourite child, the strongest in courage and industry. (Mh.: 123)]

In App. III, A.2.2, a selection of metaphors relating to royalty and aristocracy are listed which depict human beings as superior to other living beings, and Germans or Aryans as superior to other races. Hitler believed that man's power over other beings was the achievement of the Aryan, 'der Begründer höheren Menschentums überhaupt' [the founder of all higher humanity], and that man had thus risen *(emporsteigen)* to a position of mastery over all other beings on earth ('Beherrscher der anderen Wesen dieser Erde', *MK*: 317; Mh.: 263). The Aryan was, indeed, the 'Urtyp dessen (...), was wir unter dem Worte „Mensch" verstehen' [the prototype of all that we understand by the word 'man'] (*MK*: 317; Mh.: 263). The German people are portrayed in *MK* as the 'Herren der Erde' whose genius and courage give them their elevated position as defenders of the world (*MK*: 739; Mh.: 596); they are a physically, morally and culturally superior 'Herrenvolk' [master people] (*MK*: 438; Mh.: 360). Naturally, it is the NS movement which will lead the German people as their master: 'Nicht Knecht soll sie der Masse sein, sondern Herr!' [It must not become the servant of the masses, but their master!] (*MK*: 520; Mh.: 422).

Adherents of the NS *Weltanschauung* will have to behave like heroes (App. III, A.2.4). Hitler depicted the disintegration of the German Reich as poison being driven into the Aryan *Heldenleib* [heroic body] by its enemies, especially the Jews (*MK*: 169; Mh.: 141). He saw it as his role to help reinstate Germany as a player on the world stage, to be a heroic leader like the figure depicted in the following quotation:

> Wer dazu nicht fähig oder für das Ertragen der Folgen seines Tuns zu feige ist, taugt nicht zum Führer. Nur der Held ist dazu berufen. (*MK*: 379) [Anyone who is not equal to this or is too cowardly to bear the consequences of his acts is not fit to be leader; only the hero is cut out for this. (Mh.: 313)]

Not all heroes have to be of this stature: even the weakest of mothers can be a heroine in the service of her country. Hitler's image of a mother rescuing her child may also be understood metaphorically as the State, however weak it may be (*MK*.: 168; Mh.: 140).

In *MK*, metaphors expressing political power and bravery are accompanied by those that underline the nobility of German cultural and spiritual virtues. Hitler uses the adjective *edel* to refer to the State's responsibility to succour all that is noble in the German people, the **'edelsten Bestandteile unseres Volkstums, ja der ganzen Menschheit'** [*the most noble elements of our nationality, indeed of all mankind*] (*MK*: 439; Mh.: 361). Kings and queens appear less frequently than masters and mistresses in *MK* (cf. the two entries under *Königin*, App. III, A.2.2), but their crowns stand for superior behaviour, values and endeavours. The ultimate self-sacrifice of giving one's life for one's nation is, for Hitler, the crowning of all sacrifices ('die Krönung alles Opfersinns', *MK*: 327; Mh.: 271). The crowning glory of the folkish State's work in education will be the burning of racial instinct into the hearts and minds of the young:

> **Die gesamte Bildungs- und Erziehungsarbeit des völkischen Staates muß ihre Krönung darin finden, daß sie den Rassesinn und das Rassegefühl instinkt- und verstandesmäßig in Herz und Gehirn der ihr anvertrauten Jugend hineinbrennt.** (*MK*: 475f.) [*The crown of the folkish state's entire work of education and training must be to burn the racial sense and racial feeling into the instinct and the intellect, the heart and the brain of the youth entrusted to it.* (Mh.: 389)]

Hitler uses designations for a variety of professions, occupations and roles to represent mainly lower-order human characteristics and, in the case of *Drahtzieher* ('wire-puller') (*MK*: 706; Mh.: 571), specifically Jews (see App. III, A.2.3). Many of the lower-order occupations function as pejorative epithets, such as: *Handlanger* ('handyman') (*MK*: 716; Mh.: 577f.), *Lederhändler* ('leather-merchant') (*MK*: 88; Mh.: 74), *Sattlermeister* ('saddlers') and *Handschuhmacher* ('glove-makers', i.e. parliamentarians (*MK*: 762; Mh.: 613), *Schildknappe* ('squire', i.e. Jew) (*MK*: 752; Mh.: 605), *Schneiderlein* ('little tailor') (*MK*: 770; Mh.: 619), *Schutzpolizist* ('constable') (*MK*: 741; Mh.: 597), *Sterngucker* ('stargazer'), *Parteiastrologe* ('party astrologer') (*MK*: 410; Mh.: 339). Higher professions are seen as a part of a 'höhere Bestimmung' [high calling] (*MK*: 36; Mh.: 33) and the white race as a 'kulturell hochbegnadetes Volk' [people highly endowed with culture] when contrasted with Negro peoples (*MK*: 436; Mh.: 359). Other higher-order roles include *Fronvogt* ('task-master') and *Herold* (both *MK*: 716; Mh.: 577f.), and *Athlet* ('athlete') (*MK*: 770; Mh.: 619). The *"Masse der Mitte"* ('masses in the middle'), furthermore, are particularly despised.

Lower-ranking people are often referred to with common personal names in German and Hitler uses a selection of men's names to represent "ordinary chaps": *Johannes* (*MK*: 398; Mh.: 329), *Hänschen* (*MK*: 544; translated by Mh. as 'little rank-and-filers': 442), *Hinz* and *Peter* (*MK*: 88; translated by Mh. as 'Tom', 'Dick' and 'Harry': 75). Also, *Poilu* refers to the French soldiers of the First World War and *Tommy* to English soldiers (*MK*: 216f.; Mh.: 180).

3.4.3.2.2 Personification

Professions and human roles are frequently personified in *MK* (see App. III, A.2.3.1). Hitler portrays the NS movement as occupying a higher-order role, having a duty as a 'Vorkämpferin' ('pioneer') and 'Repräsentantin' ('representative') of its philosophy (*MK*: 514, Mh.: 419). It is guided by reason, its 'alleinige Führerin' [sole guide] (*MK*: 753; Mh.: 606), and is the victor *(Siegerin)* over other folkish groups (*MK*: 575; Mh.: 467). Hitler's intention as expressed in *MK* was that the NS philosophy would never be the servant *(Dienerin)* of individual federated States but would be mistress (*Herrin*, translated by Mh. as 'master') of the entire German nation (*MK*: 648; Mh.: 526). This situation would echo the order of the natural world, where stronger elements have power over weaker ones:

> (...) in einer Welt (...) in der immer nur die Kraft Herrin der Schwäche ist und sie zum gehorsamen Diener zwingt (...) (*MK*: 267) [(...) where force alone forever masters weakness, compelling it to be an obedient slave (...) (Mh.: 223)]

Useful occupations and roles occasionally represent higher-order human activities and emotional properties in *MK*. Historical education, for example, is a 'stiller Mahner (...) von neuer Zukunft' (*MK*: 11; translated by Mh. as an agent which 'whispers softly of a new future' p. 13), and sentiment *(Gefühl)* was the most loyal guardian and sentinel ('treuester Wächter und Warner') of Hitler's reason while his political views were developing (*MK*: 59; Mh.: 51). Lower-order roles are also personified: Social Democracy is ironically referred to as a 'Menschheitsfreundin' [friend of humanity] (*MK*: 53; Mh.: 46), and prostitution is seen as the 'Schrittmacherin' [which prepares the way] for syphilis (*MK*: 280; Mh.: 232). Civilisation is personified as the enemy *(Feindin)* of a truly high standard of thinking and living ('wahrer Geistes- und Lebenshöhe', *MK*: 282; Mh.: 234), and the German government is portrayed as sinking from a relatively neutral role to one of a beggar:

> Sie ist (...) nur die Vollstreckerin des jeweiligen Mehrheitswillens. (...) Sie sinkt (...) zu einer Bettlerin gegenüber der jeweiligen Majorität. (*MK*: 95) [In every case it does nothing but carry out the momentary will of the majority. (...) Thereby it sinks (...) to the level of a beggar confronting the momentary majority. (Mh.: 80)]

The Personification of Human Capacities

Human emotions, sensations and capacities are of a high order within the GREAT CHAIN (see App. III, B.2.1.2 for a selection from *MK*); they are considered more complex and refined than those experienced by non-human sentient beings. Hitler had his own views on the ranking of higher human capacities, with *Gefühl* ('feelings, sentiments') rating highly and contrasting with reason *(Verstand, Vernunft)*, which should accompany sentiment:

> (...) erst nach monatelangem Ringen zwischen Verstand und Gefühl begann der Sieg sich auf die Seite des Verstandes zu schlagen. Zwei Jahre später war das Gefühl dem Verstande gefolgt, um von nun an dessen treuester Wächter und Warner zu sein. (*MK*: 59) [(...) only after months of battle between my reason and my sentiments did my reason begin to emerge victorious. Two years later, my sentiment had followed my reason, and from then on became its most loyal guardian and sentinel. (Mh.: 51)]

Occasionally, however, the heart conquers reason and reality, as it did for Hitler when he decided to leave Vienna for Munich: 'das Herz weilte woanders' [my heart dwelt elsewhere] (*MK*: 135; Mh.: 113). Reason, according to Hitler, was the sole guide ('alleinige Führerin') of the NS movement (*MK*: 753; Mh.: 606), and *Wille* ('will') a helper in the achievement of his personal goals and those of the movement. In *MK*, Hitler writes that his will to defend and champion his nation ('der Wille zum Widerstand') was strengthened during his early days in Vienna by hunger and hardship: hardship is personified as the 'Göttin der Not' [Goddess of Suffering] and *Wille* as victorious over her: 'endlich blieb der Wille Sieger' [in the end this will was victorious] (*MK*: 20; Mh.: 19). Care *(Sorge)* and hunger are similarly personified (*MK*: 20f. and 27; Mh.: 20 and 25). Hitler personifies National Socialism as a 'junge sieghafte Idee' [young victorious idea] which will 'reject any fetter which might paralyse its activity' (*MK*: 648; Mh.: 526, cf. 'missionshaften Idee' *MK*: 751; Mh.: 605).

Higher-order capacities such as human emotions and sensations also have an internal ranking, with capacities such as suffering and the causing of pain to others rated as of a low order within them. In *MK*, Hitler describes Germany's fate as permanently accompanied by the personified lower-order emotions *(Sorge)* and lower-order conditions *(Not, Elend)*:

Not und Sorge sind seitdem die ständigen Begleiter unseres Volkes geworden, und unser einziger treuer Verbündeter ist das Elend. (*MK*: 762) [(...) since then hardship and care have been the constant companions of our people, and our one faithful ally has been misery. (Mh.: 612)]

The fact that many of the professions, roles and capacities exemplified in this section involve the use of feminine nouns leads to their personification as female beings: for example strength *(Kraft)*, the economy *(Wirtschaft)* and the German *Reich* (note that *Reich* is a neuter noun) are personified as mistresses *(Herrin)* over weaker entities (*MK*: 267, 437f. and 255f.; Mh.: 223, 360 and 213). America is portrayed ironically as 'eine neue Herrin der Welt' [a new master of the world] (*MK*: 722; Mh.: 582).

3.4.3.2.3 The Human Anatomy

While basic anatomical characteristics are shared by humans and animals, it is human anatomy which is central to our bodily experience and therefore used as the basis for most metaphors. Within the higher-order human anatomy there is a hierarchy of anatomical features, although it is likely that producers of discourse have their own favourites. The body is a significant source of metaphors for political discourse as a whole and for Hitler in particular (cf. Chapter 3.4.1.2: A STATE IS A BODY). The notion of a "national body" as a single organism divided into parts like an actual body stems from the French Revolution (Schmitz-Berning: 667). In *MK*, the *Körper* stands for the German people and is frequently compounded as *Volkskörper*, a word which is difficult to render in English but might be translated 'the body of the people'. Manheim uses, for example, 'body politic' (Mh.: 43), which I consider a rather narrow interpretation, and 'nation' (Mh.: 43) which I find inadequate; he translates *Körperschaft* as 'great comprehensive body' (*MK*: p. 536; Mh.: 435), which I find better. Hitler represents the State as a living organism *(Organismus*, see App. III, B.1.1) and the *Reich* as a body with a heart *(Herz)*, a bloodstream *(Kreislauf)*, and a pulse *(Pulsschlag)*; a State has to have a healthy heart, i.e. a prosperous capital city, in order to survive (*MK*: 109; Mh.: 92). On a more mundane level, the economy is metaphorized as a *Wirtschaftskörper* (*MK*: 51f., translated by Mh. with an architectural metaphor, 'economic edifice': 45), and the Rhine is referred to as a *Lebensader* [vital artery] (*MK*: 711; Mh.: 574).

For Hitler, the blood and the heart predominate among his anatomical metaphors, and these are indeed commonly considered to be of the highest order in the bodily make-up of humans (see App. III, B.1.2.1). To the National Socialists, blood had several metaphorizations (see App. III, B.1.2.1.2). In *MK*, it represents the life-blood of the nation, the lives of German heroes who died for their nation (*MK*: 219; Mh.: 182), and, most significantly, the German race, whose blood had to be kept pure. A nation and a *Volkskörper* can be drained of blood (*Ausblutung*, *verbluten*, *Weißbluten*, *MK*: 581, 632, 633; Mh.: 473, 513, 514), most notably by blood-sucking creatures that represent Jews (see App. III, B.1.3.11), or it can be poisoned *(Blutvergiftung)* (*MK*: 169, 268, 270, 316; Mh.: 141, 262, 225, 224). The preservation of racial purity was of paramount importance to the National Socialists. Intermarriage between Jews and Aryans was considered *Blutschande* ('racial desecration'), and Hitler disapproved of many types of racial mixture, such as that within the Austrian Empire between Serbs, Croats, Czechs and Poles (*MK*: 135; Mh.: 113). In *MK*, Hitler recommends that schools should sift out the most promising "blood" to be of use to the population as a whole; the higher-order intellectual classes would then be renewed by an influx of blood from below ('durch frische Blutzufuhr von unten', *MK*: 481f.; Mh.: 393).

The heart as the container of human emotions has been considered above. The sophistication of human emotions, or rather the fact that human beings can identify and describe these emotions, is a major reason for our belief that we are of a higher order than animals in the GREAT CHAIN: we assume that animal emotions are simple and therefore lower. The heart may be contrasted with the head or the brain as the metonymical representatives of human intellect, or the heart and the brain may be seen to complement one another. Hitler describes one of his most successful speeches as having been particularly effective because of its appeal to both the emotions and the intellect:

> Wieder war aus Herzen und Gehirnen einer nach Tausenden zählenden Menge eine große Lüge herausgerissen und dafür eine Wahrheit eingepflanzt worden. (*MK*: 524) [Again a great lie had been torn out of the hearts and brains of a crowd numbering thousands, and a truth implanted in its place. (Mh.: 425f.)]

It was vital to Hitler that his message, particularly that of the significance of racial purity, should be burnt into the hearts and minds of young people in particular: **'instinkt- und verstandesmäßig in Herz und Gehirn'** [*into the instinct and intellect, the heart and brain*] (*MK*: 475.; Mh.: 389). From an anatomical point of view, the nerves are vital to life, and Hitler writes of the *Nervenzentren* and the *Nervenzentrale* of the German State as vital for its functioning, and as something over which the NS movement should have total control (see App. III, B.1.2.1.4).

Due to its position at the top of the human body and its function of as a container for the brain, the head is frequently used as a metonym. In *MK*, *Kopf* (pl. *Köpfe*) stand for people with good brains, 'kleine Köpfe' for people with small minds or brains, and *Schädel* for brains and their owners, who might have higher or lower abilities (Hitler calls the former *Einser* and the latter *Nullen*, *MK*: 90; Mh.: 76).

The anatomical importance of the neck and the backbone, both of which hold up the body of the State and both of which can be broken, is discussed above (A STATE IS A BODY). Hands, arms, feet and legs follow in importance. Hands are particularly significant of the higher-order status of human beings, as no other animals are able to make such delicate use of their fingers. Hands and arms are metaphorized in *MK* in both positive and negative roles: hands may help and protect, but they may also hurt and threaten; arms may enclose a person in a loving or protective way, or in a manner which stifles or imprisons. When Hitler was a young man in Vienna the Goddess of Suffering took him into her arms, but the boundary between a caring and a dangerous embrace was very fine—in the end Hitler benefited from the Goddess's care and his will was strengthened (*MK*: 20; Mh.: 19). In a more sinister vein, an alliance with Russia is described in *MK* as a 'giftige Umarmung' [poisonous embrace] (*MK*: 752; Mh.: 605) and Marxism is portrayed as the 'Umarmung dieser giftigen Seuche' [embrace of this venomous plague] (*MK*: 184f.; Mh.: 154). Hands are usually helpful and may be used to pull someone up and out of a difficult situation, as in the following example:

> Mit der Besetzung des Ruhrgebiets hat das Schicksal noch einmal dem deutschen Volk die Hand zum Wiederaufstieg geboten. (*MK*: 767) [With the occupation of the Ruhr, Fate once again held out a hand to help the German people rise again. (Mh.: 617)]

Hands can, however, become tools of treachery: the tactics of Marxism are metaphorized in *MK* as one hand reaching out to offer friendship while the other reaches for a dagger: 'Während sie die kaiserliche Hand noch in der ihren hielten, suchte die andere schon nach dem Dolche' [While they still held the imperial hand in theirs, their other hand was reaching for the dagger] (*MK*: 225; Mh.: 187). The hand is more menacing when it is shaped into a fist *(Faust)*. It tends to be brutal *(roh, brutal)* rather than gentle, and functions as a metonym for physical force. In the following sentence, the fist stands for physical force, which in turn metaphorizes the Jewish practices which Hitler considered corrupt: 'Kein Volk entfernt diese Faust anders von seiner Gurgel als durch das Schwert' [No nation can remove this hand from its throat except by the sword] (*MK*: 738; Mh.: 595); Jewish non-physical force will, according to Hitler, have to be answered by physical violence, metaphorized as a sword. A brutal fist can protect a people, but it generally has to be assisted by human intelligence: 'Die Fäuste, das deutsche Volk zu beschützen, sie wären selbst damals noch dagewesen, nur die Schädel für den Einsatz hatten gefehlt' [The fists to protect the German people would have been available even then, but the heads to play the game were lacking] (*MK*: 550; Mh.: 447).

Feet and legs are of a lower order than hands and arms. They are less useful than these, indeed we can survive without legs and arms, but they are metaphorized as supports for our bodies and as weapons with which we can kick and trample (see App. III, B.1.2.1.8, where various common idioms are listed). The remaining parts of the human anatomy recorded in App. III, B.1.2 are largely common idiomatic expressions which are a popular type of metaphor in German and frequently have close or exact counterparts in English (see Chapter 3.2.3 above for examples). Of the remaining bodily metaphors used by Hitler in *MK*, the *Schoß* ('lap') stands out as the most commonly occurring and interesting. Manheim appropriately translates this word as 'bosom' (558) and 'womb' (449), the first occurrence referring to the *Reich* and the second to "war" in a positive sense: 'die Flagge [war] selbst aus dem Schoße des Krieges geboren worden' [the flag itself had been born from the womb of war] (*MK*: 552; Mh.: 448f.; interestingly, the noun *Krieg* is masculine). A third example depicts a more frightening 'Schoß des ewig Unbekannten' [womb of the eternal unknown] (*MK*: 144; Mh.: 121) to which

Nature sends back unhealthy human beings who are not able to withstand certain of the trials that she sets them.

The organs of seeing are the eyes, which are frequently metaphorized as our source of understanding (see Rash 1996: 182). Hitler uses a number of conventional metaphors involving the eyes in MK (see App. III, B.1.2.1.6), the most provocative referring to his "seeing the light" regarding the supposed Jewish involvement in Social Democracy: 'Indem ich den Juden als Führer der Sozialdemokratie erkannte, begann es mir wie Schuppen von den Augen zu fallen' [When I recognized the Jew as leader of the Social Democracy, the scales dropped from my eyes] (*MK*: 64; Mh.: 56).

Bodily Functions and Physical Size
In *MK*, most metaphors and idioms based on human physiology and size are conventional and frequently found in political discourse. The common conceptual metaphor, IDEAS ARE FOOD, is linked to feelings of hunger and thirst, just as these two compelling bodily experiences are linked with the desire for inspiration and knowledge. This metaphor is attested in *MK*, for example: 'Welche Kost aber hat die deutsche Presse der Vorkriegszeit den Menschen vorgesetzt?' [But what food did the German press of the pre-War period dish out to the people?] (*MK*: 264; Mh.: 220f.). As one may feel hunger or thirst for ideas or knowledge, one can also feel thirst for freedom, as in the following example from *MK*: 'ein ebenso kühner Wille eines freiheitsdurstigen Volkes' [an equally bold will on the part of a people thirsting for freedom] (*MK*: 716; Mh.: 578). Other common metaphors of bodily size and function in *MK* include: *in Atem halten* ('to hold one's breath'), *einer Sache keine Tränen nachweinen* ('to shed no tears over sth.'); *schlummern* ('to slumber, to lie dormant/hidden') and *verdauen* ('to digest, to understand') (see App. III, B.1.2.2 and B.1.2.3). *Schleim*, referring to Jews, may be regarded as a bodily substance if it is translated as 'mucus'; Mh., however, translated as 'slime'. Finally, *Riese* may stand for something large and important or admirable, and *Knirps* and *Zwerg* for something small and insignificant (see App. III, B.1.2.3).

Sickness and Health
The ability to recognize and heal illnesses is a specifically human and therefore higher-order achievement. Illnesses may be physical or mental, and, as far as Hitler was concerned, moral or racial:

> Denn die Erkrankung des Leibes ist hier nur das Ergebnis einer Erkrankung der sittlichen, sozialen und rassischen Instinkte. (*MK*: 280) [For in this case the sickening of the body is only the consequence of a sickening of the moral, social, and racial instincts. (Mh.: 232f.)]

Hitler saw it as his responsibility to recognize each infecting agent *(Erreger)* and find a cure, and warned more than once of the danger of concentrating on the disease while ignoring its cause: 'Manchmal dokterte man wohl auch an der Krankheit herum, verwechselte jedoch dann die Formen der Erscheinung mit dem Erreger' [Sometimes they tinkered around with the disease, but confused the forms of the phenomenon with the virus that had caused it] (*MK*: 171; Mh.: 143).

The metaphorization of the State as a body, which may be either healthy or ill, has been dealt with above. It was noted in particular that in *MK* Jews, and to a lesser extent Marxists and other groups despised by Hitler, are portrayed as plague-like sicknesses *(Pest, Pestilenz, Verpestung, Seuche)* which might infect the German State and its people. Hitler was obsessed with the fear that the entire German *Volk* was sick and in need of a cure. In one passage he accuses the cinema, the theatre and the press, all supposedly under Jewish control, of infecting the German people: 'Das war Pestilenz, geistige Pestilenz, schlimmer als der schwarze Tod von einst, mit der man da das Volk infizierte' [This was pestilence, spiritual pestilence, worse than the Black Death of olden times, and the people was being infected with it!] (*MK*: 62; Mh.: 54). The active voice of the German, with its use of *man*, may be a veiled reference to the fact that in the Middle Ages it was the Jews who were accused of spreading the plague.

After the plague, Hitler favoured metaphors involving leprosy (*MK*: 446; Mh.: 366), paralysis (App. III, B.2.1.1.2), blindness (Section B.2.1.1.4), and tumours (App. III, B.2.1.1.6). Paralysis is seen as especially frightening if it is progressive, as was, in Hitler's opinion, Marxism, '(der) fortschreitenden pazifistisch-marxistischen Lähmung unseres Volkskörpers' [the progressing pacifist-Marxist paralysis of our national body] (*MK*: 361; Mh.: 298). In particular the people could suffer from a paralysis of their power to reason ('gesunde Vernunft'), of their instinct of self-preservation ('des einfachen Selbsterhaltungstriebes') (*MK*: 169; Mh.: 141), and of their capacity to think progressively. It was the duty of National Socialists to restore all of these: **'Im übrigen wird eine junge sieghafte Idee jede Fessel ablehnen müssen, die ihre Aktivität im Vorwärtstreiben ihrer Gedanken lähmen könnte'** *[Moreover, a young victorious idea will have to reject any fetter which might paralyse its activity in pushing forward its conceptions]* (Mh.: 526; *MK*: 648). A people's physical movement and mental or spiritual progress may also be inhibited by general decrepitude and old age, metaphorized by Hitler using expressions such as: *Altersschwäche* ('senility'), *erstarren* ('to become rigid'), and *Verknöcherung* and *Verkalken* (both 'calcification').

Blindness is a disability that can befall anyone. Hitler accused various political and religious groups of not being able or not wanting to see, of being blinkered ('mit Scheuklappen behangen', *MK*: 296; Mh.: 246). The following quotation refers to the politicians of the old *Reich* who were unwilling or unable to see the political and social decrepitude around them:

> Wie mit Blindheit geschlagen wandelten sie an der Seite eines Leichnams und glaubten in den Anzeichen der Verwesung gar noch Merkmale „neuen Lebens" zu entdecken. (*MK*: 14) [As though stricken with blindness, they lived by the side of a corpse, and in the symptoms of rottenness saw only the signs of 'new' life. (Mh.: 15)]

Cancers, tumours and abscesses could eat at society but might also be cured by right-minded politicians and movements (*MK*: 49; Mh.: 43; App. III, B.2.1.1.6). The very worst type of deformity, however, namely racial mixture, could only be prevented, never cured: it would be necessary to raise **'Ebenbilder des Herrn'** *[images of the Lord]* and not **'Mißgeburten zwischen Mensch und Affe'** *[monstrosities halfway between man and ape]* (*MK*: 445; Mh.: 366. Cf. *MK*: 434, where Hitler declares that a State which does not encourage the physical and mental improvement of a homogeneous Aryan race is a *Mißgeburt*). Hitler was, of course, chiefly concerned with deterring intermarriage between Aryans and Jews. One of the best medicines for any type of illness was, according to Hitler, propaganda (*MK*: 216f.; Mh.: 180; App. III, B.2.1.1.9). The main precondition for German political health was a robust instinct for self-preservation *(Selbsterhaltungstrieb, MK*: 366; Mh.: 302). Cures for social and political wounds involved drastic action, such as cauterization or closure, or, for smaller wounds, simply time:

> Überlassen wir dann ruhig die Heilung unserer kleineren Wunden den mildernden Wirkungen der Zeit, wenn wir die größte auszubrennen und zu schließen vermögen. (*MK*: 757) [Then if we can cauterise and close the biggest wound, we can calmly leave the cure of our slighter wounds to the soothing effects of time. (Mh.: 609)]

3.4.3.2.4 Human Attributes and Capacities

The sophistication of human society puts human beings high above lower animals in the GREAT CHAIN. Humans rely less on their instinctive natures than do other animals, and they are able to develop their intellects and senses to a very high level, a faculty further aided by their ability to use language to exchange ideas and store knowledge.

The human ability to smell, taste and hear is shared with other animals, but humans are able to express their opinions about the things that they sense in this way. The embodied experiences of smells, tastes and noises may awaken strong feelings of a positive or negative nature, and it is such feelings that make sensual experiences suitable for metaphorization in general and for use as metaphors in political discourse in particular. Unpleasant tastes and smells were especially useful to a politician like Hitler, who disliked so many different categories of opponent, and in *MK* he applied the adjective *bitter* to a wide variety of objects and situations in *MK*. As usual, it was the Jews who were the most severely criticized group: they were accused of having invented an aesthetic *"Kulturparfüm"* [cultural perfume] (*MK*: 196; Mh.: 163), and of having a smell of foreignness about them ('den Geruch des allzu Fremden', *MK*: 346; Mh.: 286). Marc Weiner (1995) writes of the long-standing association of sulphurous smells with Jews, and of Wagner's depiction of Alberich as a *Schwefelgezwerg* ('sulphurous dwarf'): Hitler also refers to 'die Schwefeleien der Juden' [the drivel of the Jews] (*MK*: 336; Mh.: 278; cf. 'Schwefel und Pech', *MK*: 271). Religion was seen as having had an unpleasant taste *(Beigeschmack)* in Germany before the First World War (*MK*: 294; Mh.: 244), and the press was said to have poured drops of wormwood

(Wermuttropfen) on German enthusiasm at the beginning of the War (*MK*: 183; Mh.: 153). Unpleasant and pleasant noises are less common sources of metaphors in *MK*. Hitler writes of the noise made by the multitude of languages spoken in the Austrian parliament as a *Sprachentohuwabohu* [linguistic Babel] (*MK*: 39; Mh.: 35), and of the colours of the Nazi flag as being in harmony (*MK*: 555; Mh.: 451; App. III, A.2.13.3). Furthermore, the manner of speaking of the Jews was referred to as *radebrechen* (*MK*: 342; Mh.: 283) and *mauscheln* (*MK*: 342; Mh.: 283).

Human beings generally feel distaste for dirt on their bodies and in their surroundings; their preference for cleanliness may be used to metaphorize approval or disapproval (see App. III, A.2.11.9). Hitler accused the Jews, democracy, parliamentarians and the arts of dirtiness. In *MK,* Jews are declaimed as literally and metaphorically dirty: they are portrayed as people who hate washing ('keine Wasserliebhaber'), and as having moral stains 'moralische Schmutzflecken' (*MK*: 61; Mh.: 53). They are accused of besmirching their own history (*MK*: 65; Mh.: 56) and of pouring dirt over other, "cleaner", people from the 'Schmutzkübel niedrigster Verleumdungen und Ehrabschneidungen' [garbage pails full of the vilest slanders and defamations] (*MK*: 93; Mh.: 79). Jews are also accused of a damaging involvement in German democracy: 'Nur der Jude kann eine Einrichtung preisen, die schmutzig und unwahr ist wie er selber' [Only the Jew can praise an institution which is as dirty and false as he himself] (*MK*: 99; Mh.: 83), while the term *Abschaum* ('scum') refers to revolutionaries, whom Hitler believed were controlled by Jews (*MK*: 583; Mh.: 474). Democracy is heaped with similar scorn. Quoting from Goethe's *Faust*, Hitler calls it a „Spottgeburt aus Dreck und Feuer" [monstrosity of excrement and fire] (*MK*: 85; Mh.: 72), and he denounces bourgeois politicians for wallowing in the 'Korruptionsschlamm der Republik' [muck of republican corruption] (*MK*: 592; Mh.: 481). A rare mention of cleanliness takes the form of an ironic reference to the 'sprichwörtliche Sauberkeit der deutschen Verwaltung' [proverbial incorruptibility of the German administration] (*MK*: 305; Mh.: 253).

3.4.3.2.5 Human Society and Culture

Human Relationships and Rituals
Within the GREAT CHAIN, human kith and kin relationship systems, and rituals such as baptism, marriage and burial are seen as specifically human characteristics and therefore of a higher order. It could be argued that animals form binding relationships, but these are not as sophisticated as human relationships, nor do they enjoy the same official recognition.

Within the family, parents are the progenitors of future generations and tend to take on the role of protectors and rule-makers. Hitler metaphorizes mothers and fathers in a conventional manner in *MK*: a country can be a mother or a father (see App. III, A.2.11.1), and a colony (America) is regarded as the child of an originally more powerful parent. The more important parent is usually the father, and Hitler refers to the German *Reich* as the 'Vaterhaus' (*MK*: 136; Mh.: 114). The *Bruderzwist* [fratricidal quarrel] between Prussia and Austria (*MK*: 572; Mh.: 466) is reminiscent of the biblical quarrel between Cain and Abel in the Book of Genesis, also used as a source domain in *MK* (583; Mh.: 474; cf. Musolff 2004: 13–19 on FAMILY scenarios).

Human courtship and coupling are seen as a type of complex, higher-order behaviour which sets humans above animals. In *MK*, Hitler portrays his attempts to win the hearts of the German population for National Socialism as wooing *(werben, Bewerbung)* (see App. III, A.2.11.2). Failed attempts to recruit soldiers to defend the '„antimilitaristische" Republik' ['anti-militaristic' Republic] during its infancy are portrayed as 'vergebliche Liebesmühe' [love's labour lost] (*MK*: 584; Mh.: 475). *Liebeswerbung* and *Buhlen* (both meaning 'courting') are also used in a negative sense, described with the adjective *jämmerlich* ('miserable'), to refer to the political methods of Social Democracy (*MK*: 39f.; Mh.: 36). The institution of marriage may metaphorize either positive or negative situations in *MK*. On one occasion it is portrayed as an 'intimate coupling' ('innige Vermählung') of nationalism and social justice (*MK*: 474f.; Mh.: 388); elsewhere it represents political corruption: 'für einen Ministerstuhl gingen sie wohl auch die Ehe mit dem Teufel ein' [for a minister's chair they would even enter into marriage with the devil] (*MK*: 294; Mh.: 244). Baptism, too, is used in a negative sense to signify a "baptism of fire" *(Feuertaufe)* (App. III, A.2.11.3).

The human means of dealing with death involve ritual, such as funerals and burials. These mark humans out as superior to other animals, who have no conception of death. Metaphors associated with funerals tend to describe disagreeable events and situations in *MK* (App. III, A.2.11.5): the *Reichstag* is condemned as the 'Totengräber der deutschen Nation' [gravedigger of the German nation] (*MK*: 297; Mh.: 246) and the bourgeois political parties are derided for wanting to attend Germany's *Leichenschmaus* [funeral feast] (*MK*: 774; Mh.: 622). Supporters of a federal Germany are portrayed as having dug the ideal's own grave: 'Indem der föderative Gedanke solcherart belastet wurde, schaufelten ihm seine eigenen Anhänger das Grab' [By thus compromising the federative idea, its own supporters were digging its grave] (*MK*: 627; Mh.: 510).

Politics
Within the metaphorical category of POLITICS IS WAR, nations can be seen as composed of armies led by political commanders; the ideas and policies of these nations are their weapons, and their political goal is victory (Kövecses: 62). When he wrote *MK*, Hitler already saw his own political struggle in terms of *Kampf* (cf. Chapter 2.3.6). The metaphorization of politics as war is commonly exemplified with reference to Clausewitz's famous assertion that war is simply the continuation of politics by other means: 'Der Krieg ist eine bloße Fortsetzung der Politik mit anderen Mitteln' (Clausewitz, *Vom Kriege*, Book 1, Section 24). Hitler, who quotes from Clausewitz in *MK*, must have been familiar with this statement. In *MK*, wars between political leaders, between cultures, and between the holders of philosophical, social and religious points of view are rendered as wars and as campaigns and battles within wars, e.g.: *Kriegserklärung* ('declaration of war'), *Lügenfeldzug*, *Pressefeldzug* ('campaign of lies' and 'press campaign') and *Redeschlacht* ('battle of words'). The "battles" are fought with various types of metaphorical weapon: *(geistige) Waffe* ('(spiritual or intellectual) weapon'), *Schwert* ('sword'), *Speer* ('spear'), *Dolch* ('dagger'), and *Ramme* ('battering-ram').

The aggressive tone of *MK* seems to suggest that Hitler saw his political career as a battle or as a sequence of battles within a war, as yet metaphorical. It was a war fought with love: **'Und kämpfen kann ich nur für etwas, das ich liebe, lieben nur, was ich achte, und achten, was ich mindestens**

kenne' *[And I can only fight for something that I love, love only what I respect, and respect only what I at least know]* (*MK*: 34f.; Mh.: 31). When Hitler writes of his political efforts in terms of a war, the line between metaphor and literality sometimes becomes blurred: often it seems as though Hitler sees his very existence as imbued with war, including real battles instigated by his *"Ordnertruppe"*.

Propaganda was a major weapon of Hitler's "war" of the 1920s and 1930s, and *MK* is primarily a work of propaganda, steeped in martial vocabulary and brutal images:

> **Die Propaganda bearbeitet die Gesamtheit im Sinne einer Idee und macht sie reif für die Zeit des Sieges dieser Idee, während die Organisation den Sieg erficht durch den dauernden, organischen und kampffähigen Zusammenschluß derjenigen Anhänger, die fähig und gewillt erscheinen, den Kampf für den Sieg zu führen.** (*MK*: 653) [*Propaganda works on the general public from the standpoint of an idea and makes them ripe for the victory of this idea, while the organisation achieves victory by the persistent, organic, and militant union of those supporters who seem willing and able to carry on the fight for victory.* (Mh.: 530)]

In *MK*, Hitler stresses the importance of formulating a declaration of war against the existing social and political order: 'die Formulierung einer Kriegserklärung gegen eine bestehende Ordnung' (*MK*: 508; Mh.: 414). Whether literally or metaphorically, Hitler saw life and biological selection as a battle for existence *(Existenzkampf, Lebenskampf, Kampf ums Dasein)* (*MK*: 312f.; Mh.: 259). His political philosophy, backed by the NS movement, was to fight a battle for the Aryan race and thus for Germany. The outcome of Hitler's political programme would be a literal battle for German lebensraum and freedom from subjugation by her enemies. Any physical force would be supported by 'alle Waffen, die menschlicher Geist, Verstand und Wille zu erfassen vermögen' [all weapons which the human spirit, reason, and will can devise] *MK*: 68; Mh.: 59). Hitler's battle would be against Jews, Marxists, the press, and all enemies of German culture and society, a *(Kulturkampf, MK*: 128; 'cultural battle'). National Socialists were 'Verfechter einer neuen Weltanschauung' [champions of a new philosophy of life] (*MK*: 434; Mh.: 358), and the NS movement was seen as *kampfesfreudig* [militant] (*MK*: 658; Mh.: 533), *kampffähig* [capable of struggle] (*MK*: 513; Mh.: 418), and *kampfkräftig* [fighting] (*MK*: 508; Mh.: 414). In a broader sense, the NS fight was for freedom, human rights and progress; it was a *Klassenkampf* ('class war') (*MK*: 51), a *Lohnkampf* ('struggle over pay') and a *Tarifkampf* ('struggle over wage scales') (*MK*: 677). In order to achieve freedom for the German *Volk,* the movement would have to fight against parliamentary democracy, which Hitler saw as no more than a *Redeschlacht* [battle of words] (*MK*: 245; Mh.: 205). Economic independence and freedom from Jewish *"Finanzkapital"* also had to be won (*MK*: 233 and 257; Mh.: 194 and 214), and there was also a moral fight to be fought against sexually transmitted diseases (*MK*: 274 and 280; Mh.: 228 and 232). The consequences of not fighting would be appalling:

> Wird dieser Kampf aber aus Bequemlichkeit oder auch Feigheit nicht ausgefochten, dann möge man sich in 500 Jahren die Völker ansehen. (*MK*: 280) [But if out of smugness, or even cowardice, this battle is not fought to its end, then take a look at the peoples five hundred years from now. (Mh.: 233)]

Hitler's political warriors would need: 'bedingungslosen Glaubens, gepaart mit dem fanatischen Kampfesmut' [the persuasive force of absolute belief (...) coupled with a fanatical courage to fight] (*MK*: 414; Mh.: 343). Fighters appeared as *Kämpfer, Kämpe* ('knight'), *Bataillon* ('battalion'), *Heer* ('army'), *Phalanx, Ritter* ('knight'), *Soldat* ('soldier'), *Verfechter* ('champions'), and *Held(in)* ('hero(ine)'). Their duty was to attack their enemies, and to defend their ideas and their nation. National Socialism would be the **'junge sieghafte Idee'** [*young victorious idea*] (*MK*: 648; Mh.: 526) which would ensure a happy future for Germany and her people. A gigantic battle, a *Riesenkampf* (*MK*: 409), would be necessary to give life and strength to the new *Weltanschauung* of National Socialism. Victory would only be possible if the utmost brutality were exercised:

> **Wird der Sozialdemokratie eine Lehre von besserer Wahrhaftigkeit, aber gleicher Brutalität der Durchführung entgegengestellt**, wird diese siegen, wenn auch nach schwerstem Kampfe. (*MK*: 44f.) [*If Social Democracy is opposed by a doctrine of greater truth, but equal brutality of methods, the latter will conquer,* though this may require the bitterest struggle. (Mh.: 40)]

Germany's enemies were portrayed as cruel and ruthless, their actions being rendered by metaphors of destruction and devastation, such as *abdrosseln* ('to throttle'), *ersticken* ('to suffocate'), *fressen* ('to devour'), *anfressen* and *zerfressen* ('to corrode'), and *würgen* ('to strangle') (App. III, A.2.10). Hitler's most feared and hated enemies were the Jews, whom he attacked either explicitly or implicitly by reference to Marxists and the "Jewish" press (cf. Chapter 2.3.3 on the construction of a *"Feindbild"*). Germany is frequently portrayed as a victim *(Opfer)* in *MK*, with the Jew putting to sleep *(einschläfern)* (*MK*: 346; Mh. has 'lull': 286) or dissolving *(auflösen)* her people: 'Er wird dadurch „zum Ferment der Dekomposition" von Völkern und Rassen und im weiteren Sinne zum Auflöser der menschlichen Kultur' [He becomes 'a ferment of decomposition' among peoples and races, and in the broader sense a dissolver of human culture] (*MK*: 498; Mh.: 406). In particular, the Jew is portrayed in *MK* as fighting with poison against the German race and the fabric of German society (App. III, A.2.9):

> (...) er kämpft mit seinen Waffen, mit Lüge und Verleumdung, Vergiftung und Zersetzung, den Kampf steigernd bis zur blutigen Ausrottung der ihm verhaßten Gegner. (*MK*: 751) [(...) he fights with his weapons, with lies and slander, poison and corruption, intensifying the struggle to the point of bloodily exterminating his hated foes. (Mh.: 604)]

Jews are seen as 'internationale Vergifter' [international poisoners] (*MK*: 372; Mh.: 307) and 'Volksvergifter' (*MK*: 185; Mh.: 155), as they were in nineteenth-century anti-Semitic literature (Cobet 1973). They are accused of poisoning Aryan blood through intermarriage *(Blut(s)vergiftung)* (*MK*: 270 and 316; Mh.: 225 and 262). Similarly, Marxists are mentioned as poisoners of the world and Germany with the 'Leichengift marxistischer Vorstellungen' [the deadly poison of Marxist ideas] (*MK*: 361; Mh.: 298), and the press and the arts are depicted as pouring bucketfuls of poison into the *Volk*, watched by the bourgeoisie who complain about the decline of moral standards:

> Sie sieht, wie im Theater und Kino, in Schundliteratur und Schmutzpresse Tag für Tag das Gift kübelweise in das Volk hineingeschüttet wird (...) (*MK*: 34) [Day by day, in the theatre and in the movies, in backstairs literature and the yellow press, they see the poison poured into the people by bucketfuls (...) (Mh.: 31)]

Enemy propaganda is labelled *Giftpropaganda* and *Vergiftungspropaganda* (*MK*: 212 and 519; Mh.: 176 and 422). Any type of poison must be countered with *Gegengift* [an antidote] (*MK*: 371; Mh.: 306), and a defending party must learn 'gegen Giftgas mit Giftgas zu kämpfen' [to combat poison gas with poison gas] (*MK*: 46; Mh.: 41). The Weimar Republic is portrayed in *MK* as a *Sklavenkolonie* [slave colony] (*MK*: 640; Mh.: 520) suffering under the terms of 'Entwaffnungs- und Versklavungsedikte' [edicts of disarmament (...) edicts of enslavement, i.e. the Treaty of Versailles and the Dawes Plan] (*MK*: 639 and 762; Mh.: 520 and 612). Germans who allow themselves to be subjugated and pull others down with them are accused of dragging others into an abyss (*in den Abgrund reißen/zerren*, see App. III, B.2.1.3.1.9).

The War of the Races
Hitler's views on racial hierarchy have already been explored in Chapter 2.3.5. From this exploration one might deduce that, had Hitler been asked to explain the GREAT CHAIN OF BEING, he would have placed Aryans above Jews and close to God. The notion of a GREAT CHAIN OF BEING as a philosophical concept dating back to neo-Platonism was, of course, not itself a direct influence on Hitler's use of metaphorical expressions. Possibly a more important feature of Hitler's *Weltanschauung*, which had a bearing on his choice of metaphors, was that he saw Nature as involved in a perpetual struggle between species and races, in which the weaker would succumb to the stronger. This is where metaphors of movement and location, such as IMPORTANCE IS UP and PROGRESS IS MOVEMENT UPWARDS, merge with the GREAT CHAIN (see Section 3.4.2 above). As the highest, as Hitler claimed, of the high-level living beings, the Aryan rose to supremacy because he could make lower races work for him (*MK*: 323; Mh.: 268). The lower races are depersonalized as the Aryans' first technical instruments ('das erste technische Instrument im Dienste einer werdenden Kultur' (*MK*: 323f.; Mh.: 268; App. III, A.2.8). In general, however, it is the Jews that we hear of as having subjugated, or having tried to subjugate, other races. Hitler frequently portrays Jews and Marxists as the imprisoners and enslavers of Germany and other nations, especially Russia (App. III, A.2.8); this is the 'internationale Völkerversklavung' [international enslavement of peoples] which he blames chiefly on the Jews (*MK*: 738; Mh.: 595). The Jews are shown as forcing Germany into the 'Sklavenlos einer dauernden Unterjochung' [slave's lot of permanent subjugation] (*MK*: 358; Mh.: 296); Hitler writes of the 'Joch der

Sklaverei' [yoke of slavery] (*MK*: 195; Mh.: 163) as the most 'unbeautiful thing there can be in human life'. In *MK*, Hitler promises to fight personally on Germany's behalf against Jews, a battle which he saw as God's work: **'Indem ich mich des Juden erwehre, kämpfe ich für das Werk des Herrn'** *[by defending myself against the Jew, I am fighting for the work of the Lord]* (*MK*: 70; Mh.: 60).

As a superior race, Aryans, according to Hitler, had the right, indeed the duty, to improve their own racial stock. Jews, on the other, hand, as a discrete race, should not attempt to improve their race by intermarriage with Aryans. Clauses eight and nine of the statutes of the *Alldeutscher Verband*, which must have influenced Hitler either directly or indirectly, read as follows:

> 8) planmäßige rassische Höherentwicklung des deutschen Volkes durch Auslese und Förderung aller im Sinn guter deutscher Art hervorragend Begabten;
> 9) Bekämpfung aller Kräfte, welche die völkische Entwicklung des deutschen Volks hemmen oder ihr schaden, insbesondere Fremdensucht und der auf fast allen staatlichen, wirtschaftlichen und kulturellen Gebieten bestehenden jüdischen Vorherrschaft. (*Alldeutscher Blätter*, 1919, 29: 310) (8. planned racial progression of the German *Volk* by means of the selection and encouragement of those who are superbly gifted in the good German sense;
> 9. the fight against all forces that hamper or harm the folkish development of the German *Volk*, especially xenophilia and the Jewish hegemony which is evident in all areas of culture, business and the State.)

The coupling of these two recommendations could have served to justify racial conflict for any early twentieth century anti-Semite who sought vindication and supported Hitler's war-cry against "inferior" races (see also *Artifacts and technologies* below on genetic metaphors).

Sports and Games
Similar to POLITICS IS WAR are the metaphors POLITICS IS A HUNT, POLITICS IS A GAME and POLITICS IS A RACE. A hunt is similar to a war insofar as similar tactics are used ('entrapment, lying in wait, chasing') and similar goals are set ('defeat, slaughter'). In *MK* the German nation was portrayed as the prey *(Beute)* of its enemies, especially of Jews and Communists (see App. III, A.2.14.7), and the enemies were metaphorized as wolves or packs of hounds *(Meute)*, as in the 'jüdische Pressemeute' [the wolves of the Jewish press] (*MK*: 544; Mh.: 442). The Jews are depicted holding out a limed twig

to ensnare the German simpleton ('wobei so mancher gute deutsche Gimpel dem Juden bereitwilligst auf die hingehaltene Leimrute flog') (*MK*: 706; Mh.: 571).

Competition, sport and gambling are akin to war. Raymond Gibbs demonstrates how sporting metaphors may be used to describe politics as a rule-governed contest between two opponents, that is within a two-party political system seen as fielding opposing teams (Gibbs 1994: 140). Dealings and negotiations, such as political and business affairs, have been commonly metaphorized as games since the eighteenth century (Spalding: 2297), and such metaphors were also favoured by Hitler (see App. III, A.2.14). In *MK*, he portrays Ernst Pöhner as willing to take personal risks ('seine persönliche Existenz aufs Spiel setzen') in order to save the German people (*MK*: 403; Mh.: 333). He dismisses parliamentary dealings as a *Gaukelspiel* [jugglery] (*MK*: 413; Mh.: 342), and describes France as a *Tummelplatz* [playground] for hordes of Negroes (*MK*: 711; Mh. has 'hunting ground': 574). The unpredictable aspects of politics are seen as a game of dice, in many ways out of human control (App. III, A.2.14.2). Other types of games depend upon human intelligence or strength for a positive outcome. Hitler likens Europe to a chessboard ('dem allgemeinen europäischen Schachbrett', *MK*: 716; Mh.: 578) upon which Germany would have to win the right to play. The sporting competitions of ancient Greece are evoked in images of pace-setters (*Schrittmacher*; translated by Mh. as those who 'open the way' or 'prepare the way'), marathon-runners and winners of laurel wreaths:

> Freilich sind die Großen nur die Marathonläufer der Geschichte; der Lorbeerkranz der Gegenwart berührt nur mehr die Schläfen des sterbenden Helden. (*MK*, 232) [To be sure, these great men are only the Marathon runners of history; the laurel wreath of the present touches only the brow of the dying hero. (Mh.: 193)]

Hitler belittles the efforts of his political opponents and of the bourgeoisie by likening them to players of card-games or members of insignificant clubs such as a 'literarischer Teeklub' [literary tea-club], a 'spießbürgerliche Kegelgesellschaft' [shopkeepers' bowling society], a 'gähnender Kartenspielklub' [yawning bridge club] or a 'bürgerlicher Träträklub' (*MK*: 378, 538 and 392; Mh.: 312 and 437, the final example is not found in Mh.'s translation of the first edition of *MK*[5]). Hitler also uses two bull-fighting metaphors as negative epithets: 'bürgerliche Verleumdungstoreadore' [bourgeois meeting-hall toreadors] (*MK*: 548; Mh.: 445) and 'die Matadoren der Revolution' [the matadors of the revolution] (*MK*: 584; Mh.: 475).

Commercial and Legal Metaphors
For human societies to function, more or less sophisticated organisations have to be formed, of which mechanisms for trade and commerce are vital. This has led to the establishing of a set of source domains for metaphors, the most significant of these being associated with money (see App. III, A.2.16). Low monetary denominations, such as the *Heller* and *Groschen*, may symbolize poverty, whereas treasure *(Schatz)* frequently symbolizes an object or situation which is highly valued, like the certificates of racial origin that Hitler called 'ein kostbarer höchster Schatz des Volksganzen' [a precious national treasure to the entire nation] (*MK*: 449; Mh.: 368). The payment of a particular price *(Quittung, Preis)* for an object is used in political discourse to metaphorize unfavourable results of a transaction or situation, as in the following quotation from *MK*:

> Immer dann, wenn Völker in ihrer militärischen Niederlage die Quittung für ihre innere Fäulnis, Feigheit, Charakterlosigkeit, kurz Unwürdigkeit erhalten. (*MK*: 250) [(...) always, when military defeat is the payment meted out to peoples for their inner rottenness, cowardice, lack of character, in short, unworthiness. (Mh.: 209)]

One may also receive a bitter reward *(Lohn, Lehrgeld)*, or a matter may be put on one's bill *(Schuldkonto)* if one is at fault. A person, a State, or a race may be sold out *(verkauft)* by its enemies (*MK*: 607; Mh.: 494), but a movement may have the monopoly on a good idea, just as the NS movement laid claim to the folkish philosophy: **'Nicht nur gepachtet, sondern für die Praxis geschaffen'** [*Not only a monopoly, but a working monopoly*] (*MK*: 515; Mh.: 419). The common metaphor of cattle-trading (*Kuhhandel*, translated by Mh. with the English metaphor 'horse-trading') provides another pejorative image

---

[5] Pechau documents *Träräklub* for the 6th edition of 1930 (p. 93). The word is supposedly an onomatopoeic representation of the sound of a trumpet and intended to trivialize the activity of the "club" by using "baby-talk".

of parliamentary dealings (*MK*: 414f.; *Mh*.: 343). There are few legal metaphors in *MK* and these are recorded along with the metaphor *Schule* in App. III, A.2.12. This is perhaps surprising if one considers Hitler's view of himself as the bringer of justice to an unjust world.

3.4.3.2.6 Artifacts and Technologies

One of the characteristics that puts humans above other animals in the GREAT CHAIN is their ability to make use of the objects in the world around them, to train animals to work for them, to invent and form objects from inert materials, to create artifacts, and to farm the resources of the world for their own benefit. Human beings organize themselves into societies and share the objects that they create. They live together in households and share public spaces where they meet for social purposes and display or exchange the material objects that are of value to them. This section will illustrate the way in which such results of human creative abilities are metaphorized in political discourse as exemplified in *MK*.

The Arts

The human ability to produce works of art for pure enjoyment is perhaps the highest of the higher-order capacities which differentiate humans from other beings. In order to produce art of any type we make use of one or more sophisticated faculties, such as our ability to use language, our manual dexterity, our imaginations and our general intellect. Hitler used metaphors from a number of fields of art, although, surprisingly when one considers his view of himself as an artist, not in great quantities. The connection between literary characters and metaphor has been introduced in Section 3.2.5. above. Like myths and mythological figures, literary characters and stories help human beings to categorize the world they live in. Myth originated in preliterate times and literature later, but both belong to the realm of human creations and thus the GREAT CHAIN OF BEING. Hitler used figures from legend, brought to life in medieval literature, as examples of pure and honourable Germans. He also quoted from great German authors, most notably Goethe and Schiller. Such literary references, recorded in App. III, A.2.13.1, would have appealed to any reader who had enjoyed a good, basic education. Hitler also made use of music, the plastic arts and the theatre. Perhaps the most conventional of his political metaphors were the references to political situations and parliamentary activities as plays: 'Verhandlungskomödien' [comic-opera negotiations] and 'dieses entwürdigende Schauspiel', [this degrading spectacle] *MK*: 770; Mh.: 619), and 'jämmerliches Schauspiel' [lamentable comedy] (*MK*: 83; Mh.: 71). In a less conventional vein, Hitler depicts countries as mosaics; in the following quotation he develops a small tableau to illustrate the danger in which the Austrian mosaic found itself before the First World War:

> Österreich war damals wie ein altes Mosaikbild, dessen Kitt, der die einzelnen Steinchen zusammenbindet, alt und bröcklig geworden; solange das Kunstwerk nicht berührt wird, vermag es noch sein Dasein weiter vorzutäuschen, sowie es jedoch einen Stoß erhält, bricht es in tausend Scherbchen auseinander. (*MK*: 135) [Austria was then like an old mosaic; the cement, binding the various little stones together, had grown old and begun to crumble; as long as the work of art is not touched, it can continue to give a show of existence, but as soon as it receives a blow, it breaks into a thousand fragments. (Mh.: 113)]

One might have expected that Hitler, as a lover of music, would have made greater use than he did of metaphors taken from the field of music, but those he used were quite commonplace such as: *Intermezzo*, *Virtuosin* and *Akkord* (harmony) (see App. III, A.2.13.3); *Tanz*, *Komödie* and *Schauspiel* also appear in conventional senses (App. III, A.2.13.5/6).

Clothing

A significant aspect of human thinking and behaviour is the perceived need for clothing and the ability of people to clothe themselves. Both of these aspects of clothing are higher-order behaviours, as is the shame felt at nakedness. In both English and German the adjective *nackt* ('naked') has long been used as a metaphor for something blatant or undisguised, usually in a negative sense. Examples from *MK* include: 'nackter Vaterlandsverrat' [naked treason] (*MK*: 780; Mh.: 626), 'mit der Waffe der nackten Gewalt' [with the weapons of naked force] (*MK*: 188; Mh.: 157), and 'nackter Egoismus' [naked egoism] (*MK*: 331; Mh.: 274). Similarly, Russia is depicted as divested of its

Germanic upper class, 'seiner germanischen Oberschicht entkleidet' (*MK*: 748; Mh.: 602).

Clothes function as metaphors in a variety of ways, and Hitler uses a number of chiefly conventional clothing metaphors in *MK*. The most important aspect of clothing is its protective function. Clothes protect our modesty and protect us from cold; they may also be used to proclaim our identity or to hide it. Hitler's favourite clothing metaphors are the coat or cloak *(Mantel)* and the veil *(Schleier)*. Jews are accused of hiding themselves under various cloaks, such as social ideas and war societies; swindlers hide themselves under the *Schutzmantel* ('protective cloak') of anonymity; and prudes cover themselves in a saint's cloak *(Heiligenmantel)* (see App. III, A.2.11.6). Tyranny is accused of hiding itself in the 'Mäntelchen einer sogenannten „Legalität"' [cloak of so-called 'legality'] (*MK*: 105; Mh.: 89), and Social Democrats hide under the veil of erroneous conceptions ('die Schleier irriger Vorstellungen' *MK*: 54; Mh.: 47). Nature is excused her hidden mysteries, although mankind has always tried to understand these:

> (...) daß der Mensch die Natur noch in keiner Sache überwunden hat, sondern höchstens das eine oder andere Zipfelchen ihres ungeheuren, riesenhaften Schleiers von ewigen Rätseln und Geheimnissen erwischte und emporzuheben versuchte (...) (*MK*: 314) [(...) that man has never yet conquered Nature in anything, but at the most has caught hold of and tried to lift one or another corner of her immense gigantic veil of eternal riddles and secrets (...) (Mh.: 261)]

Futhermore, politicians are blamed of hiding behind the skirts *(Rockschößen)* of democracy (*MK*: 554 and 89; Mh.: 450 and 75), and kid gloves *(Glacéhandschuhe)* are considered too soft to perform actions which will alter the destinies of nations (*MK*: 773; Mh.: 621). As well as functioning to protect and hide, clothes can be used to assist in the adoption of a false identity, as in the following instance:

> Wie leicht es einer Tyrannei aber ist, sich das Mäntelchen einer sogenannten „Legalität" umzuhängen, zeigte wieder am klarsten und eindringlichsten das Beispiel Österreichs. (*MK*: 105) [How easy it is to cover itself with the cloak of so-called 'legality' is shown most clearly and penetratingly by the example of Austria. (Mh.: 89)]

Science and Technology

According to Cornelia Schmitz-Berning, Hitler used very few metaphors from the field of technology in *MK*. She claims that it was Goebbels who later developed the technical metaphors which are now seen as a speciality of NS discourse, and that it was he who was thus responsible for the 'Technisierung des Menschen' (technologization of mankind) (Berning 1962: 111). Human beings were, however, depersonified in *MK* as non-living entities under the control of other humans. Nouns referring to human beings as non-human entities include *Maschine*, *Mechanismus* and *Instrument*, which also occur as the second element of compound nouns, e.g. 'jüdische Welteroberungs-*maschine*' [Jewish machine for world conquest] (*MK*: 528; Mh.: 429), 'Massenerziehungs*maschine*' [machine for educating the masses = the press] (*MK*: 93), 'Rasse*bestandteile*' (*MK*: 437), 'Misch*produkt*' (*MK*: 443) (App. III, A.2.17.1.2). Substances invented by humans and used in their technologies include *Extrakt* and *Stoff* (App. III, A.2.17.1.1). A particularly odious example is that of the Jewish *Schleudermaschine* ('centrifuge') which is portrayed as splashing filth over humanity (*MK*: 62; Mh.: 54; Mh. adds to the image by translating *Schleudermaschine* as 'garbage separator'). The State is described as a 'Monstrum von menschlichem Mechanismus' [monstrosity of human mechanism] (*MK*: 425f.; Mh.: 351); it is at risk from becoming 'volksfremd' ('alien to the people') when it should be a 'völkischer Organismus' [national organism] (*MK*: 362; Mh.: 299). As a mechanism has no life in it, it cannot spread a superior *Weltanschauung* to its people:

> Aus einem toten Mechanismus, der nur um seiner selbst willen da zu sein beansprucht, soll eine lebendiger Organismus geformt werden mit dem ausschließlichen Zwecke: einer höheren Idee zu dienen. (*MK*: 439) [From a dead mechanism which only lays claim to existence for its own sake, there must be formed a living organism with the exclusive aim of serving a higher idea. (Mh.: 362)]

A variety of scientific and mechanical processes is recorded in Sections A.2.17.2 and A.2.17.3. Human beings can be sifted *(sieben)* according to their capacities and knowledge, and political views can be hammered *(einhämmern)*, drilled *(eindrillen)*, funnelled or pumped into them *(eintrichtern, einpumpen)* (cf. container metaphors above); people can be pinned down *(festnageln)* and their destinies forged together *(aneinanderschmieden)*; popular opinion can be kneaded *(kneten)*; a *Volksseele* (soul of the people) can boil *(kochen)*, and an audience can be electrified *(elektrisieren)*. Races, social and political groups and coalitions can be brewed *(zusammenbrauen)* or fused together in a number of ways *(zusammenkleistern, zusammenschmelzen, zusammenschweißen)*, ideas can be moulded and re-moulded *(umgießen)*, and an electrical metaphor *(ausschalten*, literally 'to switch off') expresses the possibility of destroying or excluding certain concepts or groups of people. The N.S.D.A.P. "crystallized out" *(herauskristallisieren)* in 1920 (*MK*: 429; Mh.: 354) and its future of fighting for Germany had to begin with the forging of a sword, as in Wagner's *Siegfried*:

> **Dieses Schwertslime zu schmieden, ist die Aufgabe der innerpolitischen Leitung eines Volkes; die Schmiedearbeit zu sichern und Waffengenossen zu suchen, die Aufgabe der außenpolitischen.** (*MK*: 689) [*To forge this sword is the task of a country's internal political leadership; to safeguard the work of forging and seek comrades in arms is the function of diplomatic leadership.* (Mh.: 558)]

Genetics and Breeding

The scientific technologies associated with genetics and breeding furnish a vocabulary to describe the possible improvement of the Aryan race, an ambition for which Hitler and the National Socialists are well known (Berning 1963: 99; Schmitz-Berning 1998: 708). We may note here that Hitler made no recommendations for improving the Jewish "race" and that his main goal was to prevent Jews from contaminating Aryan blood through marriage. In *MK*, Hitler recommends that a pure breeding stock could be taken from the peasant classes as the basis for a strong, healthy race ('Ein fester Stock kleiner und mittlerer Bauern', *MK*: 151; Mh.: 126). This could then be bred selectively *(Höherzüchtung)* to improve its inherent physical and mental qualities (*MK*: 449; Mh.: 369). The result would be that the entire Aryan race would enjoy the blessing of being the highest of all human cultures, 'des Segens eines hochgezüchteten Rassengutes' [the blessing of a highly bred racial stock] (*MK*: 448; Mh.: 368).

Agriculture and Horticulture

Breeding is also an important aspect of horticultural science, and in *MK* Hitler writes of the *Propagierung* ('propagation') of a successful political party (*MK*: 656; Mh.: 532), and of the possibility of grafting *(aufpfropfen)* the "leader principle" on to the State organism *(Staatsorganismus)* (*MK*: 673; Mh.: 546; see App. III, A.2.19.3). We may also note lines 1–5 of Jahn's text (App. I, Text 2) in which he describes the *Volk* as a body *(Leib)*, likened in turn to a many-branched tree from which the branches can be separated with a knife ('ein vielgliedriger Leib, von dem sich nicht nach Beleiben durch das Trennmesser mehrere Leiblein ablegen lassen').

Agriculture involves the planting and reaping of crops and the care of food-producing animals. A variety of emotions and beliefs can be planted into *(eingepflanzt)* people's hearts and minds (*MK*: 524; Mh.: 425f.). Similarly an idea can be sown into a person or a society and later be reaped: 'Die heutige Gegenwart erntet nur, was die letzte Vergangenheit gesät hat' [The present time is only harvesting what the immediate past has sown] (*MK*: 292; Mh.: 242; App. III, A.2.19.1). Once plants are sown they have to be cared for, as does society, and Hitler uses a common image of "weeding out" any unwelcome growth, such as criminals: 'brutal und rücksichtslos die wilden Schößlinge herauszuschneiden, das Unkraut auszujäten' [brutally and ruthlessly to prune off the wild shoots and tear out the weeds] (*MK*: 30; Mh.: 28). Growth which is too rapid is as undesirable as weeds, and Hitler considers a hot-house *(Treibhaus)* a dangerous place, describing the public life of his day as akin to a 'Treibhaus sexueller Vorstellungen und Reize' [hothouse for sexual ideas and stimulations] (*MK*: 278; Mh.: 231). Hitler notes in *MK* that political parties which accept compromises or mergers are unlikely to enjoy success. He likens such movements to hot-house plants *(Treibhauspflanzen)*: 'Sie schießen empor, allein ihnen fehlt die Kraft, Jahrhunderten zu trotzen und schweren Stürmen zu widerstehen' [They shoot up, but they lack the strength to defy the centuries and withstand heavy storms] (*MK*: 385; Mh.: 318). Furthermore, the growth of valuable plants can be impeded by weeds, which must be torn out as soon as they are seen. Similarly, weak and degenerate people must be removed from society as soon as the nation can put past guilt aside in order to 'brutal und rücksichtslos die wilden Schößlinge herauszuschneiden, das Unkraut auszujäten' [brutally and ruthlessly (...) prune off the wild shoots and tear out the weeds] (*MK*: 30; Mh.: 28). The verb *überwuchern* ('to choke out, run riot') is also used to metaphorize unwelcome situations (*MK*: 114f. and 168; Mh.: 96 and 140).

Fields which bear crops must also be fertilized and occasionally left to lie fallow. Hitler uses both of these images (App. III, A.2.19.1), although his use of the terms *Dünger* ('fertilizer, dung') and *Mist* ('manure') are pejorative, referring to non-Germans or non-Aryans whom he accuses of using these selfishly rather than for the common good:

> (...) ja, manchmal ist seine Wohltat wirklich nur mit dem Dünger zu vergleichen, der auch nicht aus Liebe zum Feld auf dieses gestreut wird, sondern aus Voraussicht für das spätere eigene Wohl. (*MK*: 344) [(...) sometimes, indeed, his charity is really comparable to fertilizer, which is not strewn on the field for love of the field, but with a view to the farmer's own future benefit. (Mh.: 285)]

The plough is an important symbol for Hitler, standing as a metonymy for "farming" and the "farmers" who will be responsible for building a new Germany once new land has been won by the sword (*MK*: 743; Mh.: 598f.; cf. *Scholle* ('the sod') as a metonymy for 'agriculture', *MK*.: 25; Mh.: 24).

The *Futterkrippe* or *Futtertrog* (both meaning 'feeding-trough') is perhaps Hitler's most striking metaphor from the field of animal husbandry. He portrays potentially "heroic" and despotic political parties as abandoning their struggle for a *Weltanschauung* due to the narrowness of their programmes. Instead they seek a place at the 'Futtertrog bestehender Einrichtungen' [feeding-trough of existing institutions] (*MK*: 507; Mh. 413); once there, they try to push rivals aside to secure their own position 'um endlich, koste es auch ihre heiligste Überzeugung, sich an der geliebten Nährquelle laben zu können' [even at the cost of their holy conviction, towards refreshing themselves at the beloved swill pail] (*MK*: 507f.; Mh. 414). A further interesting image from the field of animal farming is that of Marxists cackling in excitement before their plans had taken any kind of shape:

> Sie konnten nicht dicht halten, wenn sie so etwas ausgebrütet hatten, und zwar pflegten sie meistens schon zu gackern, ehe noch das Ei gelegt war. (*MK*: 545) [They couldn't keep it to themselves when they hatched out such a plan, and as a rule they began to cackle even before the egg was laid. (Mh.: 442)]

Other, more conventional metaphors associated with animal husbandry include 'parliamentary cattle-trading' *(Kuhhandel, MK*: 414; Mh.: 343); the 'blinkers' *(Scheuklappen)* worn by Hitler during his petit-bourgeois upbringing (*MK*: 22;

Mh.: 22); and the 'pigsty' *(Saustall)* over which Kurt Eisner presided for a short while in Bavaria before Hitler's appointment as an Education Officer (*MK*: 235; Mh.: 196).

Household Objects and Tools
Many dead metaphors and common idioms have furniture as their source domains, e.g. the idioms *zwischen zwei Stühlen sitzen* ('to fall between two stools') and *(sich an einen) Tisch setzen mit jemandem* ('to sit down at the table with somebody'). Items of furniture do not, however, occur commonly as metaphors in *MK*. As far as specific machines and tools are concerned, Hitler's metaphors are also generally conventional. Fate had its scales *(Waagschale)* and a hammer; progress was portrayed as the climbing of a ladder *(Leiter)*; and human opinion was said to swing back and forth like a pendulum *(Pendel)*. As tools do not have wills, they made a very useful source domain with which Hitler could denigrate Jews: 'Er sieht die heutigen europäischen Staaten bereits als willenlose Werkzeuge in seiner Faust' [He already sees the present-day European states as will-less tools in his fist] (*MK*: 723; Mh.: 583).

3.4.3.3 *Zoological metaphors*

Non-human living creatures follow human beings within the hierarchy of the GREAT CHAIN OF BEING. Their attributes and behaviour are considered to be of a lower order, even though it is widely recognized that their instincts are more highly developed than those of human beings. Within the animal world there is a hierarchy based on the anatomical complexity and (often corresponding) size of the animal. A monkey, for example, is obviously more intelligent than a fish. The difference in intellect between a fish and a snake is, however, less apparent. Animals are popular sources of metaphors in European languages, and nowhere more so than in German (cf. Rash 1993: 607–609 on animal epithets).

Within the GREAT CHAIN, monkeys and apes are seen as closest to human beings; in evolutionary terms they are considered to be our closest relatives. This has led racists to use them as metaphorical sources for the portrayal of certain groups of people as sub-human. In *MK*, Hitler portrays Jews as **'Mißgeburten zwischen Mensch und Affe'** *[monstrosities halfway between man and ape]* (*MK*, pp. 445; Mh., pp. 366). He condemns it as criminal lunacy ('ein verbrecherischer Wahnsinn') to drill 'Hottentotten und Zulukaffern' to take on high-level professions: 'einen geborenen Halbaffen so lange zu dressieren, bis man glaubt, aus ihm einen Advokat gemacht zu haben' [to keep drilling a born half-ape until people think they have made a lawyer out of him] (*MK*, p. 479; Mh., p. 391).

In adversarial discourse, many other animals are employed as metaphors for the dehumanization of human beings. Donkeys are typically stubborn, lazy and stupid, sheep patient and stupid, foxes sly, bees hard-working, dogs eager to please their masters, geese noisy, and so on. Humans are liable to be likened to all of these animals if they exhibit these characteristics. In *MK*, Hitler uses a varied selection of mostly conventional animal images for the purposes of dehumanization. His favoured targets for pejorative epithets using lower-order animals as source domains are politicians, the bourgeoisie, Marxists and Jews, the latter being represented most frequently by lower-order creatures such as snakes, spiders, leeches, parasites and bacteria. Unscrupulous people in general, and politicians in particular, may be portrayed as hyenas, wolves and jackals, which are generally considered less likeable than, for example, sheep and cattle. The former hunt in packs *(Rudel)* and are carnivorous, and the latter live in herds or flocks *(Herde)*; pack animals are generally metaphorized as more dangerous than herd animals. Hitler portrays the herd and the herd instinct *(Herdeninstinkt, Herdentrieb)* as potentially good or bad. It can be beneficial to live in a herd if one makes the most of the mutual support and protection that it provides, but a herd is easy to control and subjugate, a fact relied upon, in Hitler's opinion, by the Jews who prefer their opponents to be a 'morsche, unterjochungsfähige Herde' [rickety herd capable of being subjugated] (*MK*: 353; Mh.: 292). The "herd animal" is also derided in *MK* as a generally lower-level being, such as the 'Hammelherde von Hohlköpfen' [herd of sheep and blockheads] (*MK*: 86; Mh.: 73), and the 'Durchschnitt unserer parlamentarischen Politikaster und der großen stupiden Hammelherde unseres schafsgeduldigen Volkes' [the average parliamentary politicasters, and the great stupid sheep's herd of patient lamblike people] (*MK*: 685; Mh.: 555).

The fact that stronger animals hunt and kill weaker ones provides sources for some metaphors of particular value to political discourse, as, for example, when Hitler likens the predatory behaviour of cats to the natural instinct of the Marxist press to lie: 'ihnen ist das Lügen genau so Lebensnotwendigkeit wie der Katze das Mausen' [to them lying is just as vitally necessary as catching mice for a cat] (*MK*: 265; Mh.: 221). The strength and weakness of certain animals in comparison with others aid exemplification within the field of eugenics. Hitler believed that races should be kept pure and separate, so that superior traits could not be diluted by those of inferior races: 'Der Stärkere hat zu herrschen und sich nicht mit dem Schwächeren zu verschmelzen, um so die eigene Größe zu opfern' [The stronger must dominate and not blend with the weaker, thus sacrificing his own greatness]. He gives the cat and the fox as examples of natural enemies who will never have "humane" feelings for one another or intermix in any way (*MK*: 312; Mh.: 259). He explains that animals only mate with members of the same species, so human beings should follow their example and only marry people of the same race: Meise geht zu Meise, Fink zu Fink, der Storch zur Störchin, Feldmaus zu Feldmaus, Hausmaus zu Hausmaus, der Wolf zur Wölfin usw. [The titmouse seeks the titmouse, the finch the finch, the stork the stork, the field mouse the field mouse, the dormouse the dormouse, the wolf the she-wolf, etc.] (*MK*: 311; Mh.: 258). This argument depends, of course, on a deliberate conflation of species and race.

Certain animals fill human beings with particular revulsion, and Hitler often used them as source domains when writing about people and behaviour that he despised. In *MK,* he portrayed Jews as 'eine sich blutig bekämpfende Rotte von Ratten' [a horde of rats, fighting bloodily among themselves] (*MK*: 331; Mh.: 274); political opponents are depicted as rats eating the small amount of knowledge that the masses have learnt at school: 'Die Ratten der politischen Vergiftung unseres Volkes fressen auch dieses wenige aus dem Herzen und der Erinnerung der breiten Masse heraus' [The rats that politically poison our nation gnaw even this little from the heart and memory of the broad masses] (*MK*: 32; Mh.: 29).

Other animals are praised in *MK* for their innate superiority, such as the greyhound *(Windhund)*, a creature to be admired for its speed. Men with true military virtues would have to be: 'Flink wie Windhunde, zäh wie Leder und hart wie Kruppstahl' [swift as greyhounds, tough as leather, and hard as Krupp steel] (*MK*: 392; Mh.: 324). Hitler was to use this well-known series of similes in later speeches (Domarus I, 533).

The noises made by animals and birds may sound unpleasant to the human ear, such as the gabbling of geese, or be judged pointlessly effusive, such as the cackling of hens. Hitler likens parliamentarians to gabbling geese (*MK*: 57 and 245; Mh.: 50 and 205) and protesters' shouts to the cackling of hens in the following passage:

> Ich glaube, wenn ein Fuchs in einen Hühnerstall einbräche, könnte das Gegacker kaum ärger sein und das In-Sicherheit-Bringen des einzelnen Federviehs nicht beschleunigter erfolgen als das Ausreißen einer solchen prachtvollen „Protestvereinigung". (*MK*: 708) [I think if a fox were to break into a chicken-coop the cackling could hardly be worse, or the rush of the feathered fowl for safety any quicker, than the flight of such a splendid 'protest rally'. (Mh.: 572)]

Just as dogs may produce unpleasant and cowardly noises, pacifists and other enemies of the State can be heard whining *(Winseln)*, whimpering *(Flennen)* and yapping *(Gebell, Gekläff)* (*MK*: 438, 642, 757; Mh.: 360, 522, 609).

The snake is a lower-order creature within the GREAT CHAIN and has few admirers among the human race. Snakes have symbolized the devil in Germany since the Middle Ages and have been used as metaphors for dangerous, treacherous people since Luther's Bible translation. Christoph Cobet records the nineteenth-century use of *Schlangennatur* to refer to Jews. Snake metaphors are reserved chiefly for Jews in *MK* but are also used to refer to other enemies of the German *Volk*, such as Marxists and the press, which Hitler in any case considered to be run by Jews (App. III, B.1.3.9). Hitler's snakes are generally poisonous (*Viper, Kreuzotter, Natter*, all of which are designations for vipers), although he refers to Bolshevism as the 'Umstrickung dieser internationalen Schlange' [the snares of this international serpent] (*MK*: 751; Mh.: 605). The Jews are similarly metaphorized as octopuses which ensnare the entire earth (*MK*: 703; Mh.: 568).

Ornithological Metaphors
Hitler made use of an interesting array of ornithological metaphors in *MK* (App. III, B.1.3.7). Typical characteristics of a variety of birds stand as metaphors for similar human behaviour; thus an eagle soars higher than most

men's spirits (*MK*: 452; Mh.: 371), Germans are accused of hiding their heads in the sand like ostriches before their defeat in the First World War (*MK*: 250; Mh.: 209), revolutionaries are portrayed as sharp-clawed vultures (*Revolutionsgeier*, *MK*: 589; Mh.: 479), and parliamentary swindlers are less honest than the traditionally thieving magpie, who has no conception of property rights (*MK*: 707; Mh.: 571). People who try to base new political movements on ideas stolen from their comrades are likened to sparrows:

> Genau wie Sperlinge, die, scheinbar gänzlich uninteressiert, in Wirklichkeit aber dennoch, aufs äußerste gespannt, einen glücklichen Genossen, der ein Stückchen Brot gefunden hat, dauernd beobachten, um plötzlich in einem unbedachten Augenblick zu räubern, so auch diese Menschen. (*MK*: 574) [These people are just like sparrows who, apparently uninterested, but in reality more attentive, keep watching a more fortunate comrade who has found a piece of bread, in hopes of suddenly robbing him in an unguarded moment. (Mh.: 467)]

Geese are a common source of epithets for stupid people, usually women, in German as in English, and Hitler introduces the male *Gänserich* as a pejorative term for parliamentarians (*MK*: 57; Mh.: 50). The mating cry of a capercaillie ('(das) Balzen eines Auerhahns') denotes the behaviour of the press towards the royal court (*MK*: 57; Mh.: 50), and the swelling of a cock's comb is used as a metaphor for arrogant people (*MK*: 709; Mh.: 573). Birds' nests are treated as container metaphors under A STATE IS A BUILDING above.

Insects

A small selection of insects metaphorizes an assortment of chiefly negative human characteristics in *MK*. Drones *(Drohnen)* represent people who live off the efforts of others, as in English, and Hitler uses this metaphor for Jews and swindlers (*MK*: 165 and 400; Mh.: 138 and 331). An *Eintagsfliege* ('fly-by-night', literally 'a fly that only lives for one day') and a *Nachtfalter* (moth) are similarly used in a pejorative sense (*MK*: 562 and 400; Mh.: 457 and 330). Hitler also uses some rather less conventional images of caterpillars and butterflies when writing disparagingly of parliamentarians:

> Damit verwandelt sich der Volksmann und Kandidat der schaffenden Stände wieder in die parlamentarische Raupe und frißt sich am Gezweig des staatlichen Lebens weiter dick und fett, um sich nach vier Jahren wieder in den schillernden Schmetterling zu verwandeln. (*MK*: 412) [Thus, the man of the people and the candidate of the working

classes turns himself back into the parliamentary caterpillar and again fattens on the foliage of State life, and again after four years turns back into a gleaming butterfly. (Mh.: 341)]

In a rare positive insect metaphor, Hitler refers to his stormtroopers as a swarm of hornets ('Schwarm von Hornissen') swooping down on troublemakers at one of his meetings (*MK*: 551; Mh.: 447).

Blood-sucking Creatures, Parasites and Microscopic Organisms
As we descend through the hierarchy of THE GREAT CHAIN OF BEING we notice among the images used a higher proportion of metaphors referring to Jews. Blood-sucking creatures (App. III, B.1.3.11), parasites (App. III, B.1.3. –12) and microscopic organisms (App. III, B.1.3.13) appear in a number of guises, and are obviously intended to provoke revulsion in the reader. *Ungeziefer* is a general term for vermin and is used to metaphorize Jews (*MK*: 186; Mh.: 155). Blood-sucking creatures have been accorded a category of their own in App. III, B.1.3, although they are in fact parasitic. Only two instances of blood-sucking creatures quoted in B.1.3.11 do not refer to Jews, one the *Blutegel* ('leech'), and the other the *Parlamentswanze* ('parliamentary bedbug'); only one other parasite, a roundworm *(Spulwurm)*, does not refer to Jews. Cornelia Schmitz-Berning suggests that Herder first used the term *Parasit* to refer to Jews in 1787 (Schmitz-Berning 1998: 460), and Hitler readily adopted images of parasitism, claiming that the Jewish parasite had to be destroyed if its host were to survive, and that the Jews were intent on increasing their numbers: 'Sein Sich-Weiterverbreiten aber ist eine typische Erscheinung für alle Parasiten; er sucht immer neuen Boden für seine Rasse' [His spreading is a typical phenomenon for all parasites; he always seeks a new feeding ground for his race] (*MK*: 334; Mh.: 276). Such an expansion would have to be prevented if the Aryan race were to survive. The likening of the Jew to a maggot is one of the most disgusting images in both the original German and the English translation of *MK*:

Sowie man nur vorsichtig in eine solche Geschwulst hineinschnitt, fand man, wie die Made im faulenden Leibe, oft ganz geblendet vom plötzlichem Lichte, ein Jüdlein. (*MK*: 61) [If you cut even cautiously into such an abscess, you found, like a maggot in a rotting body, often dazzling with sudden light—a kike! (Mh.: 53)].

The bacillus is a type of bacterium discovered by Robert Koch in 1878. The term has been used to refer to vices since the early twentieth century, and most instances in *MK* refer to Jews. The following quotation illustrates the use of three related types of metaphor as derogatory designations for Jews in one sentence:

> Er ist und bleibt der typische Parasit, ein Schmarotzer, der wie ein schädlicher Bazillus sich immer mehr ausbreitet, sowie nur ein günstiger Nährboden dazu einlädt. (*MK*: 334)
> [He is and remains the typical parasite, a sponger who like a noxious bacillus keeps spreading as soon as a favourable medium invites him. (Mh.: 277)]

The danger for the hosts *(Wirtsvolk)* of such a "sponger" is that they inevitably die. Hitler also referred to Jews with the Germanic term for a bacterium, namely *Spaltpilz*, which is infelicitously translated by Mh. as 'mushroom': 'zwischen allem aber als ewiger Spaltpilz der Menschheit—Juden und wieder Juden' [and everywhere, the eternal mushroom of humanity—Jews and more Jews] (*MK*: 135; Mh.: 113).

3.4.3.4 *Botanical Metaphors*

Plants follow the lowest animal species in the GREAT CHAIN OF BEING and, like animals, they have their own internal hierarchy, with larger more complex organisms, such as trees, generally viewed as superior to herbs or grasses, in their turn superior to fungi or plankton. Plants are similar to animals in that they are organic and grow; they are different in that they are not conscious, sentient organisms. In App. III, metaphors associated with plant growth are recorded as botanical metaphors in Section B.1.4, and metaphors sourced from human intervention in plant growth are listed in Section A.2.19.3. The former are described below (Section 3.4.4.2) and the latter under **Human artifacts and technologies** above. The metaphor A STATE IS A PLANT, according to which parliament is depicted as a caterpillar growing fat on the foliage of the State, is, perhaps, one of Hitler's more unusual images (quoted under *Insects* on pp. 154f. above).

3.4.3.5 Non-living Entities

Inert entities such as metals and rocks have essential attributes very different to those of intelligent, sentient beings, even those of the most basic type. They vary according to their strength, resilience, flexibility and size, and their usefulness to human beings and animals. People may be dehumanized as non-specific, presumably inert, elements and materials: 'antinationale Elemente' [anti-national elements] (*MK*: 684; Mh.: 554), 'rassische Elemente' [racial elements] (*MK*: 430; Mh.: 355), 'revolutionäre Kampfelemente' [revolutionary fighting elements] (*MK*: 580; Mh.: 472); 'Führermaterial' [leader material] (*MK*: 383; Mh.: 317), 'Sklavenmaterial' [slaves] (*MK*: 41; Mh.: 37), 'Menschenmaterial' [human material] (*MK*: 424; Mh.: 350), and the 'Material niederer Völker' [the material provided by lower peoples] (*MK*: 433; Mh.: 357) (see App. III, A.2.17.1.1). The destructive criticism heaped upon Germany by Marxists prior to the First World War is described in *MK* as an 'ewig fressende Säure' [persistent corrosive acid] (*MK*: 505; Mh.: 412).

Strong, hard materials are generally considered most valuable and are common sources of metaphors for positive human character traits and behaviour in political discourse. Hitler favoured certain metals and minerals to express both good and extreme qualities in people (their behaviour, emotions and beliefs), and in political and social groups. Granite, iron *(Eisen)* and steel *(Stahl)* and the general term 'rock' *(Fels)* represent strength, hardiness, a firm will and health (App. III, B.2.2.1). The foundations of a State, writes Hitler, should be as *graniten* ('like granite') as the basis of his own convictions (*MK*: 362 and 170; Mh.: 299 and 142). The principles of a political movement should likewise be as firm as granite (*MK*: 512; Mh.: 417), and the NS movement should be guided by an iron fist ('eiserne Faust') (*MK*: 24; Mh.: 24). Extreme stupidity is like granite, but so is honesty ('granitene Redlichkeit'), as was the case with Ernst Pöhner who, according to Hitler, took personal risks in order to save Germany (*MK*: 403; Mh.: 334). Logic could be like iron (*MK*: 763; Mh.: 613), and Hitler praised his father's diligence as iron-like (*MK*: 5; Mh.: 7). Sport and gymnastics could train young people's bodies and therefore their wills to an 'eiserne Abhärtung' [hardness of iron] (*MK*: 277; Mh.: 230); a resilient, steel-like *(stählern)* body was similarly desirable among the young (*MK*: 278; Mh.: 231). The human will was healthy if it was like steel (*MK*: 715; Mh.: 577), and Germany's many wars had made the *Volk* as hard as steel ('ein stahlharter, gesunder Volkskörper') (*MK*: 773; Mh.: 621). Bronze and rocks are favoured metaphors in similar contexts, with the two combining in an ideal political party as an 'eherner Fels einheitlicher glaubens- und willensmäßiger Verbundenheit' [brazen cliff of solid unity in faith and will] (*MK*: 419; Mh.: 346). Lead, on the other hand, is generally present in images of something good being weighed down and thus unable to improve, for example by spinelessness (*Charakterlosigkeit*), as in the following example: 'Sie kann zum furchtbaren Bleigewicht werden, das ein Volk dann kaum mehr abzuschütteln vermag' [It can become a terrible lead weight, a weight which a nation is not likely to shake off] (*MK*: 761; Mh.: 612).

Hitler used a large number of common water metaphors in *MK*. Water collects in masses of smaller or greater amounts and can be used to metaphorize volumes. Furthermore it can be contained and it can break out of its container for a variety of reasons, such as a break in the container or an increase in its volume beyond that of the container. For this reason certain metaphors associated with water have already been dealt with in Section 3.4.1 (e.g. the verbs *überquellen*, *überfließen*, *überschäumen* and *ergießen*). Water is essential for organic life and is a valuable source for metaphors applied to the giving and maintenance of life, or its cessation. In *MK* Hitler used some conventional metaphors associated with crowds of people who formed a stream *(Strom)* (*MK*: 406; Mh.: 336), a sea *(Menschenmeer)* (*MK*: 561; Mh.: 456) or waves ('eine wogende Masse voll heiligster Empörung und maßlosester Grimm' [a surging mass full of the holiest indignation and boundless wrath], *MK*: 524; Mh.: 425). Large quantities of a substance or large numbers of people may be metaphorized as a flood or tide *(Flut)*, as in *Marxistenflut* ('Marxist flood') (*MK*: 361; Mh.: 298), or a stream *(Strom)*, as in *Giftstrom* ('stream of poison') (*MK*: 169; Mh.: 141). *Flut* is a common metaphor for dangerous situations: for example Hitler depicted German traitors and cowards as a plague which grew into a stifling flood and then drowned Germany's respected position in the world (*MK*: 251; Mh.: 210). Another term for a flood in German is *Überschwemmung* (verb *überschwemmen*), and this is used in *MK* to metaphorize unwanted people or ideas (*MK*: 465, 87 and 208; Mh.: 381, 74 and 172). Ideas, both good and bad, may also be depicted as waves, as in '(dem) Wellenspiel einer freien Gedankenwelt' [the shifting waves of a free thought-world] (*MK*: 419; Mh.: 346); a political movement may also be portrayed as a wave, such as the 'bolschewistische Welle' [Bolshevistic wave] (*MK*: 277; Mh.: 230). People may also swim with the current of accepted ideas *(im Strom schwimmen)* or against it *(gegen den Strom schwimmen)*: Hitler explains that Germans must stand up to the current of political views that have been bewitched *(betört)* by Jewish guile, however rough the water may be:

> (...) wohl branden manches Mal die Wogen arg und böse um uns, allein, wer im Strome schwimmt, wird leichter übersehen, als wer sich gegen die Gewässer stemmt. Heute sind wir eine Klippe, in wenigen Jahren schon kann das Schicksal uns zum Damm erheben, an dem der allgemeine Strom sich bricht, um in ein neues Bett zu fließen. (*MK*: 757f.)
> [(...) sometimes, it is true, the waves break harshly and angrily about us, but who swims with the stream is more easily overlooked that he who bucks the waves. Today we are a reef; in a few years, fate may raise us up as a dam against which the general stream will break, and flow into a new bed. (Mh.: 609)]

The sources of water, such as springs *(Quellen)* and wells *(Brunnen)*, make ideal metaphors for new beginnings, most usually of a beneficial nature, as in the poetic description of history as the 'unerschöpfliche Quell des Verständnisses für das geschichtliche Handeln der Gegenwart' [inexhaustible source of understanding for the historical events of the present] (*MK*: 14; Mh.: 15). Fast-moving and foaming water may be used to portray dangerous or confusing situations, such as the 'sogenannte „öffentliche Meinung", deren Schaum dann die parlamentarische Aphrodite entsteigt' [so-called 'public opinion', from whose foam the parliamentarian Aphrodite arises] (*MK*: 94; Mh.: 79), or the 'Strudel eines Völkerbabylons' [maelstrom of a Babylon of nations] which is Hitler's description of Austria before the First World War (*MK*: 79; Mh.: 67).

The physical make-up of the world and its universe provides the rhetorician with a useful set of metaphors, as documented in App. III, B.2.2.2 (Geography), B.2.2.3 (Geology) and B.2.2.4 (Astronomy and Astrology). The metaphors *Grund* and *Boden* are extremely important for Hitler's documentation of his *Weltanschauung*. As houses and philosophies have foundations, so do they have ground or soil upon which to stand and in which to grow (*MK*: 522; Mh.: 424). A good ground must be firm in order to support ideas and it should not be possible to dig under and therefore undermine those ideas (*den*

Boden abgraben, unterhöhlen). A State may similarly be undermined, and before the First World War the individual German States were, according to Hitler, undermining one another: 'Die einzelnen Staaten begannen immer mehr Unternehmen zu gleichen, die sich gegenseitig den Boden abgraben' [The various nations began to be more and more like private citizens who cut the ground from under one another's feet] (*MK*: 172; Mh.: 144).

Just as a firm ground is indispensible for growth of all that is good, an unsteady or swampy ground is a dangerous environment. Hitler portrays various human character flaws and unhealthy situations as swamps *(Sumpf)*, such as corruption (*MK*: 107; Mh.: 90), base mentality ('niedrige Gesinnung') (*MK*: 355; Mh.: 293), and the swamp of an 'um sich greifenden Verweichlichung und Verweibung' [universally spreading softening and effeminization] (*MK*: 308; Mh.: 255). Groups of people may also be depicted as swamps—the proletariat (*MK*: 479; Mh.: 391), for example, or the physically degenerate:

> Wenn ein Volk aber in seiner Masse aus körperlichen Degeneraten besteht, so wird sich aus diesem Sumpf nur höchst selten ein wirklich großer Geist erheben. (*MK*: 452) [But if the mass of a people consists of physical degenerates, from this swamp a really great spirit will very seldom arise. (Mh.: 371)]

A swamp is a lowly place, but higher ground surrounds it. In *MK* Hitler writes of priests as being like islands who stand up above the 'allgemeinen Sumpfe' [general morass] (*MK*: 126; Mh.: 106).

Mountains commonly function as metaphors in political discourse. In *MK*, a summit *(Gipfel)* is generally a positive image, such as the 'Gipfel ihres Ruhmes' [apogee of its glory] reached by the Christian Social Party (*MK*: 107; Mh.: 90). An avalanche may become a positive or a negative metaphor of movement, as can a volcano. Hitler applies both metaphors to political movements (*MK*: 106 and 116; Mh.: 89 and 98). In *MK* we also encounter great historical *Lawinen* ('avalanches') as forces for positive change, set in motion by the spoken word (*MK*: 116; Mh.: 98), and the French Revolution as a 'furchtbare Vulkanausbruch (...), der ganz Europa in Schrecken erstarren ließ' [that terrible volcanic eruption which held all Europe rigid with fear] (*MK*: 532; Mh.: 432).

The sun, the moon and the stars all give light to the world, and the stars make it possible for people to find their way around the world (cf. *Leitstern* and *Polarstern*; App. III, B.2.2.4). Important or popular people may be likened to the sun or stars, as when Hitler compares Frederick the Great with Friedrich Ebert:

> Der Held von Sanssouci verhält sich zum ehemaligen Bremenser Kneipenwirt ungefähr wie die Sonne zum Mond; erst wenn die Strahlen der Sonne verlöschen, vermag der Mond zu glänzen. Es ist deshalb auch der Haß aller Neumonde der Menschheit gegen die Fixsterne nur zu begreiflich. (*MK*: 286) [The hero of Sans-Souci is to the former Bremen saloon keeper approximately as the sun to the moon; only when the rays of the sun die can the moon shine. Consequently, the hatred of all new moons of humanity for the fixed stars is only too comprehensible. (Mh.: 237)]

Hitler also refers to the Star of David *(Davidstern)* in order to derogate Jews and invents pejorative epithets for old parliamentarians ('Sterngucker und Parteiastrologen' [stargazers and party astrologers] *MK*: 410; Mh.: 339). The term *kometenähnlich* (comet-like) refers to the upward social movement of stateless people (*MK*: 488; Mh.: 399). Finally in this section, the poles and magnets are portrayed as metaphors for constancy and attraction respectively (*MK*: 513, 23, 129 and 414; Mh.: 417f., 22, 108 and 343).

3.4.4 Natural Elements, Forces and Processes

3.4.4.1 Meteorological Metaphors, Fire, Light and Colours

The elements are natural forces which cause movements of air, changes of temperature and precipitation in the world without any human intervention: they move as if by the hand of God. Violent weather conditions are particularly popular features of political discourse, the storm being one of the commonest metaphors for war and other political upheavals. Writing about the Balkan War, Hitler described a scene of a storm brewing, speaking of the 'Ruhe vor dem Sturme' [quiet before the storm] like a 'faules Siechtum' [lingering disease], accompanied by a 'fahle Schwüle' [livid sultriness], as though a hurricane *(Orkan)* were on its way. The heat intensified to a 'fiebrige Tropenglut' [feverish tropical heat], light and darkness alternated, and a gust of wind blew over a nervous Europe awaiting a catastrophe. Then the first flash of lightning struck the earth, presumably a metaphor for a real attack.

This signalled the outbreak of the First World War in which the thunder of Heaven ('Donner des Himmels') merged with a real roar of batteries ('Dröhnen der Batterien des Weltkriegs') (*MK*: 173; Mh.: 145; cf. App. I, Text 8). As well as signifying war, a storm is an ideal source metaphor for strong emotions, for passion, and for the trials of life itself. Examples are 'der Sturm des Lebens' [the storm of life] (*MK*: 144; Mh.: 121), 'ein Sturm von heißer Leidenschaft' [a storm of hot passion] (*MK*: 116; Mh.: 98), 'zum rauschenden Sturm des Beifalls' [a wild storm of applause] (*MK*: 376; Mh.: 310) and 'stürmische Begeisterung' [stormy enthusiam] (*MK*: 177; Mh.: 148).

As with weather conditions, we experience the light of day and the darkness of night with our bodies, the former being more likely to bring a sense of wellbeing than the latter. Light, brightness and clarity are major sources of metaphors in many types of discourse, connoting truth, happiness, optimism, knowledge, intelligence, civilisation and numerous other positive emotions and situations. An excess of light may dazzle or blind a person, but brilliance is more commonly beneficial than negative. In *MK* Hitler praises 'kristallklare Ziele' [crystal-clear aims] (*MK*: 230; Mh.: 191), 'hellseherische Begabung' ['prophetic gift', literally 'light-seeing gift'] (*MK*: 113; Mh.: 95), and a conviction *(Überzeugung)* which is 'hell und klar' [bright and clear] (*MK*: 779; Mh.: 626). In Hitler's opinion even the working classes can "glow" with the light *(Lichter)* of 'Opferwilligkeit, treuester Kameradschaft, außerordentlicher Genügsamkeit und zurückhaltender Bescheidenheit' [willingness to make sacrifices, of loyal comradeship, astonishing frugality, and modest reserve] (*MK*: 47; Mh.: 41). Light provides yet another positive metaphor for superior races, such as the Master Race who brought light to humanity: 'aufgehellt durch die gebliebenen Schöpfungen der einstigen Lichtbringer' [illuminated by the remaining creations of the former light-bringers] (*MK*: 320; Mh.: 265). Light metaphors may also be used ironically, as in the following:

> Man muß damals wirklich das Leuchten dieser bürgerlichen parteipolitischen Schimmelkulturen angesichts einer solchen genialen Parole gesehen haben! (*MK*: 776) [The way these mouldy political party cheeses glowed at the sound of such a brilliant slogan was something to behold! (Mh.: 623)];
> (...) den in der Literatur schillernden Phrasen von Freiheit, Schönheit und Würde (...) (*MK*: 43) [(...) the glittering phrases about freedom, beauty, and dignity in the theoretical literature (...) (Mh.: 39)]

The verbs *beleuchten, einleuchten, aufhellen, aufklären, aufdämmern* (in the sense of 'to throw light on, elucidate') are so commonly used in any type of discourse that they may almost be considered dead metaphors. Their use in *MK* is, however so frequent that the political message is given a positive glow. As can be seen in App. III, B.2.2.6.5, Mh. has often neglected to translate these metaphors with equivalent metaphors of light, rendering *beleuchten* and *einleuchten*, for example, with 'presented', 'realize' and 'seemed plausible'.

High levels of light may have a positive or negative effect, as in 'blendende Beredsamkeit' [dazzling eloquence] (*MK*: 12; Mh.: 13) and 'blendenden Pracht' [dazzling glamour] (*MK*: 23; Mh.: 22), but 'demokratisch-marxistischer Verblendung' [democratic-Marxist blindness] (*MK*: 700; Mh.: 566) and 'verblendete Pazifisten' [blinded pacifists] (*MK*: 438; Mh.: 360). Superfluous light may prevent people seeing, but in general the right amount of light helps us to see, and therefore understand. Light also symbolizes progress and optimism, as in Hitler's description of Joseph II: 'Einem einzigen unter ihnen hielt das Schicksal noch einmal die Fackel über die Zukunft seines Landes empor, dann verlosch sie fur immer' [For only a single one of them did Fate once again raise high the torch over the future of his country, then it was extinguished forever] (*MK*: 79; Mh.: 67).

Darkness may be associated with mystery and lack of reason or understanding, light with knowledge, vision, understanding and reason. Hitler described the darkness of an age without culture as a 'dunkler Schleier' [dark veil] (*MK*: 421; Mh.: 348) and an age without virtue as a 'schwarzbehangenes Firmament' [overcast firmament] (*MK*: 713; Mh.: 576). A guilty conscience is portrayed as a haunting shadow ('Schatten des eigenen Schuldbewußtseins') (*MK*: 30; Mh.: 28). One way in which Hitler portrays Jews as essentially dishonest is to describe them as "murky" people who shun the daylight ('das Tagelicht scheuender Schliefer' [of the sort that shun the light of day]) (*MK*: 99; Mh.: 83). Other 'lichtscheues Gesindel' ('light-shy rabble') are deserters and pimps, doubtless, in Hitler's mind, influenced by Jews (*MK*: 583; Mh.: 474). The antithesis of the Jew is the Aryan, who, according to Hitler, brings the light of goodness, reason and civilization to the world (cf. App. III, B.2.2. –6.5, especially the reference to the 'einstiger Lichtbringer'). Hitler paints a terrible picture of what would happen if the Aryan were annihilated: 'Man schalte ihn aus—und tiefe Dunkelheit wird vielleicht schon nach wenigen

Jahrtausenden sich abermals auf die Erde senken' [Exclude him—and perhaps after a few thousand years darkness will again descend on the earth] (*MK*: 317f.; Mh.: 263; Mh. renders *ausschalten* as 'exclude' whereas I would have chose 'switch off' or 'extinguish').

    Heat and cold are closely linked to darkness and light in the physical world. Warmth and light are usually felt to be positive forces, bringing a sense of well-being; darkness and cold may cause discomfort or fear. All are part of our embodied experience, with cold commonly extended to represent reason and lack of emotion, and heat often metaphorizing strong emotions, such as the *Siedehitze* [white heat] of the first NS mass meetings (*MK*: 625; Mh.: 508) and Hitler's 'heiße Liebe' [ardent love] for Austria (*MK*: 14; Mh.: 15). The weak enthusiasm of cowards and traitors is portrayed as *lau* ('luke-warm') in *MK* (*MK*: 10; Mh.: 11); Hitler himself claiming never to have been one of the *Lauen* (*MK*: 10; Mh.: 12). Coldness is used in many languages to metaphorize lack of emotion, cruelty and "cool" reason. Hitler wrote of the determination and 'eisige Kühle der Überlegung' [icy cool presence of mind] of heroes (*MK*: 321; Mh.: 266) and the 'eisig kalte und freche Stirn' [cold and brazen gall] of the Jews and the Hapsburgs over the issue of South Tyrol (*MK*: 709; Mh.: 573).

    Fire is another natural force which is of great value to rhetoricians. Hitler used fire as the source of a large number of metaphors, in particular those representing strong emotions and opinions. In the following quotation he writes of the passions of the masses which need to be kept aglow:

> Ich kannte die Psyche der breiten Masse nur zu genau, um nicht zu wissen, daß man hier mit „ästhetischer" Gehobenheit nicht das Feuer würde schüren können, das notwendig war, um dieses Eisen in Wärme zu halten. Man war in meinen Augen verrückt, daß man nichts tat, um die Siedehitze der Leidenschaft zu steigern (...) (*MK*: 184; cf. 206) [I knew the psyche of the broad masses too well not to be aware that a high 'aesthetic' tone would not stir up the fire that was necessary to keep the iron hot. In my eyes it was madness on the part of the authorities to be doing nothing to intensify the glowing heat of passion (...) (Mh.: 153)]

In *MK*, we also encounter 'flammende Empörung' [flaming indignation] (*MK*: 705; Mh.: 570), '„flammende" Protestkundgebung' ['flaming' protest demonstration] (*MK*: 708; Mh.: 572), **'flammende Nationalbegeisterung'** *[the flame of national enthusiasm]* (*MK*: 711; Mh.: 574), **'den glühenden Willen'** [*a glowing will*] (*MK*: 769; Mh.: 618), 'glühende Vaterlandsliebe' [fervent love of their fatherland] (*MK*: 582; Mh.: 473), and 'mein brennendster Herzenswunsch' [my most ardent and heartfelt wish] (*MK*: 136; Mh.: 114). Cultural progress is also presented as a fire or as a light ('die Fackel des menschlichen Kulturfortschrittes' [the torch of human progress] *MK*: 320; Mh.: 265). Genius is likened to fire as well as the light it emits: the Aryan race is portrayed as a Prometheus from whose forehead a spark of genius emanated ('der göttliche Funke des Genies'), kindling *(entzündend)* a fire of knowledge to illuminate the night of silent mysteries ('das als Erkenntnis die Nacht der schweigenden Geheimnisse aufhellte'), and enabling mankind to rule other living beings on earth (*MK*: 317; Mh.: 263). The flames of emotions, opinions or disputes may be fanned *(schüren, anfachen)* and blaze *(auflammen, lichterloh brennen)*, but sudden blazes (such as rage) are dangerous, and if they represent progress of any type, their flames should be kept under control. Hitler likened the spread of German lebensraum to a controlled fire:

> Die Besiedlung von Grund und Boden ist ein langsamer Prozeß, der oft Jahrhunderte dauert; ja, darin ist ja gerade seine innere Stärke zu suchen, daß es sich dabei nicht um ein plötzliches Aufflammen, sondern um ein allmähliches, aber gründliches und andauerndes Wachsen handelt (...) (*MK*: 156) [The settlement of land is a slow process, often lasting centuries; in fact, its inner strength is to be sought precisely in the fact that it is not a sudden blaze, but a gradual yet solid and continuous growth (...) (Mh.: 130f.)]

Similarly, *Strohfeuer* ('burning straw') metaphorizes political movements which rapidly burn out (*MK*: 177; Mh.: 148). Something good may also be extinguished *(auslöschen, verlöschen)* or burn out *(ausbrennen)* (App. III, B.2.2.6.2.1). Hitler was concerned, for example, that Aryan blood could be corrupted or extinguished ('verdorben oder ausgelöscht') (*MK*: 735; Mh.: 592).

The colours most commonly used metaphorically in *MK* are black and red, the colours of the Nazi flag. Black tends to be used in the same way as darkness and bad weather conditions; red is the conventional metaphor for Communism and Socialism. Examples from *MK* include 'rote Drohungen' [Red threats] (*MK*: 613; Mh.: 498), 'nur rote Zeitungen, (...) nur rote Versammlungen, (...) nur rote Bücher' [only Red papers, (...) only Red meetings, (...) only Red books] (*MK*: 44; Mh.: 39), and, referring to the

General Strike, 'ein grellrotes Licht' [a flaming red light] (*MK*: 216; Mh.: 179). Hitler recognized various shades of red: 'die Parteiorganisationen des Marxismus aller Schattierungen' [the party organisations of all shadings of Marxism] (*MK*: 601; Mh.: 489). Needless to say, he despised all of them.

3.4.4.2 *Growth and the Processes of Decay*

Organic growth is an inevitable force in nature and frequently used by Hitler to metaphorize what he saw as the natural growth of the NS movement and his own ideas. He wrote, no doubt with himself in mind, of 'das ersichtliche organische Wachsen des Führers' [the visible, organic growth of the leader] (*MK*: 72; Mh.: 62).

The Growth of Plants
Higher-level plants have seeds from which they germinate, take root and, unless adverse circumstances intervene, can grow. The conceptual metaphor PROGRESS IS GROWTH represents our sense of analogy between plant growth and development within human society. In *MK*, Hitler uses plants to metaphorize the State, the NS movement and ideas in general. A seed may grow into a beneficial or a harmful plant. Hitler writes of the 'Erhaltung dieser Keimzelle des Reiches' [the preservation of this nuclear cell of the Empire [= Austria]] (*MK*: 74; Mh.: 63), but also of the destructive 'Keimzellen des Entdeutschungsprozesses' [germ-cells of the de-Germanisation process] (*MK*: 119; Mh.: 100), and of seeds which fail to germinate, ('im Keime ersticken', *MK*: 213). In *MK*, Hitler advises that ideas or actions which are considered wrong are best destroyed before they have a chance to germinate, giving as an example his own actions when rivals threatened to disrupt his political meetings (*MK*: 546; Mh.: 443; Mh.'s translation of 'im Keim unmöglich gemacht' as 'forestalled in the bud' is a rather infelicitous rendering of the equivalent English metaphor "nipped in the bud").

The German *Kern* may be translated into English as 'kernel', 'core' or 'nucleus'. While Mh. prefers 'nucleus', the representation of political movements or a particular race as having a living core or kernel seems more appropriate. The image of a kernel certainly seems the best match for Hitler's view of his responsibility to 'remove his core ideas from their shell' (*herausschälen*, translated by Mh. as 'extracting') and to present them in an understandable form to the German people:

> Deshalb sah ich meine eigene Aufgabe besonders darin, aus dem umfangreichen und ungestalteten Stoff einer allgemeinen Weltanschauung diejenigen Kernideen herauszuschälen in mehr oder minder dogmatische Formen umzugießen (...) (*MK*: 423f.) [Therefore I saw my own task especially in extracting those nuclear ideas from the extensive and unshaped substance of a general world view and remoulding them into more or less dogmatic forms (...) (Mh.: 350)]

Once a seed has germinated, roots develop which will support the plant and form the basis for its future growth. Only strong, healthy roots will allow vigorous growth, just as, within the A STATE IS A BUILDING metaphor, the foundations of an edifice are vital if it is to remain standing for any length of time. Any unhealthy state of affairs is best rectified at root level, before harmful growth is allowed to continue. Hitler suggests that the Austrian parliament should have been destroyed in this way, from within, before the First World War:

> Auch schien es einzuleuchten, daß der Angriff an der Wurzel des Übels erfolgreicher sein müsse als das Anstürmen von außen. (*MK*: 112) [Besides, it seemed plausible that attacking the root of the evil was bound to be more successful than storming it from outside. (Mh.: 94)]

Race is conventionally metaphorized as "roots" in German as in English. If it is not to succumb to its enemies, a nation such as Germany must take care of its racial roots ('die ihm von der Natur gegebenen und in seinem Blute wurzelnden Eigenschaften seines Wesens') [the Nature-given qualities of its being which root in its blood] (*MK*: 359; Mh.: 297).

Once the roots of a plant take hold, the stem and leaves will sprout and develop. The young plant is tender and easy to bend—it is at this stage that a plant or tree may be formed into its future shape. The youth of the German nation are often metaphorized as young shoots *(Sproß, Spro̊ßling, Reis)* in *MK*. It is particularly important to care for young people as they develop, for, according to Hitler, it is while they are young that they enjoy a certain youthful genius ('Genialität der Jugend') which will eventually blossom and bear valuable fruit: 'die in unerschöpflicher Fruchtbarkeit Gedanken und Ideen ausschüttet' [which pours out thoughts and ideas with inexhaustible fertility] (*MK*: 21; Mh.: 21). Hitler saw the NS movement as capable of leading the German Reich to a new blossoming, 'zu neuer Blüte' (*MK*: 753); it would bring to fruition a superior culture supported by the German State: 'die Frucht eines durch die lebendige staatliche Zusammenfassung gesicherten kulturschöpferischen Volkstums' [the fruit of a culture-creating nationality safeguarded by a living integration through the state] (*MK*: 435f.; Mh.: 359). A stem or trunk of a plant is also important as a provider of support as it grows (*MK*: 657; Mh.: 532).

Mistletoe, a parasitic plant, is conceived in *MK* as weakening its host. Hitler likens the rulers of Russia to mistletoe in order to illustrate the impossibility of any German treaty with them:

> Wenn der Mensch glaubt, mit Parasiten verträgliche Bindungen eingehen zu können, so ähnelt dies dem Versuche eines Baumes, zu eigenem Vorteil mit einer Mistel ein Abkommen zu schließen. (*MK*: 750) [If a man believes that he can enter into profitable connections with parasites, he is like a tree trying to conclude for its own profit an agreement with mistletoe. (Mh.: 604)]

The Jews are likened to dead chaff: 'Was nicht gute Rasse ist auf diese Welt, ist Spreu' [All who are not of good race in this world are chaff] (*MK*: 324; Mh.: 369), and bourgeois political parties to mould *(Schimmelkultur)*, a plant growth of the lowest order (*MK*: 776; rendered by Mh. as the extraordinary 'mouldy political party cheeses'(623)).

Images of Decay and Transience
All that is organic and able to grow must eventually decay. Some of Hitler's strongest images are based on this notion; indeed, one of his best-known metaphors, and one which has possibly caused more offence than any other, is his portrayal of the Jews as a 'Ferment der Dekomposition' which he claims to be a quotation from Mommsen (*MK*: 498 and 743; Mh.: 406 and 598). In *MK* the adjective *faul* ('rotten') is applied to the bourgeois world (*MK*: 409; Mh.: 339), states of peace, particularly those which are artificially cultivated (*MK*: 773; Mh.: 621), and the corpses of states other than Germany ('die fauligen staatlichen Leichname') (*MK*: 756; Mh.: 608). In his recommendations for State education, Hitler claims that a good mind can only exist in

a healthy body, for **'ein verfaulter Körper wird durch einen strahlenden Geist nicht im geringsten ästhetischer gemacht'** [*a decayed body is not made the least more aesthetic by a brilliant mind*] (*MK*: 453; Mh.: 371). Inner rottenness ('innere Fäulnis') is listed with other character faults ('lack of character and cowardice') as unworthy and un-Germanic. The synonymous loan-word, *dekadent*, is also attested. The Reich is portrayed as having shown signs of *Verwesung* ('rottenness', *MK*: 14; Mh.: 15) and *Verfall* ('decay') (*MK*: 282; Mh.: 234), and the world is described as *verkommend* ('decomposing') (*MK*: 420; Mh.: 347). Finally, two pseudo-scientific terms *entarten* and *ausarten*, both meaning 'to degenerate', refer respectively to the adverse results of intermarriage (*MK*: 275; Mh.: 229) and to a possible negative development of Marxism (*MK*: 589; Mh.: 479). Hitler also used the metaphor of the soap-bubble *(Seifenblase)* to indicate transience (*MK*: 156; Mh.: 131).

3.4.4.3   Other natural forces

The NS movement is described as having a magnetic attraction: 'jene große magnetische Anziehung, der die breite Masse immer nur folgt' [that great magnetic attraction which alone the masses always follow] (*MK*: 414; Mh.: 343). Hitler also uses some conventional and well-worn metaphors for the passing of time, such as 'das Rad der Geschichte' [the wheel of history] (*MK*: 642; Mh.: 522) and 'Der Zeiger der Weltuhr ist seitdem weiter vorgerückt' [The hand of the world clock has moved on since then] (*MK*: 753; Mh.: 606).

3.5   How Conventional were Hitler's Metaphors?

Hitler obviously intended *MK* to fit into the tradition of political rhetoric which uses metaphors and similes for adornment and effect; he wanted to use aesthetic means to persuade, instruct and move his audience. Well-read in political literature, he reproduced metaphors from a wide range of sources. As stated in Chapter 2 of this book, he may also have adopted metaphors from literature and opera, although research has not yet been able to identify all of these sources. When George Orwell wrote in 1946 that "political writing is bad writing" he was in part referring to the over-use of stale metaphors and hackneyed idioms (Orwell 1946: 6). He claimed that 'one almost never finds (...) a fresh, vivid, homemade turn of speech', a feeling which may be shared by anyone who has read *MK*. While many politicians make use of very novel, non-conventionalized metaphors, the majority of Hitler's metaphors show little originality and most are immediately understandable: as well as being well-worn in political rhetoric, they are used for everyday purposes by ordinary people (e.g. LIFE IS A JOURNEY). A small number of the metaphors used in *MK* are, however, located further along Kövecses's "scale of conventionality": they are less conventionalized and require more cognitive effort on the part of the decoder. It is the purpose of this section to make some general remarks about Hitler's use of metaphors and similes as well as to identify instances of less conventional usage.

Hitler used a large quantity of chiefly common source domains for his metaphors: the human body; animals (both wild and domestic); birds; fish; insects; plants; metals and minerals; the sun, the moon and the stars; rivers and the sea; the weather; fire, heat, light and day; darkness, cold and night; height and depth; decay; disease and healing; warfare; social categories and domestic life; the Bible; history; mythology; literature; music; art; magic; travel; farming and gardening; architecture; science, technology and medicine; sport, games and hunting; finance; violence, restraint and robbery; unpleasant smells and poisons; dirt and cleanliness. He had a stock of more frequently used metaphors, his personal favourites, which were the most prone to repetition, for example: Jews are snakes; Jews, Marxists and the produce of the Press are poisons; Jews, Marxism and the Press are diseases; Jews are parasites.

Hitler's choice of metaphors within individual source domains, such as those of cold, darkness, gardening, sport and the human body, are widely varied. If we take one example, the human body, we encounter: blood, arteries, nerves, the heart, the brain, the head, the throat, the neck, hands, fingers, fists, arms, feet, legs, eyes, eyelashes, ears, the nose, the tongue, the lap, the backbone, the shoulders and the breast. If we examine one more example, in more detail this time, namely darkness, we meet with an assortment of nouns, verbs and adjectives: *dunkel* ('dark'), *trüb* ('gloomy'), *schwarz* ('black'), *lichtscheu* ('shunning the light'); *auslöschen* ('to extinguish'), *trüben* ('to darken'), *das Tagelicht scheuen* ('to shun the daylight'), *die Sonne scheuen* ('to avoid the sun'); *Schatten* ('shade'), *Nacht* ('night'), *Zwielicht* ('twilight'), *(dunkler) Schleier* ('(dark) veil'), *Auslöschung* ('extinguishing, extinction').

A large proportion of Hitler's metaphors are recorded in Keith Spalding's *An Historical Dictionary of German Figurative Usage* (1952–2000), although Spalding did not use *MK* as one of his sources. Many of the metaphors entered the German language between the Middle Ages and the eighteenth century and a large number would have typified political rhetoric at the time when Hitler was reading nationalistic literature and listening to political speeches. It is thus not so much the types of metaphor used in *MK* that are of interest as their density, as well as the fact that they include almost every possible source domain used in political discourse. While Hitler's metaphors were mostly conventional, he used some in unconventional ways or modified or blended them (some would say that he simply forgot the conventional usage), as in: 'in einem Zeitungsartikel die Finger wund zu schmieren' (*MK*: 709), translated by Mh. as 'wear your fingers to the bone writing a newspaper article' (Mh.: 573); this is a composite metaphor based on *sich die Finger wund schreiben* ('to write/work one's fingers to the bone', Spalding: 791) and *schmieren* ('to grease sb.'s palm', Spalding: 2155). I believe this to be a deliberate satirization of the press. Another feature of Hitler's language was his tendency to combine metaphors and similes in novel ways, such the well-known trio of similes: 'Flink wie Windhunde, zäh wie Leder und hart wie Kruppstahl' [swift as greyhounds, tough as leather, and hard as Krupp steel] (*MK*: 392; Mh.: 324). This combination is better known from his later speeches (Domarus I, 533). Spalding records *flink wie ein Wiesel* ('as agile as a weasel', 2667), *flink wie ein Reh* ('as fleet of foot as a deer', which has a biblical source: 2 Chron. 13, 8 and 2 Sam. 2,18: 1969); *zäh wie Leder* ('as hard as nails, tough as old boots', 1598); and *wie stahl* ('strong, tough' since MHG: 2328). This complex and unique image was destined to become one of Hitler's most memorable contributions to Nazi discourse. Further interesting mixtures include: 'der strahlendste Akkord' [the most brilliant harmony] (*MK*: 555; Mh.: 451); 'eine wahrhaft niederdrückenden „Höhe"' [a really depressing level] (*MK*: 83; Mh.: 71)l and 'jenes Feuer entzündend, das als Erkenntnis die Nacht der schweigenden Geheimnisse aufhellte' [forever kindling that fire of knowledge which illuminated the night of silent mysteries] (*MK*: 317; Mh.: 263). The image of heartless arms ('herzlose Arme') with which poverty embraced Hitler during much of his time in Vienna is especially idiosyncratic.

In *MK*, Hitler showed a preference for certain groups of metaphor. His personifications, for example of Nature, Fate, history, and of human roles, capacities and emotions, are varied and possibly his most unusual and individual metaphorizations. The would-be artist believed that he had a special gift for architecture and, while it may be going too far to claim that any of his building metaphors were novel, he certainly ventured into less well-known territory with some of them. They are: MANKIND IS A BUILDING, THE *VOLK* IS A BUILDING, HUMAN PROGRESS IS A BUILDING and AN ERA IS A BUILDING. Hitler was also extremely fond of animals and used domestic and wild creatures as sources for his similes and metaphors (see App. III, B.1.3). Most of his animal metaphors were very conventional, (such as *Schafsgeduld, Hornvieh, Hasenfuß*), and some may be classed as dead metaphors, (such as *jem. beim Ohr nehmen* ('to lead someone by the ears' (like a donkey), although Hitler revivifies this by writing of 'seinen langen Ohren' ('his long ears'), and *jem. an der Nase herumführen* ('to lead someone by the nose'). Other animal metaphors are more obscure. Manheim considered one metaphor, *enthörnt* ('dehorned'), either too difficult or too embarrassing to translate, rendering it as 'worn-out' and providing a footnote to the effect that it really meant 'to sow one's wild oats' (*MK*: 275; Mh.: 229; cf. Murphy 1939: 218, who avoids the problem by translating: 'the poor girl finds no difficulty in getting a mate of this description'). Hitler frequently used animal behaviour to metaphorize human behaviour, both current and desired, for example when he explained that animals only mate with members of the same species and that human beings should follow their example (*MK*: 311; Mh.: 258). Another interesting set of images caused Mh. difficulties (a *Maikäfer* is a May-bug, not a butterfly):

> So wie der Engerling nicht anders kann, als sich zum Maikäfer zu verwandeln, so verlassen diese parlamentarischen Raupen das große gemeinsame Puppenhaus und flattern flügelbegabt hinaus zum lieben Volk. (*MK*: 411) [Just as a caterpillar cannot help turning into a butterfly, these parliamentary larvae leave their parliamentary cocoons and, endowed with wings, fly out among the beloved people. (Mh.: 341)]

Thus we can see that, while his metaphors were not unique in themselves, Hitler combined groups of metaphors in unique, sometimes entertaining, ways.

In *MK* we also encounter interesting combinations of metaphors such as LOVE IS HEAT and LOW IS BAD: 'heiße Liebe zu meiner deutschösterreichischen Heimat, tiefen Haß gegen den österreichischen Staat' [ardent love for my German-Austrian homeland, deep hatred for the Austrian state] (*MK*: 14; Mh.: 15). Hitler was obviously not aware that he was using what Lakoff, Johnson and Turner class as conceptual metaphors based on embodied experience, but his need to hammer his message home by every possible means, hyperbole being one of these, caused him to heap up metaphorical expressions even within the shortest of sentences: 'Es ist notwendig, daß wir uns diese *bittere* Wahrheit *kühl* und *nüchtern* vor Augen halten' [We must bear this *bitter* truth *coolly* and *soberly* in mind] (*MK*: 731; Mh.: 590). In the following longer passage we find an effective variety of ways to describe old and inflexible civil servants: 'Nicht in dem verkalkten Sinn alter, verknöcherter Beamtenseelen, im Dienste der toten Autorität eines toten Staates' [Not in the calcified sense of old, ossified officials serving the *dead authority* of a *dead state*] (*MK*: 550; Mh.: 447). Metaphors from different categories may be combined in *MK* in unusual ways to contrast or compare different situations, as in the following two examples, the first an antithesis, the second a comparison: **'Ein VERFAULTER Körper wird durch einen STRAHLENDEN Geist nicht im geringsten ästhetischer gemacht'** *[A DECAYED body is not made the least more aesthetic by a BRILLIANT mind]* (*MK*: 453; Mh.: 371) and '(ich) verglich den AUFSTIEG des Reiches mit dem DAHINSIECHEN des österreichischen Staates' [I compared the RISE of the Reich with the WASTING AWAY of the Austrian state] (*MK*: 57; Mh.: 50). In other instances, metaphorical expressions are aligned with literal expressions to good effect, as in the following description of the Ruhr region:

(...) oder man schuf dem deutschen Volk, mit dem Blicke auf das Gebiet der glühenden Essen und qualmenden Öfen, zugleich den glühenden Willen, diese ewige Schande zu beenden (...) (*MK*: 769) [(...) or, directing the eyes of the German people to this land of glowing smelters and smoky furnaces, we inspired them with a glowing will to end this eternal disgrace (...) (Mh.: 618)]

Allegorical tableaux constructed for series of metaphors and similes are one of Hitler's specialities in *MK*. The following example includes the personification of a tree's relationship with the mistletoe which feeds on it:

> Wenn der Mensch glaubt, mit Parasiten verträgliche Bindungen eingehen zu können, so ähnelt dies dem Versuche eines Baumes, zu eigenem Vorteil mit einer Mistel ein Abkommen zu schließen. (*MK*: 750) [If a man believes that he can enter into profitable connections with parasites, he is like a tree trying to conclude for its own profit an agreement with mistletoe. (Mh.: 604)]

Hitler had the freedom to write a very long book and was thus able to indulge himself in flourishes of rhetoric that are not often found in political texts of average length. Hitler's description of the political situation in the Balkans before 1918 (App. I, Text 8) is examined in Section 3.4.4.1 above. In App. I, Text 9 makes use of the LIFE IS A JOURNEY conceptual metaphor, showing important tasks (long journeys) as comprising numerous smaller trips, and portraying the masses as liable to grow weary of the smaller journeys because they cannot see the ultimate goal. A good leader will show the traveller the different sections of the longer journey so that he can attack each one as if it were his only goal. While Text 8 is stylistically quite pleasing, Text 9 repeats the same message twice using a limited variety of travel metaphors. Further interesting allegorical passages are recorded in App. I, 12 and 13. Such passages taken out of the context of Hitler's long-winded and repetitive work give the impression of a skilled rhetorician at work. Unfortunately the book as a whole is very much less entertaining.

Sadly, Hitler's most repulsive metaphors are his most imaginative, and his most imaginative and distinctive images are of Jews (slime, maggots, bacteria). His animal metaphors are also among his most creative, and one can discern genuine interest in and knowledge of animals in many of them; but the fact that he reserved lower-order and less agreeable animals, such as leeches, to metaphorize Jews, while showing admiration for higher-order animals, such as greyhounds, epitomizes Hitler's depraved view of the world.

Conclusion

Since the end of the Second World War, *MK* has been denounced as an 'Unbuch' (an "unbook"), 'ein Buch, das nicht sein darf' (a book which cannot be allowed to exist) (Podak 1991, 16). But it does exist, and it belongs to the political discourse of one of the most dangerous periods in history, and of one of history's most influential figures. It is therefore an important historical and linguistic document and should be read, however unpleasant the experience might be. The present book is based on a close reading of the text; and whilst it is not an exhaustive record of relevant linguistic features, it provides a broad survey of the most important aspects of Hitler's language and the *Weltanschauung* that it expresses.

As early as 1935 the language of National Socialism, including that of *MK*, was dubbed a *Gewaltstil* (language of violence) by Manfred Pechau, who judged Hitler's rhetoric in a positive light (Pechau 1935: 95f.). *MK* is, indeed, a book of violent emotions and extremes, both in its language and content, just as its author was a man of extremes. The language of *MK* was the expression of a decided mind. Hitler hated half-heartedness *(Halbheit)*, and there is no half-heartedness in his book. His "all-or-nothing" stance could be seen as a continuation of the German attitude to a potential German victory at the end the First World War, exemplified in the pronouncements of General Erich Ludendorff and Admiral Alfred von Tirpitz (Mann 1997: 634 and 640).

While not mentioning Hitler explicitly, Ernst Cassirer likened leaders of totalitarian States to the sorcerers of primitive societies. Writing before his death in April 1945, Cassirer claimed that such leaders were responsible for a shift from a semantic to a magical use of language for political purposes in order to 'produce effects and to change the course of events' (Cassirer 1946: 283). Rather than furnishing logical descriptions, this kind of discourse uses "magic words" to stir up emotions and feelings of violence. Such words work on the imagination and are more effective than compulsion in moving the masses of a population (Cassirer: 289). Totalitarian rulers supplement magical words and political actions with various rituals that have the effect of lulling 'all our active forces, our power of judgment and critical discernment'

(Cassirer: 284). *MK* and Hitler's later speeches and rallies are examples of such a technique. In Cassirer's terms, Hitler was a *homo magus* and a *homo divinans*: he was the "medicine man" and the "soothsayer" who 'reveals the will of the gods and foretells the future' (Cassirer: 288). His regime eventually relieved the German people of the burden of freedom (in the Kantian sense of the ethical imperative to create one's own freedom) and personal responsibility in that he took both freedom and responsibility from them and claimed to bear both on their behalf.

MK was, however, addressed to a readership assumed to be responsible. Hitler merged argumentational rhetoric with more "magical" figures of speech, such as repetition and hyperbole. Having made successful speeches before writing *MK*, he knew what type of language would be effective. The book was a call to arms aimed at the German nation and a warning of what would befall the *Volk* if the call went unheeded. Hitler believed he held the key to the future of Germany, and that Jews were the principal source of all the ills of the world. *MK* contained his anti-Semitic doctrine: almost every problem that he identified was traced back to Jewish originators. The German press, all left-wing political movements, and the arts were all supposedly under Jewish control. Other problems were the fault of the German population who, in Hitler's view, were too apathetic or stupid to recognize the Jewish threat.

In Chapter 2.3, I analyzed a large linguistic database (App. II) and concluded that the totalitarian discourse of *MK* aimed to achieve the following:

1. To identify an enemy and encourage fear and hatred of it, using aggressive language, hyperbole, antithesis, dehumanization, pejorative epithets, and metaphors (chiefly from the group known as THE GREAT CHAIN OF BEING);
2. To provoke action, using martial vocabulary and metaphors;
3. To present Hitler's mission as hallowed, and his *Volk* as having divine rights (at the expense of other people), using hyperbole, and religious language and metaphors;
4. To depict the Aryan race as superior to others, especially the Jews, using hyperbole, antithesis, positive epithets and metaphors.

Hitler's rhetoric also demonstrates various aspects of his personal character and political position:

1. Hatred of *"Halbheit"*, an unwillingness to negotiate or compromise, and a tendency to polarize;
2. Aggression and desire for power, expressed with violent and apocalyptic vocabulary;
3. Arrogant self-righteousness, expressed with emphatic language and statements of "universal truths";
4. Belief that he was an expert rhetorician, emphasized by his flamboyant use of adjectives and metaphors;
5. Belief that the masses were stupid, expressed by his recommendations for the language of propaganda and his own use of repetitive figures of speech.

A detailed comparison of Hitler's language with that of authors who may have influenced him, most notably Richard Wagner and Houston Stewart Chamberlain, has yet to be undertaken, and it is hoped that the present volume will contribute to future work in this direction. Brigitte Hamann (1999: 201) draws attention to the fact that Hitler read widely and internalized the words of others as though they were his own, fitting them into his *Weltanschauung* as he saw fit: 'als Mosaiksteinchen in dem allgemeinen Weltbilde' [like the stone of a mosaic (...) into the general world picture] (*MK*, p. 36; Mh., p. 33). This image of Hitler's *Weltanschauung* as a mosaic or patchwork of other people's ideas is fitting so long as one recognizes Hitler's personal contribution in the form of violent, bombastic language, and an uncompromising, arrogant, megalomaniacal attitude. By the time he wrote *MK* he knew what he believed, and stated his beliefs boldly and with apparent pleasure.

Hitler's language in *MK*, particularly his use of metaphorical expressions, serves to highlight the strength of his opinions and the extreme polarity of his *Weltanschauung*. Those of his followers who read the book will have understood his polarized stance *vis-à-vis* Jews and the so-called Aryan race. They would not have been able to ignore the message, which may have operated on a subliminal level in the case of less attentive readers, that the Jews were evil, dishonest, lower-level human beings, and that they were an enemy to be feared and destroyed. Such a message was supported by metaphors of darkness, dirt, unpleasant locations, low-level life forms, hell and the devil. Aryans were portrayed as the opposite, having high-level natures and inborn goodness. Metaphors of light, cleanliness, higher-level animals and heaven supported the message that Aryans were God's preferred race: a reversal of the traditional view of Jews as an *Auserwähltes Volk* (Chosen People). The following list illustrates the binary oppositions which even a detached reader must have noticed: Aryan/Jew; *Volk*/non-German; nationalism/internationalism; tradition/modernity; high-level natures/low-level natures; heroism/cowardice; courage/fear; light/darkness; white or blonde/black; pleasant locations/unpleasant locations; cleanliness/dirt; truth/lies; construction/destruction; antidote/poison; inside/outside; belonging/foreign; heaven/hell; God/the devil; life/death.

Similar to the Aryan/Jew antithesis was Hitler's polarization of the qualities of his fellow Germans, who could display German/folkish or un-German/unfolkish attitudes and behaviour. The good folkish German would react passionately and aggressively to the danger to which he was exposed. It was the duty of all Germans to despise unworthy compatriots as well as the more clearly dangerous Jews. Epithets and personifications combine with metaphors to emphasize personal qualities. Animal metaphors are particularly favoured by Hitler and emphasize cowardice (*Hasenfuß* = hare's foot), patience (sheep), stupidity (donkeys, long ears), dishonesty (jackals, hyenas), slyness (foxes), obsequiousness (dogs, yelping, whimpering, cringing, licking), aggression in the wrong cause (foxes, rats), officialdom (*Hornvieh* = cattle), the bourgeoisie (*Wahlstimmvieh* = voting cattle), and herd or pack behaviour *(Rudel, Herdentier)*. The following paired expressions illustrate Hitler's view of the extremes of the German character, the first of each pair being positive, the second negative: *völkisch/unvölkisch*; *deutsch/undeutsch*; high-level natures/low-level natures; heroic and brave/unheroic and cowardly; duty/irresponsibility; sacrifice of the self for the benefit of the group/individualism; idealism/intellect; aggression/pacifism; strength/weakness; enthusiasm and passion/apathy; determination and excess/compromise and moderation; totalitarianism/democracy; hatred of an enemy/charity towards the unworthy; anger/tolerance; desire for victory/acceptance of defeat; good/evil.

The masses are frequently referred to in a derogatory sense as 'die Masse der Mitte' (the masses in the centre). In Hitler's mind, those who stuck to the middle ground were unworthy. The "middle road" trod by the bourgoisie is also portrayed as shallow and unfulfilling: 'nur die Schalheit eines bürgerlichen Gemüts kann die mittlere Linie als den Weg ins Himmelreich betrachten' [only the shallowness of a bourgeois mind can regard the middle course as the road to heaven] (*MK*, p. 371; Mh., p. 306). The mixing of races was a particularly contemptible meeting of extremes, as were compromise and treaties, such as that of Versailles. Hitler preached that Germany was faced with a choice between survival as a superior power and destruction: **'Deutschland wird entweder Weltmacht oder überhaupt nicht sein'** *[Germany will either be a world power or there will be no Germany]* (*MK*: 742; Mh.: 597). It would either *be* or *not be (Sein oder Nichtsein)*, depending upon whether it heeded Hitler's call to arms. This message follows a tradition of similar admonitions (see App. I), but it is nevertheless Hitler's own. He gives no direct personal promise to save Germany nor specific detailed advice as to how the German *Volk* might regain the freedom they lost after the First World War. He warns of present dangers and promises a glorious future, stressing the need to fight, although (as I have shown in Chapter 2.3.6) he does not specify what form this fight will take. All of this is expressed in vivid, often terrifying language intended to shake Germany out of its apathy and encourage it to fight to regain its national pride.

When *MK* was published as a single volume, having previously been published as two, the work took on the appearance of a Bible; in fact copies were eventually presented to newly-wed couples in place of the Bible, no doubt as a spur to national regeneration. Hitler clearly thought of his message as an optimistic one, as expressed in words such as the following:

> **Dann wird dereinst ein Volk von Staatsbürgern erstehen, miteinander verbunden und zusammengeschmiedet durch eine gemeinsame Liebe und einen gemeinsamen Stolz, unerschütterlich und unbesiegbar für immer.** (*MK*: 474f.) [*Then a people of citizens will some day arise, bound to one another and forged together by a common love and a common pride, unshakable and invincible forever.* (Mh.: 388)]

While this vision of a glorious German future rarely shines out from behind the long tracts of repetitive, aggressive ranting, many of Hitler's followers saw *MK* as the work of a latter-day Messiah. This view is illustrated by the words of Hans Wendt written ten hours after Hitler's accession to power:

> In seinem Buch „Mein Kampf" (...) findet man wichtige Aufschlüsse für Wesen und Methoden dieses Mannes, der in vielem an die Propheten der Bibel, die Gewissensmahner und Führer ihres Volkes, erinnert. (In his book 'Mein Kampf' (...) one finds important information about the character and strategy of this man who in many ways reminds one of the prophets of the Bible who led their people and were the voices of their conscience.) (Wendt 1933: 19)

One clue to the central idea of *MK* may lie in its original title, *Viereinhalb Jahre gegen Lügen, Dummheit und Feigheit (Four and a Half Years of Struggle against Lies, Stupidity and Cowardice)*. Hitler was obviously angry with those people whom he considered responsible for Germany's defeat at the end of the First World War. He aimed to create a new political system which would lift the nation out of the doldrums which followed.

In 1941, Kenneth Burke wrote of Hitler's self-imposed role as the architect of National Socialism and his 'fury at the dialectics of those who opposed him when his structure was in the stage of scaffolding' (Burke 1973: 199). *MK* is, indeed, the work of an angry man; a man who has been (in his own view unjustly) incarcerated in the middle of his ascent to power; and this in spite of his seemingly altruistic promises to unite a nation in a state of impoverishment (both economic and moral), disunity and chaos. Hitler was an obsessive personality with a burning need to speak his mind and be listened to, but he had been prevented from reaching his audience; while writing the first volume of *MK* he had only his fellow prisoners to preach to. On the other hand, his imprisonment gave him the opportunity to indulge himself and give the speech of a life-time as he dictated the first volume of *MK*. Burke writes of the "medicine" of creating a scapegoat to blame for one's misfortunes, and Hitler chose to inculpate the entire Jewish race. He allocated a "devil-function" to the Jews, thus misappropriating that aspect of Christian doctrine which sees the "Prince of Evil" as a non-material force. Burke claims that Hitler suffered from a "persecution mania", as identified by Freud, and that through *MK* he was able to transform himself from the persecuted to the persecutor. Hitler would not have understood the curative function of this role-reversal in Freudian terms, but if he felt its benefit he would have wished to offer the same "medicine" to his fellow Germans. Burke poses the question of whether Hitler's methods of persuasion were sincere and spontaneous, fuelled by his anger, or whether his weighty rhetoric was deliberate; was he a drastic but honest paranoid or a shrewd demagogue or both? I suggest that Hitler was both sincere and calculating, and that his immoderate personality and anger served him well in his attempt to spread what he believed to be a sane message by means of skilful rhetoric.

APPENDIX I

Sample Texts

Text 1

Was Einzelheiten sammelt, sie zu Mengen häuft, diese zu Ganzen verknüpft, solche steigernd zu immer größern verbindet, zu Sonnenreichen und Welten eint, bis all sämtlich das große All bilden—diese *Einigungskraft* kann in der höchsten und größesten und umfassendsten Menschengesellschaft, im Volke, nicht anders genannt werden als—*Volkstum*. Es ist das Gemeinsame des Volks, sein inwohnendes Wesen, sein Regen und Leben, seine Wiedererzeugungskraft, seine Fortpflanzungsfähigkeit. Dadurch waltet in allen Volksgliedern ein *volkstümliches* Denken und Fühlen, Lieben und Hassen, Frohsein und Trauern, Leiden und Handeln, Entbehren und Genießen, Hoffen und Sehnen, Ahnen und Glauben. Das bringt alle die einzelnen Menschen des Volks, ohne daß ihre Freiheit und Selbständigkeit untergeht, sondern gerade noch mehr gestärkt wird, in der Viel- und Allverbindung mit den übrigen zu einer schönverbundenen Gemeinde.
(Friedrich Ludwig Jahn, *Von deutschem Volkstum*, 1810: 6f.)

Text 2

Ein Volk ist einem festgewurzelten, hochstämmigen Baume vergleichbar, der, wenn er auch vielastig und vielzweigig ein dichtes, vielblättriges Laubdach wölbt, doch immer ein und derselbe Baum bleibt; ein vielgliedriger Leib, von dem sich nicht nach Beleiben durch das Trennmesser mehrere Leiblein ablegen lassen.

Der einzelne Mensch und die Gesamtheit des Volks gehorchen darin gleichem Gesetz, daß sie zu ihrem Auswachsen und Wohlsein Bewegung und freien Spielraum bedürfen, sollen sie nicht verkrüppeln. Soll darum ein Volk als völlige Gemeinde seine Vollkommenschaft erlangen, so muß es sich regen und rühren. Es darf nicht auf einer einzigen Scholle kleben, an *einem* Strome entlang ufern, in einem einzigen Gau hocken, in einem einzigen Tale hausen. Durch jede solche alleinige Eigenheit müßte es verkümmern und verbauern. Nur durch die Mannigfaltigkeit des Lebens sichert es sein Dasein und Wesen.
(Friedrich Ludwig Jahn, *Von deutschem Volkstum*, 1810: 23)

Text 3

Der Antisemit beachtet zwei Dinge nicht: erstens, daß der Jude niemals ein reiner Semit war, noch ist, und daß er somit manche vermittelnde Elemente in seinem Blut enthält, woraus folgt, daß man zwischen Juden und Juden unterscheiden muß und nicht übersehen darf, daß mancher Jude sich ebensosehr wie wir nach der Erlösung aus semitischen Vortstellungen sehnt; zweitens, daß zwar der jüdische Halbsemit durch die Gewalt seines Willens und durch die Verknüpfung zu einer geschlossenen internationalen Nation das auffallendste „fremde" Element in unserer Mitte ist, beileibe aber nicht das einzige. Ich nannte den Semiten, weil er allein in der Geschichte der Ideen eine Rolle gespielt hat, vergleichbar an Bedeutung derjenigen der Indoarier und der diesen geistig—vielleicht auch leiblich—verwandten Europäer; doch gibt es andere fremde Elemente, die namenlos bleiben und darum nur um so gefährlicher sind, Menschen, die uns äußerlich ziemlich ähnlich sehen, innerlich jedoch eine spezifisch andere Seele besitzen, und die nun alles, was sie von uns erhalten und woran sie mit uns gemeinsam teilnehmen, nicht völlig umwandeln, wie das der Semit tut, sondern inwendig verderben, vergiften, hierdurch den Segen zum Fluch kehrend. Nicht allein lehrt uns die Geschichte, daß der eigentliche Europäer (der Indogermane) auf seinem Zug nach Westen und Süden sich in fremde, ethnisch stark vermischte und geistig minderwertige Elemente hineinkeilte, die er nie austilgte, sondern die Anthropologe bezeugt das Dasein und die allmähliche Zunahme der Nachkommen uralter Einwohner Europas, die teils vor dem Homo europaeus in die höchsten Gebirge geflohen, teils von ihm als Sklaven unterjocht worden waren, und nunmehr, durch eine mit relativer geistiger Beschränktheit gepaarte physische und namentlich sexuelle Kraft begünstigt, sich stark vermehren und nach und nach den germanischen Stock durchsetzen. Dazu dann die starke Vermischung mit mongolischen Elementen, welche nach Buschans Untersuchungen eine nachweisbare Abnahme der Schädelkapazität, der Hirngröße und somit auch der Kulturfähigkeit—kurz, auf deutsch, eine Verdummung—ganze Völkerschaften herbeigeführt hat. Ignatius von Loyola, der Baske, das Kind und der Typus dieser geborenen Feinde unserer Kultur, ist ihr tausendmal gefährlicher als der Jude. Wie sollen wir nun, wie können wir uns schützen? Wie sollen wir in diesem durchaus berechtigten, ja heiligen Kampf—dem Kampf um das eigene Dasein—bestehen? Erstens, indem wir die Notwendigkeit des Kampfes einsehen lernen, zweitens, indem wir uns auf unserer Eigenart besinnen und sie dadurch vollkommen bewußt erfassen. Ein ganzes Jahrhundert haben wir der Marotte einer unbeschränkten Toleranz geopfert; wir haben das Gefühl für die unersetzliche Bedeutung der Grenzen, für die Bedeutung der Persönlichkeit, des Niewiederkehrenden, aus

dem allein Schöpfungen und große Taten hervorgehen, fast verloren; wir steuern auf das Chaos zu. Es ist hohe Zeit, daß wir zur Besinnung erwachen; nicht um anderen ihre geistige Freiheit zu schmälern, sondern damit wir Herren im eigenen Hause werden, was wir heute nicht sind.
(Houston Stewart Chamberlain, *Arische Weltanschauung*, 1905: 30–32)

Text 4

(...) Alle offenkundige und heimliche Feindschaft von Ost und West, von jenseits der See haben wir bisher ertragen im Bewußtsein unserer Verantwortung und Kraft. Nun aber will man uns demütigen. Man verlangt, daß wir mit verschränkten Armen zusehen, wie unsere Feinde sich zu tückischem Überfall rüsten, man will nicht dulden, daß wir in entschlossener Treue zu unserem Bundesgenossen stehen, der um sein Ansehen als Großmacht kämpft und mit dessen Erniedrigung auch unsere Macht und Ehre verloren ist. So muß denn das Schwert entscheiden. Mitten im Frieden überfällt uns der Feind. Darum auf! zu den Waffen! Jedes Schwanken, jedes Zögern wäre Verrat am Vaterlande. Um Sein oder Nichtsein unseres Reiches handelt es sich, das unsere Väter sich neu gründeten. Um Sein oder Nichtsein deutscher Macht und deutschen Wesens. Wir werden uns wehren bis zum letzten Hauch von Mann und Roß, und wir werden diesen Kampf bestehen auch gegen eine Welt von Feinden. Noch nie ward Deutschland überwunden, wenn es einig war. Vorwärts mit Gott, der mit uns sein wird, wie er mit den Vätern war!
(Kaiser Wilhelm II, 'An das deutsche Volk', 6.8.1914)

Text 5

Auf Grund der Haager Konvention von 1899 galt die Verwendung von Geschossen für unzulässig, deren alleiniger Zweck die Verbreitung von erstickenden oder betäubenden Gasen ist. Das in Worten stets von Humanität übertriefende England, das mit widerwärtiger Grausamkeit auch die berüchtigten Dumdumgeschosse verwendet, kehrte sich im selben Augenblicke nicht an diese Bestimmungen, als deren Nichtbeachtung ihm von Nutzen sein konnte. Solche Gesetze sind ja nach angelsächsischer Anschauung immer nur für die anderen bindend, denen man dann sogar die Versenkung eines Truppentransportdampfers als völkerrechtswidrige Greueltat anrechnet, wie von amerikanischer Seite geschehen. Rücksichtslos setzten sich die Engländer in ihren Kämpfen im

Sudan und besonders im Burenkriege über die Haager Bestimmungen hinweg und bedienten sich der grauenhaft tückischen Lydditgranaten, die im Umkreise von hundert Meter alles Lebende dem Erstickungstode überlieferten.

(O. Th. Stein, 'Gase als Kampfmittel', 1919: 135)

Text 6

Zum vierten Male zwingt mich das Schicksal, den Neujahrsaufruf im Kriege an das deutsche Volk zu richten. In diesen vier Jahren ist aber auch dem deutschen Volke klar geworden, daß es in diesem Kampf, der uns, wie so oft in der deutschen Geschichte, von den habgierigen alten Feinden aufgezwungen worden war, wirklich um Sein oder Nichtsein geht. Wenn in früheren Jahrhunderten dynastische Streitigkeiten die Welt mit ihrem Kriegslärm erfüllten, dann waren die Resultate eines solchen Kampfes für Sieger und Besiegte in ihren Folgen oft doch nur sehr bescheiden. Dennoch ist nach einem jahrhundertelangen Verfall der ersten Deutschen Reiches unser Volk infolge seiner inneren Zersplitterung und der daraus entsprungenen Ohnmacht von seiner einst achtungsgebietenden Stellung in Europa heruntergesunken und für lange Zeiten nur zum Kulturdünger der anderen Welt geworden. Ungezählte Millionen Deutscher waren gezwungen, um das tägliche Brot zu finden, die Heimat zu verlassen. Gerade sie haben unbewußt mitgeholfen, jenen Kontinent aufzubauen, der nunmehr Europa zum zweiten Male mit Krieg zu überziehen versucht.

(...) Hätte das deutsche Volk im Jahre 1918, statt den verlogenen heuchlerischen Phrasen Wilsons zu glauben, den Kampf in eiserner Entschlossenheit weitergeführt, so wäre schon damals die feindliche Umwelt zusammengebrochen.

(part of Hitler's speech on New Year's Day 1943, quoted from Domarus II: 1967f.)

Text 7

Wir Deutschen können stolz sein auf all die berühmten Persönlichkeiten unserer Geschichte. Und wir müssen uns von niemandem einreden lassen, dass wir minderwertig, kriminell oder rechtsradikal sind. Radikal sind die, die uns vernichten wollen, zum Beispiel die Zweckverbände als Handlanger der Politik.

Erkennen Sie bitte die Zusammenhänge! Erkennen Sie bitte auch die Funktion der Medien! Diese werden von den Machthabern benutzt und manupuliert, um das einfache Volk zu steuern. Wenn die Machthaber jetzt nicht endlich die Wahrheit sagen, entfachen sie einen Krieg im eigenen Lande. Ich frage die Verantwortlichen: Können Sie das verantworten? Wollen Sie es so weit kommen lassen? Denken Sie an die Not, das Elend, den Hunger, die Tragödien, das Blutvergießen! Schützen Sie unsere Kinder!!! Bitte!!!

Sagen Sie endlich die Wahrheit, haben Sie den Mut, retten Sie Deutschland vor den vernichtenden Folgen weiteren Schweigens!

Die Wahrheit kommt immer ans Licht, früher oder später. Tragen Sie dazu bei und wir bekommen alle die Chance für einen Neubeginn. Einen Neubeginn mit einer ehrlichen, aufrichtigen Regierung, die dem Wohle des Deutschen Volkes und aller Menschen auf der ganzen Welt dient.

Wie alle dienen einem ehrlichen, aufrichtigen Staat! Wir sind Bürger des Deutschen Reiches!
('Der größte Betrug seit Bestehen des Universums?', Martina Pflock, Vereinsvorsitzende „ Abwasser—Abzocke! Nein Danke!", 5.10.2004; www. abwasser—abzocke.de/text/text13.htm).

Text 8

Seitdem waren viele Jahre verflossen, und was mir einst als Junge wie faules Siechtum erschien, empfand ich nun als Ruhe vor dem Sturme. Schon während meiner Wiener Zeit lag über dem Balkan jene fahle Schwüle, die den Orkan anzuzeigen pflegt, und schon zuckte manchmal auch ein hellerer Lichtschein auf, um jedoch rasch in das unheimliche Dunkel sich wieder zurückzuverlieren. Dann aber kam der Balkankrieg, und mit ihm fegte der erste Windstoß über das nervös gewordene Europa hinweg. Die nun kommende Zeit lag wie ein schwerer Alpdruck auf den Menschen, brütend wie fiebrige Tropenglut, so daß das Gefühl der herannahenden Katastrophe infolge der ewigen Sorge endlich zur Sehnsucht wurde: der Himmel möge endlich dem Schicksal, das nicht mehr zu hemmen war, den freien Lauf gewähren. Da fuhr denn auch schon der erste gewaltige Blitzstrahl auf die Erde nieder: das Wetter brach los, und in den Donner des Himmels mengte sich das Dröhnen der Batterien des Weltkriegs. (*MK*: 173) [Since then many years have passed, and what as a boy had seemed to me a lingering disease, I now felt to be the quiet before the storm. As early as my Vienna period, the Balkans were immersed in that livid sultriness which customarily announces the hurricane, and from time to time a beam of brighter light flared up, only to vanish again in the spectral darkness. But then came the Balkan War and with it the first gust of wind swept across a Europe grown nervous. The time which now followed lay on the chests of men like a heavy

188   The Language of Violence

nightmare, sultry as feverish tropical heat, so that due to constant anxiety the sense of the approaching catastrophe turned at last to longing: let Heaven at last give free rein to the fate which could no longer be thwarted. And then the first mighty lightning flash struck the earth; the storm was unleashed and with the thunder of Heaven there mingled the roar of the World War batteries. (Mh.: 145)]

Text 9

Dieser Grundsatz gilt also auch für den einzelnen Menschen, sofern er große Ziele erreichen will. Auch er wird dies nur in stufenförmigen Abschnitten zu tun vermögen, auch er wird dann immer seine gesamten Anstrengungen auf die Erreichung einer bestimmt begrenzten Aufgabe zu vereinigen haben, so lange, bis diese erfüllt erscheint und die Absteckung eines neuen Abschnittes vorgenommen werden kann. Wer nicht diese Teilung des zu erobernden Weges in einzelne Etappen vornimmt und diese dann planmäßig unter schärfster Zusammenfassung aller Kräfte einzeln zu überwinden trachtet, wird niemals bis zum Schlußziel zu gelangen vermögen, sondern irgendwo auf dem Wege, vielleicht sogar abseits desselben, liegen bleiben. Dieses Heranarbeiten an das Ziel ist eine Kunst und erfordert jeweils den Einsatz aber auch der letzten Energie, um so Schritt für Schritt den Weg zu überwinden.

Die allererste Vorbedingung also, die zum Angriff auf ein so schwere Teilstrecke des menschlichen Weges not tut, ist die, daß es der Führung gelingt, der Masse des Volkes gerade das jetzt zu erreichende, besser zu erkämpfende Teilziel als das einzig und allein der menschlichen Aufmerksamkeit würdige, von dessen Eroberung alles anhänge, hinzustellen. Die große Menge des Volkes kann ohnehin nie den ganzen Weg vor sich sehen, ohne zu ermüden und an der Aufgabe zu verzweifeln. Sie wird in einem gewissen Umfang das Ziel im Auge behalten, den Weg aber nur in kleinen Teilstrecken zu übersehen vermögen, ähnlich dem Wanderer, der ebenfalls wohl das Ende seiner Reise weiß und kennt, der aber die endlose Straße besser überwindet, wenn er sich dieselbe in Abschnitte zerlegt und auf jeden einzelnen losmarschiert, als ob er schon das ersehnte Ziel selber wäre. (*MK*: 273f.) [This principle applies also to the individual man in so far as he wants to achieve great goals. He, too, will be able to do this only in steplike sections, and he, too, will always have to unite his entire energies on the achievement of a definitely delimited task, until this task seems fulfilled and a new section can be marked out. Anyone who does not divide the road to be conquered into separate stages and does not try to conquer these one by one, systematically with the sharpest concentration of all his forces, will never be able to reach the ultimate goal, but will be left lying somewhere along the road, or perhaps even off it. The gradual working up to a goal is an art, and to conquer the road step by step in this way you must throw in your last ounce of energy.

The very first prerequisite needed for attacking such a difficult stretch of the human road is for the leadership to succeed in representing to the masses of the people the partial goal which now has to be achieved, or rather conquered, as the one which is solely worthy of attention, on whose conquest everything depends. The great mass of the people cannot see the whole road ahead of them without growing weary and despairing of the task. A certain number of them will keep the goal in mind, but will only be able to see the road in small, partial stretches, like the wanderer, who likewise knows and recognises the end of his journey, but is better able to conquer the endless highway if he divides it into sections and boldly attacks each one as though it represented the desired goal itself. (Mh.: 227f.)]

APPENDIX II

Rhetorical Devices

1   Superlatives

In his description of NS language *("LTI")*, Victor Klemperer differentiates between (a) adjectives in their superlative form, which I will call grammatical superlatives, (b) superlative meanings inherent in words, and (c) 'ganz superlativisch durchtränkte Satzgebilde' (clauses and sentences saturated with hyperbole) (Klemperer 1966: 233). In *MK* these categories seldom appear alone, with a fusion of (a) and (b) the commonest type of superlative (see Section 1.3 below).

1.1   Grammatical superlatives

'mein brennendster Herzenswunsch' (*MK*: 136) [my most ardent and heartfelt wish (Mh.: 114)], 'teuerstes Blut' (*MK*: 219) [the most precious blood (Mh.: 182)], 'mit brutalster Rücksichtslosigkeit' (*MK*: 392) [with brutal ruthlessness (Mh.: 324)], '(Rot) ist die aufpeitschendste' (*MK*: 402) [(red) is the most exciting (Mh.: 332)], 'die schwersten, blutigsten Verfolgungen' (*MK*: 778) [the gravest, bloodiest persecutions (Mh.: 625)], 'die humanste Tat der Menschheit' (*MK*: 279) [the most human act of mankind (Mh.: 232)]; 'Da haben sie erbärmlichst und jämmerlichst versagt' (*MK*: 537) [they miserably and wretchedly failed (Mh.: 436)].

Constructions with *auf das ...-ste, am ...-sten, bei ...-stem, vom ...-sten* or *in der ...-sten Weise*:

'am allerbesten' (*MK*: 252) [most of all (Mh.: 210)], 'auf das ernsteste' (*MK*: 248) [gravely (Mh.: 207)], 'auf das schlagendste' (*MK*: 282) [striking (Mh.: 234)], 'auf das rücksichtsloseste' (*MK*: 370) [ruthlessly (Mh.: 305)], 'wen sie am tödlichsten hassen' (*MK*: 386) [the man they hate worst (Mh.: 319)], 'auf das unseligste rächen' (*MK*: 771) [to pay most catastrophically (Mh.: 620)], 'auf das ungeheuerlichste' (*MK*: 120) [enormously (Mh.: 101)], 'vom allerärgsten Mißgriff' (*MK*: 260) [from the worst possible mistakes (Mh.: 217)], 'bei gründlichstem Abriechen' (*MK*: 94) [after the most careful sniffing (Mh.: 79)], 'in der schurkenhafteste Weise' (*MK*: 94) [in the most contemptible fashion (Mh.: 79)], 'in der wahrhaft genialsten Weise' (*MK*: 201) [most brilliantly (Mh.: 167)].

Common prefixes and suffixes include:

aller-: allerschlechtest (*MK*: 200), '(dem) Allereinfältigsten' (*MK*: 100), *allerverlogenst* (*MK*: 99), *allergenialst* (*MK*: 199);
-los: rücksichtslos (*MK*: 158: 401), *bedingungslos* (*MK*: 414), *bodenlos* (*MK*: 142), *grenzenlos* (*MK*: 301), *endlos* (*MK*: 218), *rettunglos* (*MK*: 212), *im Uferlosen* (*MK*: 513);
riesen-: riesenhaft (*MK*: 314), *riesengroß* (*MK*: 355), *Riesenkampf* (*MK*: 409), *Riesenorganismus* (*MK*: 481), *Riesenmuschel* (*MK*: 560);
-reich: tränenreich (*MK*: 438), *siegreich* (*MK*: 438);
über-: übermenschlich (*MK*: 252), *überwälzendst* (*MK*: 486), *überschäumend* (*MK*: 475), *überwältigendst* (*MK*: 124);
un-: unermeßlich (*MK*: 301), *unglaublich* (*MK*: 87), *unsäglich* (*MK*: 483), *unvergleichlich* (*MK*: 301), *ungeteilt* (*MK*: 153), *unermeßlich* (*MK*: 301), *unwahr* (*MK*: 698), *Unmasse* (262), *Unnatur* (*MK*: 65);
ur-: urgesund (*MK:* 9), *urewig* (*MK*: 296, cf. 129), *urwüchsig* (*MK*: 139), *Urelemente* (*MK*: 438);
-voll: schandvoll (*MK*: 701), *schmachvoll* (*MK*: 714), *verhängnisvoll* (*MK*: 751), *wundervoll* (*MK*: 435).

1.2 Superlative Meanings

ewig (eternal) (*MK*: 9: 168), 'immer und ewig' (*MK*: 286) [always (Mh.: 237)], *fanatisch*, as in **'fanatischer, ja hysterischer Leidenschaften'** (*MK*: 475) [*fanatical, yes, hysterical passion* (Mh.: 388)], 'fanatische Vaterlandsliebe' (*MK*: 611) [fanatical love of their country (Mh.: 497)], *felsenfest* (*MK*: 405), *flammend* (*MK*: 705); *genial* (*MK*: 510), *gigantisch* (*MK*: 729), *heilig*, as in 'heilige Aufgabe' (*MK*: 626) [sacred mission (Mh.: 509)], *heldenhaft* (heroic) (*MK*: 546), *heldisch* (heroic) (*MK*: 103), *himmleschreiend*, as in 'in himmelschreiender Weise' (*MK*: 700) [in a way that cries to high Heaven (Mh.: 566)], *himmelweit* (*MK*: 415) [yawning (Mh.: 344), literally 'as wide as the sky'], *infernalisch* (*MK*: 520), *kolossal* (*MK*: 559), *kometähnlich* (comet-like) (*MK*: 488), *kübelweise* (by bucketfuls) (*MK*: 34), *leidenschaftlich* (passionate) (*MK*: 142), *monumental* (*MK*: 413), *unendlich* (infinite) (*MK*: 767), *ungeheuer*, as in 'ungeheuer, riesenhaft' (*MK*: 314) [immense gigantic (Mh.: 261)], *ungeheuerlich* (immense) (*MK*: 457), *Krönung*, as in 'die Krönung alles Opfersinnes' (*MK*: 327) [the crown of all sense of self-sacrifice (Mh.: 271)], *Mustervorbild*, as in 'von dem Mustervorbild aller Verantwortungslosigkeit' (*MK*: 306) [the model prototype of all irresponsibility (Mh.: 254)], *Welt* in compounds such as 'jüdische Welteroberungsmaschine' (*MK*: 528) [Jewish machine for world conquest (Mh.: 429)], 'des internationalen Weltfinanzjudentums' (*MK*: 702) [of international world finance (Mh.: 568)], 'das jüdische Weltsatrapenreich' (*MK*: 723) [the world empire of Jewish satrapies (Mh.: 584)].

1.3 Grammatical Superlatives with Words of Superlative Meaning

'Was mir zu allererst und am allermeisten zu denken gab' (*MK*: 85) [What gave me most food for thought (Mh.: 73)];
'als weitaus furchtbarste' (*MK*: 351) [by far the most terrible (Mh.: 291)];
'die absolute Führung des extrembesten Teiles' (*MK*: 581) [*the absolute leadership of the extreme best part* (Mh.: 472)];
'das Ungeheuerlichste an Rechtswidrigkeit (...), das man sich vorstellen kann' (*MK*: 545) [the most monstrous form of injustice that can be conceived of (Mh.: 442f.)];
'vor der erbärmlichsten Kapitulation aller Zeiten' (*MK*: 59) [the most wretched capitulation of all time (Mh.: 51)];
'das Gewaltigste, was die Erde bisher je gesehen' (*MK*: 249) [the mightiest that the earth had ever seen (Mh.: 208)];
'die entsetzlichste Gewißheit meines Lebens' (*MK*: 222) [the most terrible certainty of my life (Mh.: 184f.)];
'die überlegendste Führung und zugleich die diszipliniertheste, blindgehorsamste, bestgedrillte Truppe' (*MK*: 510) [the most superior leadership and at the same time the most disciplined, blindly obedient, best-drilled troop (Mh.: 416)];
'durch den sträflichen Leichtsinn dieser Verantwortungslosesten der Nation' (*MK*: 301) [the criminal frivolity of these most irresponsible among irresponsibles (Mh.: 250)];
'die unglaubliche Überschwemmung des gesamten politischen Lebens mit den minderwertigsten Erscheinungen unserer Tage' [= Jews] (*MK*: 87) [the incredible inundation of all political life with the most inferior, and I mean the most inferior, characters of our time (Mh.: 74)];
'Wer Führer sein will, trägt bei höchster unumschränkter Autorität auch die letzte und schwerste Verantwortung' (*MK*: 379) [Any man who wants to be leader bears, along with the highest unlimited authority, also the ultimate and heaviest responsibility (Mh.: 313)].

1.4 Superlatives of Size and Amount

kübelweise, as in 'wie (...) das Gift kübelweise in das Volk hineingeschüttet wird' (*MK*: 34) [the poison poured into the people by bucketfuls (Mh.: 31)], *kolossal* (*MK*: 559), *gigantisch* (*MK*: 729), *ungeheur* (immense) (*MK*: 314), 'jämmerlich zwergenhaft' (*MK*: 774) [miserable and dwarfish (Mh.: 622)], 'Am Gegner aber war unendlich viel zu lernen' (*MK*: 199) [There was no end to what could be learned from the enemy (Mh.: 166)], *himmelweit* (*MK*: 415) [yawning (Mh.: 344)], *unermeßlich* (immeasurable) (*MK*: 301), and compounds with *riesen-* as listed above.

1.5 Numerical Superlatives

'all die Hunderttausende' (*MK*: 363) [all the hundreds of thousands (Mh.: 300)], 'hunderttausend und aber hunderttausend Menschen' (*MK*: 449) [hundreds and hundreds of thousands of people (Mh.: 369)], 'in tausend und aber tausend Formen' (*MK*: 80) [in thousands and thousands of forms (Mh.: 68)], 'Millionen, ja Milliarden von menschlichen Lebewesen' (*MK*: 496) [millions, nay, billions of human creatures (Mh.: 405)];
'Was wir brauchten und brauchen, waren und sind nicht hundert oder zweihundert verwegene Verschwörer, sondern hunderttausend und aber hunderttausend fanatische Kämpfer für unsere Weltanschauung' (*MK*: 608) [*What we needed and still need were and are not a hundred or two hundred reckless conspirators, but a hundred thousand and a second hundred thousand fighters for our philosophy of life* (Mh.: 494)].

1.6 Time Superlatives

ewig, as in 'die Souveränität des ewigen Judenreiches' (*MK*: 704) [the sovereignty of the eternal Jewish empire (Mh.: 569)], 'seit urewig' (*MK*: 116) [from time immemorial (Mh.: 98)], 'jetzt und in allen Zeiten der Zukunft' (*MK*: 99) [now and in all ages of the future (Mh.: 83)], **'unerschütterlich und unbesiegbar für immer'** (*MK*: 475) [*unshakable and invincible for ever* (Mh.: 388)], 'vielleicht jahrhunderttausendlange Arbeit' (*MK*: 313) [work of perhaps hundreds of thousands of years (Mh.: 260)], 'von wirklicher, weltgeschichtlicher Größe' (*MK*: 773) [of real world-historical import (Mh.: 621)], 'den gemeinsten Landesverrat, ja die erbärmlichste Schurkentat der deutschen Geschichte überhaupt' (*MK*: 607) [the vilest treason, nay, the most wretched piece of villainy in all German history (Mh.: 493)].

2 Repetition

2.1 Phonetic Repetition

2.1.1 Alliteration

'**Wir wollen wieder Waffen!**' (*MK*: 715) [*Give us arms again!* (Mh.: 577)];
'Geschrei und Geschimpfe' (*MK*: 90) [hue and cry (Mh.: 76)];
'hehr und hoch' (*MK*: 117) [lofty and noble (Mh.: 98)];
'stumpf und stumm' (*MK*: 223) [in dull silence (Mh.: 186)];
'und flattern flügelbegabt hinaus' (*MK*: 411) [endowed with wings, fly out (Mh.: 341)];
'wich nicht und wankte nicht' (*MK*: 220) [neither gave ground nor wavered (Mh.: 183)];
'eine Koalition von Krüppeln' (*MK*: 747) [a coalition of cripples (Mh.: 602)];
'wer rastet—rostet' (*MK*: 440) [he who rests—rusts (Mh.: 362)].

2.1.2 Assonance

'die zum Idol gewordene Idee' (*MK*: 122) [to an idea which has become an idol (Mh.: 103)];
'daß besagte Angriffe nur die Abwehr von Angriffen der anderen Seite waren!' (*MK*: 125) [that these attacks are only a defence against the attacks from the other side! (Mh.: 105)];
'zur lockenden Ursache der Unterjochung und Unterdrückung' (*MK*: 168) [the seductive cause of subjugation and oppression (Mh.: 140)].

2.1.3 Rhyming

'Sang- und klanglos' (*MK*: 779) [Quietly and ingloriously (Mh.: 626)];
'Nun lungert er hungernd herum' (*MK*: 26) [Now he walks the streets, hungry (Mh.: 25)];
'Er selbst ist kein Element der Organisation, sondern ein Ferment der Dekomposition' [= the Jew] (*MK*: 743) [He himself [the Jew] is no element of organisation, but a ferment of decomposition (Mh.: 598)].

2.2 Morphological Repetition

'ausgerottet und ausgelöscht' (*MK*: 743) [exterminated and extinguished (Mh.: 598)], 'versetzt und verkauft' (*MK*: 26) [pawns and sells (Mh.: 25)], '**verfemt und verdammt**' (*MK*: 642) [*outlawed and damned* (Mh.: 522)], 'Unterjochung und Unterdrückung' (*MK*: 168) [subjugation and oppression (Mh.: 140)], 'dem

Ausgange zuwälzte, zuschob und zudrängte' (*MK*: 406) [to move, shove and press towards the exit (Mh.: 336)], 'Einigkeit und Einheit' (*MK*: 574) [unification and unity (Mh.: 467)].

2.3 Grammatical Repetition

2.3.1 Anaphora

Anaphora is the repetition of the first word of a phrase or clause in each sequential construction (Nash: 112).

At the beginning of phrases:

> 'Jede jüdische Verleumdung und jede jüdische Lüge ist eine Ehrennarbe am Körper unserer Kämpfer' (*MK*: 386) [Every Jewish slander and every Jewish lie is a scar of honour on the body of our warriors (Mh.: 319)];
> 'Der gleiche Vortrag, der gleiche Redner, das gleiche Thema wirken ganz verschieden (...)' (*MK*: 530) [The same lecture, the same speaker, the same theme have an entirely different effect (...) (Mh.: 430)];
> '(der) brutalen Forderung, nur rote Zeitungen zu halten, nur rote Versammlungen zu besuchen, rote Bücher zu lesen usw.' (*MK*: 44) [the brutal demand that I read only Red papers, attend only Red meetings, read only Red books, etc. (Mh.: 39)].

At the beginning of clauses and sentences:

> '(...) allein ich wende mich an die, denen das Schicksal entweder bisher dieses Glück verweigert oder in grausamer Härte wieder genommen hat; ich wende mich an alle die, die losgelöst vom Mutterlande, selbst um das heilige Gut der Sprache zu kämpfen haben (...); ich wende mich an alle diese und weiß: Sie werden mich verstehen!' (*MK*: 136) [(...) but I address myself to those to whom Fate has either hitherto denied this, or from whom in harsh cruelty it has taken it away; I address myself to all those who, detached from their mother country, have to fight even for the holy treasure of their language (...); I address myself to all these, and I know that they will understand me! (Mh.: 114)].

At the beginning of paragraphs:

> 'Das Heer erzog zur unbedingten Verantwortlichkeit (...).
> Das Heer erzog zur Entschlußkraft (...).
> Das Heer erzog zum Idealismus und zur Hingabe an das Vaterland und seine Größe (...)' (*MK*: 306f.)
> [The army trained men for unconditional responsibility (...).

The army trained men in resolution (...).
The army trained men in idealism and devotion to the fatherland and its greatness (...) (Mh.: 254f.)];

'Halb war alles, was irgendwie dem Einfluß dieses Parlaments unterstand (...).
Halb und schwach war die Bündnispolitik des Reiches (...).
Halb war die Polenpolitik (...)
Halb war die Lösung der elsaß-lothringischen Frage' (*MK*: 297)
[Half-hearted was everything that was subject in any way to the influence of this parliament (...).
Half-hearted and weak was the alliance policy of the Reich (...).
Half-hearted was the Polish policy (...)
Half-hearted was the solution of the Alsace-Lorraine question (...) (Mh.: 246f.)].

2.3.2 Anadiplosis

Here the last word of a phrase or clause becomes the first word of the next (Nash: 112), as follows:

'In diesem Falle blieb als letzte Rettung noch der Kampf, der Kampf mit allen Waffen (...)' (*MK*: 68) [In this case the only remaining hope was struggle, struggle with all the weapons (...) (Mh.: 59)];
'In diesen Nächten wuchs mir der Haß, der Haß gegen die Urheber dieser Tat' (*MK*: 225) [In these nights hatred grew in me, hatred for those responsible for this deed (Mh.: 187)].

2.3.4 Chiasmus

The name of this figure is based on the Greek word for the letter **X** and describes a two-clause sentence in which the second clause is an inverted parallel of the first (Nash: 114). This figure is not common in *MK*:

'Fast jeder Schreiber ein Jude und jeder Jude ein Schreiber' (*MK*: 211) [Nearly every clerk was a Jew and nearly every Jew was a clerk (Mh.: 175)].

2.3.5 Polyptoton

This figure involves the repetition of a word in different inflectional forms:

'Da nicht der Jude der Angegriffene, sondern der Angreifer ist, gilt als sein Feind nicht nur der, der angreift, sondern auch der, der ihm Widerstand leistet' (*MK*: 355) [Since the Jew is not the attacked but the attacker, not only anyone who attacks passes as his enemy, but also anyone who resists him (Mh.: 293)];

'Es ging auf Biegen und Brechen. Und Deutschland bog sich gleich zu Beginn, um später dann beim vollständigen Bruch zu enden' (*MK*: 767) [It was a question of bending and breaking. Germany bent at the very outset, and ended up by breaking completely later (Mh.: 616)];

'Verbände und Verbändchen, Gruppen und Grüppchen' (*MK*: 515) [clubs and clublets, groups and grouplets (Mh.: 419)].

2.4 Lexical Repetition

'mehr und mehr' (*MK*: 47) [steadily (Mh.: 41)], 'oft und oft' (*MK*: 545) [many and many a time (Mh.: 442)], 'immer und immer wieder' (*MK*: 13) [again and again (Mh.: 14)], 'Pfui Teufel und wieder Pfui Teufel!' (*MK*: 540) [Phooey, I say, and again phooey! (Mh.: 439)], '(ich) wiederholte und wiederholte' (*MK*: 524) [I repeated and repeated them (Mh.: 426)], 'Juden und wieder Juden' (*MK*: 135) [Jews and more Jews (Mh.: 113)], 'hunderttausend und aber hunderttausend Menschen' (*MK*: 449) [hundreds and hundreds of thousands of people (Mh.: 369)], 'Für sie ist eben Geschichte Geschichte und Wahrheit Wahrheit' (*MK*: 260) [For them history remains history and the truth the truth (Mh.: 217)]; 'Denn jüdisches Interesse ist es heute, die völkische Bewegung in dem Augenblick in einem religiösen Kampf verbluten zu lassen, in dem sie beginnt, für den Juden eine Gefahr zu werden. Und ich betone das Wort verbluten lassen (...)' (*MK*: 632) [For it is to the Jewish interest today to make the folkish movement bleed to death in a religous struggle at the moment when it is beginning to become a danger for the Jew. And I expressly emphasise the words bleed to death (...) (Mh.: 513f.)].

Extreme cases of lexical repetition are reminiscent of oral rhetoric, such as:

'Ich vergesse nicht die dauernde freche Bedrohung, die das damalige panslawistische Rußland Deutschland zu bieten wagte; ich vergesse nicht die dauernden Probenmobilmachungen (...); ich kann nicht vergessen die Stimmung der öffentlichen Meinung in Rußland (...), kann nicht vergessen die große russische Presse, die immer mehr für Frankreich schwärmte als für uns' (*MK*: 753) [I have not forgotten the insolent threat which the pan-Slavic Russia of that time dared to address to Germany; I have not forgotten the constant practice mobilisations (...); I cannot forget the mood of public opinion in Russia (...); I cannot forget the big Russian newspapers, which were always more enthusiastic about France than about us (Mh.: 606)];

'**Freiwillige** vor die Front, **freiwillige** Patrouillengänger, **freiwillige** Meldegänger, **Freiwillige** für Telephontrupps, **Freiwillige** für die Brückenübergänge, **Freiwillige** für U-Boote, **Freiwillige** für Flugzeuge, **Freiwillige** für Sturmbataillone usw.—immer und immer wieder durch viereinhalb Jahre hindurch bei tausend Anlässen Freiwillige und wieder Freiwillige—' (*MK*: 582) [*volunteers* to the front, *volunteer* patrols, *volunteer* dispatch carriers, *volunteers* for telephone squads, *volunteers* for bridge crossings, *volunteers* for U-boats, *volunteers* for airplanes, *volunteers* for storm battalions, etc.—again and again through four and a half years, on thousands of occasions, *volunteers* and more *volunteers* (Mh.: 473)].

2.5 Semantic Repetition

'**Grund und Boden**' (*MK*: 754) [*soil* (Mh.: 607)], 'Mord und Totschlag' (*MK*: 559) [murder and homicide (Mh.: 455)], 'immer und ewig' (*MK*: 286) [always (Mh.: 237)], 'der internationale Weltjude' (*MK*: 675) [the international world Jew (Mh.: 548)], 'immer und jederzeit, an jeder Stelle und an jedem Orte' (*MK*: 550) [always and forever, at all times and places (Mh.: 447)], 'rein gefühlsmäßige Empfindungen' (*MK*: 131) [purely emotional feeling (Mh.: 110)], 'die heutige Gegenwart' (*MK*: 292) [the present time (Mh.: 242)], 'eines zentralen Mittelpunktes' (*MK*: 381) [of a focal centre (Mh.: 315)], 'dem Ausgange zuwälzte, zuschob und zudrängte' (*MK*: 406) [to move, shove and press towards the exit (Mh.: 336)], 'alle acht Tage, also wöchentlich einmal' (*MK*: 518) [every seven days; in other words, once a week (Mh.: 421)], '**vier Millionen emsig arbeitenden, fleißigen, schaffenden Menschen**' (*MK*: 628) [*four million hard-working, producing people* (Mh.: 510)], 'zu althergebracht, zu abgedroschen, dann wieder zu überlebt usw.' (*MK*: 202) [too old-fashioned, too hackneyed, too out-of-date (Mh.: 168)].

Lexical and semantic repetition:

'Es war alles umsonst gewesen. Umsonst all die Opfer und Entbehrungen, umsonst der Hunger und Durst von manchmal endlosen Monaten, vergeblich die Stunden, in denen wir, von Todesangst umkrallt, dennoch unsere Pflicht taten, und vergeblich der Tod von zwei Millionen, die dabei starben' (*MK*: 223f.) [And so it had all been in vain. In vain all the sacrifices and privations; in vain the hunger and thirst of months which were often endless; in vain the hours in which, with mortal fear clutching at our hearts, we nevertheless did our duty; and in vain the death of two millions who died (Mh.: 186)].

Semantic repetition and intensification:

With *besser (gesagt)*:

'Ähnliches ansehen zu können, besser gesagt, ansehen zu müssen' [= prostitution] (*MK*: 63) [to see similar things, or, better expressed, forced them to see them (Mh.: 55)];

'festzustellen, warum dies nicht geschah, oder, besser, warum man dies nicht getan' (*MK*: 78) [to ascertain why this did not occur, or rather, why it was not done (Mh.: 66)];
'Denn auch hier ist alles entlehnt, besser gestohlen' [= the concept of a Jewish religious community] (*MK*: 336) [For here, too, everything is borrowed or rather stolen (Mh.: 278)].

With *richtiger ausgedrückt:*

'aus der Tatsache des Zusammenstehens der Juden im Kampfe, richtiger ausgedrückt in der Ausplünderung ihrer Mitmenschen' (*MK*: 331) [the fact that they stand together in struggle, or, better expressed, in plundering of their fellow men (Mh.: 274)].

Semantic repetition and summarization:

With *kurz (gesagt):*

'innere Fäulnis, Feigheit, Charakterlosigkeit, kurz Unwürdigkeit' (*MK*: 250) [inner rottenness, cowardice, lack of character, in short, unworthiness (Mh.: 209)];
'die Elemente der Gemeinheit, der Niedertracht und der Feigheit, kurz die Masse des Extrems des Schlechten' (*MK*: 582) [the elements of baseness, treachery, cowardice, in short, the mass of the bad extreme (Mh.: 473)].

Introducing repetition:

'Das heißt mit anderen Worten folgendes: (...)' (*MK*: 654) [This, in other words, means the following: (...) (Mh.: 531)].

3 Accumulation *(Häufung)*

This figure is extremely common in *MK*. Only a small selection is recorded below.

3.1 Idiomatic Pairs *(Zwillingsformeln)*

'auf Schritt und Tritt' (*MK*: 63) [at every step (Mh.: 55)];
'auf Biegen und Brechen' (*MK*: 564) [through thick and thin (Mh.: 459)];
'Grund und Boden' (*MK*: 154) [land (Mh.: 128)];
'Hirn und Seele' (*MK*: 356) [mind and soul (Mh.: 294)];
'Zeter und Mordio (jammern)' (*MK*: 46) [cry bloody murder Mh.: 41)];
'Not und Harm' (*MK*: 3) [suffering and care (Mh.: 5)];

'Not und Jammer' (*MK*: 32) [poverty and suffering (Mh.: 29)];
'Not und Sorge' (*MK*: 762) [hardship and care (Mh.: 612)];
'Not und Verderben' (*MK*: 780) [misery and ruin (Mh.: 627)];
'Unheil und Verderben' (*MK*: 676) [rack and ruin (Mh.: 548)];
'Unglück und Jammer' (*MK*: 29) [misery and despair (Mh.: 27)];
'Elend und Jammer' (*MK*: 20) [hardship and misery (Mh.: 20)].

3.2 Figures of Three (*Dreierfiguren*)

'**die Kämpfer, die Lauen und die Verräter**' (*MK*: 10) [*The fighters, the lukewarm, and the traitors* (Mh.: 11)];
'Einsicht, Willenskraft und Tatentschlossenheit' (*MK*: 169) [insight, will power, and active determination (Mh.: 141)];
'**Treue, Opferwilligkeit, Verschwiegenheit** sind Tugenden' (*MK*: 461) [*Loyalty, spirit of sacrifice, discretion* are virtues (Mh.: 378)];
'neun Zehntel alles literarischen Schmutzes, künstlerischen Kitsches und theatralischen Blödsinns' [= of Jewish] (*MK*: 62) [nine tenths of all literary filth, artistic trash, and theatrical idiocy (Mh.: 54)];
'Dieser Kampf gegen die eigene Art, das eigene Nest, die eigene Heimat' [= of the Jews] (*MK*: 65) [This struggle against their own species, their own clan, their own homeland (Mh.: 56)];
'dem Ausgange zuwälzte, zuschob und zudrängte' (*MK*: 406) [began to move, shove, press towards the exit (Mh.: 336)]
'beschimpft und besudelt und beschmutzt' (*MK*: 552) [reviled, befouled, and soiled (Mh.: 449)];
'einfach, bestimmt und klar' (*MK*: 5) [simple, definite, and clear (Mh.: 7)];
'unbedingte, freche, einseitige Sturheit' [= of a lie] (*MK*: 201) [rabid, impudent bias and persistence (Mh.: 168)];
'**ein gesundes, lebensfähiges, natürliches Verhältnis**' (*MK*: 728) [*a healthy, viable natural relation* (Mh.: 587)];
'Flink wie Windhunde, zäh wie Leder und hart wie Kruppstahl' (*MK*: 392) [swift as greyhounds, tough as leather, and hard as Krupp steel (Mh.: 324)].

3.3 Figures of Four

'von Not und Sorge, von Schmach und Elend' (*MK*: 388) [of distress and care, of disgrace and misery (Mh.: 320)];
'mit Ach und Krach und Mühe und Nöten' (*MK*: 605) [with puffing and blowing, with trouble and grief (Mh.: 492)];
'mit Worten wie Schuft, Schurke, Lump und Verbrecher' (*MK*: 301f.) [by words such as 'scoundrel', 'villain', 'scum', and 'criminal' (Mh.: 250)];

'innere Fäulnis, Feigheit, Charakterlosigkeit, kurz Unwürdigkeit' (*MK*: 250) [inner rottenness, cowardice, lack of character, in short, unworthiness (Mh.: 209)];
'Diebstahl, Wucher, Raub, Einbruch usw.' (*MK*: 326) [theft, usury, robbery, burglary, etc. (Mh.: 270)];
'zehn- oder zwölftausend Volksverräter, Schieber, Wucherer und Betrüger' (*MK*: 772) [ten or twelve thousand traitors, profiteers, usurers, and swindlers (Mh.: 620)];
'mit einem Haufen von Straßenstrolchen, Deserteuren, Parteibonzen und jüdischen Literaten' (*MK*: 413) [a band of bums, deserters, party bosses, and Jewish journalists (Mh.: 342)].

3.4 Figures of Five

'im verschiedenen Maße der Kraft, der Stärke, der Klugheit, Gewandheit, Ausdauer usw.' (*MK*: 312) [in the varying measures of force, strength, intelligence, dexterity, endurance, etc. (Mh.: 259)];
'Repräsentanten der Lüge, des Betrugs, des Diebstahls, der Plünderung, des Raubes' [= Jews] (*MK*: 750) [champions of deceit, lies, theft, plunder, and rapine (Mh.: 604)];
'in einer Gesellschaft von Zuhältern, Dieben, Einbrechern, Deserteuren, Drückebergern usw.' (*MK*: 584) [the society of pimps, thieves, burglars, deserters, slackers, etc. (Mh.: 475)].

3.5 Enumeration

'Man kann dabei ihre Leser im großen und ganzen in drei Gruppen einteilen: erstens in die, die alles, was sie lesen glauben;
zweitens in solche, die gar nichts mehr glauben;
drittens in die Köpfe, welche das Gelesene kritisch prüfen und danach beurteilen' (*MK*: 262);
[Its readers, by and large, can be divided into three groups:
First, into those who believe everything they read;
second, into those who have ceased to believe anything;
third, into the minds which critically examine what they read, and judge accordingly (Mh.: 219)].

4 Aggressive and Apocalyptic Vocabulary

Compounds with *Kampf-*, *-kampf* and *-kämpfer*:

kampfbestimmend (*MK*: 748) [decisively (Mh.: 603)], *Kampfelemente* (*MK*: 580) [fighting elements (Mh.: 472)], *Kampfesentschlossenheit* (*MK*: 761) [determination for struggle (Mh.: 611)], *kampfesfreudig* (*MK*: 658) [militant (Mh.: 533)], *Kampfesmission* (*MK*: 776) [mission of their struggle (Mh.: 624)], *Kampfesmut* (*MK*: 414) [courage to fight (Mh.: 343)], *kampffähig* (*MK*: 513) [capable of struggle (Mh.: 418)], *Kampffaktor* (*MK*: 417) [fighting factor (Mh.: 345)], *Kampffeld* (*MK*: 109) [the field (Mh.: 92)], *Kampfgemeinschaft* (*MK*: 550) [combat group (Mh.: 447)], *Kampfkraft* (*MK*: 109) [fighting power (Mh.: 92)], *kampfkräftig* (*MK*: 508) [fighting (organisation) (Mh.: 414)], *Kampfruf* (*MK*: 10) [battle-cry (Mh.: 11)], *Kampfschatz* (*MK*: 10) [battle fund (Mh.: 11)], *Kampftruppe* (*MK*: 52) [shock troops (Mh.: 45)], *Kampfwille* (*MK*: 109) [will to fight (Mh.: 91)].

Entscheidungskampf (*MK*: 766) [decisive struggle (Mh.: 616)], *Existenzkampf* (*MK*: 5) [struggle for existence (Mh.: 7)], *Freiheitskampf* (*MK*: 177) [fight for freedom (Mh.: 148)], *Heldenkampf* (*MK*: 102) [heroic struggle (Mh.: 86)], *Klassenkampf* (*MK*: 80) [class struggle (Mh.:)], *Lebenserhaltungskampf* (*MK*: 495) [struggle for self-preservation (Mh.: 404)], *Lebenskampf* (*MK*: 29) [the hardship of my own life (Mh.: 27)], *Lohnkampf* (*MK*: 677) [struggles over pay (Mh.: 549)], *Massenkampf* (*MK*: 677) [mass struggle (Mh.: 549)], *Riesenkampf* (*MK*: 409) [gigantic struggle (Mh.: 339)], *Ringkampf* (*MK*: 532) [wrestling bout (Mh.: 432)], *Schicksalskampf* (*MK*: 155) [struggle for the destiny [= of the whole nation] (Mh.: 130)], *Seelenkampf* (*MK*: 64) [soul struggle (Mh.: 56)], *Tarifkampf* (*MK*: 677) [struggles over (...) wage scales (Mh.: 549)], *Titanenkämpfe* (*MK*: 578) [titanic struggles (Mh.: 470)], *Verleumdungskampf* (*MK*: 355) [slanderous struggle (Mh.: 293)].

Barrikadenkämpfer (*MK*: 592) [barricade fighters (Mh.: 481)], *Hauptkämpfer* (*MK*: 575) [chief fighter (Mh.: 468)], *Vorkämpfer* (*MK*: 485) [vanguard fighters (Mh.: 396)].

Other Violent Vocabulary:

This vocabulary is most usually applied to Jews, or combinations of groups which Hitler takes to include Jews, such as the press and Marxists. Mh.'s rendition is given only when this differs from the generally accepted translation:

abdrosseln (to throttle) (*MK*: 265), *die Gurgel abdrücken* (to strangle) (*MK*: 521), *abwürgen* (to stifle, Mh. has 'slaughter') (*MK*: 750), *abzapfen* (to tap off (blood)) (*MK*: 340), *anfressen* (to corrode) (*MK*: 310), *auflösen* (to dissolve) (*MK*: 765), *aufzwingen* (to force upon) (*MK*: 648), *ausbluten* (to drain of blood, Mh. has 'bled white') (*MK*: 749), *Ausblutung* (bleeding dry) (*MK*: 581), *aushöhlen* (to erode, Mh. has 'threaten') (*MK*: 111), *auslöschen* (to extinguish) (*MK*: 743), *Ausmerzung* (annihilation) (*MK*: 764), *ausplündern* (to plunder) (*MK*: 122), *Ausplünderung* (plundering) (*MK*: 585), *auspressen* (to squeeze) (*MK*: 343), *Auspressung* (squeezing, Mh. has 'sweating', *MK*: 703), *ausschalten* (to switch off, Mh. has 'exclude') (*MK*: 317), *ausrotten* (to exterminate) (*MK*: 331), *Ausrottung* (extermination) (*MK*: 155), *aussaugen* (to suck (blood)) (*MK*: 340 and 343), *zum Einsturz bringen* (to bring to collapse) (*MK*: 505), *entreißen* (to snatch) (*MK*: 155), *erobern* (to conquer) (*MK*: 315), *Erschütterung* (shaking) (*MK*: 676), *herausfressen* (to eat out) (Mh. has 'gnaw') (*MK*: 32), *herauspressen* (to squeeze) (*MK*: 341), *herausschinden* (to extract, Mh. has 'grind') (*MK*: 341), *hineinzerren* (to force into) (*MK*: 586), *niederdreschen* (Mh. has 'thrash') (*MK*: 601), *rauben* (to rob) (*MK*: 757), *ruinieren* (to ruin) (*MK*: 765), *sabotieren* (to sabotage) (*MK*: 265), *steinigen* (to stone) (*MK*: 521), *stürzen* (to overthrow) (*MK*: 327), *überfallen* (to attack, ambush) (*MK*: 330), *überschwemmen* (to flood) (*MK*: 528), *überwuchern* (to choke) (*MK*: 168), *umgarnen* (to grip, ensnare) (*MK*: 345), *Umgarnung* (ensnarement) (*MK*: 340), *umklammern* (to ensnare) (*MK*: 345), *Umstrickung* (snaring) (*MK*: 751), *Unheil und Verderben* (rack and ruin) (*MK*: 676), *Unterdrückung* (oppression) (*MK*: 168), *unterhöhlen* (to undermine) (*MK*: 265), *unterjochen* (to subjugate) (*MK*: 319), *Unterjochung* (subjugation) (*MK*: 168), *unterwerfen* (to subject) (*MK*: 315), *verführen* (to seduce) (*MK*: 402), *vergiften* (to poison) (*MK*: 346), *Vergiftung* (poisoning) (*MK*: 751), *verhetzen* (to incite) (*MK*: 402), *Verhetzer* (agitator) (*MK*: 185), *sich verkrümeln* (to crumble away) (*MK*: 582), *verbastardiert* (bastardized) (*MK*: 421), *vernichten* (to destroy) (*MK*: 327), *Vernichtung* (destruction) (*MK*: 187), *Verpestung* (contamination) (*MK*: 630), *verseuchen* (to contaminate) (*MK*: 358), *verzehren* (to consume, exhaust) (*MK*: 397), *würgen* (to strangle) (*MK*: 757), *zerbrechen* (to smash (to pieces), Mh. has 'crushing') (*MK*: 267), *Zerbrechung* (destruction, Mh. has 'smash') (*MK*: 214), *Zerfall* (decay) (*MK*: 80), *zerfetzen* (to tear to pieces, Mh. has 'disorganised') (*MK*: 39), *zerfressen* (to corrode, Mh. has 'infected') (*MK*: 580), *Zerfressung* (corrosion, Mh. has 'erosion') (*MK*: 80), *zerlegen* (to dismantle, to take to pieces, Mh. has 'divide') (*MK*: 338), *zermürben* (to wear down, Mh. has 'undermined') (*MK*: 505), *Zermürbungsarbeit* ('wearing down', Mh. has 'softening up') (*MK*: 352), *zerpflücken* (to pull apart) (*MK*: 522f), *zerreiben* (to crush) (*MK*: 27), *zerreißen* (to tear) (*MK*: 232), *Zerreißung* (tearing, Mh. has 'partition') (*MK*: 175), *in den Abgrund zerren* (to drag into the abyss) (*MK*: 414f.), *zerschießen* (to shoot to pieces) (*MK*: 582), *Zersetzung* (corruption, disintegration) (*MK*: 751), *zersplitternd* (splintering) (*MK*: 512), *Zersplitterung* (fragmentation) (*MK*: 395), *Zerstörung* (destruction) (*MK*: 187), *zertreten* (to crush underfoot, Mh. has 'trample') (*MK*: 606), *zertrümmern* (to shatter) (*MK*: 120), *Zertrümmerung* (shattering) (*MK*: 676), *zunichte machen* (to shatter, to ruin, Mh. has 'nullify') (*MK*: 712), *zurückdrängen* (to repress) (*MK*: 155), *zwingen* (to force, to compel) (*MK*: 267).

5 Epithets and Evaluations

5.1 Neutral Epithets

(die breite) Masse (the broad masses); 'Proletariermassen' (*MK*: 413) [proletarian masses (Mh.: 342)], 'der Durchschnittsdeutsche' (*MK*: 149) [the average German (Mh.: 124)], 'Durchschnittsköpfe' (*MK*: 679) [average minds (Mh.: 551)].

5.2 Positive Epithets and Evaluations

5.2.1 Positive Epithets

For fighters:

Held, Kämpfer, Kämpe (*MK*: 261), 'Kampfnaturen' (*MK*: 441) [fighting natures (Mh.: 363)], 'den deutschen Recken' (*MK*: 214) [the German warrior (Mh.: 178)].

For Aryans:

'Herrenvolk' (*MK*: 422) [master people (Mh.: 348f.)], 'höherstehende(n) Rassereinen' (*MK*: 443) [higher racial element (Mh.: 364)], **'Ebenbilder des Herren'** (*MK*: 445) [*images of the Lord* (Mh.: 366)], 'eines hochgezüchteten Rassengutes' (*MK*: 448) [(of) a highly bred racial stock (Mh.: 368)], **'Kulturträger', 'Kulturbegründer', 'Kulturschöpfer'** (all *MK*: 444) [*culture-bearer, culture-founder, culture-creator* (all Mh.: 365)].

5.2.2 Good Qualities, Activities and Behaviour

Common nouns referring to any social group (page references are not provided as the words occur frequently):

Angriffsgeist (spirit of attack), *Angriffsmut* (courage to attack), *Aufopferungssinn* and *Aufopferungswille* (willingness for self-sacrifice), *Ausdauer* (stamina), *Ausharren* (perseverance), *Autorität* (authority), *Begeisterung* (enthusiasm), *Beharrungsvermögen* (power of perseverance), *Bluteinsatz* (the sacrifice of one's blood), *Einheit* (unity), *Elastizität* (flexibility), *Entbehrung* (privation), *Entschlußkraft* (decisiveness), *Fleiß* (diligence), *Freiheitsdurst* (thirst for freedom), *Genialität* (genius), *Gutmeinen* (well-meaning), *Heldenmut* and *Heroismus* (heroism), *Hingabe* (dedication), *Hinopferung* (sacrifice), *Idealismus* (idealism), *Kameradschaft* (comradeship), *Kraft* (strength), *Lebensenergie* (energy for life), *Leidenschaft* (passion), *Manneswürde* (honour as a (gentle) man), *Nationalbegeisterung* (national enthusiasm/pride), *Opferbereitschaft* and *Opfersinn* (willingness for self-sacrifice), *Ordnung* (orderliness), *Pflichterfüllung* (performance of one's duty), *Rassegefühl* and *Rassesinn* (sense of (one's) race), *Reinhaltung des Blutes* (keeping one's blood pure), *Ruhm* (fame), *Selbstbehauptung* (self-reliance), *Selbstbewußtsein* and *Selbstvertrauen* (self-confidence), *Stählung* (hardening oneself), *Standhalten* (steadfastness), *Stolz* (pride), *Todesmut* (death-defying courage), *Treue* (loyalty), *Vaterlandsliebe* (love of one's country), *Verantwortung* (sense of responsibility), *Verpflichtung* (duty), *Versöhnung* (reconciliation), *Verzicht* (renunciation), *Virtuosität* (virtuosity), *Willenskraft* (will power), *Wohlwollen* (goodwill).

Nouns with the suffixes *-heit* or *-keit*:

Aufmerksamkeit (attention, concentration), *Aufnahmefähigkeit* (receptivity, ability to take things in), *Aufopferungsfähigkeit* (ability to sacrifice oneself), *Beharrlichkeit* (persistence), *Bereitwilligkeit* (willingness), *Bescheidenheit* (modesty), *Besorgtheit* (concern), *Brüderlichkeit* (brotherliness), *Einheitlichkeit* (uniformity), *Entschlossenheit* (determination), *Entschlußfreudigkeit* (decisiveness), *Ergriffenheit* (capacity to be moved, involvement), *Fähigkeit* (capability), *Freiheit* (freedom), *Genügsamkeit* (contentment), *Geradlinigkeit* (straightforwardness, sincerity), *Geschicklichkeit* (skill), *Gechlossenheit* (unity, uniformity), *Geschmeidigkeit* (adaptability), *Gewandheit* (skill, expertise), *Gleichmäßigkeit* (uniformity), *Heldenhaftigkeit* (heroism), *Herrlichkeit* (magnificence, masterful behaviour), *Kampfentschlossenheit* (determination to fight), *Klugheit* (intelligence), *Opferwilligkeit* (willingness for self-sacrifice), *Rassenreinheit* (racial purity), *Redlichkeit* (honesty, integrity), *Rücksichtslosigkeit* (ruthlessness), *Sauberkeit* (uprightness), *Schlichtheit* (simplicity), *Tüchtigkeit* (industry, efficiency), *Überlegenheit* (superiority), *Tapferkeit* (bravery), *Unabhängigkeit* (independence), *Uneigennützigkeit* (selflessness), *Verantwortungsfreudigkeit* (sense of responsibility), *Vertrauensseligkeit* (trustfulness), *Vertrauenswürdigkeit* (trustworthiness), *Wehrhaftigkeit* (ability to defend oneself), *Weisheit* (wisdom), *Widerstandsfähigkeit* (robustness, toughness), *Zähigkeit* (toughness, tenacity).

A selection of compound adjectives:

arisch-nordisch (*MK*: 735) [Aryan-Nordic (Mh.: 592)]; *aufopferungsbereit* (*MK*: 114) [prepared to make sacrifices (Mh.: 96)]; *bündnismöglich* (*MK*: 720) [possible for alliance (Mh.: 581)]; *deutschvölkisch* (*MK*: 746) [German-folkish (Mh.: 601)]; *einzigschön* (*MK*: 553) [uniquely beautiful (Mh.: 449)]; *erfolgverheißend* (*MK*: 644) [promising success (Mh.: 523)]; *felsenfest* (*MK*: 163) [firm as rock (Mh.: 136)]; *jugendfrisch* (*MK*: 553) [fresh, youthful (Mh.: 450)]; *kampfkräftig* (*MK*: 127) [militant (Mh.: 107)]; *kristallklar* (*MK*: 230) [crystalclear (Mh.: 191)]; *kultur- und wertebildend* (*MK*: 430) [(the forces) which build culture and values (Mh.: 355)]; **kulturbegründend** (*MK*: 319) [*culture-founding* (Mh.: 264)]; *kulturell-schöpferisch* (*MK*: 387) [cultural and creative (Mh.: 320)]; **kulturtragend** (*MK*: 319) [*culture-bearing* (Mh.: 264)]; *tiefinnerlichst* (*MK*: 271) [profound (used ironically, Mh.: 226)]; *todesmutig* (*MK*: 114) [willing to die (Mh.: 96)]; *überglücklich* (*MK*: 561) [overjoyed (Mh.: 456)]; *völkisch-nationalsozialistisch* (*MK*: 492) [folkish National Socialist (Mh.: 402)].

Hitler's view of himself:

'von stürmischer Begeisterung' (*MK*: 177) [by stormy enthusiasm (Mh.: 148)], 'nationale Begeisterung' (*MK*: 178) [national enthusiasm (Mh.: 149)], 'mit größtem Feuereifer' (*MK*: 57) [with ardent zeal (Mh.: 49)].

The qualities of a *Führer*:

'Führereigenschaft und Führertüchtigkeit' (*MK*: 650) [*the qualities and abilities of a leader* (Mh.: 528)], 'Führerfähigkeit' (*MK*: 650) [ability as a leader (Mh.: 528)], 'alle Führergenialität und aller Führerschwung' (*MK*: 651) [all the genius and energy of a leader (Mh.: 528)], 'Führerpflicht und Führerkönnen' (*MK*: 661) [leader's duty and leader's ability (Mh.: 536)].

Reproduction of the Aryan race:

Compounds with *-erhaltung* (preservation), such as *Selbsterhaltung, Erhaltungswille, Selbsterhaltungswille, Forterhaltung, Forterhaltungswille, Arterhaltung,* 'die Instinkte der Erhaltung der Art' (*MK*: 168) [the instincts of preservation of the species (Mh.: 140)], 'Vermehrung und Erhaltung der Art und Rasse' (*MK*: 275f.) [the increase and preservation of the species (Mh.: 229)], 'der normalen rassereinen Vermehrung' (*MK*: 443) [of normal, racially pure reproduction (Mh.: 365)], 'naturgesetzliche Vorgänge des Dranges der Selbsterhaltung und Mehrung von Art und Rasse' (*MK*: 310) [processes relating to the selfpreservation and propagation of the species and the race and subject to the laws of Nature (Mh.: 257)]; *Selbsterhaltungstrieb* (often with the adj. *völkisch* cf. *MK*: 104 = the national instinct for self-preservation (Mh.: 88)), 'Selbsterhaltungs- und Selbstverteidigungstrieb(es) des deutschen Heeres' (*MK*: 734) [the German army's instinct for self-preservation and self-defence (Mh.: 592)].

Self-sacrifice and loyalty:

'Aufopferungsfähigkeit und Aufopferungswille des einzelnen für die Gesamtheit' (*MK*: 167) [the ability and will of the individual to sacrifice himself for the totality (Mh.: 140)], (von) großer Opferwilligkeit wie zäher Kampfkraft' [= Lueger's new party] (*MK*: 109) [whose spirit of sacrifice was as great as its fighting power (Mh.: 92)], **'in verzichtsfreudiger Opferbereitschaft'** (*MK*: 470) [*in a spirit of sacrifice and joyful renunciation* (Mh.: 385)], '**Treue, Opferwilligkeit, Verschwiegenheit** sind Tugenden' (*MK*: 461) [*Loyalty, spirit of sacrifice, discretion* are virtues (Mh.: 378)].

German courage and heroism:

'heldische Tugend' (*MK*: 168) [heroic virtues (Mh.: 140)], 'strahlendes Heldentum' (*MK*: 169) [resplendent heroism (Mh.: 141)], 'unsterblichen Heldentums' (*MK*: 245) [(for) immortal heroism (Mh.: 205)], 'in vorbildlichem Heldentum' (*MK*: 583) [with exemplary heroism (Mh.: 474)], 'in seiner heldischen Gesinnung' (*MK*: 103) [whose heroic convictions (Mh.: 87)], 'mit unerschütterlichem Mute' (*MK*: 112) [with unflinching courage (Mh.: 94)], '(eines) heroischen Todesmutes' (*MK*: 366) [(of) heroic death-defying courage (Mh.: 302)], 'blindes, rücksichtsloses Einstehen' (*MK*: 401) [blindly and ruthlessly fighting (Mh.: 331)], '**entschlossen und angriffsweise**' (*MK*: 655; cf. 111) [*resolutely and aggressively* (Mh.: 531)];

Was haben unsere Regierungen getan, um in dieses Volk wieder den Geist stolzer Selbstbehauptung, männlichen Trotzes und zornigen Hasses hineinzupflanzen? (*MK*: 714) [*What have our governments done to reimplant the spirit of proud self-reliance, manly defiance, and wrathful hatred in this people?* (Mh.: 576)].

and the following formations with *held-* and *sieg-*:

heldisch, heldenhaft, heldenmütig (heroic); 'heldische Tugenden' (heroic virtues) alongside 'ideelle Tugenden' (ideal virtues) (*MK*: 166f.); *sieghaft* ('**eine junge sieghafte Idee**', *MK*: 648 = *a young victorious idea* (Mh.: 648)), *siegreich* (*MK*: 361, 575) [victorious (Mh.: 298)], **unerschütterlich und unbesiegbar** (*MK*: 475) [*unshakable and invincible* (Mh.: 388)].

Honesty, selflessness, steadfastness, idealism and general moral superiority:

'Uneigennützigkeit und Redlichkeit' [= the government of the Second Reich] (*MK*: 309) [selflessness and honesty (Mh.: 257)]], 'Höhe und Würde' [= of the Germans] (*MK*: 430) [lofty dignity (Mh.: 355)], 'unbestechlich ehrenhafte

Gesinnung' (*MK*: 308) [incorruptible honesty (Mh.: 256)], 'moralisches Standhalten' (*MK*: 201) [moral steadfastness (Mh.: 167)], 'bei immer gleichbleibender Beharrlichkeit' (*MK*: 394) [with steady perseverance (Mh.: 325)], 'sagenhafte Überlegenheit' (*MK*: 299) [legendary superiority (Mh.: 248)], '(der) moralischen Widerstandsfähigkeit' (*MK*: 366) [(from) moral capacity for resistance (Mh.: 302)], 'stählerne Willenskraft' (*MK*: 481) [iron will-power (Mh.: 393)], **'im disziplinierten Gehorsam'** (*MK*: 510) [*in (the) disciplined obedience* (Mh.: 415)], 'emsig und fleißig' (*MK*: 713) [diligently and industriously (Mh.: 576)], 'der bisher blindgläubigen Soldaten' (*MK*: 215) [of the soldiers who had hitherto believed blindly (Mh.: 179)], 'Ein Mann von granitener Redlichkeit, von antiker Schlichtheit und deutscher Geradlinigkeit' [= Ernst Pöhner] (*MK*: 403) [A man of granite honesty, of antique simplicity and German straightforwardness (Mh.: 334)].

The mental agility of the Germans:

'der geistigen Gelenkigkeit' [= used ironically to refer to parliamentarians] (*MK*: 413) [mental dexterity (Mh.: 342)], 'der geistigen Elastizität und schöpferischen Fähigkeit' (*MK*: 443) [of spiritual elasticity and creative ability (Mh.: 364)], 'blitzschnelle Entschlußkraft' (*MK*: 454) [lightning decisions (Mh.: 373)].

German health, strength and will:

'Kraft und Stärke' [= the government of the Second Reich] (*MK*: 308) [power and strength (Mh.: 256)], 'Gesundheit und Widerstandskraft' (*MK*: 313) [health and power of resistance (Mh.: 259)], 'Wille und Kraft' (*MK*: 371) [will and power (Mh.: 307)], 'Willens- und Tatkraft' [= of a leader] (*MK*: 384) [will and energy (Mh.: 317)], 'Willen und Entschlossenheit' (*MK*: 158) [will and determination (Mh.: 132)], 'Einsicht, Willenskraft und Tatentschlossenheit' (*MK*: 169) [insight, will power, and active determination (Mh.: 141)], 'im verschiedenen Maße der Kraft, der Stärke, der Klugheit, Gewandheit, Ausdauer usw.' (*MK*: 312) [in the varying measures of force, strength, intelligence, dexterity, endurance etc. (Mh.: 259)].

Ruthlessness and brutality:

'brutal und rücksichtslos' (*MK*: 30) [brutally and ruthlessly (Mh.: 28)], 'mit rücksichtsloser Brutalität' (*MK*: 229) [with ruthless brutality (Mh.: 191)], 'rücksichtslose Führung' (*MK*: 158) [ruthless pursuit of this struggle (Mh.: 132)], 'rücksichtslose Energie' (*MK*: 541) [ruthless energy (Mh.: 440)], 'rücksichtslose Nüchternheit' (*MK*: 128) [cold ruthlessness (Mh.: 107)], 'brutales Draufgängertum' (*MK*: 541) [brutal activism (Mh.: 440)], '(der) Energie und brutalen Entschlossenheit' (*MK*: 188) [(from) energy and brutal determination (Mh.: 157)], 'rücksichtslos und ohne zu Schwanken' (*MK*: 279) [ruthlessly and without wavering (Mh.: 231)], 'rücksichstlose und fanatisch einseitige Einstellung auf das nun einmal zu erstrebende Ziel' (*MK*: 370) [ruthless and fanatically one-sided orientation towards the goal to be achieved (Mh.: 306)].

Fanaticism and hysteria:

'in einem sie beseelenden Fanatismus und manchmal in einer sie vorwärtsjagenden Hysterie' [= the masses] (*MK*: 371) [in a fanaticism which inspired them and sometimes in a hysteria which drove them forward (Mh.: 306)], 'mit dem fanatischen Kampfesmut' (*MK*: 414) [with a fanatical courage to fight (Mh.: 343)], 'in einer fanatischen Weltanschauung' (*MK*: 188) [in a fanatical outlook (Mh.: 157)], **'fanatischen Glaubens'** (*MK*: 597) [*of a fanatical faith* (Mh.: 485)];

'(...) wenn ihre Triebkraft statt fanatischer, ja hysterischer Leidenschaften nur die bürgerlichen Tugenden der Ruhe und Ordnung gewesen wären' (*MK*: 475) [*if their motive force, instead of fanatical, yes, hysterical passion, had been merely the bourgeois virtues of law and order* (Mh.: 388)].

National feelings:

'von glühender Vaterlandsliebe' (*MK*:582) [filled with love of their fatherland (Mh.: 473)], 'nationale Willenskraft' (*MK*: 457) [national will-power (Mh.: 375)], 'flammende Nationalbegeisterung' (*MK*: 711) [*the flame of national enthusiasm* (Mh.: 574)], 'Hingabe an das Vaterland' (*MK*: 307) [devotion to the fatherland (Mh.: 255)].

Physical superiority:

'zu stählerner Geschmeidigkeit' [= the body] (*MK*: 454) [in steel dexterity (Mh.: 373)], 'die notwendige Stählung für das spätere Leben' [= young people] (*MK*: 453) [the necessary steeling for later life (Mh.: 372)], 'die Rasse, welche die Probe nicht besteht, wird sterben und gesünderen oder doch zäheren und widerstandsfähigeren den Platz räumen' (*MK*: 272) [the race which cannot stand the test will simply die out, making place for healthier or tougher and more resisting races (Mh.: 226)], *kerngesund* [= blood] (*MK*: 47) [healthy (Mh.: 42)], *kerngesund* [= the body) (*MK*: 452) [absolutely healthy (Mh.: 371)], *kraftstrotzend* (*MK*: 308) [vigorous (Mh.: 255)].

5.3 Pejorative Epithets and Evaluations

5.3.1 Pejorative Epithets

5.3.1.1 Ubiquitous Epithets Referring to any Social Group

Bandit (bandit), *Bastard* (bastard), *Betrüger* (swindler), *Bursche* (boy, lout), *Dieb* (thief), *Drahtzieher* (wirepuller), *Esel* (donkey), *Faulpelz* (lazy so-and-so), *Feigling* (coward), *Gauner* (scoundrel, rogue), *Gesindel* (rabble, riff-raff), *Handlanger* (lackey), *Hanswurst* (fool, clown), *Herrschaften* (gentlemen, usually used ironically, e.g. *MK*: 412), *Hetzer* and *Verhetzer* (agitator), *Idiot* (idiot), *Kerl* (nasty so-and-so, rogue), *Klub* (club), *Kreatur* (creature), *Lump* (scoundrel, rogue), *Nullen* (nonentities), *Pack* (pack), *Plünderer* (plunderer), *Schieber* (black-marketeer), *Schleicher* (toadying hypocrite), *Schurke* (rogue, villain), *Schwätzer* (windbag), *Schwindler* (swindler), *Spießer* and *Spießbürger* ((petit) bourgeois), *Spitzbube* (scoundrel, rogue), *Tropf* (twit, moron), *Trottel* (fool, wally), *Verbrecher* (criminal).

5.3.1.2 Jews

Compounds and derivatives with *Jude(n)*:

'Jüdlein' (*MK*: 61) [kike (Mh.: 53)], 'Judenschaft' (*MK*: 60) [Jews (Mh.: 52)], 'Judentum' (*MK*: 61) [Jews (Mh.: 53)], 'Judenheit' (*MK*: 131) [Jewry (Mh.: 110)], 'Judenjungen' (*MK*: 221) [Jewish youths (Mh.: 184)], 'Judenvolk' (*MK*: 337) [Jewish people (Mh.: 279)], 'Judenkopf' (*MK*: 337) [Jewish brain (Mh.: 279)], '(dem) Hofjuden' (*MK*: 343) [the court Jew (Mh.: 284)], 'der Volksjude' (*MK*: 343: 358) [the people's Jew (Mh.: 284)], 'der Blutjude' (*MK*: 358) [the blood-Jew (Mh.: 296)], 'zum nächstbesten Bankjuden' (*MK*: 256) [with some old bank Jew (Mh.: 214)], 'des internationalen Weltjuden' (*MK*: 498; cf. 675) [of the international world Jew (Mh.: 407)], 'Warenhausjüdin' (*MK*: 270) [department store Jewess (Mh.: 225)], 'krummbeinige, widerwärtige Judenbankerte' (*MK*: 458) [bow-legged, repulsive Jewish bastards (Mh.: 375)], 'des internationalen Börsenjudentums' (*MK*: 702) [of the international stock exchange Jews (Mh.: 567)], 'das Reich der bolschewistischen Kampftruppe des internationalen Weltfinanzjudentums' (*MK*: 702) [the Bolshevistic shock troop of international Jewish world finance (Mh.: 568)].

With *jüdisch*:

'das jüdisches Gesindel' (*MK*: 365) [the Jewish rabble (Mh.: 302)], 'der jüdischen Pressemeute' (*MK*: 544) [the wolves of the Jewish press (Mh.: 442)], 'die jüdischen Drahtzieher' (*MK*: 589) [the Jewish wirepullers (Mh.: 478)], '(von) jüdischen Literaten' (*MK*: 413) [(of) Jewish journalists (Mh.: 342)], **'das Gezische der jüdischen Welthydra'** (*MK*: 721) [*the hissing of the Jewish world hydra* (Mh.: 581)], 'das jüdisches Führerpack' (*MK*: 185) [the gang of Jewish leaders (Mh.: 154)], 'das jüdische Weltsatrapenreich' (*MK*: 723) [the world empire of Jewish satrapies] [(Mh.: 584)], 'dieser blut- und geldgierigen jüdischen Völkertyrannen' (*MK*: 703) [of these blood-thirsty and avaricious Jewish tyrants of nations (Mh.: 568)].

Other race-specific epithets:

'dieser hebräischen Volksverderber' (*MK*: 772) [of these Hebrew corrupters of the people (Mh.: 620)], 'dieser völkischen Ahasvere' (*MK*: 397) [of these folkish wandering Jews (Mh.: 328)].

The Jews as outsiders:

'von Volksfremden und Volksfeinden' (*MK*: 269) [of aliens and enemies of the people (Mh.: 224)].

Liars and cheats:

'nur den allerverlogensten und zugleich besonders das Tagelicht scheuenden Schliefer' (*MK*: 99) [the biggest liars and sneaks of the sort that shun the light of day (Mh.: 83)], 'der unerbittliche Todfeind jedes Lichtes' (*MK*: 346) [the inexorable mortal enemy of all light (Mh.: 286)], 'gewissenloser Schacherer' (*MK*: 257) [for unscrupulous Jewish business men (Mh.: 214)].

Behaviour, attributes and appearance:

'Börsenbanditen' (*MK*: 358) [stock exchange bandits (Mh.: 296)], 'Völkertyrann' (*MK*: 358) [tyrant over peoples (Mh.: 296)], 'Verführer unseres Volkes' (*MK*: 66) [the seducer of our people (Mh.: 57)], 'Verführer und Verderber' (*MK*: 68) [seducer and corrupter (Mh.: 59)], 'Kaftanträger' (*MK*: 61) [caftan-wearers (Mh.: 53)], 'keine Wasserliebhaber' (*MK*: 61) [no lovers of water (Mh.: 53)], 'Schmierer' (*MK*: 62) [scribblers (Mh.: 54)], 'der Herr von Bastarden' (*MK*: 357) [master over bastards (Mh.: 295)], **'Nomaden'** (*MK*: 333) [*nomads* (Mh.: 275)], 'Spießgesellen'(*MK*: 94) [accomplices (Mh.: 79)], 'so ein Bursche' (*MK*: 94) [one of these scoundrels (Mh.: 79)], 'Scheusale' (*MK*: 341) [monsters (Mh.: 282)], 'die ganze betrügerische Genossenschaft dieser jüdischen Volksvergifter' (*MK*: 185) [the whole treacherous brotherhood of these Jewish poisoners of the people (Mh.: 155)], 'Nachäffer' (*MK*: 332) [ape (Mh.: 275)], 'Nachahmer' (*MK*: 332) [imitator (Mh.: 275)], 'Zerstörer der arischen Menschheit' (*MK*: 632) [the destroyer of Aryan humanity (Mh.: 514)], 'der Hasser jeder wahren Kultur' (*MK*: 346) [hater of all true culture (Mh.: 286)], **'der große Hetzer'** (*MK*: 702) [*the great agitator* (Mh.: 568)], 'jedem

Appendix II   213

spanischen Schatzschwindler' (*MK*: 149) [by any gold-brick salesman (Mh.: 125)].

Ironic epithets:

'Apostel' [(Mh.: 67)], '„Gaukler"' (*MK*: 332) ['juggler' (Mh.: 275)], '„Wohltäter" der Menschheit' (*MK*: 343) ['benefactor' of mankind (Mh.: 284)], '„Freund der Menschen"' (*MK*: 344) ['friend of mankind' (Mh.: 284)], 'diese Zierden des menschlichen Geschlechtes' (*MK*: 341) [these ornaments of the human race (Mh.: 282)].

Animal and metaphors:

'von der internationalen Völkermade' (*MK*: 623) [from the international maggot of nations (Mh.: 506)], 'Drohnen' (*MK*: 165) [drones (Mh.: 138)], 'Ungeziefer' (*MK*: 186) [vermin (Mh.: 155)], 'Blutegel' (*MK*: 340) [blood-sucker (Mh.: 282)], *Parasit* and compounds, e.g. 'Völkerparasit' (*MK*: 358) [parasite upon the people (Mh.: 296)], *Pack* and compounds, e.g. 'Lumpenpack' (*MK*: 94) [rabble (Mh.: 94)], **'Mißgeburten zwischen Mensch und Affe'** (*MK*: 445) [*monstrosities halfway between man and ape* (Mh.: 366)], 'eine sich blutig bekämpfende Rotte von Ratten' (*MK*: 331) [a horde of rats, fighting bloodily among themselves (Mh.: 274)].

Metaphors of illness and decay:

Bazillus and compounds, e.g. 'Bazillenträger schlimmster Art' (*MK*: 62), [germ-carriers of the worst sort (Mh.: 54)], 'Spaltpilz der Menschheit' (*MK*: 135) [the eternal mushroom of humanity (Mh.: 113; a correct translation of *Spaltpilz* would have been 'bacterium')], 'Schmarotzer' (*MK*: 334) [sponger (Mh.: 277)], '„Ferment der Dekomposition"' (*MK*: 498) ['a ferment of decomposition' (Mh.: 406)], 'Seuche' (*MK*: 266) [plague (Mh.: 221)], *Pest* (plague), compounds and derivatives, e.g. 'diese Verpestung unseres Blutes' (*MK*: 630).

5.3.1.3 Marxists and Revolutionaries (usually including the Jews)

Seuche (plague) (e.g. *MK*: 184), 'Pestilenz' (*MK*: 184) [pestilence (Mh.: 154)] 'roter Terror' (*MK*: 616) [the Red terror (Mh.: 500)], 'rote Bonzen' (*MK*: 616) [Red bosses (Mh.: 500)], 'die rote Meute' (*MK*: 602) [the Red mob (Mh.: 489)], 'marxistische Kirchenväter' (*MK*: 529) [of the Marxist church fathers (Mh.: 429)], 'bei diesen marxistischen Freibeutern' (*MK*: 583) [these Marxist gangsters (Mh.: 474)], 'in seinem weniggeistigen Menschenmaterial' (*MK*: 509f.) [with their unintellectual human material (Mh.: 415)], 'die Matadoren der Revolution' (*MK*: 584) [the matadors of the revolution (Mh.: 475)], 'den marxistischen Wegelagerern' (*MK*: 618) [(of) the Marxist highwaymen (Mh.: 502)], 'mit den marxistischen Todfeinden' (*MK*: 773) [with Marxism (Mh.: 621)], 'den internationalen Volksverrätern und Vaterlandsfeinden' (*MK*: 613) [of the international traitors and enemies of the fatherland (Mh.: 498)], 'den marxistischen Landesverrätern und Volksmördern' (*MK*: 771) [of the Marxist traitors and murderers (Mh.: 620)], 'den hinterlistigen Meuchelmördern der Nation' (*MK*: 186) [treacherous murderers of the nation (Mh.: 155)], 'die kanaillösen Führerkreaturen des Jahres 1918' (*MK*: 771) [the scoundrelly leaders of 1918 (Mh.: 620)], 'feiger Revolutionskreaturen' (*MK*: 607) [(of) cowardly creatures of the revolution (Mh.: 493)], 'Revolutionsgeier' (*MK*: 589) [revolutionary vultures (Mh.: 479)], 'revolutionärer Mordbrenner, Volksausplünderer und Nationalverräter' (*MK*: 607) [(of) revolutionary pyromaniac murderers, plunderers of the people and traitors (Mh.: 493)], 'Revolutionswanzen' (*MK*: 610) [revolutionary bedbugs (Mh.: 495)], 'Rucksackspartakisten' (*MK*: 610) [knapsack Spartacists (Mh.: 495)], 'Weltversöhnungsapostel' (*MK*: 248) [apostles of world conciliation (Mh.: 207)], 'Vergewaltiger der Nation' (*MK*: 607) [rapers of the nation (Mh.: 494)], 'die revolutionierenden Novemberlumpen' (*MK*: 481) [the revolutionist November scoundrels (Mh.: 393)], 'die geistigen Zyklopen unserer Novemberparteien' (*MK*: 705) [these intellectual Cyclopses of our November parties (Mh.: 570)].

5.3.1.4 The Press (usually including the Jews)

'Tintenfisch' (*MK*: 94) [octopus (Mh.: 79)], 'Presselumpen' (*MK*: 94) [scoundrels of the press (Mh.: 79)], 'Schundpresse' (*MK*: 34) [yellow press (Mh.: 31)], 'Schundliteratur und Schmutzpresse' (*MK*: 34) [back-stairs literature and the yellow press (Mh.: 31)], **'die jüdische Börsen- und Marxistenpresse'** (*MK*: 703) [*the press of the Jewish stock exchange and Marxists* (Mh.: 568)], 'solch einem geistigen Raubritter' (*MK*: 94) [these spiritual robber-barons (Mh.: 79)], 'das Brudervolk von links' (*MK*: 548) [the brethren on the left (Mh.: 445)].

5.3.1.5 Politicians, Civil Servants and the Bourgeoisie

Beamten/beamtet:

'Beamtenhuren' (*MK*: 602) [official whores (Mh.: 489)], 'alter, verknöcheter Beamtenseelen' (*MK*: 550) [of old, ossified officials (Mh.: 447)], 'von diesen beamteten Staatslenkern' (*MK*: 185) [of these official guides of the state (Mh.: 154)], 'des beamteten Kalbskopfes' (*MK*: 547) [of the official bonehead (Mh.: 444)], 'beamtete Kreatur' (*MK*: 547) [official toady (Mh.: 444)].

Parlamentarier/parlamentarisch/Parlaments-:

'diese parlamentarischen Gänseriche' (*MK*: 57) [these parliamentarian imbeciles (Mh.: 50)] *Gänseriche* translates literally as 'ganders', 'parlamentarische Parteilumpen' (*MK*: 297) [parliamentary rabble (Mh.: 247)], 'solch einem parlamentarischen Taugenichts und Tagedieb' (*MK*: 125) [one of these parliamentarian good-for-nothings and lounge-lizards (Mh.: 105)], 'einen solchen parlamentarischen Ehrenmann' [= ironic] (*MK*: 763) [these parliamentary honourables (Mh.: 613)], 'eines solchen parlamentarischen Zauberpriesters bürgerlicher Demokratie' (*MK*: 413) [one of these parliamentary medicine-men of bourgeois democracy (Mh.: 342)], 'dieser parlamentarischen Medizinmänner der weißen Rasse' (*MK*: 412) [these parliamentary medicine-men of the white race (Mh.: 341)], 'einer parlamentarischen Schwätzervereinigung' (*MK*: 99) [in a parliamentary bull session (Mh.: 83)], 'unserer parlamentarischen Politikaster' (*MK*: 685) [(of) our parliamentary politicasters (Mh.: 555)], 'die parlamentarischen Strauchdiebe' (*MK*: 707) [the parliamentary sneak-thieves (Mh.: 572)], 'beutehungrige Parlamentarier' (*MK*: 701) [hungry parliamentarians (Mh.: 567)], '(bestehend aus) Parlamentsschwätzern (*MK*: 708) [(consisting of) parliamentary big-mouths (Mh.: 572)], **'die Zungenfertigkeit geschliffener parlamentarischer Mäuler'** (*MK*: 710) [*sharp parliamentary big-mouths and their glibness of tongue* (Mh.: 574)], '(diese Sorte von) Parlamentswanzen' (*MK*: 72) [(this sort of) parliamentary bed-bug (Mh.: 62)], 'die größten parlamentarischen Strohköpfe, wirklicher Gevatter Sattlermeister und Handschuhmacher—nicht bloß dem Beruf nach' (*MK*: 762) [the greatest parliamentary thick-heads, regular saddlers and glove-makers—and not only by profession (Mh.: 613)].

Partei-/partei-:

'das ganze politische Parteipack' (*MK*: 218) [the whole political party rabble (Mh.: 181)], 'parteipolitisches Strauchrittertum' (*MK*: 425) [political crooks (Mh.: 351)], 'Sterngucker und Parteiastrologen' (*MK*: 410) [stargazers and party astrologers (Mh.: 339)], 'Parteihyänen' (*MK*: 583) [party hyenas (Mh.: 474)], 'dieser bürgerlichen parteipolitischen Schimmelkulturen' (*MK*: 776) [these mouldy political party cheeses (Mh.: 623)], 'dieses gesamte politisierende Parteigesindel' (*MK*: 707) [all the politics-playing party rabble (Mh.: 572)].

Politiker/politisch/politisierend:

'(all den anderen) politischen Knirpsen' (*MK*: 609) [(all the other) political midgets (Mh.: 495)], 'politisierende „Bourgeois"-Gilde' (*MK*: 451) [political 'bourgeois' guild (Mh.: 370)], 'einem solchen politisierenden Dreikäsehoch' (*MK*: 414) [one of (sic) political twerps (Mh.: 343)], 'ein solcher politischer Kleptomane' [= imitators of the N.S.D.A.P.] (*MK*: 576) [these political kleptomaniacs (Mh.: 469)], 'solch einen politischen Strauchdieb' (*MK*: 89) [one of these political bandits (Mh.: 75)].

Other descriptions of politicians, parliamentarians and statesmen:

'Völkerapostel' (*MK*: 413) [people's apostles (Mh.: 342)], 'einer alten, ausgetrockneten Ministerseele' (*MK*: 773) [(of) some dried-up old minister (Mh.: 621)], 'dieser Auserkorenen der Nationen' (*MK*: 84) [(of) the elect of the peoples (Mh.: 71)], 'dieser Auserwählten der Völker' (*MK*: 91) [(of) the elect of the peoples (Mh.: 77)], 'dieser Prachterscheinungen unseres öffentlichen Lebens' (*MK*: 91) [(of) these ornaments of our public life (Mh.: 77)], 'unserer gelahrten Regierungsheroen' (*MK*: 37) [(of) our learned and highly placed government heroes (Mh.: 34)], 'unfähige Zwerge oder gar minderwertige Subjekte' (*MK*: 121) [incapable dwarfs or really inferior characters (Mh.: 102)], 'unsere geistfreien „Staatsmänner"' (*MK*: 202) [our feather-brained 'statesmen' (Mh.: 168)], 'Staatsparasiten' (*MK*: 685) [government parasites (Mh.: 685)], 'staatlicher Fetischinsulaner' (*MK*: 106) [(of) fetish-worshipping isolationists in the government (Mh.: 89)], 'Kurpfuscher und Salbader' [= statesmen] (*MK*: 257f.) [quacks and big-mouths (Mh.: 215)], 'die Väter unseres demokratischen Parlamentsunsinns jüdischer Prägung' (*MK*: 690) [the fathers of our democratic parliamentary nonsense of the Jewish variety (Mh.: 559)].

Democrats:

'Objektivitäts-Fanatiker' (*MK*: 121) [fanatical objectivist (Mh.: 102)], 'Prinzipienbock' (*MK*: 121) [principle-monger (Mh.: 102)].

Bürger/bürgerlich:

'von jenen bürgerlichen Gimpeln' (*MK*: 536) [by those bourgeois simpletons (Mh.: 435)], 'gemäßigt-bürgerliche Elemente' (*MK*: 111) [moderate bourgeois elements (Mh.: 93)], 'bürgerliche Versammlungstoreadoren' (*MK*: 548) [bourgeois meeting-hall toreadors (Mh.: 445)], 'unserer vom Juden geführten bürgerlichen Wortpatrioten' (*MK*: 712) [(by) the Jewish-led bourgeois patriots of the word (Mh.: 574)], 'des bürgerlichen Wahlstimmviehs' (*MK*: 375) [the bourgeois voting cattle (Mh.: 309)], 'die bürgerlichen Schwätzerorganisationen' (*MK*: 594) [the bourgeois talking clubs (Mh.: 483)], 'bürgerliche Schwachköpfe auf Ministerstühlen' (*MK*: 599) [feeble-minded bourgeois in ministerial chairs (Mh.: 487)], 'die bürgerlichen „Staatsmänner"' (*MK*: 595) [the bourgeois 'statesmen'(Mh.: 484)], 'ein neubürgerlicher Patriot' (*MK*: 607) [a neo-bourgeois patriot (Mh.: 493)], 'unserer politisierenden bürgerlichen Einfaltspinsel' (*MK*: 706) [our political bourgeois simpletons (Mh.: 571)], 'aufgeblasener Vereinspatrioten und spießbürgerlicher Kaffeehauspolitiker' (*MK*: 718) [(of) inflated parlour patriots and petit bourgeois café politicians (Mh.: 579)].

5.3.1.6 The Proletariat

'das „proletarische" Stimmvieh' (*MK*: 412) [the 'proletarian' voting cattle (Mh.: 341)], '(zum) verkommenen Proleten' (*MK*: 445) [(into a) depraved proletarian (Mh.: 366)].

5.3.1.7 The General Population (most usually implying Germans)

The incapable, stupid and ignorant:

'dieser unfähigen und verbrecherischen Nichtskönner oder Nichtswoller' (*MK*: 206) [(of) the incapable and criminal incompetents or scoundrels (Mh.: 171)], 'von Nichtswissern und Nichtskönnern' (*MK*: 97) [of ignoramuses and incompetents (Mh.: 81)], 'Nichtskönner und Nichtstuer' (*MK*: 399) [incompetents and do-nothings (Mh.: 330)], 'Nichtskönner und Schwächlinge' (*MK*: 100) [incompetents and weaklings (Mh.: 84)], 'die Büttel blöder Nichtskönner und Schwätzer' (*MK*: 88) [the stooges of idiotic incompetents and big-mouths (Mh.: 75)], 'geistige Halbwelt' (*MK*: 97) [intellectual *demi-monde* (Mh.: 81)], 'Dilettanten' (*MK*: 97) [dilettantes (Mh.: 81)], 'einer Hammelherde von Hohlköpfen' (*MK*: 86) [(to) a herd of sheep and blockheads (Mh.: 73)], 'der Dummkopf und Unfähige' (*MK*: 90) [the simpleton and incompetent (Mh.: 76)], 'eine Schar geistig abhängiger Nullen' (*MK*: 99) [a band of mentally dependent nonentities (Mh.: 83)], 'der Haufe der Einfältigen und Leichtgläubigen' (*MK*: 264) [the mob of the simple and credulous (Mh.: 220)], 'von diesen Halbnarren und Gaunern' (*MK*: 287) [these half-wits and scoundrels (Mh.: 238)], 'Hansdampfgesellen' (*MK*: 128) [jacks-of-all-trades (Mh.: 108)], 'Hansdampfe in allen Gassen' (*MK*: 242) [jacks-of-all-trades (Mh.: 202)], 'der windigste Murkser' (*MK*: 762) [the most incompetent windbag (Mh.: 613)].

The generally lazy, weak and degenerate:

'**ein geistreicher Schwächling**' (*MK*: 452) [*clever weakling* (Mh.: 371)], 'die Lauen' (*MK*: 10) [the lukewarm (Mh.: 11)], 'Druckpöstchen' (*MK*: 204) [slackers (Mh.: 169)], 'Wahlmüden' (*MK*: 364) [those who are weary of elections (Mh.: 300)], 'der denkfaul Gleichgültigen' (*MK*: 441) [of the mentally lazy and indifferent (Mh.: 363)], 'seitens körperlich Degenerierter und geistig Erkrankter' (*MK*: 448) [on the part of the physically degenerate and mentally sick (Mh.: 368)], 'geistiger Degeneraten' (*MK*: 287f.) [of spiritual degenerates (Mh.: 238)], 'den Wankelmütigwerdenden und den Schwachen' (*MK*: 781) [the wavering and the weak (Mh.: 627)], 'eine faulige Bastardbrut' (*MK*: 446) [a rotten brood of bastards (Mh.: 367)], 'Dulder' (*MK*: 740) [(patient sufferers), (Mh. has 'nations': 741)], 'Unglücksraben' (*MK*: 213) [Calamity Janes (Mh.: 176)], 'aus solchen Jämmerlingen' (*MK*: 89) [of such vile creatures (Mh.: 75)],

'Jammerlappen' (*MK*: 399) [poor wretches (Mh.: 329)], 'eine Generation von Stubenhockern' (*MK*: 453) [a generation of hothouse plants (Mh.: 372), *Stubenhocker* is more usually translated as 'stay-at-home'], 'faule Herumlungerer' (*MK*: 574) [lazy loiterers (Mh.: 467)], 'dieses körperlich verhunzten und damit natürlich auch geistig verlumpten Jammerpacks' (*MK*: 446) [(at) this physically botched and hence spiritually degenerate rabble (Mh.: 366)].

Cowards and pacifists:

'aus vorsichtigen Pfeffersäcken' (*MK*: 451) [of cautious pepper sacks [= small tradesmen] (Mh.: 370)], 'Angsthase' (*MK*: 210) [coward (Mh.: 174)], 'Hasenfüße' (*MK*: 261) [poltroons (Mh.: 217)], 'Schwächlinge und zaghafte Naturen' (*MK*: 658) [weaklings and hesitant characters (Mh.: 533)], 'keusche Jungfrauenvereinigungen' (*MK*: 555) [chaste virgins' clubs (Mh.: 451)], 'körperlich verkommene und verkrüppelte, im Charakter willensschwache, schwankende, feige Subjekte' (*MK*: 453) [physically degenerate and crippled, weak-willed, wavering and cowardly individuals (Mh.: 371)], 'verblendete Pazifisten' (*MK*: 438) [blinded pacifists (Mh.: 360)], 'pazifistische Narren' (*MK*: 323) [pacifistic fools (Mh.: 268)], **'tränenreicher pazifistischer Klageweiber'** (*MK*: 438) [*of tearful, pacifist female mourners* (Mh.: 360)].

Crawlers, climbers and hangers-on at Court:

'Diese „alleruntertänigsten" Kreaturen' (*MK*: 259) [These 'most humble' creatures (Mh.: 216)], 'ein Schleicher und charakterloser Kriecher' (*MK*: 259) [a sneak and a spineless lickspittle (Mh.: 216)], 'Kriecher und Speichellecker' (*MK*: 261) [cringers and lickspittles (Mh.: 218)], 'der nächstbeste unwürdige Streber und moralische Drückeberger' (*MK*: 100) [any old climber or moral slacker (Mh.: 83)], 'Hofgaul' (*MK*: 57) [every rickety horse in the Court (Mh.: 50)], 'ein geadelter oder auch ungeadelter Spulwurm' [= monarchists] (*MK*: 259) [ennobled or even unennobled tapeworms (Mh.: 216)].

Liars, cheats, traitors and thieves:

'Lumpen und Lügner' (*MK*: 263) [scoundrels and liars (Mh.: 219)], 'dieser verlogenen, heimtückischen Duckmäuser' (*MK*: 400) [(of) these lying, treacherous sneaks (Mh.: 330f.)], 'Diese frechen Lügenmäuler' (*MK*: 294) [These insolent liars (Mh.: 244)], 'gerissene Betrüger' (*MK*: 288) [slimy swindlers (Mh.: 238)], 'ein listiger Fuchs' (*MK*: 125) [sly fox (Mh.: 105)], 'einen schuftigen Waffenverräter' (*MK*: 610) [a scoundrelly armaments stool-pigeon (Mh.: 496)], 'eine verräterische kleine Kreatur' (*MK*: 610) [a traitorous petty creature (Mh.: 496)], 'in einer Gesellschaft von Zuhältern, Dieben, Einbrechern, Deserteuren, Drückebergern usw.' (*MK*: 584) [in the society of pimps, thieves, burglars, deserters, slackers, etc. (Mh.: 475)].

Appendix II   219

General rabble and scoundrels:

'Gelichter' (*MK*: 219) [gang (Mh.: 182)], 'Kanaillen' (*MK*: 610) [scoundels (Mh.: 496)], 'Blutsauger und Handlanger (der Entente)' (*MK*: 236) [leeches and stooges (of the Entente) (Mh.: 197)], 'mit einem Haufen von Straßenstrolchen, Deserteuren, Parteibonzen und jüdischen Literaten' (*MK*: 413) [with a band of bums, deserters, party bosses, and Jewish journalists (Mh.: 342)], 'Hanswurste' (*MK*: 544) [clowns (Mh.: 442)].

5.3.1.8 The "Intelligentsia", Artists, Writers, Aesthetes

'Neunmalklugen' (*MK*: 306) [know-it-alls (Mh.: 254)], '„Köpfe"' (*MK*: 97) ['thinkers' (Mh.: 81)], 'Intelligenzler' (*MK*: 377) [member of the intelligentsia (Mh.: 311)], 'Geisteskämpfer' (*MK*: 455) [spiritual fighters (Mh.: 455)], 'Der bebrillte Theoretiker' (*MK*: 105) [The bespectacled theoretician (Mh.: 89)], 'aller theoretischen Prinzipienreiter (*MK*: 106) [(of) all theoretical pedants (Mh.: 89)], 'eine Kolonie friedsamer Ästheten' (*MK*: 455) [a colony of peaceful aesthetes (Mh.: 373)], 'Ästheten oder Blasierten' (*MK*: 202) [aesthetes or people who have become blasé (Mh.: 168)], 'blasierte Herrchen' (*MK*: 203) [blasé young gentlemen (Mh.: 169)], 'literarische Teegesellschaften' (*MK*: 202) [literary teas (Mh.: 168)], 'literarischer Teeklub oder spießbürgerliche Kegelgesellschaft' (*MK*: 378) [a literary tea-club or a shopkeepers' bowling society (Mh.: 312)], 'der bolschewistischen Kunstapostel' (*MK*: 287) [(by) the apostels of Bolshevistic art (Mh.: 238)], 'Ritter mit dem „geistigen" Schwert' (*MK*: 399) [knights of the 'spiritual sword' (Mh.: 329)], 'die schriftstellernden Ritter und Gecken' (*MK*: 116) [fops and knights of the pen (Mh.: 97f.)], 'ästhetisierender Literaten und Salonhelden' (*MK*: 116) [(of) literary aesthetes and drawing-room heroes (Mh.: 98)], 'ein normaler deutscher Tintenritter' (*MK*: 533) [an average German knight of the ink-pot (Mh.: 433)], 'das durchschnittliche Spatzenhirn einer deutschen, wissenschaftlich natürlich höchst gebildeten Schreiberseele' (*MK*: 533) [the average sparrow brain of a German scribbler, equipped, it goes without saying, with a high scientific education (Mh.: 433)].

5.3.1.9 *Völkisch* Used in a Pejorative or Ironic Sense

'diese völkischen Komödianten' (*MK*: 397) [these folkish comedians (Mh.: 328)], 'dieser völkischen Johanesse' (*MK*: 398) [(of) these folkish Saint Johns (Mh.: 329)], 'dieser völkischen Schlafwandler' (*MK*: 399) [(of) these folkish sleepwalkers (Mh.: 329)], 'ein völkischer Nachtfalter' (*MK*: 400) [these folkish moths (Mh.: 330)], cf. 'dieser völkischen Ahasvere' [= Jews] (*MK*: 397),

'Scheinvölkische' (*MK*: 516) [those (...) pretending to be folkish (Mh.: 420)], 'vor jenen deutschvölkischen Wanderscholaren' (*MK*: 395) [against those *deutschvölkisch* wandering scholars (Mh.: 326f.)].

Epithets used in connection with folkish ideas:

'Altertumsschwärmer' (*MK*: 399) [antiquity enthusiasts (Mh.: 329)], 'unfruchtbare Theoretiker' (*MK*: 516) [sterile theoreticians (Mh.: 420)], 'verheerende Schwadroneure' (*MK*: 516f.) [disastrous braggarts (Mh.: 420)], 'urgermanisches Getue' (*MK*: 517) [primeval Teutonic gestures (Mh.: 420)].

5.3.2 Bad Qualities, Activities and Behaviour

5.3.2.1 General Terms

Common nouns (page references are not provided as the words occur frequently):

Anarchie (anarchy), *Banditentum* (banditry), *Barbarei* (barbarism), *Betrug* (deception) and *Volksbetrug* (deception of the people), *Blödsinn* (stupidity), *Brutalität* (brutality), *Dekadenz* (decadence), *Diebstahl* (theft), *Drückebergerei* (shirking), *Egoismus* (egoism), *Eigennutz* (self-interest), *Einbildung* (conceit), *Entfremdung* (alienation), *Erpressung* (blackmail), *Erstarrung* (ossification), *Fälschung* (falsification), *Furcht* (fear), *Grauen* (horror), *Habsucht* (greed), *Haß* (hate), *Indolenz* (indolence), *Infizierung* (infection), *Konzilianz* (accommodation), *Kriecherei* (grovelling), *Lähmung* (paralysis), *Landesverrat* (treason), *Lügen* (lying), *Lumperei* (trickery), *Menschenverführung* (leading people astray), *Nachgeben* (submissiveness), *Neid* (envy), *Nichtstun* (indolence), *Niedertracht* (malice, despicableness), *Nihilismus* (nihilism), *Ohnmacht* (impotence), *Perfidie* (perfidy), *Pflichtverletzung* (breach of duty), *Phantasterei* (having pipe dreams), *Primitivität* (crudeness), *Raub* (robbery), *Schmeichelei* (flattery), *Schwäche* (weakness), *Schwindel* (swindle, fraud), *Spiegelfechterei* (sham), *Terrorisierung* (terrorization), *Vereinsmeierei* (enthusiasm for club life), *Verknöcherung* (fossilization), *Verleumdung* (slander), *Verpestung* (pollution), *Verprassung* (squandering), *Versagen* (failure), *Verwüstungen* (devastation), *Verzagtsein* (despondency), *Wahnsinn* (lunacy), *Widerwille* (aversion), *Wortklauberei* (hairsplitting), *Wucher* (profiteering), *Zweifel* (doubt).

Nouns with the suffixes *-heit* or *-keit*:

Ärmlichkeit (meagreness, shabbiness), *Aufdringlichkeit* (insistency, pushiness), *Bedeutungslosigkeit* (meaninglessness), *Bequemlichkeit* (laziness), *Beschränktheit* (lack of intelligence, limitedness), *Borniertheit* (bigotry), *Charakterlosigkeit* (lack of character), *Denkfaulheit* (mental laziness), *Derbheit* (courseness), *Dummheit* (stupidity), *Eingebildetheit* (conceit), *Entschlußlosigkeit* (indecisiveness), *Fehlerhaftigkeit* (imperfection), *Feigheit* (cowardice), *Frechheit* (impudence), *Fügsamkeit* (obedience), *Gesinnungslosigkeit* (lack of conviction), *Gewissenlosigkeit* (lack of conscience), *Gleichgültigkeit* (indifference), *Halbheit* (half-heartedness), *Harmlosigkeit* (mildness), *Hoffnungslosigkeit* (hopelessness), *Instinktlosigkeit* (lack of instinct), *Jämmerlichkeit* (pitifulness, contemptibility, uselessness), *Leblosigkeit* (lifelessness), *Leichtsinnigkeit* (carelessness, recklessness), *Mundfertigkeit* (eloquence), *Niederträchtigkeit* (maliciousness), *Ratlosigkeit* (helplessness), *Roheit* (brutishness, courseness), *Schalheit* (staleness, emptiness), *Schamlosigkeit* (shamelessness), *Schlappschwänzigkeit* (weediness), *Schlechtigkeit* (badness, wickedness), *Schwerfälligkeit* (ponderousness), *Sittenlosigkeit* (immorality), *Sturheit* (obstinacy), *Teilnahmslosigkeit* (indifference, apathy), *Trägheit* (lethargy), *Trottelhaftigkeit* (feeble-mindedness), *Unaufrichtigkeit* (insincerity), *Unfähigkeit* (incompetence), *Unfreiheit* (bondage), *Unsicherheit* (unsureness), *Unterwürfigkeit* (obsequiousness), *Unverschämtheit* (impertinence), *Unvollständigkeit* (incompleteness), *Unwahrhaftigkeit* (untruthfulness), *Unwirksamkeit* (ineffectiveness), *Unwürdigkeit* (unworthiness), *Unzulänglichkeit* (inadequacy), *Verantwortungslosigkeit* (irresponsibility), *Verderbtheit* (corruptness, depravity), *Vergeßlichkeit* (forgetfulness), *Verlogenheit* (mendacity), *Verworfenheit* (depravity), *Verzagtheit* (despondency, despair), *Weltfremdheit* (unworldliness), *Zerfahrenheit* (distractedness), *Zerrissenheit* (being at odds with oneself), *Ziellosigkeit* (aimlessness), *Zweideutigkeit* (ambiguity), *Zwerghaftigkeit* (dwarfishness).

Common adjectives:

beamtet (official), *bureaukratisch* (bureaucratic), *bezopft* and *zopfig* (old fashioned), *defekt* (defective), *denkfaul* (mentally lazy), *egoistisch* (egoistic), *fanatisch* (fanatical), *faul* (lazy), *feige* (cowardly), *gelahrt* (learned), *geschminkt* (*MK*: 328) [camouflaged (Mh.: 272)], *liberal*, *modern*, *niederträchtig* (malicious, vile), *pazifistisch* (*MK*: 110), *primitiv* can also have positive connotations (cf. 367), *undeutsch* (un-German), *unfähig* (incapable), *unvölkisch* (unfolkish), *völkisch* can be pejorative, *verbrecherisch* (criminal), *verludert* (debauched).

A selection of less common compound adjectives describing human beings and their activities:

blitzdumm (*MK*: 208) [idiotic (Mh.: 172)]; *bekannt borniert-kurzsichtig* (*MK*: 367) [well-known narrow-minded and short-sighted (Mh.: 303)]; *deutschfeindlich* (*MK*: 131) [anti-German (Mh.: 110)]; *dividendenhungrig* (*MK*: 370) [dividend-hungry (Mh.: 306)]; *fluchwürdigst* (*MK*: 421) [most execrable (Mh.: 348)]; *gottverlassen* (*MK*: 633) [God-forsaken (Mh.: 514)]; *gutmütig-dumm* (*MK*: 626) [good-natured fools (Mh.: 509)]; *haßaufwühlend* (*MK*: 532) [hate-fomenting (Mh.: 432)]; *hochnäsig-arrogant* (*MK*: 727) [supercilious, arrogant

(Mh.: 587)]; *kindlich-blödsinnig* (*MK*: 505) [absurd childish (Mh.: 412)]; *kindlich-naiv* (*MK*: 738) [childish and naïve (Mh.: 595)]; *kleinherzig-partikularistisch* (*MK*: 644) [small-hearted, particularistic (Mh.: 523)]; *marxistisch-jüdisch* (*MK*: 616) [Marxist-Jewish (Mh.: 590)]; *pazifistisch-marxistisch* (*MK*: 361) [pacifist-Marxist (Mh.: 298)]; *sadistisch-pervers* (*MK*: 704) [perverted sadistic (Mh.: 569)]; *schafsgeduldig* (*MK*: 685) [patient lamblike (Mh.: 555)]; *siegestrunken* (*MK*: 393) [drunk with victory (Mh.: 324)]; *streikgleichgültig* (*MK*: 26) [indifferent (about strikes) (Mh.: 25)]; *streiklustig* (*MK*: 26) [enthusiastic about strikes (Mh.: 25)]; *todgefährlich* (*MK*: 149) [mortally dangerous (Mh.: 125)]; *überbildet* (*MK*: 480 [*overeducated* (Mh.: 392)]); „*verantwortlichseinsollend*" (*MK*: 685) [should be responsible (Mh.: 555)]; *volksbelügend* and *volksbetrügerisch* (*MK*: 547) [treachery (Mh.: 444)]; *volksfremd* (*MK*: 480) [alien to the people (Mh.: 392)]; *weniggeistig* (*MK*: 509) [unintellectual (Mh.: 415)]; „*weltbürgerlich*", *pazifistisch-ideologisch* (*MK*: 703) [cosmopolitan, pacifistic-ideological (Mh.: 569)]; *witzig-ulkig* (*MK*: 489) [cute and kittenish (Mh.: 400), *ulkig* would normally be translated as 'peculiar']; *wutentbrannt* (*MK*: 560) [burned up with rage (Mh.: 455)].

5.3.2.2 Jews

Criticism of a positive stereotype:

> 'Es ist also grundfalsch aus der Tatsache des Zusammenstehens der Juden im Kampfe, richtiger ausgedrückt in der Ausplünderung ihrer Mitmenschen, bei ihnen auf einen gewissen idealen Aufopferungssinn schließen zu wollen' (*MK*: 331) [So it is absolutely wrong to infer any ideal sense of sacrifice in the Jews from the fact that they stand together in struggle, or, better expressed, in plundering of their fellow men (Mh.: 274)];
> 'zu ihrer klugen Vorsicht (sprich „Feigheit")' (*MK*: 365) [for their wily caution (read cowardice) (Mh.: 302)].

The desire of Jews to expand their race:

> 'Sein Sich-Weiterverbreiten aber ist eine typische Erscheinung für alle Parasiten; er sucht immer neuen Boden für seine Rasse' (*MK*: 334) [His spreading is a typical phenomenon for all parasites; he always seeks as new feeding ground for his race (Mh.: 276)];
> '(...) das ahnungslose Mädchen, das er mit seinem Blute schändet und damit seinem, des Mädchens Volke raubt' (*MK*: 357) [the unsuspecting girl whom he defiles with his blood, thus stealing her from her people (Mh.: 295)].

Appendix II 223

Desire for world domination:

'dieser jüdischen Welteroberungstendenz' (*MK*: 703) [(of) this Jewish tendency of world conquest (Mh.: 568)], 'Auspressung der deutschen Arbeitskraft im Joche der jüdischen Weltfinanz' (*MK*: 703) [the sweating of the German working class under the yoke of Jewish world finance (Mh.: 568)], **'Weltbeherrschung'** (*MK*: 704) [*Jewish world domination* (Mh.: 569)], 'der jüdischen Herrschaftsanmaßung' (*MK*: 355) [(to) the Jewish presumption to dominate (Mh.: 293)], **'die jüdische Weltbolschewisierung'** (*MK*: 752) [*Jewish world Bolshevisation* (Mh.: 605)], '(im Dienste) des jüdischen Welteroberungsgedankens und -kampfes' (*MK*: 761) [(in the service of) the Jewish idea and struggle for world conquest (Mh.: 611)], 'ihrer internationalen Weltbegaunerei' (*MK*: 356) [(for) their international world swindle (Mh.: 294)], 'dieser internationalen Weltvergiftung' (*MK*: 521) [(to) this international world poisoning (Mh.: 423)], 'wirtschaftliche Eroberung der Welt' (*MK*: 352) [economic conquest of the world (Mh.: 291)].

Danger to Germany and the Aryan race:

'Entweihung und Zerstörung' (*MK*: 630) [desecration and destruction (Mh.: 512)], 'die Versklavung und damit die Vernichtung aller nichtjüdischen Völker' (*MK*: 351) [the enslavement and with it the destruction of all non-Jewish peoples (Mh.: 290)], 'seine blutsaugerische Tyrannei' (*MK*: 339) [his bloodsucking tyranny (Mh.: 281)], 'Unterjochung' (*MK*: 358) [subjugation (Mh.: 296)], 'Ausrottung' (*MK*: 703) [extermination (Mh.: 568)], 'wie er sie immer von neuem unbarmherzig auspreßte und aussog' (*MK*: 343) [how he squeezed and sucked their blood again and again (Mh.: 284)], 'Umgarnung' (*MK*: 340) [ensnarement (Mh.: 282)], 'Umstrickung' (*MK*: 703) [snares (Mh.: 568)], 'Umklammerung' (*MK*: 703) [embrace (Mh.: 568)], 'Zerstörungsarbeit' (*MK*: 352) [work of disintegration (Mh.: 291)], 'der jüdisch-freimaurerischen Umklammerung' (*MK*: 521) [from the Jewish-Masonic embrace (Mh.: 423)].

Dishonesty, deception, theft, slander, hypocrisy, lack of conscience:

'Lug und Trug' (*MK*: 386) [lies and deception (Mh.: 319)], 'die unverschämtesten Versprechungen' (*MK*: 354) [the most shameless promises (Mh.: 292)], 'der dialektischen Verlogenheit dieser Rasse' (*MK*: 67) [of this race of dialectical liars (Mh.: 58)], 'kraft seiner verlogenen dialektischen Gewandheit und Geschmeidigkeit' (*MK*: 530, cf. 338) [thanks to his lying dialectical skill and suppleness (Mh.: 430)], 'ihre Zungenfertigkeit oder ihre Kunst der Lüge' (*MK*: 67) [the agility of their tongues or their virtuosity at lying (Mh.: 58)], 'dieses jüdischen Lügenfeldzugs' (*MK*: 356) [(for) this Jewish campaign of lies (Mh.: 294)] (Houston Stewart Chamberlain refers to a British *Lügenfeldzug* (1925: 20)), 'Meister im großen Lügen' (*MK*: 386) [the great master in lying (Mh.: 319)], 'der allgemeinen Verlogenheit und Verleumdungstendenz'

[= politicians as well as Jews] (*MK*: 709) [(with) the general hypocrisy and slanderous tendencies (Mh.: 573)], 'ihrer volksbelügenden und volksbetrügerischen Tätigkeit' [= the "Jewish" press] (*MK*: 547) [the treachery with which they deceived and lied to the people (Mh.: 444)], '(er) heuchelt Mitleid' (*MK*: 350) [(he) simulates pity (Mh.: 289)], 'Schwindel' (*MK*: 341) [swindle (Mh.: 282)], 'keinerlei Gewissensbisse' (*MK*: 353) [no pangs of conscience (Mh.: 292)], 'Verbalhornisierung oder geistiger Diebstahl' (*MK*: 332) [patchwork or intellectual theft (Mh.: 275)], 'diese infame jüdische Art, ehrlichen Menschen (...) aus die Schmutzkübel niedrigster Verleumdungen und Ehrabschneidungen über das saubere Kleid zu gießen' (*MK*: 93) [this vile Jewish technique of emptying garbage pails full of the vilest slanders and defamations (...) on the clean garments of honourable men (Mh.: 79)], 'Jede jüdische Verleumdung und jede jüdische Lüge ist eine Ehrennarbe am Körper unserer Kämpfer' (*MK*: 386) [Every Jewish slander and every Jewish lie is a scar of honour on the body of our warriors (Mh.: 319)], 'Repräsentanten der Lüge, des Betrugs, des Diebstahls, der Plünderung, des Raubes' (*MK*: 750) [champions of deceit, lies, theft, plunder, and rapine (Mh.: 604)].

Seduction, luring, exploitation and imitation of other races:

'bei der teuflischen Gewandheit dieser Verführer' (*MK*: 67) [the diabolical craftiness of these seducers (Mh.: 58)], 'Ausplünderung ihrer Mitmenschen' (*MK*: 331) [the plundering of their fellow men (Mh.: 274)], 'Menschenausbeutung' (*MK*: 340) [human exploitation (Mh.: 281)], 'Ausplünderung seiner Opfer' (*MK*: 339) [to plunder his victims (Mh.: 281)], 'Zur Maskierung des Treibens und zur Einschläferung seiner Opfer' (*MK*: 346) [To mask his activity and lull his victims (Mh.: 286)], 'der jüdischen Lockung' (*MK*: 354) [the Jewish lures (Mh.: 292)], 'Unter einem Geseires von schönen Tönen und Redensarten lullen sie dieselben in den Glauben ein (...)' (*MK*: 268) [Amid a *Gezeires* of fine sounds and phrases they lull their readers into believing (...) (Mh.: 223), *Gezeires* is a Yiddish word meaning 'arbitrary decrees'], 'Wie sehr der Jude nur nachempfindend, besser verderbend fremde Kultur übernimmt' (*MK*: 332) [To what extent the Jew takes over foreign culture, imitating or rather ruining it (Mh.: 275)]; 'der „Gaukler", besser der Nachäffer' (*MK*: 332) [a 'juggler', or rather an ape (Mh.: 275)].

Subversion and agitation:

'Wühlarbeit' (*MK*: 703) [agitational efforts (Mh.: 568)], 'wüste Aufpeitschung der Masse' (*MK*: 353) [wild incitement of the masses (Mh.: 292)], 'die Heranbildung einer ihm blind ergebenden wirtschaftlichen Kampftruppe zur Zertrümmerung der nationalen wirtschaftlichen Unabhängigkeit' (*MK*: 353) [in training an economic storm troop, blindly devoted to him, with which to destroy the national economic independence (Mh.: 292)].

Selfishness and cowardice:

'eines krassesten Egoismus' (*MK*: 331) [of the crassest egoism (Mh.: 274)], 'nackter Egoismus des einzelnen' (*MK*: 331) [naked egoism of the individual (Mh.: 274)], 'der sich in ihrer Feigheit ausdrückende restlose Mangel jedes Aufopferungssinnes' (*MK*: 331) [the absolute absence of all sense of self-sacrifice, expressing itself in their cowardice (Mh.: 274)], 'zu ihrer klugen Vorsicht (sprich „Feigheit")' (*MK*: 365) [for their wily caution (read cowardice) (Mh.: 302)].

Greed:

'mit fiebernder Gier' (*MK*: 343) [with feverish avidity (Mh.: 284)], 'Seine Gewandtheit, besser Skrupellosigkeit in allen Geldangelegenheiten versteht es, immer neue Mittel aus den ausgeplünderten Untertanen herauszupressen, ja herauszuschinden' (*MK*: 341) [With his deftness, or rather unscrupulousness, in all money matters he is able to squeeze, yes, to grind, more and more money out of the plundered subjects (Mh.: 282)].

Brutality:

'Seiner ganzen inneren raubgierigen Brutalität entsprechend' (*MK*: 354) [In keeping with all his inner rapacious brutality (Mh.: 292)], 'die Völker diktatorisch mit brutaler Faust zu unterjochen und zu regieren' (*MK*: 357) [to subjugate and govern the peoples with a dictatorial and brutal fist (Mh.: 295)], 'den abgehäuteten Opfern' (*MK*: 343) [to his flayed victims (Mh.: 284)], 'das liebe Volk bis zur Verzweiflung quälen' (*MK*: 341) [torment the 'beloved people' to despair (Mh.: 282)], 'bestialische Grausamkeit mit unfaßlicher Lügenkunst' (*MK*: 750) [bestial cruelty and an inconceivable gift for lying (Mh.: 604)].

Impertinence, flattery and slyness:

'eine wahrhaft jüdische Frechheit' (*MK*: 248) [truly Jewish effrontery (Mh.: 207)], 'echt judenhaft frech, aber ebenso dumm' (*MK*: 314) [as truly Jewish in its effrontery as it is stupid (Mh.: 260)], 'dieser jüdischen Anmaßung und Frechheit' (*MK*: 388) [(to) this Jewish arrogance and effrontery (Mh.: 320)], 'in übelster Schmeichelei umkriechen' (*MK*: 341) [by crawling around them with the vilest flattery (Mh.: 282)], cf. *sich anbiedern* (make friends with) on the same page, 'die Schlauheit des Juden' (*MK*: 596) [the slyness of the Jew (Mh.: 485)], '(die Juden) betölpeln abermals die dummen Gojim auf das gerissenste' (*MK*: 356) [the Jews again slyly dupe the dumb *Goyim* (Mh.: 294)], 'Mätzchen und Tricks' (*MK*: 332) [twists and tricks (Mh.: 275)], 'von jüdischer Hinterlist' (*MK*: 758) [by Jewish guile (Mh.: 609)], 'der eisig kalten Überlegung des Juden' (*MK*: 704) [with the ice-cold calculation of the Jew (Mh.: 569)].

The Jews' influence on Germany's cultural life:

'Kulturell verseucht er Kunst, Literatur, Theater, vernarrt das natürliche Empfinden, stürzt alle Begriffe von Schönheit und Erhabenheit, von Edel und Gut und zerrt dafür die Menschen herab in den Bannkreis seiner eigenen niedrigen Wesensart' (*MK*: 358) [Culturally he contaminates art, literature, the theatre, makes a mockery of natural feeling, overthrows all concepts of beauty and sublimity, of the noble and the good, and instead drags men down into the sphere of his own base nature (Mh.: 296)].

The Jew speaking:

'Da er vom Deutschtum wirklich nichts besitzt als die Kunst (...) zu radebrechen' (*MK*: 342) [Since of Germanism he possesses really nothing but the art of stammering its language (Mh.: 283)], '(deutsch) mauscheln' (*MK*: 342, cf. 430) [jabbering German (Mh.: 283)], salbadern (*MK*: 94) [to shoot off his mouth (Mh.: 79)], 'die Schwefeleien der Juden' (*MK*: 336) [the drivel of the Jews themselves (Mh.: 278)].

Intolerence:

'daß diese Art von Unduldsamkeit und Fanatismus geradezu jüdischer Wesensart verkörpere' and 'von infernalischer Unduldsamkeit' (both *MK*: 506) [that this type of intolerance and fanaticism positively embodies the Jewish nature; infernal intolerance (Mh.: 413)].

Lists of faults:

'vom Juden verfolgt, gelästert, verleumdet, beschimpft, beschmutzt' (*MK*: 386) [persecuted, reviled, slandered, abused, befouled (Mh.: 319)];
'Kriechende Unterwürfigkeit nach „oben" und arrogante Hochnäsigkeit nach „unten" (...) himmelschreiende Borniertheit (...) manchmal geradezu erstaunliche Einbildung' (*MK*: 352) [Cringing submissiveness to superiors and high-handed arrogance to inferiors (...) a narrow-mindedness that often cries to high Heaven (...) a self-conceit that is sometimes positively amazing (Mh.: 291)];
'In ihrem Besitz [der Presse] setzt er sich mit aller Zähigkeit und Geschicklichkeit. Mit ihr beginnt er langsam das ganze öffentliche Leben zu umklammern und zu umgarnen, zu leiten und zu schieben (...)' (*MK*: 345) [With all his perseverance and dexterity he seizes possession of it [the press]. With it he slowly begins to grip and ensnare, to guide and to push all public life (...) (Mh.: 286)];
'Er geht seinen Weg, den Weg des Einschleichens in die Völker und des inneren Aushöhlens derselben, und er kämpft mit seinen Waffen, mit Lüge und Verleumdung, Vergiftung und Zersetzung, den Kampf steigernd bis zur blutigen Ausrottung der ihm verhaßten Gegner' (*MK*: 751) [He goes his way, the way

of sneaking in among the nations and boring from within, and he fights with his weapons, with lies and slander, poison and corruption, intensifying the struggle to the point of bloodily exterminating his hated foes (Mh.: 604)].

5.3.2.3 Marxists and the Press

'in demokratisch-marxistischer Verblendung' (*MK*: 700) [in democratic-Marxist blindness (Mh.: 566)], 'einer kurpfuscherischen Salbaderei' [= Marxism] (*MK*: 171) [bungling quackery (Mh.: 143)], 'in einem geradezu fanatischen Verleumdungskampf' [= the press] (*MK*: 355) [fanatical and slanderous struggle (Mh.: 293)], 'so elend ungeschickt, ja verbrecherisch dumm' [= the behaviour of the press] (*MK*: 205) [conducted itself with such miserable awkwardness, nay, criminal stupidity (Mh.: 170)], 'einer wahrhaft balkenbiegenden Lügenvirtuosität' [= the press] (*MK*: 43) [lying with a virtuosity that would bend iron beams (Mh.: 39)].

5.3.2.4 The General Population (most usually implying Germans)

Halbheit:

'Halbheit und Feigheit' (*MK*: 262) [half-heartendness and cowardice (Mh.: 219)], 'Halbheit und Schwäche' (*MK*: 301) [half-heartendness and weakness (Mh.: 250)], 'durch Halbheiten, durch schwaches Betonen eines Objektivitätsstandpunktes' (*MK*: 370) [by half-measures, by weakly emphasising a so-called objective standpoint (Mh.: 306)], 'gemäßigt-bürgerliche Elemente' (*MK*: 111) [moderate bourgeois elements (Mh.: 93)], 'Jede Halbheit ist das sichtbare Zeichen des inneren Verfalls, dem der äußere Zusammenbruch früher oder später folgen muß und wird' (*MK*: 269) [Every half-measure is a visible sign of inner decay which must and will be followed sooner or later by outward collapse (Mh.: 224)].

Lack of *Wille*:

'Mangel an Wille' (*MK*: 463) [lack of will (Mh.: 379)], **'das Fehlen einer geschlossenen Zusammenarbeit brutaler Macht mit genialem politischen Wollen'** [= Germans] (*MK*: 596) [*the lack of a unified collaboration of brutal force with brilliant political will* (Mh.: 484)], 'so wenig Wille zur Freiheit' (*MK*: 715) [so little will for freedom (Mh.: 577)].

Treason and anti-German/un-German behaviour:

'den gemeinsten Landesverrat, ja die erbärmlichste Schurkentat der deutschen Geschichte überhaupt' (*MK*: 607) [the vilest treason, nay, the most wretched piece of villainy in all German history (Mh.: 493)], **'antideutsche Psychose'** [= of other countries] (*MK*: 716) [*anti-German psychosis* (Mh.: 578)], 'ihrer willenlosen, nachgiebigen, in Wahrheit aber verräterischen Politik' [= left-wing politicians] (*MK*: 365) [of their spineless, compliant, actually treasonous policy (Mh.: 302)], 'antinationale, verbrecherische Politik' [= left-wing politicians] (*MK*: 365) [anti-national, criminal policy (Mh.: 302)], '(in) schandvoller Unterdrückung nationaler Tugenden' (*MK*: 701) [(in) disgraceful oppression of national virtues (Mh.: 567)], 'in einer solchen mangelhaften nationalen Entschlossenheit' (*MK*: 122) [in such a lack of national determination (Mh.: 103)], 'einer ebenso mangelhaften Erziehung zum Deutschtum' (*MK*: 122) [of an inadequate education in Germanism (Mh.: 103)].

Weakness, cowardice and unmanliness:

'faul und feige' [= the bourgeoisie] (*MK*: 409) [rotten and cowardly (Mh.: 339)], **'träge und feige'** [= most of humanity] (*MK*: 652) [*lazy and cowardly* (Mh.: 529)], 'mit zitternder Feigheit' (*MK*: 364) [with trembling cowardice (Mh.: 301)], 'dank ihrer jämmerlichen Feigheit' (*MK*: 365) [thanks to their miserable cowardice (Mh.: 302)], 'eurer elenden Jämmerlichkeit' (*MK*: 365) [of you miserable villainy (Mh.: 302)], 'in einer zum Himmel schreienden Feigheit' (*MK*: 266) [in a cowardice crying to high Heaven (Mh.: 221)], 'feige Duldung' (*MK*: 292) [cowardly tolerance (Mh.: 242)], 'bürgerliche Schlappschwänzigkeit' (*MK*: 550) [bourgeois cowardice and shilly-shallying (Mh.: 447)], 'ein Bild jämmerlichster Unfähigkeit, pazifistischer Feigheit' (*MK*: 700) [a picture of the most wretched incompetence and pacifistic cowardice (Mh.: 566)], 'Mangel an Entschlossenheit und Mut' (*MK*: 166) [lack of determination and courage (Mh.: 139)], 'in der mangelnden Zivilcourage' (*MK*: 463) [lack of civil courage (Mh.: 380)], 'ihrer eigenen geringen Heldenhaftigkeit' (*MK*: 656) [(of) their own scanty heroism (Mh.: 532)], 'Verweichlichung und Verweibung' (*MK*: 308) [softening and effeminization (Mh.: 255)], 'von jeder unmännlichen prüden Unaufrichtigkeit' (*MK*: 279) [from all unmanly, prudish hypocrisy (Mh.: 232)].

Compliance and submission:

'hündische Verehrung' (*MK*: 426) [dog-like veneration (Mh.: 352)], 'hündische Unterwürfigkeit' (*MK*: 590) [doglike submissiveness (Mh.: 480)], 'Winseln und Flennen' (*MK*: 123) [whimpering and whining (Mh.: 104)], 'das jämmerliche Buhlen' and 'Liebeswerbung' [= of the Slavs] (*MK*: 39) [disgraceful courting; declaration of love (Mh.: 36)], 'willenlose Fügsamkeit' (*MK*: 305) [spineless compliance (Mh.: 253)], 'ein würdeloses Nachgeben und Erfüllen' (*MK*.: 101) [undignified submissiveness and acquiescence (Mh.: 85)].

Stupidity, frivolity and incompetence (especially of the masses):

'dumme Schafsgeduld' (*MK*: 51) [sheeplike patience (Mh.: 45)], 'verbrecherisch leichtsinnig' (*MK*: 275) [criminal frivolity (Mh.: 229)], 'durch den sträflichen Leichtsinn dieser Verantwortungslosesten der Nation' (*MK*: 301) [by the criminal frivolity of these most irresponsible among irresponsibles (Mh.: 250)], 'geheimrätliche Dummheit oder Harmlosigkeit' (*MK*: 266) [a stupidity and innocence such as only privy councillors are capable of (Mh.: 222)], 'unwissend und nichtskönnend' (*MK*: 308) [ignorant and incompetent (Mh.: 256)], 'bei der primitiven Einfalt ihres Gemütes' [= of the masses] (*MK*: 252) [in view of the primitive simplicity of their minds (Mh.: 211)], 'Bei der geringen Denkfähigkeit' [= of the masses] (*MK*: 52) [In view of the great masses' small capacity for thought (Mh.: 46)], 'jämmerlichster Unfähigkeit' (*MK*: 700) [of the most wretched incompetence (Mh.: 566)], '„staatsmännischen" Murkserei' (*MK*: 88) ['statesmanlike' bungling (Mh.: 75)], 'bei der ebenso denkfaulen wie manchmal anmaßenden Masse' (*MK*: 355) [Since the masses are as mentally lazy as they are sometimes presumptuous (Mh.: 293)], 'Mangel an Klugheit' (*MK*: 166) [lack of astuteness (Mh.: 139)].

Lunacy:

'verbrecherischer Wahnwitz' (*MK*: 479) [criminal lunacy (Mh.: 391)].

Indolence and failure to do one's duty:

'infolge einer unglaublichen Indolenz' (*MK*: 451) [an incredible indolence (Mh.: 370)], 'Faulheit und Unvermögen' (*MK*: 399f.) [laziness and inability (Mh.: 330)], 'in gottverblendeter Pflichtvergessenheit' (*MK*: 621) [in their damnable blindness and disregard of duty (Mh.: 505)], **'pflichtvergessenes Verbrechen'** (*MK*: 693) [*criminal neglect of duty* (Mh.: 561)].

Sentimentality:

'Phantastische Sentimentalität' (*MK*: 712) [*Fantastic sentimentality* (Mh.: 575)], 'in jämmerlicher Sentimentalität' (*MK*: 29) [in tearful sentimentality (Mh.: 27)].

Dishonesty, trickery, slyness and hypocrisy:

'**Lüge** und Fälschung' [= of left-wing politicians] (*MK*: 365) [*lies* and falsification (Mh.: 302)], 'verlogenste Heuchelei' (*MK*: 523) [vile hypocrisy (Mh.: 425)], 'der allgemeinen Verlogenheit und Betrügerei' (*MK*: 98) [of general falsehood and deceit (Mh.: 82)], 'listige Verschlagenheit' (*MK*: 168) [cunning craftiness (Mh.: 140)], 'Wortklauberei und Spiegelfechterei' (*MK*: 395) [hair-splitting and shadow-boxing (Mh.: 326)], 'einer so ungeheuren Frechheit der infamsten Verdrehung' (*MK*: 252) [(of) such monstrous effrontery and infamous misrepresentation (Mh.: 211)], 'Feilschen und Handeln' [= politicians] (*MK*: 91) [haggling and bargaining (Mh.: 77)], 'unmenschlich und ausbeuterisch' [= employers] (*MK*: 374) [inhuman exploiting (Mh.: 309)], 'dieses Instrument einer maßlosen Erpressung und schmachvollsten Erniedrigung' (*MK*: 714) [This instrument of boundless extortion and abject humiliation (Mh.: 577)].

Greed and extravagance:

'Habgier und Kurzsichtigkeit' (*MK*: 352) [greed and shortsightedness (Mh.: 291)], 'Habsucht und Materialismus' (*MK*: 307) [greed and materialism (Mh.: 255)], 'Überdruß und Prasserei' (*MK*: 208) [abundance and high-living (Mh.: 173)], 'dieser geistigen Verprassung des Heldentums der Armee' (*MK*: 205) [to this spiritual squandering of the army's heroism (Mh.: 170)].

Envy and ambition:

'in der traurigen Mischung von Neid, Eifersucht, Ehrgeiz und diebischer Gesinnung' (*MK*: 573) [in the sorry mixture of envy, jealousy, ambition, and thievish mentality (Mh.: 466)].

Arrogance and criticism of others:

'Arroganz und eingebildete Frechheit' (*MK*: 400) [arrogance and conceited effrontery (Mh.: 330)], 'mit ungezogenster Eingebildetheit' (*MK*: 774) [with boorish arrogance (Mh.: 622)], 'Nörgeln und Kritisieren' (*MK*: 111) [grumbling and criticising (Mh.: 93)], 'nichtssagendes Glotzen und Kopfschütteln, ein überlegenes Lächerlichfinden' (*MK*: 450) [meaningless staring and headshaking, a supercilious ridicule (Mh.: 370)].

Brutality and violence:

'unbändiges Randalieren' (*MK*: 590) [unruly rowdyism (Mh.: 480)], 'wahnwitzige Verhetzung' (*MK*: 625) [insane incitement (Mh.: 508)].

Bourgeois behaviour:

'in ihrer lächerlichen Spießerhaftigkeit' (*MK*: 238) [in their absurd philistinism (Mh.: 198)].

Unacceptable verbal behaviour:

'von einem widerlichen Gekläff' (*MK*: 642) [for a repulsive yelping (Mh.: 522)], 'dem haßerfüllten Gebell der Feinde' (*MK*: 757) [the hateful yapping of the enemies (Mh.: 609)], 'Geflenne' (*MK*: 701) [whimpering (Mh.: 567)], 'leere Geflunker' (*MK*: 717) [empty bragging (Mh.: 578)], 'albernes Geschwätz' (*MK*:

718) [silly gossip (Mh.: 579)], 'diese unsinnigsten Ergüsse' (*MK*: 718) [the senseless outpourings (Mh.: 579)].

Cosmopolitanism:

'von völkischen Allerweltsgefühlsduseleien' (*MK*: 741) [by cosmopolitan folkish drivel (Mh.: 597)], 'dumme internationale Einstellung' [= of the masses] (*MK*: 190) [stupid international attitude (Mh.: 159)], '(diesem) „weltbürgerlichen", pazifistisch-ideologischen Gedanken' [= learnt from the Jews] (*MK*: 703) ['cosmopolitan', pacifistic-ideological ideas (Mh.: 569)].

Lack of a sense of justice:

'(mit) mangeldem Rechts- und Billigkeitsgefühl' (*MK*: 49) [with a deficient sense of justice and propriety (Mh.: 43)].

General depravity:

'**gewollte** Schlechtigkeit' (*MK*: 451) [*deliberate* malice (Mh.: 370)], 'der allmählichen Verlumpung' (*MK*: 607) [(to) the gradually increasing depravity (Mh.: 493)], 'grenzlose Schmach und Schande' (*MK*: 301) [boundless shame and disgrace (Mh.: 250)], 'jämmerlich zwerghaft' (*MK*: 774) [miserable and dwarfish (Mh.: 622)], 'niederschmetternd schmachvoll' (*MK*: 779) not in Mh., 'innere Fäulnis, Feigheit, Charakterlosigkeit, kurz Unwürdigkeit' (*MK*: 250) [inner rottenness, cowardice, lack of character, in short, unworthiness (Mh.: 209)];
'die Elemente der Gemeinheit, der Niedertracht und der Feigheit, kurz die Masse des Extrems des Schlechten' (*MK*: 582) [the elements of baseness, treachery, cowardice, in short, the mass of the bad extreme (Mh.: 473)];
'Man weiß ja nicht, was in dieser bürgerlichen Welt größer ist, die Trottelhaftigkeit, die Schwäche und Feigheit oder die durch und durch verlumpte Gesinnung' (*MK*: 772) [We never know which is greater in this bourgeois world, the imbecility, weakness, and cowardice, or their deep-dyed corruption (Mh.: 621)].

One fault can be marginally better than another:

'Lieber noch etwas zofpig, aber redlich und treu, als aufgeklärt und modern, aber minderwertig von Charakter und (...) unwissend und nichtskönnend' (*MK*: 308) [It is better to be a little old-fashioned, but honest and loyal, than enlightened and modern, but of inferior character and (...) ignorant and incompetent (Mh.: 256)].

6   Antithesis

'Sein oder Nichtsein' (*MK*: 178) [for life or death (Mh.: 149)];
'die Schicksalsfrage von Sein oder Nichtsein' (*MK*: 195) [the question of destiny, 'to be or not to be' (Mh.: 162)];
'Aus einem toten Mechanismus (...) soll ein lebendiger Organismus geformt werden' (*MK*: 439) [From a dead mechanism (...) there must be formed a living organism (Mh.: 362)];
'Damit aber ist der Staat ein völkischer Organismus und nicht eine wirtschaftliche Organisation' (*MK*: 165) [(...) thus the state is a national organism and not an economic organisation (Mh.: 138)];
'In politischen Angelegenheiten entscheidet nicht selten das Gefühl richtiger als der Verstand' (*MK*: 190) [In political matters feeling often decides more correctly than reason (Mh.: 159)];
'(...) das eine ergibt dann eben arische Arbeits- und Kulturstaaten, das andere jüdische Schmarotzerkolonien' (*MK*: 168) [(...) the one results in Aryan states based on work and culture, the other in Jewish colonies of parasites (Mh.: 140)].

Constructions with *nicht ... sondern ..., kein ... sondern, nie/niemals ... sondern* or *niemals ... immer, lieber ... als*:

'Völker befreit man nicht durch Nichtstun, sondern durch Opfer' (*MK*: 777) [*People are not freed by doing nothing, but by sacrifices* (Mh.: 624)];
'Mit dem Juden gibt es kein Paktieren, sondern nur das harte Entweder-Oder' (*MK*: 225) [There is no making pacts with Jews; there can only be the hard: either—or (Mh.: 187)];
'Zeiten, in denen nicht der Geist, sondern die Faust entscheidet' (*MK*: 277) [(Mh.:)] [In times when not the mind but the fist decides (Mh.: 230)];
'nicht für den Augenblick, sondern für die Ewigkeit bestimmt' [= monuments] (*MK*: 290) [(...) made, not for the moment, but for eternity (Mh.: 240)];
'Nicht Knecht soll sie der Masse sein, sondern Herr!' [= the N.S.D.A.P.] (*MK*: 520) [It must not become the servant of the masses, but their master! (Mh.: 422)];
'Die Frage lautet ja doch nie: was kann der Mensch, sondern was hat er gelernt?' (*MK*: 243) [The question has never been: What are the man's abilities? but: What has he learned? (Mh.: 203)];
'ein Staat (...) der nicht einen volksfremden Mechanismus wirtschaftlicher Belange und Interessen, sondern einen völkischen Organismus darstellt' (*MK*: 362) [a state (...) which represents, not an alien mechanism of economic concerns and interests, but a national organism (Mh.: 299)];
'Für mich war es dann keine vorübergehende Spielerei, sondern blutiger Ernst' (*MK*: 242) [For me is was no passing game, but grim earnest (Mh.: 202)];

'Diese sind aber immer heldische Tugenden und niemals krämerischer Egoismus' (*MK*: 166) [And these are always heroic virtues and never the egoism of shopkeepers (Mh.: 138)];

'Die Nationalisierung der breiten Masse kann niemals erfolgen durch Halbheiten, durch schwaches Betonen eines Objektivitätsstandpunktes, sondern durch rücksichstlose und fanatisch einseitige Einstellung auf das nun einmal zu erstrebende Ziel' (*MK*: 370) [The nationalisation of the broad masses can never be achieved by half-measures, by weakly emphasising a so-called objective standpoint, but only by a ruthless and fanatically one-sided orientation towards the goal to be achieved (Mh.: 306)];

'Daher wird sein Intellekt niemals aufbauend wirken, sondern zerstörend und in ganz seltenen Fällen vielleicht höchstens aufpeitschend' [= the Jew] (*MK*: 332) [Hence his intellect will never have a constructive effect, but will be destructive, and in very rare cases perhaps will at most be stimulating (Mh.: 275)];

'(...) er war deshalb auch nie Nomade, sondern immer nur **Parasit** im Körper anderer Völker' [= the Jew] (*MK*: 334) [(...) for that reason he was never a nomad, but only and always a *parasite* in the body of other peoples (Mh.: 276)];

'Lieber noch etwas zopfig, aber redlich und treu, als aufgeklärt und modern, aber minderwärtig von Charakter und (...) unwissend und nichtskönnend' (*MK*: 308) [It is better to be a little old-fashioned, but honest and loyal, than enlightened and modern, but of inferior character and (...) ignorant and incompetent (Mh.: 256)].

7 Irony

7.1 Ironic Quotation Marks

Jews:

'Angehörige des „auserwählten Volks"' (*MK*: 65) [members of the 'chosen people' (Mh.: 57)], 'ein paar Judenjungen waren die „Führer" in diesem „Kampf um die Freiheit, Schönheit und Würde" unseres Volksdaseins' (*MK*: 221) [a few Jewish youths were the 'leaders' in this struggle for the 'freedom, beauty, and dignity' of our national existence (Mh.: 184)], 'Er gilt heute als „gescheit"' (*MK*: 329) [Today he passes as 'smart' (Mh.: 273)], '„Freund der Menschen"' (*MK*: 343) ['friend of mankind' (Mh.: 284)], '„Wohltäter" der Menschheit' (*MK*: 343) ['benefactor' of mankind (Mh.: 284)], 'Während er von „Aufklärung", „Fortschritt", „Freiheit", „Menschentum" überzufließen scheint, übt er selber strengste Abschließung seiner Rasse' (*MK*: 346) [While he seems to overflow with 'enlightenment', 'progress', 'freedom', 'humanity', etc. he himself practices the severest segregation of his race (Mh.: 286)].

Other groups:

'des (...) Herrn „Volksvertreters"' (*MK*: 113) [fellow 'representative of the people' (Mh.: 95)], '(den) „Friedensvertrag von Versailles"' (*MK*: 523) [the 'Peace Treaty of Versailles' (Mh.: 425)], 'die „Friedensverträge von Brest-Litowsk und Versailles"' (*MK*: 523) [the 'Peace Treaties of Brest-Litovsk and Versailles' (Mh.: 425)], 'höhere „Intelligenzschichten"' (*MK*: 43) [educated 'classes' (Mh.: 39)], 'der Gedankengang dieses „bedeutenden" „nationalen" „Staatsmannes", den man (...) zu „seinem Volk" reden ließ' [= Cuno] (*MK*: 776) [this 'eminent' 'national' 'statesman', who (...) was allowed to address *his people* (Mh.: 623)], 'die „große Kulturnation"' [= France] (*MK*: 58) [the 'great cultural nation' (Mh.: 51)], 'eine dieser „Weltzeitungen"' (*MK*: 58) [one of these 'world newspapers' (Mh.: 51)], 'schwatzt von „journalistischer Pflicht" und ähnlichem verlogenen Zeug' (*MK*: 94) ['prates about journalistic duty' and such-like lies (Mh.: 79)], 'der journalistischen „Ehre"' (*MK*: 94) [(of) 'honour', to wit, the journalistic variety (Mh.: 79)], 'Die „internationale" Sozialdemokratie' (*MK*: 257) ['International' Social Democracy (Mh.: 215)], 'in der „wirtschaftsfriedlichen" Eroberung der Welt' [= Germany's expansionist policy] (*MK*: 157) [In the 'peaceful economic' conquest of the world (Mh.: 131f.)], 'zur „Verteidigung" des schon benannten „Weltfriedens" und der „friedlichen" Eroberung der Welt' (*MK*: 157) [for the 'defence' of our old friend 'world peace' and 'peaceful' conquest of the world (Mh.: 131f.)].

With *sogenannt*:

'der große Durchschnitt unserer sogenannten „Intelligenz"' (*MK*: 36) [the average member of our so-called 'intelligentsia' (Mh.: 33)], 'unseres sogenannten „Führertums"' (*MK*: 89) [our so-called 'leadership' (Mh.: 75)], 'Dann kommen die Sterngucker und Parteiastrologen, die sogenannten „erfahrenen" und „gewiegten"' (*MK*: 410) [Then come the stargazers and party astrologers, the so-called 'experienced', 'shrewd' men (Mh.: 339)].

7.2 Irony Without Inverted Commas

Often with *diese(r)* (the irony may lost in translation if *dies* is translated as *the*):

'diese Herrschaften' (*MK*: 97) [these gentry (Mh.: 81)], 'diese Zierden des menschlichen Geschlechts' [= Jews] (*MK*: 341) [these ornaments of the human race (Mh.: 282)], 'diese Menschheitsfreundin' [= social democracy] (*MK*: 53) [this friend of humanity (Mh.: 46)], 'dieser Auserkorenen der Nationen' [= politicians] (*MK*: 84) [(of) the elect of the peoples (Mh.: 71)], 'dieser Prachterscheinungen unseres öffentlichen Lebens' [= politicians] (*MK*: 91) [(of) these ornaments of our public life (Mh.: 77)], 'unser deutscher Pazifist' (*MK*: 122) [our German pacifist (Mh.: 102)], 'die Herren Parlamentarier' (*MK*: 218) [the Parliamentary gentlemen (Mh.: 181)], 'in einer so illustren Gesellschaft' (*MK*: 98) [in such an illustrious company (Mh.: 82)];

'Aber freilich, was sind denn Schiller, Goethe oder Shakespeare gegenüber den Heroen der neueren deutschen Dichtkunst! Alte abgetragene und überlebte, nein, überwundene Erscheinungen' (*MK*: 285) [But after all, what are Schiller, Goethe, or Shakespeare compared to the heroes of the newer German poetic art? Old, outworn, outmoded, nay, obsolete (Mh.: 136)];

'Im Verlauf einiger Jahre bildete sich mir dann in Erkenntnis und Einsicht der Typ der würdevollsten Erscheinung der neueren Zeit in plastischer Deutlichkeit aus: der Parlamentarier' (*MK*: 84) [In the course of a few years, my knowledge and insight shaped a plastic model of that most dignified phenomenon of modern times: the parliamentarian (Mh.: 72)].

7.3   Sarcasm

'daß der Jude ein „Wohltäter und Menschenfreund" geworden ist. Welch ein eigentümlicher Wandel' (*MK*: 344) [that the Jew has become a 'benefactor and friend of mankind'. What a strange transformation (Mh.: 285)];

'Die Kanzleien waren mit Juden besetzt. Fast jeder Schreiber ein Jude und jeder Jude ein Schreiber. Ich staunte über diese Fülle von Kämpfern des auserwählten Volkes (...)' (*MK*: 211) [The office were filled with Jews. Nearly every clerk was a Jew and nearly every Jew was a clerk. I was amazed at this plethora of warriors of the chosen people (...) (Mh.: 175)];

'das durchschnittliche Spatzenhirn einer deutschen, wissenschaftlich natürlich höchst gebildeten Schreiberseele' (*MK*: 533) [the average sparrow brain of a German scribbler, equipped, it goes without saying, with a high scientific education (Mh.: 433)].

7.4   Ironic Epithets

'meine tapferen Herren Wortprotestler!' (*MK*: 710) [my brave *lip-service protesters* (Mh.: 574)];

'unsere deutschen Phantasten' (*MK*: 315) [our German visionaries (Mh.: 261)];

'den famosen Weltverbesserern unserer Tage' (*MK*: 444) [the famous world reformers of our days (Mh.: 365)].

With *erhaben, gelehrt/gelahrt, erlaucht*:

'leuchtete unseren erhabenen Lehrern professoraler Wissenschaft leider nicht ein' (*MK*: 159) [something that never occurred to our exalted professors of academic science (Mh.: 133)], 'dieser erlauchten Korporation' [= the Bavarian medical board] (*MK*: 233) [of this exalted corporation (Mh.: 194)], 'dem gelahrten Herren' (*MK*: 238) [the learned gentleman (Mh.: 199)], 'unserer gelahrten Regierungsheroen' (*MK*: 37) [of our learned and highly placed government heroes (Mh.: 34)].

8   Euphemisms

'Zwölftausend Schurken zur rechten Zeit beseitigt, hätte vielleicht einer Million ordentlicher, für die Zukunft wertvoller Deutschen das Leben gerettet' [= Jews] (*MK*: 772) [twelve thousand scoundrels eliminated in time might have saved the lives of a million real Germans, valuable for the future (Mh.: 620)];
'bei der Frage der **Beseitigung sogenannter Landesverräter (...)**' (*MK*: 610) [in the question of *eliminating so-called traitors against the nation (...)* (Mh.: 495)];
'der redliche Idealist, der für sein Volk einen schuftigen Waffenverräter beseitigt' (*MK*: 610) [the honest idealist, who puts a scoundrelly armaments stool-pigeon out of the way (Mh.: 496)];
'**durch korrigierende Beseitigung all jener Mißstände (...)**' (*MK*: 675) [*corrective elimination of all those abuses (...)* (Mh.: 548)];
'den roten Terror endgültig zu erledigen' (*MK*: 616) [to dispose of the Red terror for good (Mh.: 500)];
'Im allgemeinen pflegt schon die Natur in der Frage der rassischen Reinheit irdischer Lebewesen bestimmte korrigierende Entscheidungen zu treffen. Sie liebt Bastarde nur wenig' (*MK*: 441) [In general, Nature herself usually makes certain corrective decisions with regard to the racial purity of earthly creatures. She has little love for bastards (Mh.: 363)].

Noticing others' use of euphemisms:

'Sie nennen es eine „vorbeugende Maßnahme zur Verhinderung einer Gesetzwidrigkeit"' [= the police banning meetings at which they have been warned trouble may break out] (*MK*: 545) [They call this a 'precautionary measure for the prevention of an illegal act' (Mh.: 443)];
'Wie sehr der Jude nur nachempfindend, besser verderbend fremde Kultur übernimmt' (*MK*: 332) [To what extent the Jew takes over foreign culture, imitating or rather ruining it (Mh.: 275)];
'zu ihrer klugen Vorsicht (sprich „Feigheit")' [= Jews] (*MK*: 365) [for their wily caution (read cowardice) (Mh.: 302)].

9 Involving the Reader

9.1 Questions

Open Questions:

'Und die Heimat—?
   Allein—war es nun das einzige Opfer, das wir zu wägen hatten? War das vergangene Deutschland weniger wert? Gab es nicht auch eine Verpflichtung der eigenen Geschichte gegenüber? Waren wir noch wert, den Ruhm der Vergangenheit auch auf uns zu beziehen? Wie aber war diese Tat der Zukunft zur Rechtfertigung zu unterbreiten?
   (...) Was war der ganze Schmerz der Augen gegen diesen Jammer?' (*MK*: 224f.)
   [And what about those at home—?
   And yet, was it only our own sacrifice that we had to weigh in the balance? Was the Germany of the past less precious? Was there no obligation towards our own history? Were we still worthy to relate the glory of the past to ourselves? And how could this deed be justified to future generations?
   (...) What was all the pain in my eyes compared to this misery? (Mh.: 186)].

Inviting affirmation:

'Welche Kost aber hat die deutsche Presse der Vorkriegszeit den Menschen vorgesetzt? War es nicht das ärgste Gift, das man sich vorzustellen vermag? Wurde dem Herzen unseres Volkes nicht schlimmster Pazifismus zu einer Zeit eingeimpft, da die andere Welt sich schon anschickte, Deutschland langsam, aber sicher abzudrosseln? Hatte diese Presse nicht schon im Frieden dem Gehirn des Volkes den Zweifel an das Recht des eigenen Staates eingeflößt, um es so in der Wahl der Mittel zu seiner Verteidigung von vornherein zu beschränken? War es nicht die deutsche Presse, die den Unsinn der „westlichen Demokratie" unserem Volke schmackhaft zu machen verstand, bis dieses endlich, von all den begeisterten Tiraden gefangen, glaubte, seine Zukunft einem Völkerbunde anvertrauen zu können? Hat sie nicht mitgeholfen, unser Volk zu einer elenden Sittenlosigkeit zu erziehen? Wurden nicht Moral und Sitte von ihr lächerlich gemacht, als rückständig und spießig gedeutet, bis endlich auch unser Volk „modern" wurde? Hat sie nicht in dauerndem Angriff die Grundfesten der Staatsautorität so lange unterhöhlt, bis ein einziger Stoß genügte, um dieses Gebäude zum Einsturz zu bringen? Hat sie nicht einst gegen jeden Willen, dem Staate zu geben, was des Staates ist, mit allen Mitteln angekämpft, nicht in dauernder Kritik das Heer herabgesetzt, die allgemeine Wehrpflicht sabotiert, zur Verweigerung der militärischen Kredite aufgefordert usw. bis der Erfolg nicht mehr ausbleiben konnte?' (*MK*: 265) [But what food did the German press of the pre-War period dish out to the people? Was it not the worst poison that can even be imagined? Wasn't the worst kind of pacifism injected into the heart of our people when the rest of the world was preparing to throttle Germany, slowly but surely? Even in peacetime didn't the press inspire the minds of the people with doubt in the right of their own state, thus from the outset limiting them in the choice of means for its defence? Was it not the German press which knew how to make the absurdity of 'Western democracy' palatable to our people until finally, ensnared by all the enthusiastic tirades, they thought they could entrust their future to a League of Nations? Did it not help to teach our people a miserable immorality? Did it not ridicule morality and ethics as backward and petit-bourgeois, until our people finally became "modern"? Did it not with its constant attacks undermine the foundations of the state's authority until a single thrust sufficed to make the edifice collapse? Did it not fight with all possible means against every effort to give unto the state that which is the state's? Did it not belittle the army with constant criticism, sabotage universal conscription, demand the refusal of military credits etc., until the result became inevitable? (Mh.: 220f.)].

Questions with answers:

'An wen hat sich die Propaganda zu wenden? An die wissenschaftliche Intelligenz oder an die weniger gebildete Masse? Sie hat sich ewig nur an die Masse zu richten!' (*MK*: 196) [To whom should propaganda be addressed? To the scientifically trained intelligentsia or to the less educated masses? It must be addressed always and exclusively to the masses (Mh.: 163)];

'Lagen aber die Verhältnisse während des Weltkrieges oder zu Beginn desselben etwa anders? Leider nein' (*MK*: 190) [Were conditions different during the World War or at its beginning? Unfortunately not (Mh.: 158)];

'Hatte man nicht in vielen Kreisen in der schamlosesten Weise geradezu Freude über das Unglück des Vaterlandes geäußert? Wer aber tut dieses, wenn er nicht wirklich eine solche Strafe verdient? Ja, ging man nicht noch weiter und rühmte sich, die Front endlich zum Weichen gebracht zu haben? Und dieses tat nicht etwa der Feind, nein, nein, solche Schande luden Deutsche auf ihr Haupt! Traf sie etwa das Unglück zu Unrecht? Seit wann aber geht man dann noch her und mißt sich selbst auch noch die Schuld am Kriege zu? Und zwar wider bessere Erkenntnis und besseres Wissen!

Nein und nochmals nein (...)' (*MK*: 250f.)

[Didn't many circles express the most shameless joy at the misfortune of the fatherland? And who would do such a thing if he does not really deserve such a punishment? Why, didn't they go even further and brag of having finally caused the front to waver? And it was not the enemy that did this—no, no, it was Germans who poured such disgrace upon their heads! Can it be said that misfortune struck them unjustly? Since when do people step forward and take

the guilt for a war on themselves? And against better knowledge and better judgment!
No, and again no (Mh.: 209)].

9.2 Addressing the Reader

Direct address:

'(...) allein ich wende mich an die, denen das Schicksal entweder bisher dieses Glück verweigert oder in grausamer Härte wieder genommen hat; ich wende mich an alle die, die losgelöst vom Mutterlande, selbst um das heilige Gut der Sprache zu kämpfen haben (...); ich wende mich an alle diese und weiß: Sie werden mich verstehen!' (*MK*: 136) [(...) but I address myself to those to whom Fate has either hitherto denied this, or from whom in harsh cruelty it has taken it away; I address myself to all those who, detached from their mother country, have to fight even for the holy treasure of their language (...); I address myself to all these, and I know that they will understand me! (Mh.: 114)];

'Denn jüdisches Interesse ist es heute, die völkische Bewegung in dem Augenblick in einem religiösen Kampf verbluten zu lassen, in dem sie beginnt, für den Juden eine Gefahr zu werden. Und ich betone das Wort verbluten lassen (...)' (*MK*: 632) [For it is to the Jewish interest today to make the folkish movement bleed to death in a religous struggle at the moment when it is beginning to become a danger for the Jew. And I expressly emphasise the words bleed to death (...) (Mh.: 513f.)].

Referring to shared knowledge:

'so bitte ich nicht zu vergessen, daß (...)' (*MK*: 502) [I beg you not to forget that (...) (Mh.: 410)].

Giving personal opinions:

'Entsetzlich, aber es war so' (*MK*: 523) [Dreadful, but it was so (Mh.: 425)];
'Im übrigen ist in dieser Frage meine Stellungnahme die, daß man nicht kleine Diebe hängen soll, um große laufen zu lassen' (*MK*: 610) [Further, in this question, my position is that there is no use hanging petty thieves in order to let big ones go free (Mh.: 496)];
'**unbewußt (was ich persönlich nicht glaube)**' (*MK*: 721) [*unconsciously (which I personally do not believe)* (Mh.: 581)];
'Es ist meine felsenfeste, mich manches Mal fast beklemmende innere Überzeugung, daß (...)' (*MK*: 764) [It is my firm and heart-felt conviction, and sometimes almost a source of anguish to me, that (...) (Mh.: 614)];
'In dieser Zeit—ich gestehe es offen—faßte ich die tiefste Bewunderung für den großen Mann südlich der Alpen' [= Mussolini] (*MK*: 774) [In this

period—I openly admit—I conceived the profoundest admiration for the great man south of the Alps (Mh.: 622)].

Remembering:
> Ich vergesse nicht die dauernde freche Bedrohung, die das damalige panslawistische Rußland Deutschland zu bieten wagte; ich vergesse nicht die dauernden Probenmobilmachungen (...); ich kann nicht vergessen die Stimmung der öffentlichen Meinung in Rußland (...), kann nicht vergessen die große russische Presse, die immer mehr für Frankreich schwärmte als für uns' (*MK*: 753) [I have not forgotten the insolent threat which the pan-Slavic Russia of that time dared to address to Germany; I have not forgotten the constant practice mobilisations (...); I cannot forget the mood of public opinion in Russia (...); I cannot forget the big Russian newspapers, which were always more enthusiastic about France than about us (Mh.: 606)].

Hitler explaining his choice of vocabulary:
> 'In diesen Kampf schritt das deutsche Volk als **vermeintliche** Weltmacht. Ich sage hier vermeintliche, denn in Wirklichkeit war es keine' (*MK*: 729) [The German people entered this struggle as a *supposed* world power. I say her 'supposed', for in reality it was none (Mh.: 588)];
> 'Ich sage **zwangsläufig** deshalb, weil (...)' (*MK*: 639) [I say *inevitably* because (...) (Mh.: 520)];
> 'Das heißt freilich, nur bildlich gesprochen „gegen sich selbst"' (*MK*: 349) ['Against himself' is only figuratively speaking (Mh.: 289)];
> 'schroff ausgedrückt und ins Große übertragen' (*MK*: 461) [harshly expressed and enlarged (Mh.: 378)].

Hitler's own and so-called universal truths:
> 'Es kann nicht scharf genug betont werden, **daß** (...)' (*MK*: 149) [It cannot be emphasised sharply enough *that* (...) (Mh.: 125)];
> 'Ich betone es und bin fest davon überzeugt, daß (...)' (*MK*: 765) [I emphasise the fact, and I am firmly convinced of it (...) (Mh.: 615)];
> 'Selbst wenn dies hart wäre—es ist nun einmal so!' (*MK*: 317) [Even if this were hard—that is how it is! (Mh.: 262)];
> 'Man darf folgenden Satz als ewig gültige Wahrheit aufstellen: (...)' (*MK*: 168) [The following theorem may be established as an eternally valid truth: (...) (Mh.: 140)];
> 'Und das war gut so' (*MK*: 658) [And this was good (Mh.: 533)].

Appendix II

9.3 Appellatives

wir:

> '**Wir wollen wieder Waffen!**' (*MK*: 715) [*Give us arms again!* (Mh.: 577)];
> '**Wir Nationalsozialisten** (...)' (*MK*: 434) [*We National Socialists* (...) (Mh.: 358)];
> '**Wir, als Arier,** (...)' (*MK*: 434) [*We, as Aryans,* (...) (Mh.: 358)].

Ihr:

> 'Mit euch läßt sich das freilich nicht mehr machen, eure Welt ist dafür nicht geeignet! Ihr kennt nur **eine** Sorge: euer persönliches Leben, und **einen** Gott: euer Geld! Allein, wir wenden uns auch nicht an euch (...)' [= the bourgeoisie] (*MK*: 449) [*True, it can no longer be done with you, your world isn't fit for it! You know but one concern: your personal life, and one God: your money! But we are not addressing ourselves to you* (...) (Mh.: 369)];
> 'War dies etwa nicht so, ihr elenden und verlogenen Burschen?' [= the 1918 revolutionaries] (*MK*: 248) [*Will you claim that this was not so, you wretched, lying scoundrels?* (Mh.: 207)];
> 'Jawohl, wir versuchen nachzuholen, was Ihr in Eurer verbrecherischen Dummheit versäumt habt. Ihr habt durch die Grundsätze Eures parlamentarischen Kuhhandels mitgeholfen, die Nation in den Abgrund zu zerren' [= politicians] (*MK*: 414) [*Yes, indeed, we are trying to make up for what you in your criminal stupidity failed to do. By the principles of your parliamentary cattle-trading, you helped to drag the nation into the abyss* (Mh.: 343)].

9.4 Imperatives

> '**Duldet niemals das Entstehen zweier Kontinentalmächte in Europa! Seht in jeglichem Versuch, an den deutschen Grenzen** (...) **einen Angriff gegen Deutschland, und erblickt darin nicht nur das Recht, sondern die Pflicht** (...) **die Enstehung eines solchen Staates zu verhindern beziehungsweise einen solchen, wenn er schon entstanden, wieder zu zerschlagen! Sorgt** (...) **dafür, daß die Stärke unseres Volkes ihre Grundlagen nicht in Kolonien, sondern im Boden der Heimat in Europa erhält! Haltet das Reich nie für gesichert** (...)**!. Vergeßt nie, daß das heiligste Recht auf dieser Welt das Recht auf Erde ist** (...)' (*MK*: 754 f.) [*Never suffer the rise of two continental powers in Europe. Regard any attempt to organise a second military power on the German frontiers* (...) *as an attack on Germany, and in it see not only the right, but also the duty* (...) *to prevent the rise of such a state, or, if one has already arisen, to smash it again. —See to it that the strength of our nation is founded, not on colonies, but on the soil of our European homeland. Never*

regard the Reich as secure (...) Never forget that the most sacred right on this earth is a man's right to have earth to till (...) (Mh.: 607)].

9.5 Exclamations

'Gott bewahre!' (*MK*: 94) [God forbid! (Mh.: 79)];
'wahrhaftiger Gott' (*MK*: 184) [by God (Mh.: 154)];
'Eine **deutsche** Stadt!! Welch ein Unterschied gegen Wien!' [= Munich] (*MK*: 138) [A *German* city! What a difference from Vienna! (Mh.: 116)];
'So kam alles anders!' (*MK*: 764) [Thus everything turned out differently! (Mh.: 614)];
'Elende und verkommene Verbrecher!' (*MK*: 224) [Miserable and degenerate criminals (Mh.: 186)];
'Fürchterlich, fürchterlich!' (*MK*: 241) [Terrible, terrible! (Mh.: 201)];
'Pfui Teufel und wieder Pfui Teufel!' (*MK*: 540) [Phooey, I say, and again phooey! (Mh.: 439)];
'... Brrrr' (*MK*: 548) [... Brrr! (Mh.: 445)]. (Note Mh.'s addition of an exclamation mark).

10 Features of Colloquial Language

10.1 Clichés

um nicht zu sagen:

'von aus reinen Zweckmäßigkeit vorgebrachten Ausreden, um nicht zu sagen Lügen' [= of Jews] (*MK*: 60) [of pretexts advanced for mere reasons of expedience, not to say lies (Mh.: 53)].

sagen wir:

'eine Zahl von sagen wir fünfhundert Männern' (*MK*: 95) [a body of, let us say, five hundred men (Mh.: 80)];
'wie, sagen wir, über eine Frage hoher Außenpolitik' (*MK*: 97) [as, let us say, a question of high foreign policy (Mh.: 81)].

ich möchte sagen:

'Die erste Konsequenz dieser Erkenntnis ist zugleich die, ich möchte fast sagen gröbere' (*MK*: 492) [The first consequence of this realisation might at the same time be called the cruder one (Mh.: 402)];

'ich möchte fast sagen, mit zwangsläufiger Sicherheit' (*MK*: 494) [with almost inevitable certainty I might say (Mh.: 403)].

10.2 Modal Particles

ja:

'ja, darin ist ja gerade seine innere Stärke zu suchen, daß (...)' (*MK*: 156) [in fact, its inner strength is to be sought precisely in the fact that (...) (Mh.: 131)].

doch ja:

'so glaube man doch ja nicht, daß (...)' (*MK*: 639) [let no one suppose that (...) (Mh.: 519)].

ja auch; ja doch:

'Allein man dachte ja auch gar nicht daran, sich mit Rußland gegen England zu verbünden, sowenig wie mit England gegen Rußland, denn in beiden Fällen wäre das Ende ja Krieg gewesen, und um diesen zu verhindern, entschloß man sich ja doch überhaupt erst zur Handels- und Industriepolitik' (*MK*: 157) [But we did not think of concluding an alliance with Russia against England, any more than with England against Russia, for in both cases the end would have been war, and to prevent this we decided in favour of a policy of commerce and industry (Mh.: 131)];
'da er ja genau weiß, daß (...) sein Ende ja doch schon längst in den Sternen verzeichnet steht' (*MK*: 88) [for he well knows that (...) his end has long been written in the stars (Mh.: 75)].

ja eben:

'darin liegt ja eben der Sinn einer germanischen Demokratie' (*MK*: 100) [Germanic democracy means just this (Mh.: 83)].

ja überhaupt:

'Allein, man beschritt diesen Weg ja überhaupt nicht' (*MK*: 156) [This road, however, was not taken at all (Mh.: 130)].

allein wohl:

'Der Krieg wäre auch dann noch gekommen, allein wohl nicht mehr als Kampf gegen uns' (*MK*: 175) [Even then the war would have come, but no longer as a struggle of all against ourselves (Mh.: 147)] (*allein* occurs frequently in *MK* and is usually translated with 'but').

auch:

'Ist dies auch ein Jude?' (*MK*: 59) [Is this a Jew? (Mh.: 52)];
'Ist dies auch ein Deutscher?' (*MK*: 59) [Is this a German? (Mh.: 52)].

denn doch:

'ein denn doch sehr wesentlicher Unterschied' (*MK*: 699) [*quite an essential difference, after all!* (Mh.: 565)].

eben:

'weil er eben ein—Deutscher ist.—' (*MK*: 122) [just because he is—a German. (Mh.: 102)];
'das eine ergibt dann eben arische Arbeits- und Kulturstaaten, das andere jüdische Schmarotzerkolonien' (*MK*: 168) [the one results in Aryan states based on work and culture, the other in Jewish colonies of parasites (Mh.: 140)].

etwa:

'War dies etwa nicht so, ihr elenden und verlogenen Burschen?' (*MK*: 248) [Will you claim that this was not so, you wretched, lying scoundrels? (Mh.: 207)];
'Lagen aber die Verhältnisse während des Weltkrieges oder zu Beginn desselben etwa anders? Leider nein' (*MK*: 190) [Were conditions different during the World War or at its beginning? Unfortunately not (Mh.: 158)].

nun einmal:

'Selbst wenn dies hart wäre—es ist nun einmal so!' (*MK*: 317) [Even if this were hard—that is how it is! (Mh.: 262)].

10.3 Pauses

'meine Entscheidung (war) schnell und—falsch' (*MK*: 48) [my decision was instantaneous and—mistaken (Mh.: 43)];
'weil er eben ein—Deutscher ist.—' (*MK*: 122) [just because he is—a German. (Mh.: 102)];
'Selbst wenn dies hart wäre—es ist nun einmal so!' (*MK*: 317) [Even if this were hard—that is how it is! (Mh.: 262)];
'Und die Heimat—?
    Allein—war es nun das einzige Opfer, das wir zu wägen hatten? (*MK*: 224) [And what about those at home—?

And yet, was it only our own sacrifice that we had to weigh in the balance? Was the Germany of the past less precious? (Mh.: 186)].

11 Narrative Structure

Looking back in the text:

> 'wie schon betont' (*MK*: 321) [As already emphasised (Mh.: 266)];
> 'Wie schon erwähnt' (*MK*: 600) [As already mentioned (Mh.: 487)];
> 'Ich habe bereits geschildert, wie (...)' (*MK*: 599) [I have already described how (...) (Mh.: 487)];
> 'Zusammenfassend kann festgestellt werden: (...)' (*MK*: 430) [In summing up we can state the following: (...) (Mh.: 355)];
> 'Die erste Frage denke ich zur einen Hälfte schon genügend erörtert zu haben' (*MK*: 712) [I think I have sufficiently discussed one half of the first question (Mh.: 575)];
> 'Plakate und Flugblätter (...), deren Tendenz nach jenen Gesichtspunkten bestimmt wurde, die ich in meiner Abhandlung über Propaganda in groben Umrissen schon niedergelegt habe' (*MK*: 401f.) [posters and leaflets whose content was determined according to those guiding principles which in rough outlines I have set down in my treatise on propaganda (Mh.: 332)];
> Ich habe mich schon im ersten Band über Wesen und Zweck und über die Notwendigkeit von Gewerkschaften geäußert. (...) Ich habe dort den Standpunkt eingenommen, daß (...). Ich betonte weiter, daß (...). Ich erklärte weiterhin, daß (...); und ich zog daraus den Schluß, daß (...) (*MK*: 671) [In the first volume I have expressed myself with regard to the nature and purpose, and the necessity, of trade unions. There I espoused the viewpoint that (...). I further emphasised that (...). I further declared that (...) and from this I drew the inference that (...) (Mh.: 545)].

Looking forward in the text:

> 'Ich werde darauf noch besonders zurückkommen' [I shall return to this point in particular (Mh.: 130)];
> 'wie ich später nachweisen will' (*MK*: 569) [as I shall later demonstrate (Mh.: 463)];
> 'Und nicht nur das!' (*MK*: 315) [And not only that! (Mh.: 261)];
> 'Es kommt aber hierzu noch etwas anderes: (...)' (*MK*: 188) [Added to this there is something else: (...) (Mh.: 157)];
> 'Ich möchte diese Betrachtungen nicht beenden, ohne nochmals auf die alleinige Bündnismöglichkeit hinzuweisen, die es für uns augenblicklich in Europa gibt' (*MK*: 755) [I should not like to conclude these reflections without pointing once

again to the sole alliance possibility which exists for us at the moment in Europe (Mh.: 607)].

12   Archaisms

Bronnen 'allein schon in wenigen Jahren würde der Bronnen versiegen' (*MK*: 318) [but even in a few years the well would dry up (Mh.: 264)];
ehern (*MK*: 311) [rigid (Mh.: 258)], 'ein eherner Fels' (*MK*: 419) [a brazen cliff (Mh.: 346)];
erlaucht (*MK*: 233) [exalted (Mh.: 194)];
Fronvogt (*MK*: 716) [task-master (Mh.: 578)];
gelahrt (*MK*: 238) [learned (Mh.: 199)];
Harm, as in 'Not und Harm' (*MK*: 3) [suffering and care (Mh.: 5)];
hehr (*MK*: 415) [exalted (Mh.: 343)];
Heldenmären (*MK*: 102) [tales of heroism (Mh.: 86)];
Hellebarde (*MK*: 261) [halberd (Mh.: 218)];
Kämpe (*MK*: 261) [champions (Mh.: 218)], 'Protestkämpe' (*MK*: 718) [knights of the protest meeting (Mh.: 579)];
küren (*MK*: 103) [choose [= as Emperor] (Mh.: 87)], 'erkoren' (*MK*: 552) [chosen [= as the colours of the Imperial flag] (Mh.: 449)];
Panier (*MK*: 418) [banner (Mh.: 346)];
raunen, e.g. 'von neuer Zukunft raunen' (*MK*: 11) [whispers softly (Mh.: 13)];
Recke (*MK*: 214) [warrior [(Mh.: 178)]];
Scholle, e.g 'der bäuerlichen Scholle ernährende' (*MK*: 25) [from the peasant sod (Mh.: 24)];
Siechtum (*MK*: 173) [disease (Mh.: 145)];
sintemalen (*MK*: 57) [since (Mh.: 50)];
teutsch, as in '„teutscher" Miene' (*MK*: 776) [a Teutonic face (Mh.: 624)].

13   Foreign words (a selection; all references are from *MK*)

Agitator (66: 400), Akkord (555), appellieren (13), basta (660), Bataillone [= the S.A.] (618), Blamage (38), Bluff (414), Bourgeoisie (41), „*en canaille*" (590), defekt (279), Definition (425), degeneriert (277), dekoriert (560), demolieren (294: 350), demonstrieren (65), Deplacement (299), Deserteure (245), Desertion (587), Desorganisation (584), Despotie (505), Destrukteure (585), dezimieren (368), diffamieren (cf. Klemperer: 267), dirigieren (345), diskreditieren (546), diskriminieren (cf. Klemperer: 267), Division (588), Doktrin (105), doktrinär (121), dokumentieren (402), eklatant (769), elektrisieren (391), eminent (416), Entente (236), Etappe (275: 588), Explosion (623), *à fonds perdu* (682), Fabrikkulis (767), Farmer (156), feminin (201), *en gros*

Appendix II 247

und *en détail'* (610), Geseires (268), Glacéhandschuhe (773), grandios (552), Großstadtbohème (53), identifizieren (555), Ignorant (120), illustre (98), immens (232), impotent (570), Indolenz (451), infizieren (62), Institution (85), Intermezzo (640), Jargon (135), Kanaillen (610), kanaillös (771), kapitulieren (20: 546), Kokarden (606), Kollision (512), konsolidieren (584), Kontrolleur (345), Konzentration (23), konzentrieren (29), Konzession (513), Konzilianz (507), Korporation (604), lancieren (596), Matadoren (584), Niveau (429), okkupierend (777), oktroyieren (409), Organismus (69), paktieren (774), Parole (585), Patrouillen [= S.A.] (615), Poilu [= a French soldier during the First World War] (217), Popularität (579), Postament (679), proklamieren (737), propagieren (627), Provokation (546), provozieren (628), Prüderie (274), Refrain (540), zur Raison bringen (777), Reservoir (374), Resistenz (367), Restauration (597), revoltieren (181), Sabotage (559), sabotieren (29), Sineküre (666), spendieren (673), Stellage (663), stoppen (742), suggestiv (552), telephonisch (560), Terrorisierung (44), Tommy (217), Trancezustand (539), Trick (63), triumphieren (350), umgemodelt (409), *via triumphalis* (23), Volks*café* (43), Zeitungsjournaille [= Eisner] (624), Zivilcourage (463).

Glossary

Aryan/Arier, arisch

The designation "Aryan", which has no scientific basis, was first used as an ethnographic term in 1710. Gobineau was one of the first racial theorists to shift the meaning of *Arier* to signify a superior, white *Urrasse* (original race), and Wagner used the term *Arier* as a foil for the Jewish *Nicht-Arier* (Schmitz-Berning 1998: 54f.). The terms *Arier* and *arisch* were no longer considered acceptable in the "de-nazified" German of the post-Second World War period (Deissler 2004: 114).

Feindbild

The image of an enemy. The totality of what is understood by the term *Feind* and its synonyms, and how this is portrayed.

Kampf

The noun *Kampf* and its derivative verb *kämpfen* are two of the most difficult words to interpret in *MK*. In both Kluge (1934) and the *Sprach-Brockhaus* (1935) the noun *Kampf* is interpreted as denoting a fierce, usually physical fight. Spalding documents *kämpfen* as originally having the sense: 'to fight (physically)', but later, in the Middle Ages, extending its meaning to cover 'non-physical endeavours, struggles against the elements, emotions, somebody else's opinions, etc.' (Spalding: 1431f.). In *MK*, *Kampf* and *kämpfen* are sometimes used literally ('fight/to fight'), but often metaphorically, either hyperbolically ('struggle/to struggle', 'argument/to argue') or euphemistically ('war/to go to war'). Each instance of either word in *MK* has to be interpreted individually. *Kampf* and *kämpfen* are used frequently and forcefully in *MK*, in keeping with the conceptual metaphor POLITICS IS WAR. The force and vigour of these words in *MK* make Mh.'s translation of them as 'to struggle' inappropriate in many cases. Kenneth Burke, who wrote about *MK* in 1941, spoke of Hitler's 'battle', a term which embraced what Burke saw as the battle of persuasion that was essentialized in *MK*. To my mind, 'battle' or 'fight' is more in line with the violent vocabulary with which the words are usually associated in *MK*. Hitler himself varied *Kampf* and *kämpfen* with synonyms such as *fechten* and *ringen*, which are both translated by Mh. as 'fighting/fight' or 'struggling/struggle'.

Volk, völkisch

The terms *Volk* and *völkisch* (often translated as 'folkish') became associated with nationalist politics during the nineteenth century, their semantic value undergoing a gradual intensification in the direction of a 'racially pure, exclusively German people' (Schmitz-Berning 1998: 642). In his 1939 translation of *MK*, James Murphy prefers to leave *Volk* and *völkisch* untranslated, explaining *Volk* as meaning 'the whole body of the people without any distinction of class or caste' and 'the basic national stock' (*MK* 1939: 10). The *Sprach-Brockhaus* of 1935 documents the primary meaning of *Volk* as 'die Gemeinschaft rassisch verwandter Menschen, die durch Sprache, Geschichte und Kultur verbunden sind' and *völkisch* (2) as 'das Volkstum, bes. in seinen rassischen und sittlichen Grundlagen betreffend, betonend' (cf. Kershaw: 135f.: 'mystical notions of a uniquely German social order, with roots in the Teutonic past, resting on order, harmony, and hierarchy'). The commonest translations of *Volk* are 'people' and 'nation', neither of which adequately match the full meaning of the source lexeme. Schmitz-Berning describes the NS usage of *Volk* as referring to an 'Abstammungs- und Schicksalsgemeinschaft zugleich'.

Weltanschauung

R.H. Barry's translation of the word *Weltanschauung*, in Maser 1970 (59), is 'a view of life and definite outlook on the world'; Ian Kershaw calls it a 'world-view' (Kershaw 2001: xxviii); but, along with J. P. Stern and James Murphy, I prefer to leave the word untranslated.

Bibliography

Editions and Translations of *Mein Kampf*

Hitler, Adolf (1942), *Mein Kampf*, 11th ed. München: Zentralverlag der NSDAP.
———. (1939), *Mein Kampf. An historic document describing the aims of the National Socialist Movement*, Hutchinson's illustrated edition, unexpurgated, translated by James Murphy. London: Hurst and Blackett.
———. (1992), *Mein Kampf*, translated by Ralph Manheim with an introduction by D. Cameron Watt. London: Pimlico.

Other Sources

Alldeutsche Blätter (1919), quoted from www.gehove.de/antisem/antis_alldeutsch.html.
Allinson, Mark (2002), *Germany and Austria 1814–2000. Modern History for Modern Languages*. London: Arnold.
Appendix III is the web site: www.qmul.ac.uk/~mlw032.
Bauer, Gerhard (1988), *Sprache und Sprachlosigkeit im Dritten Reich*. Köln: Bund Verlag.
Benz, Wolfgang and Angelika Königseder (2002), *Judenfeindschaft als Paradigma. Studien zur Vorurteilsforschung*. Berlin: Metropol.
Berger, Stefan (2004), *Germany. Inventing the Nation*. London: Arnold.
Berning, Cornelia (1960–1963), 'Die Sprache der Nationalsozialisten'. In: *Zeitschrift für deutsche Wortforschung* XVI:71–118, 178–188; XVII:83–121, 171–182; XVIII: 108–118, 160–172; XIX: 92–112.
Böll, Heinrich (1983), *Was soll aus dem Jungen bloß werden? Oder: Irgendwas mit Büchern*. dtv: München.
Bork, Siegfried (1970), *Mißbrauch der Sprache. Tendenzen nationalsozialistischer Sprachregelung*. Bern und München: Francke.
Brekle, Herbert E. (1989), 'War with words'. In: Wodak, Ruth (ed.), *Language, Power and Ideology. Studies in Political Discourse*. John Benjamins: Amsterdam/Philadelphia: 81–91.
Brewer's Dictionary of Phrase and Fable. Centenary Edition (1970), ed. Ivor H. Evans. London: Cassell.
Burke, Kenneth (1973), 'The Rhetoric of Hitler's "Battle"'. In: *The Philosophy of Literary Form*, 3rd ed. Berkeley: University of California Press.
Burleigh, Michael (2001), *The Third Reich. A New History*. London: Pan Macmillan.
Chamberlain, Houston Stewart (1899), *Die Grundlagen des neunzehnten Jahrhunderts*. München: F. Bruckmann.
———. (1905), *Arische Weltanschauung*. Berlin: Bard, Marquardt & Co.

———. (1925), 'Deutsche Weltanschauung' (2nd ed.,first published in 1917). In: *Rasse und Persönlichkeit. Aufsätze von Houston Stewart Chamberlain*. München: F. Bruckmann: 7–34.
Charteris-Black, Jonathan (2004), *Corpus Approaches to Critical Metaphor Analysis*. Basingstoke: Palgrave Macmillan.
Cobet, Christoph (1973), *Der Wortschatz des Antisemitismus in der Bismarckzeit* (= Münchner Germanistische Beiträge 11). München: W. Fink.
Collins Cobuild Metaphor Dictionary (1987), ed. J. Sinclair. London: Collins.
Deissler, Dirk (2004), *Die entnazifierte Sprache. Sprachpolitik und Sprachregelung in der Besatzungszeit*. Frankfurt am Main etc.: Peter Lang.
Domarus, Max (ed.) (1962–63), *Hitler. Reden und Proklamationen 1932–1945*, 2 vols. Neustadt a.d. Aisch: Schmidt.
Ehlich, Konrad (1989), 'Über den Faschismus sprechen—Analyse und Diskurs'. In: Ehlich, Konrad (ed.), *Sprache im Faschismus*. Frankfurt am Main: Suhrkamp: 7–34.
Fairclough, Norman (1989), *Language and Power*. London and New York: Longman.
Friederich, Wolf (1966), *Moderne deutsche Idiomatik. Systemisches Wörterbuch mit Definitionen und Beispielen*. München: Max Hueber Verlag.
Frind, Sigrid (1966), 'Die Sprache als Propagandainstrument des Nationalsozialismus'. In: *Muttersprache* 76: 129–135.
Gibbs, Raymond W. (1994), *The Poetics of the Mind: Figurative Thought, Language, and Understanding*. Cambridge: C.U.P.
Goatly, Andrew (1997), *The Language of Metaphors*. London/New York: Routledge.
Gregor, Neil (2005), *How to Read Hitler*. London: Granta.
Grieswelle, Detlef (1972), *Propaganda der Friedlosigkeit. Eine Studie zu Hitlers Rhetorik 1920–1933*. Stuttgart: Ferdinand Enke Verlag.
Haffner, Sebastian (2003), *Defying Hitler. A Memoir*. London: Phoenix.
Hamann, Brigitte (1999), *Hitler's Vienna. A Dictator's Apprenticeship*. Oxford/New York: O.U.P.
Hodge, Robert and Gunther Kress (1979), *Language as Ideology*. London/New York: Routledge.
Hoffend, Andrea (1987), 'Bevor die Nazis die Sprache beim Wort nahmen'. In: *Muttersprache* 97: 259–299.
Horan, Geraldine (2003), *'Frauenkraft und Mutterwille': Female identity in National Socialist discourse. 1924–1934* (= Studia Linguistica Germanica 68). Berlin/New York: de Gruyter.
Humphrys, John (2004), *Lost for Words. The Mangling and Manipulating of the English Language*. London: Hodder and Stoughton.
Jäger, Siegfried (1989), 'Rechtsextreme Propaganda heute'. In: Ehlich, Konrad (ed.), *Sprache im Faschismus*. Frankfurt am Main: Suhrkamp: 289–322.
Jahn, Friedrich Ludwig (1810), *Von deutschem Volkstum*. Jena: Eugen Diederichs Verlag.
Johnston, Otto W. (1990), *Der deutsche Nationalmythos. Ursprung eines politischen Programms*. Stuttgart: J.B. Metzlersche Verlagsbuchhandlung.
Kässner, Frank (2004), 'Braune Nester'. In: *Die Welt*, 21. Dec. 2004: 3.
Kaufmann, Walter (1974), *Nietzsche. Philosopher, Psychologist, Antichrist*, 4th ed. Princeton: Princeton University Press.
Kershaw, Ian (1998), *Hitler 1889–1939*. London: Penguin Books.

Kinne, Michael and Johannes Schwitalla (1994), *Sprache im Nationalsozialismus*. Heidelberg: Groos.
Klemperer, Victor (1996), *'LTI'. Notizbuch eines Philologen*, 5th ed., text based on 3rd edition 1957, first published 1947. Leipzig: Reclam.
Kluge, Friedrich (1934), *Etymologisches Wörterbuch der deutschen Sprache*, 11th ed., bearbeitet von Alfred Götze. Berlin and Leipzig: Walter der Gruyter & Co.
Kövecses, Zoltàn (2002), *Metaphor. A Practical Introduction*. Oxford: O.U.P.
Lakoff, George (1987), *Women, Fire and Dangerous Things. What Categories Reveal about the Mind*. Chicago/London: University of Chicago Press.
Lakoff, George and Mark Turner (1989), *More then Cool Reason. A Field Guide to Poetic Metaphor*. Chicago/London: The University of Chicago Press.
Lakoff, George and Mark Johnson (1999), *Philosophy in the Flesh. The Embodied Mind and Its Challenge to Western Thought*. New York: Basis Books.
Lincoln, Bruce (1999), *Theorizing the Myth. Narrative, Ideology, and Scholarship*. Chicago/London: University of Chicago Press.
Lovejoy, Arthur O. (1966), *The Great Chain of Being*, 2nd ed. Cambridge, Massachusetts: Harvard University Press.
Maas, Utz (1984), *„Als der Geist der Gemeinschaft eine Sprache fand". Sprache im Nationalsozialismus. Versuch einer historischen Argumentationsanalyse*. Opladen: Westdeutscher Verlag.
———. (1991), 'Sprache im Nationalsozialismus: Macht des Wortes oder Lähmung der Sprache'. In: Bohleber, Werner and Jörg Drews, *Gift, das du unbewußt eintrinkst. Der National-sozialismus und die deutsche Sprache*. Bielefeld: Aisthesis: 25–37.
Mann, Golo (1997, first published 1958), *Deutsche Geschichte des 19. und 20. Jahrhunderts*. Frankfurt am Main: Fischer.
Maser, Werner (1970), *Hitler's 'Mein Kampf'. An Analysis*. translated by R. H. Barry. London: Faber.
———. (1983), *Adolf Hitler. Mein Kampf. Geschichte, Auszüge, Kommentare*. Rastatt: Moewig.
Michael, Robert and Karin Doerr (2002), *Nazi-Deutsch/Nazi German. An English Lexicon of the Language of the Third Reich*. Westport, Connecticut/London: Greenwood Press.
Mieder, Wolfgang (1983), 'Sprichwörter unterm Hakenkreuz'. In: *Muttersprache* 103: 1–30.
———. (1993), 'Proverbs in Nazi Germany. The Promulgation of Anti-Semitism and Stereotypes through Folklore'. In: W. Mieder (ed.), *Proverbs Are Never Out of Season. Popular Wisdom in the Modern Age*. Oxford/New York: O.U.P.
———. (1994), '«... als ob ich Herr der Sprache würde»: Zur Sprichwortmanipulation in Adolf Hitlers *Mein Kampf*'. In: *Muttersprache* 104: 193–218.
———. (1997), ' "As if I were the master of the situation". Proverbial Manipulation in Adolf Hitler's *Mein Kampf*. In: *The Politics of Proverbs. From Traditional Wisdom to Proverbial Stereotypes*. Madison, Wisconsin: University of Wisconsin Press: 9–38. See also: *De Proverbio* 1, 1995; www. deproverbio. com /DPjournal. DP, 1, 1, 95/ HITLER.html.
———. (2000), *"In lingua veritas". Sprichwörtliche Rhetorik in Victor Klemperers "Tagebüchern 1933–1945"*. Wien: Edition Praesens.
Mieder, Wolfgang and Alan Dundes (eds) (1981), *The Wisdom of Many: Essays on the Proverb*. New York: Garland.

Musolff, Andreas (2003), 'Ideological functions of metaphor: The conceptual metaphors of *health* and *illness* in public discourse'. In: *Cognitive Models of Language and Thought* (= Cognitive Linguistics Research, 24). Berlin/New York: Mouton de Gruyter: 327–352.

———. (2004a), *Metaphor and Political Discourse: Analogical Reasoning in Debates about Europe*. New York: Palgrave Macmillan.

———. (2004b), 'Metaphor and conceptual evolution'. In: *Metaphorik* 7: 55–75; www.metaphorik.de/07/musolff.pdf.

Nash, Walter (1989), *Rhetoric. The Wit of Persuasion*. Oxford/Cambridge: Blackwell.

Nietzsche, Friedrich (1956), *Werke in drei Bänden*. München: Carl Hanser Verlag.

Orwell, George (1946), *Politics and the English Language*; www.resort.com/~prime8/Orwell/patee.html.

Ottmer, Clemens (1996), *Rhetorik*. Stuttgart/Weimar: Metzler.

Paechter, Heinz (1944), *Nazi-Deutsch. A Glossary of Contemporary German Usage*. New York: Frederick Unger Publishing Co.

Pechau, Manfred (1935), *Der Nationalsozialismus und deutsche Sprache*. Greifswald: Buchdruckerei Hans Adler.

Peil, Dietmar (1983), *Untersuchungen zur Staats- und Herrschaftsmetaphorik in literarischen Zeugnissen von der Antike bis zur Gegenwart* (= Münstersche Mittelalter-Schriften 50). München: Wilhelm Fink.

Perelman, Ch. and L. Olbrechts-Tyteca (1969), *The New Rhetoric. A Treatise on Argumentation*. Notre Dame/London: University of Notre Dame Press.

Pfahl-Traughber, Armin (2003), 'Freimaurer und Juden, Kapitalisten und Kommunisten als Feindbilder rechtsextremistischer Verschwörungsideologien vom Kaiserreich bis zur Gegenwart'. In: Uwe Backes (ed.), *Rechtsextreme Ideologien in Geschichte und Gegenwart* (= Schriften des Hannah-Arendt-Instituts für Totalitarismusforschung, 23). Köln/Weimar/Wien: Böhlau Verlag.

Podak, Klaus (1991), 'Spiegel des Unheils. Hitlers *Mein Kampf*: Annäherung an ein Buch, das es nicht gibt'. In: Werner Bohleber and Jörg Drews (eds), *Gift, das du unbewußt eintrinkst. Der Nationalsozialismus und die deutsche Sprache*. Bielefeld: Aisthesis, 16-24.

Polenz, Peter von (1972), *Geschichte der deutschen Sprache* (= Sammlung Göschen, Band 4015). Berlin/New York: Walter de Gruyter.

———. (1999), *Deutsche Sprachgeschichte vom Spätmittelalter bis zur Gegenwart, Band III: 19. und 20. Jahrhundert*. Berlin/New York: Walter de Gruyter.

Pörksen, Bernhard (2000), *Die Konstruktion von Feindbildern. Zum Sprachgebrauch in neonazistischen Medien*. Westdeutscher Verlag: Wiesbaden.

Radden, G. and Zoltàn Kövecses (1999), 'Towards a theory of metonymy'. In: Panther, K. and G. Radden (eds), *Metonymy in Language and Thought*. Amsterdam: John Benjamins: 17–59.

Rash, Felicity (1993), '*Gwaggli* and *Gwagglitante*. The use of epithets for men and women in Swiss German past and present.' In: J.L. Flood, P. Salmon, O. Sayce and C.J. Wells (eds), *Das unsichtbare Band der Sprache. Studies in German Language and Linguistic History in Memory of Leslie Seiffert*. Verlag Hans-Dieter Heinz: Stuttgart 1993: 597–626.

———. (1996), 'Metaphors of Darkness and Light in Eveline Hasler's *Anna Göldin, Letzte Hexe* and *Der Riese im Baum*'. In: A. Williams, S. Parkes and J. Preece (eds), *German*

Contemporary Writers: Their Aesthetics and Their Language. Bern/Berlin/Frankfurt a.M./New York/Wien: Peter Lang: 181–200.
Schäffner, Christina (in press), 'Metaphors and Translation: Some Implications of a Cognitive Approach'. In: *Journal of Pragmatics*.
Schmidt, Josef (2004), 'In Praise of Kenneth Burke: His 'The Rhetoric of Hitler's "Battle"' Revisited'. In: *Rhetor* 1; www.cssr-scer.ca/rhetor.
Schmitz-Berning, Cornelia (1998), *Vokabular des Nationalsozialsmus*. Berlin/New York: Walter de Gruyter.
Seidel, Eugen and Ingeborg Seidel-Slotty (1960), *Sprachwandel im Dritten Reich. Eine kritische Untersuchung faschistischer Einflüsse*. Halle: Verlag Sprache und Literatur.
Shirer, William L. (1959, reprinted 1977), *The Rise and Fall of the Third Reich. A History of Nazi Germany*. London: Book Club Associates.
Simon, Gerd (1989), 'Sprachpflege im «Dritten Reich»'. In: Ehlich, Konrad (ed.), *Sprache im Faschismus*. Frankfurt am Main: Suhrkamp: 58–86.
Spalding, Keith (1952–2000), *An Historical Dictionary of German Figurative Usage*. Oxford: Blackwell.
Sprach-Brockhaus, Der: Deutsches Bildwörterbuch für Jedermann (1935). Leipzig/London: F.A Brockhaus and Sir Isaac Pitman and Sons.
Stein, O. Th. (1919), 'Gase als Kampfmittel'. In: *Bibliothek der Unterhaltung und des Wissens*, Zweiter Band. Stuttgart/Berlin/Leipzig/Wien: Union Deutsche Verlagsgesellschaft: 136–156.
Stern, J.P. (1975), *Hitler. The Führer and the People*. Glasgow: Fontana/Collins.
Sternberger, Dolf, Gerhard Storz and Wilhelm E. Süskind (1985^3), *Aus dem Wörterbuch des Unmenschen*. München: Deutscher Taschenbuch Verlag.
Thompson, John B. (1984), *Studies in the Theory of Ideology*. Cambridge: Polity Press.
Toland, John (1977), *Adolf Hitler*. London: Book Club Associates.
Ulonska, Ulrich (1990), *Suggestion der Glaubwürdigkeit. Untersuchungen zu Hitlers rhetorischer Selbstdarstellung zwischen 1920 und 1933*. Ammershut bei Hamburg: Verlag an der Lottbek.
Volmert, Johannes (1989), 'Politische Rhetorik des Nationalsozialismus'. In: Ehlich, Konrad (ed.), *Sprache im Faschismus*. Frankfurt am Main: Suhrkamp: 137–161.
Wagner, Richard (2000), *Alle Opern-Texte. Ein Richard Wagner-Lesebuch*. Vienna: Aarachne Verlag.
Weiner, Marc A. (1995), *Richard Wagner and the Anti-Semitic Imagination*. Lincoln and London: University of Nebraska Press.
Wendt, Hans (1933), *Hitler regiert*, 3rd ed. Berlin: E.S. Mittler & Sohn.
Zehnpfennig, Barbara (2002), *Hitlers Mein Kampf. Eine Interpretation*, 2nd ed. München: Wilhelm Fink Verlag.
Zentner, Christian (2004), *Adolf Hitlers Mein Kampf. Eine kommentierte Auswahl*, 17th ed. München: List Verlag.
Zschaler, Mathias (2004), 'Jung, wenig gebildet, arbeitslos'. In: *Die Welt*, 21. Dec. 2004: 3.

Index of Metaphors

Agriculture	148	Horticulture	148
Architecture	96	Household objects	150
Artifacts	143	Human anatomy	125
Arts	143	Human attributes and capacities	132
Astronomy	159	Hunting	140
Blood-sucking creatures	155	Human society and culture	134
Bodily functions	129	IDEAS ARE BUILDINGS	98
Botanical metaphors	156	IMPORTANCE IS ABOVE	104
Building metaphors	96	IMPORTANCE IS BEING AT THE CENTRE	103
Change of direction	113	Insects	154
Change of state	113	INSTRUMENT FOR PRODUCT	79
Clothing	144	KNOWLEDGE IS A BUILDING	98
CLOTHING FOR THE WEARER	80	Lack of movement	114
Colours	161	Legal metaphors	142
Commercial metaphors	142	LIFE IS A JOURNEY	105
Darkness	161	Light	161
Decay	168	Location	103
Fate	119	MEDIOCRITY IS BEING IN THE MIDDLE	103
Fire	161	Metals	157
Games	140	Meteorological metaphors	161
Genetics and breeding	147	Microscopic organisms	155
Geography	159	MIND IS A CONTAINER	100
Geology	159	MIND IS A SHIP/MOVING VESSEL	101
GOOD IS ABOVE	104	Mountains	160
GREAT CHAIN OF BEING	115	Movement inwards	112
Growth	166	Movement outwards	112
Growth of plants	166	Movement to force into	112
Health	130	Movement to surround	112
HEART IS A CONTAINER	101	NATION/STATE IS A BUILDING	96
HEART IS A ROOM	101		
Hierarchy	120		

Nature	119	Scientific metaphors	146
OBJECT FOR USER	79	Sickness	130
Ornithological metaphors	153	Size	129
Parasites	155	Sporting metaphors	140
PART FOR WHOLE	79	STATE IS A BODY	93
POLITICS IS WAR	135	STATE IS A CONTAINER	93
PROGRESS IS MOVEMENT FORWARDS	107	STATE IS A PLANT	156
		STATE IS A SHIP	100
PROGRESS IS MOVEMENT UPWARDS	109	SUPERIORITY IS ABOVE	104
		Supernatural beings	117
Putting aside/away	113	Technological metaphors	143
REGRESSION IS MOVEMENT BACKWARDS	107	Tools	150
		Transience	168
REGRESSION IS MOVEMENT DOWNWARDS	109	Unbounded movement	114
		VOLK IS A BODY	93
Relationships	134	Water	158
Rituals	134	Zoological metaphors	150
Rocks	157		

General Index

A

abscess(es), 52, 131, 156
agriculture, 147–149
Alldeutsche Bewegung, 12, 107
Alldeutscher Blätter, 140
Alldeutscher Verband, 24, 25, 140
Allinson, M., 5, 6
architecture, 11, 82, 96, 126, 170, 172
aristocracy, 120
astronomy, 159

B

backbone(s), 83, 94, 127, 170
bacteria, 60, 80, 116, 151, 174
bacterium, 13, 51, 155, 156, 213
barriers, 114
Bauer, G., 31, 85
Benz, W., x, 48
Berger, S., 86, 87
Berning, C., 30–33, 53, 125, 146, 147, 155, 249
Bible, 20, 88, 89, 91, 153, 170, 179, 180
biblical, viii, 67, 71, 84, 88, 89, 134, 171
bird(s), 84, 153, 154, 170
birth, 75, 96, 104
blasphemous, 2
blasphemy, 118
blind, 162, 224
blindness, 131, 227, 229
blood–sucking, 50, 53, 96, 126, 155, 223
bodies, 65, 76, 92, 94, 103, 128, 133, 158, 162
breeding, 39, 49, 110, 147–148

Brockhaus, 30, 249, 250
building(s), 90–92, 96–100, 112, 149, 154, 167, 172
Bürgerbräukeller, 16, 17
burial, 135
Burke, K., 1, 249
Burleigh, M., 21, 22
Burschenschaften, 5

C

Chamberlain, Houston S., 11, 17, 35–39, 59, 62, 97, 177, 185
Charteris-Black, J., 91, 92
clean, 83, 224
cleanliness, 134, 170, 178
clothing, 80, 145
Cobet, C., 37, 138, 153
cold, 77, 90, 135, 164, 170, 226
colour(s), viii, 99, 133, 161, 165, 246
competition, 27, 141
containers, 76, 92, 100, 112–114, 126

D

dams, 100
darkness, 52, 53, 60, 77, 90, 162–165, 170, 171, 178, 187
daylight, 52, 60, 163, 171
decay, viii, 26, 37, 71, 166, 168–170, 204, 213, 227
decrepitude, 131
Deissler, D., 249
destruction, 110, 138, 178, 179, 204, 205, 223
Deutsche Arbeiterpartei, 8, 14, 15, 26

Deutsches Volksblatt, 23, 32
Deutschvölkischer Schutz- und Trutzbund, 15, 25
devastation, 138, 220
devil, 44, 48, 55, 118, 135, 153, 178, 180
dirt, 28, 133, 170, 178
disease, 50, 52, 94, 95, 130, 137, 161, 170, 187
Doerr, K., 21, 37
Domarus, M., 155, 171, 186
domestic, 109, 170, 172
door(s), 90, 97, 102
Drahtzieher, 25, 122, 211

E

eating, 80, 152
Ebert, F., 6, 8, 161
edifice, 96, 98, 100, 126, 167, 238
Ehlich, K., 31
enslavement, 139, 140, 223
explosion, 246

F

farming, 79, 149, 170
Feder, G., 18, 80
Feindbild(er), x, 2, 3, 28, 40, 47–48, 52, 54, 138, 249
fish, 150, 170
foundations, 46, 80, 97–99, 157, 159, 167, 238
Frederick the Great, 26, 35, 161
Frick, W., 18
Fritsch, Th., 25
führen, 27, 83, 113, 137
Führer, 12, 17, 25, 34, 70, 108, 121, 129, 168, 180, 193, 207, 233
Führerfähigkeit, 27, 207
Führergenialität, 27, 207
Führerschwung, 27, 207

G

Germanenorden, 32
Gewaltstil, 29, 175
Gibbs, R., 77, 78, 84–86, 141
Gobineau, A. Comte de, 35, 249
Goebbels, J., 17, 18, 146
Göring, H., 18
Gregor, N., 17, 18, 23, 27, 28, 32
Grieswelle, D., 30

H

Halbheit(en), 27, 60, 69, 94, 110, 175, 177, 221, 227, 233
Hamann, B., 14, 32, 177
Hammer, Der, 25, 41
Hanfstaengel, E., 35
healing, 71, 170
health, 56, 69, 90, 130, 132, 157, 209
heat, 77, 79, 90, 92, 162, 164, 170, 173, 188
hell, 45, 54, 117, 118, 178
Hindenburg, P., 8, 9, 19
Hitlerjugend 17
Horan, G., 31
horticulture, 148
household, 150
hunting, 141, 170

I

impotence, 40, 220
imprisonment, 112, 180
insects, 53, 60, 116, 154, 170
iron, 14, 36, 114, 157, 158, 164, 227

J

Jahn, F.L., 11, 24, 37, 93, 148, 183, 184

General Index

Johnson, M., 75, 76, 91, 92, 102, 103, 173
Johnston, O., 24

K

Kapp Putsch, 7
Kässner, F., 49
Kershaw, I., 10, 12–18, 22, 23, 25, 27, 31
Kaufmann, W., 26
Klemperer, V., 1, 30, 51, 59, 71, 72, 191, 246
Königseder, A., x, 48
Kövecses, Z., 75–80, 82–86, 88, 90, 91, 135, 170

L

Lakoff, G., 75–78, 90–92, 102, 103, 173
Landvolk, 18
law, 35, 40, 210
lebensraum, 17, 27, 36, 49, 106, 136, 165
Leninist, 41
Liebenfels, J.L. von, 12, 33
Lincoln, B., 33, 35
List, G. von, xii, 12, 32, 33, 38, 50, 65, 108
Lohengrin, 33, 34
Lovejoy, A. 116
Ludendorff, E., 16, 35, 175
Lueger, K., 12, 208

M

machine(s), 52, 90, 116, 146, 150, 193
magic, 89, 170, 175
Mann, G., 175
Marxism, ix, 9, 11–13, 15, 16, 20, 115, 127, 128, 131, 169, 170, 214

Marxist, ix, 13, 61, 99, 113, 131, 138, 140, 149, 151–153, 157, 158, 163, 213, 214, 222, 227
Maser, W., 23, 250
mechanism(s), 93, 142–146, 232
metals, 80, 116, 157, 170
Michael, M., 21, 37
Mieder, W., 31, 84, 85
minerals, 157, 170
Murphy, J., 172, 250
music, 82, 144, 170
Musolff, A., 91, 92, 94, 134
myth(s), 22–26, 33, 49, 78, 85, 86, 143
mythology, 86, 170

N

Nash, W., 75, 196, 197
nakedness, 135, 144, 145
neck, 83, 94, 127, 170
Nietzsche, F., 17, 26, 31, 39, 58, 59

O

Ordnertruppe, 64, 107, 136
Ostara, 12, 33
Ottmer, C., 44

P

Paechter, H., 29
Papen, F. von, 9, 19
paralysis, 95, 115, 131, 220
parasite(s), 15, 36, 37, 49, 52, 60, 151, 155, 156, 168, 170, 174, 216, 222, 232, 233, 244
Pechau, M., 29
personification, viii, 55, 78, 80–82, 87, 89, 123–125, 174
Pfahl-Traughber, A., 25

plague, 52, 94, 95, 128–130, 131, 158, 213
poison(s), 38, 50, 51, 55, 56, 94, 101, 102, 117, 121, 138, 139, 152, 158, 170, 178, 193, 204, 227, 238
prostitution, 20, 124
Pörksen, B., 47, 48, 52
Protokolle der Weisen von Zion, 24
purgatory, 118

SS see *Schutzstaffel*
Stein, O.Th., 24, 186
Stern, J.P., 250
Sternberger, D., ix, 31
Storz, G., 31
Strasser, G., 17, 18
Sturmabteilung, 8, 15, 16, 17, 19
Stürmer, Der, 16
Süskind, W., 31

R

Radden, G., 79
Rassenfrage(n), 18, 59
Rassenkunde, 18
Reichshammerbund, 25
religion, 21, 22, 52, 100, 117, 133
resurrection, 58, 88, 96, 109, 111, 119
rock(s), 80, 157, 158, 207
Rosenberg, A., 17
route(s), 106, 107
royalty, 121

T

taste(s), 132, 133
temperature, 77, 161
theatre, 52, 130, 138, 144, 226
Thule-Gesellschaft, 32
Thüring, E., ix
Treaty of Versailles, 6, 7, 16, 18, 87, 139, 234
Treitschke, H. von, 17, 32, 35, 39
Tugendbund, 24
tumours, 131
Turner, M., 75-78, 90, 91, 173

S

SA see *Sturmabteilung*
sacred, 22, 55, 119, 242
scar, 196, 224
Schmidt, J., 1, 30
Schönerer, G. Ritter von, 12, 13
Schutzstaffel, 8, 9, 17, 19
Schwab, G., 35
Seidel, E., 30
Seidel-Slotty, I., 30
ship(s), 92, 100, 101
Shirer, W.L., 16, 35
sickness, 69, 95, 108, 109, 130
Simon, G., 31, 84
slave, 54, 111, 123
slavery, 54
smell(s), 132, 170
snake(s), 37, 53, 150, 151, 153, 170
sport, 90, 141, 157, 170

U

Ulonska, U., 31, 42, 43, 56, 89
undermine, 96, 98, 160, 204, 238
undermining, 52, 160

V

virus, 130
Völkischer Beobachter, 16
Volksgemeinschaft, 18, 61
Volmert, J., 31

W

Wagner, R., 11, 26, 33, 35, 39, 133, 147, 177, 249
wall(s), 8, 18, 97, 99
warfare, 170
water, 158, 159, 212
weather, 161, 162, 165, 170
Weiner, M., 133
Wendt, H., 66, 179, 180
Wille(n), 11, 26, 56, 58, 81, 124, 129, 136, 209, 165, 173, 227
wound(s), 132
wrestling, 47

Z

Zehnpfennig, B., 60
Zentner, C., 35
Zschaler, M., 49